AQA Certificate in Chemistry (iGCSE) Level 1/2

SCIENCE

Lawrie Ryan

Margaret Cross

Jason Murgatroyd

Carl Howe

Editor
Lawrie Ryan

Nelson Thornes

Published in 2012 by:
Nelson Thornes Ltd
Delta Place
27 Bath Road
CHELTENHAM
GL53 7TH
United Kingdom

12 13 14 15 16 / 10 9 8 7 6 5 4 3 2

A catalogue record for this book is available from the British
Library.

AQA examination questions are reproduced by permission of the
Assessment and Qualifications Alliance.

ISBN 978 1 4085 1711 6

Cover photograph © Image Source / Alamy

Page make-up by Wearset Ltd, Boldon, Tyne and Wear

Printed and bound in Spain by GraphyCems

Chemistry Contents

Welcome to AQA Level 1/2 Certificate in Chemistry

This book has been written for you by the people who will be marking your exams, very experienced teachers and subject experts. It covers everything you need to know for your exams and is packed full of features to help you achieve the very best that you can.

Figure 1 Many diagrams are as important for you to learn as the text, so make sure you revise them carefully

Key words are highlighted in the text. You can look them up in the glossary at the back of the book if you are not sure what they mean.

Learning objectives

Each topic begins with key statements that you should know by the end of the lesson.

Examiner's tip

Hints from the examiners who will mark your exams, giving you important advice on things to remember and what to watch out for.

??? Did you know ... ?

There are lots of interesting and often strange facts about science. This feature tells you about many of them.

∞ links

Links will tell you where you can find more information about what you are learning and how different topics link up.

Activity

An activity is linked to a main lesson and could be a discussion or task in pairs, groups or by yourself.

Maths skills

This feature highlights the maths skills that you will need for your Chemistry exams with short, visual explanations.

Practical

This feature helps you become familiar with key practicals. It may be a simple introduction, a reminder or the basis for a practical in the laboratory.

Summary questions

These questions give you the chance to test whether you have learned and understood everything in the topic. If you get any wrong, go back and have another look. They are designed to be increasingly challenging.

And at the end of each chapter you will find ...

Summary questions

These will test you on what you have learned throughout the whole chapter, helping you to work out what you have understood and where you need to go back and revise.

AQA Examination-style questions

These questions are examples of the types of questions you will answer in your actual exam, so you can get lots of practice during your course.

Key points

At the end of each topic are the important points that you must remember. They can be used to help with revision and summarising your knowledge.

C1.1

States of matter

Learning objectives

After this topic, you should know:

- there are three states of matter

- the arrangement and motion of the particles in each state of matter

- the names of the processes and energy changes involved in changing state.

We can classify the majority of substances as solids, liquids or gases. These are called the three **states of matter**.

Solids have a fixed shape and volume. They cannot be compressed. **Liquids** have a fixed volume, but they can flow and change their shape. Liquids occupy just slightly more space than when solid (water and ice are exceptions). **Gases** have no fixed shape or volume. They can be compressed easily.

To explain the properties of solids, liquids and gases we use the kinetic theory of matter. It is based on the fact that all matter is made up of tiny particles and describes:

- the movement of the particles, and
- the average distance between particles

within each state of matter.

Look at the diagrams to the left that represent the three states of matter.

Each particle in a solid is touching its nearest neighbours and they remain in this fixed arrangement. They cannot move around, but they do vibrate constantly.

The particles in a liquid are also very close together but they can move past each other. This results in a constantly changing, random arrangement of particles.

The particles in a gas have much more space, on average, between them. They can move around at high speeds and in any direction. This means the particles have a random arrangement. The hotter the gas is, the faster the particles move. The pressure of a gas is caused by the particles colliding with the sides of the container. The more frequent and energetic the collisions, the higher the pressure of the gas. So, in a sealed container, the pressure of the gas increases with temperature.

Changing state

If a solid is heated and changes directly to a gas without melting, i.e. it does not pass through the liquid phase, the change of state is called sublimation.

Look at the changes of state that occur when water is heated and cooled:

Solid

Particles vibrate

Liquid

Particles slip and slide over each other

Gas

Particles move very quickly in all directions; as the particles bash against the walls of the container, they exert a force that causes pressure

Figure 1 The particles in the three states of matter

Figure 2 The changes of state in water

The hotter a solid is, the faster its particles vibrate. Eventually, the vibrations will be so strong that the particles begin to break free from their neighbours. At this point the solid starts to melt and become a liquid.

The hotter a liquid is, the faster its particles move around. As the temperature rises, more and more particles gain enough energy to escape from the surface of the liquid. Its rate of evaporation increases. Eventually, the liquid boils and bubbles of gas rise and escape from within the liquid.

Each change of state is reversible. They are examples of physical changes. No new substances are formed in changes of state. For example, water molecules (H_2O) are the same in ice as they are in liquid water or in water vapour.

Energy changes during changes of state

When we monitor the temperature of a solid as we heat it to beyond its melting point, the results are surprising. The temperature stops rising at the solid's melting point. It remains constant until all the solid has melted, and only then starts to rise again.

At its melting point, the energy we provide in heating the solid is being absorbed to break the forces between the particles in the solid. Once all the solid has melted, the energy from the heat source raises the temperature of the liquid as expected.

Changes of state which involve particles becoming closer together, i.e. condensing and freezing (solidifying), release energy to the surroundings as stronger forces form between particles.

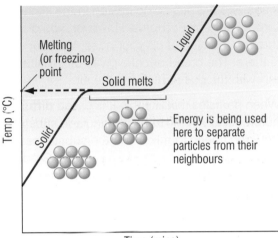

Figure 3 The heating curve of a solid

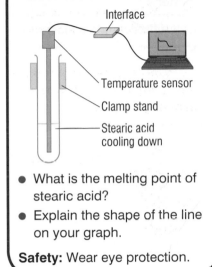
Summary questions

1 Draw a table to summarise the general properties of solids, liquids and gases, as well as the average distance, arrangement and movement of their particles.

2 Describe the changes that occur to the particles as a gas is cooled down to a temperature below its freezing point.

3 Name the following changes:
   a liquid → solid   b gas → liquid   c solid → liquid
   d liquid → gas   e solid → gas (in a single step).

4 Using the kinetic theory of matter, predict how temperature and pressure affect the density of a fixed mass of gas.

5 Explain why substances have different melting points in terms of their particles.

6 Evaporation is the change of state that occurs when a liquid changes to a gas below its boiling point. We can investigate the factors that affect the rate of evaporation using a wet paper towel on a high resolution electric balance.
   Plan an investigation into one factor that might affect the rate of evaporation of water from the paper towel, writing a brief method.

Key points

- The three states of matter are solids, liquids and gases.

- The particles in a solid are packed closely together, fixed in their positions and vibrate.

- The particles in a liquid are also close together but can slip and slide over each other in random motion.

- The particles in a gas have, on average, lots of space between them and zoom around randomly.

- Melting and boiling absorb energy as they take place, whereas freezing and condensing release energy when they occur.

C1.2 Evidence for particles

All the substances that make up our world are made of tiny particles. These particles are too small to see, although nowadays the latest powerful microscopes can show us images of particles. Scientists have developed special probes that can measure very small forces. These probes can be used to detect particles, and even position them where you want. However, long before the invention of these microscopes, people, such as the ancient Greeks, had proposed particle models to explain the properties of materials.

Diffusion

If somebody does some baking in the kitchen, the smell quickly spreads through into other rooms. However, you don't *see* any particles moving through the air and up your nose. Yet your sense of smell tells you that it really is there. The bread or cake gives off invisible particles of itself. These particles mix with the gas particles in the air.

When particles mix like this it is called **diffusion**. Diffusion happens automatically in mixtures that include substances which are liquids and gases. You don't need to mix or stir the substances. The particles in liquids and gases move constantly in a random manner. Gradually, this has the overall effect of moving particles from an area of **high** concentration to an area of **low** concentration. Eventually the particles of gas in a closed container will be evenly spread throughout the container.

Diffusion in liquids

Practical

Diffusion through a liquid

Use tweezers to pick up a few potassium manganate(VII) crystals.

Gently place them at the bottom of a beaker of water.

Observe the beaker for a few minutes.
- What do you see happen?

Leave your beaker until your next lesson.

Draw a diagram to show your results.
- Explain what you think happens to the purple particles.

Use the words **particles** and **diffuse** in your answer.

Safety: Wear eye protection. The crystals are harmful and will stain clothing and skin.

Purple colour starts spreading through the water

Potassium manganate(VII) crystals

Figure 1 Diffusion of potassium manganate(VII) through water

Practical

Does temperature affect the rate of diffusion?

Plan an investigation to see how temperature affects the rate of diffusion through a liquid.

Let your teacher check your plan before you start any practical work.

Diffusion in gases

As in liquids, the random motion of particles in a gas enables diffusion to take place.

We can show this using a coloured gas, just as we used coloured particles dissolved in water in the first practical to demonstrate diffusion in a liquid. A little bromine liquid is placed in a gas jar with a lid. Bromine vapour evaporates from the volatile liquid and fills the gas jar. Then a second gas jar of air is placed upside down on top of the original bromine-filled gas jar and the lid is removed, linking the jars together. Even though bromine vapour is much more dense than air, the bromine gas gets distributed evenly between the two gas jars after a time. The rapid, random movement of air and bromine particles (molecules) ensure complete mixing takes place.

Diffusion takes place more quickly through gases than through liquids. That is because the particles of gas are moving much more rapidly, on average, than the particles in a liquid.

We find that lighter particles of gas move faster, on average, than heavy ones at the same temperature. Therefore small, light particles diffuse faster than large, heavy ones.

Figure 2 Bromine vapour diffuses and mixes thoroughly with the air

---

Demonstration

Diffusion through a gas

Watch what happens when the stoppers from bottles of concentrated ammonia solution and hydrochloric acid are brought near each other. The reaction is:

$$\text{ammonia} + \text{hydrogen chloride} \rightarrow \text{ammonium chloride}$$
$$NH_3(g) + HCl(g) \rightarrow NH_4Cl(s)$$
$$\text{(seen as white 'smoke')}$$

Your teacher will set up the apparatus as shown below:

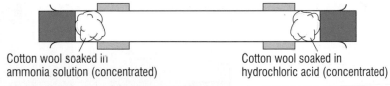

Cotton wool soaked in ammonia solution (concentrated)

Cotton wool soaked in hydrochloric acid (concentrated)

Figure 3 Diffusion of $NH_3(g)$ and $HCl(g)$ through air

- What do you see in the long tube where the $HCl(g)$ and $NH_3(g)$ particles meet?
- Which particles diffuse faster, $NH_3(g)$ or $HCl(g)$? How can you tell?

In this experiment, the particles meet nearer the acid end of the tube.

- Which particles are lighter, the $HCl(g)$ or $NH_3(g)$?

Safety: Do not inhale the gases. If you are asthmatic take particular care.

Summary questions

1 Explain each of the statements below in terms of particles:
   a You can smell a fish and chip shop from across the road.
   b Sugar dissolves faster in hot water than cold water.
   c Condensation forms on the inside of your bathroom windows in winter.
   d It is dangerous to smoke or strike a match in a petrol station.

2 a Define the word 'diffusion'.
   b Explain why diffusion takes place more quickly in a gas than in a liquid.

3 When pollen grains in water are viewed under a microscope, the grains are seen to be moving in a haphazard, jittery manner. This is called Brownian motion, after the scientist who first observed it. Explain how Brownian motion gives us evidence for the existence of particles in matter?

4 Hydrogen bromide (HBr) is a similar gas to hydrogen chloride (HCl) but its particles (molecules) are more than twice as heavy. If the demonstration 'Diffusion through a gas' in Figure 3 was done with HBr(g) instead of HCl(g), explain what you would expect to see happen.

Key points

- All substances are made up of particles.

- In liquids and gases, the random movement of particles mixes substances in a process called diffusion.

- Diffusion takes place faster in a gas than in a liquid.

- Small, light particles diffuse faster than large, heavy ones.

C1.3 Atoms

Look at the things around you and the substances that they are made from. You will find wood, metal, plastic, glass ... the list is almost endless. Look further and the number of different substances is mind-boggling.

All substances are made of **atoms**. There are about 100 different types of atom found naturally on Earth. These can combine in a huge variety of ways, giving us all those different substances.

Some substances are made up of only one type of atom. We call these substances **elements**. It follows that as there are only about 100 different types of atom, there are only about 100 different elements.

Elements can have very different properties. Elements such as silver, copper and gold are shiny, solid metals. Other elements such as oxygen, nitrogen and chlorine are non-metals, and are gases at room temperature.

Chemical symbols

The name we use for an element depends on the language being spoken. For example, the element sulfur is called *schwefel* in German and *azufre* in Spanish. However, the scientific community communicates globally so it is important that we have symbols for elements that all nationalities can understand. These symbols are shown in the **periodic table**.

- The symbols in the periodic table represent atoms. For example, O represents an atom of oxygen; Na represents an atom of sodium.

Figure 1 An element contains only one type of atom – in this case gold

Figure 2 The periodic table shows the symbols for each type of atom

- The elements in the table are arranged in columns, called **groups**. Each group contains elements with similar chemical properties.
- The 'staircase' drawn in bold black is the dividing line between metals and non-metals. The elements to the left of the line are metals. Those on the right of the line are non-metals. However, a few elements lying next to the dividing line are called metalloids or semi-metals as they have some metallic and some non-metallic characteristics. Examples include silicon (Si) and germanium (Ge) from Group 4.

Atoms, elements and compounds

Most substances we come across are not elements. They are made up of different types of atom joined together and are called **compounds**. Chemical bonds hold the atoms tightly together in compounds. Some compounds are made from just two types of atom (e.g. water, made from atoms of hydrogen and oxygen). However, most compounds consist of more than two different types of atom.

An atom is made up of a tiny central **nucleus** with **electrons** around it.

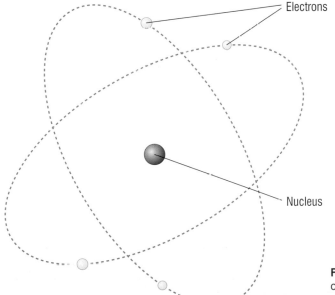

Electrons

Nucleus

Figure 3 Each atom consists of a small nucleus surrounded by electrons

∞ **links**

For more information on the periodic table of elements, see 5.1 'The periodic table'.

??? Did you know …?

Only 92 elements occur naturally on Earth. The other heavier elements in the periodic table have to be made artificially and might only exist for fractions of a second before they decay into other, lighter elements.

O

H   Chemical bonds   H

Figure 4 A grouping of two or more atoms bonded together is called a **molecule**. Chemical bonds hold the hydrogen and oxygen atoms together in the water molecule. Water is an example of a compound.

∞ **links**

For more information on what is inside an atom, see 1.4 'Atomic structure' and 1.5 'The arrangement of electrons in atoms'.

Summary questions

1 **a** Arrange these elements into a table showing metals and non-metals: phosphorus (P), barium (Ba), vanadium (V), mercury (Hg), krypton (Kr), potassium (K) and uranium (U).
   b Would you classify hydrogen as a metal or a non-metal. Why?

2 Explain why when we mix two elements together we can often separate them again quite easily by physical means; yet when two elements are chemically combined in a compound, they are usually very difficult to separate.

3 Draw diagrams to explain the difference between an element and a compound.

4 Describe the basic structure of an atom.

5 Find out the Latin words from which the symbols of the following metallic elements are derived:
   a sodium, Na   **b** gold, Au   **c** lead, Pb   **d** potassium, K

Key points

- All substances are made up of atoms.
- The periodic table lists all the chemical elements, with eight main groups each containing elements with similar chemical properties.
- Elements contain only one type of atom.
- Compounds contain more than one type of atom.
- An atom has a tiny nucleus at its centre, surrounded by electrons.

C1.4

Atomic structure

In the centre of every atom there is a very small nucleus. This contains two types of sub-atomic particle, called **protons** and **neutrons**. A third type of sub-atomic particle orbits the nucleus. We call these really tiny particles electrons.

Protons have a positive charge. Neutrons have no charge, i.e. they are neutral. So the nucleus itself has an overall positive charge. The electrons orbiting the nucleus are negatively charged. The relative charge on a proton is +1 and the relative charge on an electron is −1.

Type of sub-atomic particle	Relative charge
Proton	+1
Neutron	0
Electron	−1

Because every atom contains equal numbers of protons and electrons, the positive and negative charges cancel out and its charge is zero. So, there is no overall charge on any atom. For example, a carbon atom is neutral. It has 6 protons, so we know it must have 6 electrons.

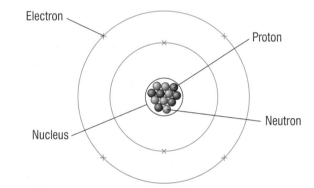

Figure 1 Understanding the structure of an atom gives us important clues to the way chemicals react together. If you look carefully, this atom of carbon has 6 protons and 6 neutrons in its nucleus, and 6 electrons orbiting the nucleus. Note that although the number of protons and electrons are always equal in an atom, the number of neutrons can differ (but in this case they are the same).

Atomic number and the periodic table of elements

All the atoms of a particular element have the same number of protons. For example, hydrogen has 1 proton in its nucleus, carbon has 6 protons in its nucleus and sodium has 11 protons in its nucleus.

We call the **number of protons** in each atom of an element its **atomic number**.

Figure 2 You read the periodic table from left to right, and from the top down – just like reading a page of writing. This is an abbreviated version of the start of the periodic table, showing the first 18 elements. The elements in the periodic table are arranged in order of their atomic number.

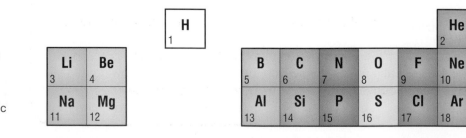

The elements in the periodic table are arranged in order of their atomic number (number of protons). If you are told that the atomic number of an element is 8, you can identify it using the periodic table. It will be the 8th element listed, i.e. oxygen.

Mass number

The **number of protons plus neutrons** in the nucleus of an atom is called its **mass number**. So, if an atom has 4 protons and 5 neutrons, its mass number will be 4 + 5 = **9**.

Given the atomic number and mass number, we can work out how many protons, electrons and neutrons are in an atom. For example, an argon atom has an atomic number of 18 and a mass number of 40.

- Its atomic number is 18 so it has **18 protons**. Remember that atoms have an equal number of protons and electrons. So argon also has **18 electrons**.
- The mass number is 40, so we know that:

    18 (the number of protons) + the number of neutrons = 40

- Therefore, argon must have **22 neutrons** (as 18 + 22 = 40).

We can summarise the last part of the calculation as:

number of neutrons = mass number – atomic number

Examiner's tip

In an atom, the number of protons is always equal to the number of electrons. You can find out the number of protons and electrons in an atom by looking up its atomic number in the periodic table.

⃝ links

For more information on the patterns in the periodic table, see 1.5 'The arrangement of electrons in atoms'.

Summary questions

1 Draw a table showing the location and relative charge of the three sub-atomic particles.

2 Look at the abbreviated periodic table in Figure 2.
   a How does the number of electrons in each atom vary going across each row (called a period) in the table?
   b What pattern do you notice in the number of protons going down Group 0?
   c Sort out the elements in the table into metals, non-metals and metalloids.

3 Explain why all atoms are neutral.

4 An atom has 27 protons and 32 neutrons. Use the periodic table in 1.3 to name this element, and give its symbol, atomic number and mass number.

5 How many protons, electrons and neutrons do the following atoms contain?
   a A nitrogen atom whose atomic number is 7 and whose mass number is 14.
   b A chlorine atom whose atomic number is 17 and whose mass number is 35.
   c A silver atom whose atomic number is 47 and whose mass number is 108.
   d A uranium atom whose atomic number is 92 and whose mass number is 235.

Key points

- Atoms are made of protons, neutrons and electrons.

- Protons have a relative charge of +1, and electrons have a relative charge of –1. Neutrons have no electric charge. They are neutral.

- Atoms contain an equal number of protons and electrons so carry no overall charge.

- Atomic number = number of protons (= number of electrons)

- Mass number = number of protons + neutrons

- Atoms of the same element have the same number of protons (and hence electrons) in their atoms.

C1.5 The arrangement of electrons in atoms

Learning objectives

After this topic, you should know:

● how the electrons are arranged in an atom

● the electronic structures of the first 20 elements in the periodic table

● how to represent electronic structures in diagrams and by using standard notation.

1
Hydrogen H

2, 3
Boron B

2,6
Oxygen O

2,8,3
Aluminium Al

2,8,8
Argon Ar

2,8,8,2
Calcium Ca

Figure 2 Once you know the pattern, you should be able to draw the energy levels (shells) and electrons in the atoms of any of the first 20 elements (given their atomic number)

The model of the atom which we use at this level has electrons arranged around the nucleus in **shells**, rather like the layers of an onion. Each shell represents a different **energy level**.

The lowest energy level is shown by the shell which is nearest to the nucleus. The electrons in an atom occupy the lowest available energy level (the shell closest to the nucleus).

Electron shell diagrams

An energy level (or shell) can only hold a certain number of electrons.

● The first, and lowest, energy level (nearest the nucleus) can hold up to 2 electrons.

● The second energy level can hold up to 8 electrons.

● Once there are 8 electrons in the third energy level, the fourth begins to fill up.

Beyond this point, i.e. after the first 20 elements in the periodic table, the situation gets more complex so is covered in higher level courses. You only need to know the arrangement of electrons in atoms of the first 20 elements.

We can draw diagrams to show the arrangement of electrons in an atom. For example, a sodium atom has an atomic number of 11 so it has 11 protons, which means it also has 11 electrons. Figure 1 shows how we can represent an atom of sodium.

Figure 1 A simple way of representing the arrangement of electrons in the energy levels (shells) of a sodium atom

To save drawing atoms all the time, we can write down the numbers of electrons in each energy level. This is called an **electronic structure**. For example, the sodium atom in Figure 1 has an electronic structure of 2,8,1. We start at the lowest energy level (innermost or first shell), recording the numbers in each successive energy level or shell.

Silicon, whose atoms have 14 electrons, is in Group 4 of the periodic table. It has the electronic structure 2,8,4. This represents 2 electrons in the lowest energy level (first shell), then 8 in the next energy level or shell. There are 4 in the highest energy level (its outermost shell).

The best way to understand these arrangements is to look at the examples in Figure 2.

Examiner's tip

Make sure that you can draw the electronic structure of the atoms for all of the first 20 elements. You will always be given their atomic number or their position in the periodic table (which tells you the number of electrons) – so you don't have to memorise these numbers.

Electrons and the periodic table

Look at the elements in any one of the main groups of the periodic table. Their atoms will all have the same number of electrons in their highest energy level. These electrons are often called the outer electrons because they are in the outermost shell. Therefore, all the elements in Group 1 have one electron in their highest energy level.

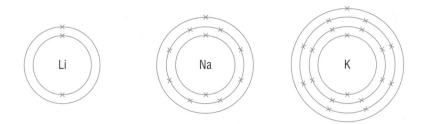

The chemical properties of an element depend on how many electrons it has. The way an element reacts is determined by the number of electrons in its highest energy level (or outermost shell). So because the elements in a particular group all have the same number of electrons in their highest energy level, they all react in a similar way.

For example:

$$\text{lithium} + \text{water} \rightarrow \text{lithium hydroxide} + \text{hydrogen}$$
$$\text{sodium} + \text{water} \rightarrow \text{sodium hydroxide} + \text{hydrogen}$$
$$\text{potassium} + \text{water} \rightarrow \text{potassium hydroxide} + \text{hydrogen}$$

The elements in Group 0 of the periodic table are called the noble gases because they are unreactive. Their atoms have a very stable arrangement of electrons. All the Group 0 elements have 8 electrons in their outermost shell, except for helium, which has only 2 electrons.

Figure 3 The Group 1 metals are all reactive metals, stored under oil

∞ links

For more information on the reactions of elements and their electronic structures, see Chapter 5 'The periodic table'.

Summary questions

1 a Which shell represents the lowest energy level in an atom?
  b How many electrons can each of the lowest two energy levels hold?

2 Using the periodic table, draw the arrangement of electrons in the following atoms and label each one with its electronic structure.
  a He **b** Be **c** Cl **d** Ar

3 a Write the electronic structure of potassium (atomic number 19).
  b How many electrons does a potassium atom have in its highest energy level (outermost shell)?

4 Give the name and symbol of the atom shown:

5 a Why do the Group 1 metals all react in a similar way with oxygen?
  b Write word equations for the reactions of lithium, sodium and potassium with oxygen to form their oxides.

Key points

● The electrons in an atom are arranged in energy levels or shells.

● The lowest energy level (1st shell) can hold up to 2 electrons and the next energy level (the 2nd shell) can hold up 8 electrons.

● The 4th shell starts to fill after 8 electrons occupy the 3rd shell.

● The number of electrons in the outermost shell of an element's atoms determines the way in which that element reacts.

C1.6 Atoms and isotopes

Learning objectives

After this topic, you should know:

- the relative masses of protons, neutrons and electrons

- how to represent an atom's atomic number and mass number

- the definition of isotopes.

??? Did you know ... ?

The volume of the nucleus of an atom can be between 10 000 and 100 000 times smaller than the volume of the atom itself.

As we have seen, an atom consists of a tiny nucleus containing positively charged protons, together with neutrons which have no charge. The negatively charged electrons are arranged in energy levels (shells) around the nucleus.

The mass of a proton and a neutron is the same so we can say that the 'relative mass' of a neutron compared with a proton is 1. Electrons are much, much lighter than protons and neutrons. They have a mass of about 1/2000 of a proton or neutron. Because of this, the mass of an atom is concentrated in its nucleus and we can ignore the tiny mass of the electrons when working out the relative mass of an atom.

Type of sub-atomic particle	Relative mass
Proton	1
Neutron	1
Electron	very small

Representing the atomic number and mass number

Remember that:

- the number of protons in an atom is its atomic number, and
- the total number of protons and neutrons in an atom is its mass number.

We can show the atomic number and mass number of an atom like this:

Mass number

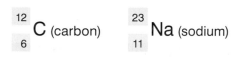
$^{12}_{6}\text{C}$ (carbon) $^{23}_{11}\text{Na}$ (sodium)

Atomic number

Given this information, we can work out the number of neutrons in the nucleus of an atom by subtracting its atomic number from its mass number. (See page 9).

number of neutrons = mass number – atomic number

For the two examples above:

Carbon has 6 protons and a mass number of 12.
So the number of neutrons in a carbon atom is (12 − 6) = 6.

Sodium has an atomic number of 11 and the mass number is 23.
So a sodium atom has (23 − 11) = 12 neutrons.
In its nucleus there are 11 protons and 12 neutrons.

$^{12}_{6}\text{C}$

- ● Proton — Number of protons gives atomic number
- ○ Neutron — Number of protons plus number of neutrons gives mass number

Figure 1 An atom of carbon

Isotopes

Atoms of the same element always have the same number of protons. However, they can have different numbers of neutrons.

We give the name **isotopes** to atoms of the same element with different numbers of neutrons.

Isotopes always have the same atomic number but different mass numbers. For example, two isotopes of carbon are $_6^{12}C$ (also written as carbon-12) and $_6^{14}C$ (carbon-14). The carbon-12 isotope has 6 protons and 6 neutrons in the nucleus. The carbon-14 isotope has 6 protons and 8 neutrons, i.e. 2 more neutrons than carbon-12.

Sometimes extra neutrons make the nucleus unstable, so it is radioactive. However, not all isotopes are radioactive – they are simply atoms of the same element that have different masses.

Samples of different isotopes of an element have different *physical* properties. For example, they will have a different density and they may or may not be radioactive. However, they always have the same *chemical* properties because their reactions depend on their electronic structures. As their atoms will have the same number of protons, and therefore electrons, the electronic structure will be same for all isotopes of an element.

For example, look at the three isotopes of hydrogen in Figure 2. The three isotopes are called hydrogen (hydrogen-1), deuterium (or hydrogen-2) and tritium (or hydrogen-3). Each has a different mass and tritium is radioactive. However, all have identical chemical properties, e.g. they all react with oxygen to make water:

$$2H_2(g) + O_2(g) \rightarrow 2H_2O(l)$$

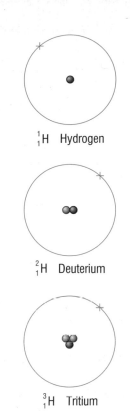

$_1^1H$ Hydrogen

$_1^2H$ Deuterium

$_1^3H$ Tritium

Figure 2 The isotopes of hydrogen – they have identical chemical properties but different physical properties, such as density

---

Summary questions

1 Draw a table to summarise the relative mass and charge of the three sub-atomic particles.

2 State how many protons and how many neutrons there are in the nucleus of each of the following elements:
 a $_5^{11}B$ b $_7^{14}N$ c $_{12}^{24}Mg$ d $_{17}^{37}Cl$ e $_{53}^{127}I$

3 Define the word isotopes.

4 a Which physical property will always differ in pure samples of each isotope of the same element?
 b Explain why the isotopes of the same element have identical chemical properties?

5 a The same volume of any gas contains the same number of molecules. If the density of hydrogen gas containing only the hydrogen-1 isotope is 0.00008 g/cm³ at 25 °C, what will be the density of the gas containing only the hydrogen-3 isotope at 25 °C?
 b Name one hazard associated with both gases containing hydrogen-1 or hydrogen-3 isotopes.
 c Name a hazard associated with the gas containing hydrogen-3 which does not apply to the hydrogen-1 sample.

Key points

- The relative mass of protons and neutrons is 1.

- We can represent the atomic number and mass number of an atom using the notation: $_{12}^{24}Mg$, where magnesium's atomic number is 12 and its mass number is 24.

- Isotopes are atoms of the same element with different numbers of neutrons. They have identical chemical properties, but their physical properties, such as density, can differ.

Summary questions

1 Arsenic (As) is a solid element that sublimes at 613 °C.

  a What is sublimation?

  b Assuming arsenic exists as atoms, draw a diagram to show the arrangement of some of its particles in boxes like the ones below:

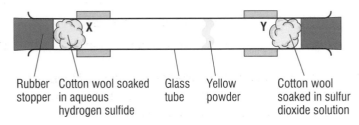

  c Which of these processes take in energy from the surroundings?

    boiling   melting   freezing   condensation   sublimation

2 Look at the experiment below:

Rubber stopper | Cotton wool soaked in aqueous hydrogen sulfide | Glass tube | Yellow powder | Cotton wool soaked in sulfur dioxide solution

Hydrogen sulfide gas is released from the cotton wool at X and sulfur dioxide gas from the cotton wool at Y.

  a The yellow powder inside the glass tube forms after 10 minutes. Explain how the yellow powder forms using the kinetic theory of matter.

  b Name the physical process that this experiment demonstrates.

  c Why is the yellow powder formed nearer to end Y of the tube?

  d Draw a long tube and show the possible path of a hydrogen sulfide particle (molecule) travelling down the tube.

  e The original experiment was carried out at 18 °C. Predict any difference you might notice if the experiment was repeated at 25 °C.

3 Look at the data in the table below:

Chemical element	Melting point (°C)	Boiling point (°C)	Density (g/cm³)
Bromine	−7	59	3.12
Caesium	29	669	1.88
Fluorine	−220	−188	0.001 58
Strontium	769	1384	2.6
Xenon	−112	−108	0.005 5

  a What is the physical state of each element in the table at 25 °C?

  b Which element exists as a liquid over the widest range of temperature?

  c Explain the large differences in the densities of the elements in the table using the kinetic theory of matter.

  d What is the chemical symbol for atoms of each element in the table?

  e Classify each element in the table as a metal or a non-metal.

4 **a** **i** Which sub-atomic particles are found in the nucleus?

    ii What is the maximum number of electrons that can occupy each of the first two energy levels or shells?

  b **i** Explain the overall charge on any atom.

    ii Define atomic number and mass number.

5 This question is about some of the elements in the periodic table.

You will need to use the periodic table at the back of this book to help you answer some parts of the question.

  a Neon (Ne) is the 10th element in the periodic table.

    i Is neon a metal or a non-metal?

    ii Are there more metals or non-metals in the periodic table?

    iii How many protons does an neon atom contain?

    iv The mass number of a neon atom is 20. How many neutrons does it contain?

    v State the name and number of the group to which neon belongs.

    vi Name two other elements in the same group as neon.

    vii Write the electronic structure of a neon atom.

    viii What is special about the electronic structure of neon and the other elements in its group?

  b The element radium (Ra) has 88 electrons.

    i How many protons are in the nucleus of each radium atom?

    ii How many electrons does a radium atom have in its highest energy level (outermost shell)? How did you decide on your answer?

    iii Is radium a metal or a non-metal?

    iv Calcium is in the same group as radium. Its atomic number is 20. Write down its electronic structure.

AQA Examination-style questions

1 Use words from the list to complete the table to show the state of matter described.

gas   liquid   solid

Description	State
particles close together but not moving around	
particles very far apart	
particles close together but continuously moving around	

(3)

2 a Explain the difference between an element and a compound. (2)

b Why is ammonia classified as a compound but air is classified as a mixture? (2)

c Name the change of state in each of these processes.
  i $H_2O(g) \rightarrow H_2O(l)$ (1)
  ii $H_2O(l) \rightarrow H_2O(g)$ (1)
  iii $I_2(s) \rightarrow I_2(g)$ (1)

3 A crystal of copper(II) sulfate is placed at the bottom of a beaker of water and left for a few days.

a Describe the appearance of the liquid in the beaker after a few days. (2)

b How does the appearance of the crystal change during the experiment? (1)

c Name **two** processes that occur during the experiment. (2)

4 The diagram shows the apparatus used in a teacher demonstration.

Cotton wool soaked in
ammonia solution (concentrated)

Cotton wool soaked in
hydrochloric acid (concentrated)

a Describe the observations you would make after a few minutes. (2)

b Use state symbols to complete the symbol equation for the reaction that occurs.

$NH_3(...) + HCl(...) \rightarrow NH_4Cl(...)$ (1)

c Explain how this experiment shows that ammonia molecules have a smaller mass than hydrogen chloride molecules. (1)

5 The atoms in a sample of neon can be represented as $^{20}_{10}Ne$ and $^{22}_{10}Ne$.

These atoms are isotopes.

a Explain the term isotopes. (2)

b Explain why isotopes have identical chemical properties. (1)

c Use numbers to complete these statements.
  i The number of protons in an atom of $^{20}_{10}Ne$ is .... (1)
  ii The number of electrons in an atom of $^{22}_{10}Ne$ is .... (1)
  iii The number of neutrons in an atom of $^{20}_{10}Ne$ is .... (1)
  iv The mass number of $^{22}_{10}Ne$ is .... (1)

d The relative atomic mass of neon is 20.2.

Which of the two isotopes is more abundant? (1)

6 Electrons in atoms are arranged in energy levels (or shells) at different distances from the nucleus. Use numbers to complete the sentences.

a The maximum number of electrons in the first shell is .... (1)

b The maximum number of electrons in the second shell is .... (1)

c Atoms of sodium have electrons in .... shells. (1)

d The number of electrons in the third shell of an atom of phosphorus is .... (1)

e The atomic number of an atom with the electronic structure 2,8,6 is .... (1)

C2.1 Relative masses and moles

∞ **links**

You can find out more about ions and bonding in 3.1 'Atoms into ions', 3.2 'Ionic bonding' and 3.3 'Giant ionic structures'.

∞ **links**

You can find out more about atoms sharing electrons and bonding in 3.4 'Covalent bonding', 3.5 'Simple molecules' and 3.6 'Giant covalent structures'.

Figure 1 The relative atomic mass of $^{12}_{6}C$ atom is 12. Compared with this, the A_r of helium is 4 and the A_r of magnesium is 24.

When different types of atom combine chemically we get a compound.

Sometimes atoms react together by **transferring** electrons to form chemical bonds. This happens when metals react with non-metals. If the reacting atoms are all non-metallic, then the atoms **share** electrons to form chemical bonds.

Forming ions

When a metal bonds with a non-metal, the metal atom gives one or more electrons to the non-metal atom. Both atoms become charged particles called **ions**.

- Metal atoms form positively charged ions. Their atoms lose electrons, e.g. Li, which contains 3 protons and 3 electrons, forms Li^+, which contains 3 protons and 2 electrons.

- Non-metal atoms form negatively charged ions. Their atoms gain electrons, e.g. F, which contains 9 protons and 9 electrons, forms F^-, which contains 9 protons and 10 electrons.

The ions formed attain the stable electronic structure of the nearest noble gas to them in the periodic table. So the electronic structure of Li^+ is 2 (the same as a helium atom) and F^- is 2,8 (the same as a neon atom).

Within these compounds made from metals and non-metals, there are strong electrostatic attractions between the positive and negative ions, forming the chemical bonds (called **ionic bonds**).

Forming molecules

Non-metal atoms bond to each other in a different way. The outermost shells of their atoms overlap and they share electrons. Each pair of shared electrons forms a chemical bond between the atoms. Molecules are formed, such as hydrogen sulfide, H_2S, and methane, CH_4.

Relative atomic masses

The mass of a single atom is so tiny that it would not be practical to use it in experiments or calculations. So instead of working with the actual masses of atoms, we use the *relative* masses of atoms of different elements. We call these **relative atomic masses (A_r)**.

We use an atom of carbon-12 ($^{12}_{6}C$) as a standard atom. We give this a 'mass' of exactly 12 units, because it has 6 protons and 6 neutrons. We then compare the masses of atoms of all the other elements with this standard carbon atom. For example, hydrogen has a relative atomic mass of 1 as most of its atoms have a mass that is one-twelfth of the mass of a $^{12}_{6}C$ atom.

The A_r takes into account the proportions of any isotopes of the element found naturally. So it is an *average* relative mass of the atoms of an element compared with the standard carbon atom. (This is why chlorine has a relative atomic mass of 35.5, although we could never have half a proton or neutron in an atom.)

Relative formula masses

We can use the A_r of the various elements to work out the **relative formula mass (M_r)** of compounds. This is true whether the compounds are made up of molecules or ions. A simple example is a substance such as sodium chloride.

We know that the A_r of sodium is 23 and the A_r of chlorine is 35.5. So the relative formula mass of sodium chloride (NaCl) is:

$$23 + 35.5 = \mathbf{58.5}$$
$$A_r\!:\!Na \quad A_r\!:\!Cl \quad M_r\!:\!NaCl$$

We can use the same approach with relatively complicated molecules such as sulfuric acid, H_2SO_4. Hydrogen has a A_r of 1, the A_r of sulfur is 32 and the A_r of oxygen is 16. This means that the M_r of sulfuric acid is:

$$(1 \times 2) + 32 + (16 \times 4) = 2 + 32 + 64 = \mathbf{98}$$

Moles

Saying or writing 'relative atomic mass in grams' or 'relative formula mass in grams' is rather clumsy. So chemists have a shorthand word to describe this amount of substance, a **mole**.

They say that the relative atomic mass in grams of carbon (i.e. 12g of carbon) is a mole of carbon atoms. **One mole is simply the relative atomic mass or relative formula mass of any substance expressed in grams**. A mole of any substance always contains the same number of atoms, molecules or ions. This is a huge number (6.02×10^{23}). So chemists prefer to use the mole when describing relative numbers of particles in a certain mass of substance. They use the equation:

$$\text{number of moles} = \frac{\text{mass (g)}}{A_r} \text{ or } \frac{\text{mass (g)}}{M_r}$$

So if we have 120 g of carbon we have 120/12 = 10 moles of C atoms, or if we have 9.8 g of sulfuric acid we have 9.8/98 = 0.1 moles of H_2SO_4 molecules.

Re-arranging the equation lets us work out the mass of a certain number of moles of substance:

$$\text{mass (g)} = \text{number of moles} \times A_r \text{ or}$$
$$\text{mass (g)} = \text{number of moles} \times M_r$$

Examiner's tip

You don't have to remember the number 6.02×10^{23}. The relative atomic masses of elements are always provided. But do practise calculating the mass of one mole of different substances from their formula and the relative atomic masses that you are given, as well as the number of moles in a given mass of substance.

Summary questions

1 a Define the term 'relative atomic mass' of an element.
  b Explain why we can have relative atomic masses which are not whole numbers, e.g. A_r of chlorine (Cl) is 35.5.

2 What is the relative formula mass of:
  a S_8 (A_r value: S = 32)
  b MgF_2 (A_r values: Mg = 24, F = 19)
  c $CuSO_4$ (A_r values: Cu = 63.5, S = 32, O = 16)
  d $C_6H_{12}O_6$ (A_r values: C = 12, H = 1, O = 16)

3 The relative atomic mass (A_r) of helium is 4, and that of sulfur is 32.
  a How many times heavier is a sulfur atom than a helium atom?
  b How many moles of helium atoms are there in:
    i 16g of helium   ii 0.02g of helium?
  c How many moles of sulfur atoms are there in:
    i 9.6g of sulfur
    ii 16 tonnes of sulfur (where 1 tonne = 1000kg)

4 What is the mass of:
  a 0.5 moles of aluminium, Al
  b 50 moles of calcium carbonate, $CaCO_3$
  c 0.05 moles of hydrogen, H_2
  d 0.6 moles of phosphorus, P_4
  (Find the A_r values needed from the periodic table at the back of this book.)

Key points

- We compare the masses of atoms by measuring them relative to atoms of carbon-12.

- We work out the relative formula mass of a compound by adding up the relative atomic masses of the elements in it, in the ratio shown by its formula.

- One mole of any substance is its relative formula mass, in grams.

- Number of moles =
$$\frac{\text{mass (g)}}{A_r} \text{ or } \frac{\text{mass (g)}}{M_r}$$

C2.2

Percentages and formulae

Learning objectives

After this topic, you should know:

- how to calculate the percentage of an element in a compound from its formula

- how to calculate the empirical formula of a compound from its percentage composition.

We can use the relative formula mass of a compound to calculate the percentage mass of each element in it.

Working out the percentage of an element in a compound

Worked example 1

What percentage of the mass of magnesium oxide is actually magnesium?

Solution

We need to know the formula of magnesium oxide: MgO.

The A_r of magnesium is 24 and the A_r of oxygen is 16.

Adding these together gives us the relative formula mass (M_r) of MgO, i.e. $24 + 16 = 40$

So in 40 g of magnesium oxide, 24 g is actually magnesium.

The fraction of magnesium in the MgO is:

$$\frac{\text{mass of magnesium}}{\text{total mass of compound}} = \frac{24}{40}$$

so the percentage of magnesium in the compound is:

$$\frac{24}{40} \times 100\% = \mathbf{60\%}$$

Worked example 2

A pure white powder is found at the scene of a crime. It could be strychnine, a deadly poison with the formula $C_{21}H_{22}N_2O_2$: but is it?

When a chemist analyses the powder, she finds that 83% of its mass is carbon. What is the percentage mass of carbon in strychnine? Is this the same as the white powder?

Solution

Given the A_r values: C = 12, H = 1, N = 14, O = 16, the relative formula mass (M_r) of strychnine is:

$$(12 \times 21) + (1 \times 22) + (14 \times 2) + (16 \times 2) = 252 + 22 + 28 + 32 = 334$$

The percentage mass of carbon in strychnine is therefore:

$$\frac{252}{334} \times 100 = \mathbf{75.4\%}$$

This is **not** the same as the percentage mass of carbon in the white powder – so the white powder is not strychnine.

Maths skills

To calculate the percentage of an element in a compound:

- Write down the formula of the compound.

- Using the A_r values from your data sheet in the exam, work out the M_r of the compound. Write down the mass of each element making up the compound as you work it out.

- Write the mass of the element you are investigating as a fraction of the M_r.

- Find the percentage by multiplying your fraction by 100.

Working out the empirical formula of a compound from its percentage composition

We can find the percentage of each element in a compound by experiments. Then we can work out the simplest ratio of each type of atom in the compound. We call this simplest (whole-number) ratio its **empirical formula**.

This is sometimes the same as the actual number of atoms in one molecule (which we call the **molecular formula**) – but not always. For example, the empirical formula of water is H_2O, which is also its molecular formula. However, hydrogen peroxide has the empirical formula HO, but its molecular formula is H_2O_2.

Worked example 3

A hydrocarbon contains 75% carbon and 25% hydrogen by mass. What is its empirical formula? (A_r values: C = 12, H = 1)

Solution

Imagine we have 100 g of the compound. Then 75 g is carbon and 25 g is hydrogen.

Work out the number of moles by dividing the mass of each element by its relative atomic mass:

For carbon: $\frac{75}{12} = 6.25$ moles of carbon atoms

For hydrogen: $\frac{25}{1} = 25$ moles of hydrogen atoms

So this tells us that 6.25 moles of carbon atoms are combined with 25 moles of hydrogen atoms.

This means that the ratio is 6.25 (C) : 25 (H).

So the simplest whole-number ratio is 1 : 4 (by dividing both numbers by the smallest number in the ratio).

In other words each carbon atom is combined with 4 hydrogen atoms.

So the empirical formula of the compound is **CH_4**.

Maths skills

To work out the formula from percentage masses:

- Change the percentages given to the masses of each element in 100 g of compound.
- Change the masses to moles of atoms by dividing the masses by the A_r values. This tells you how many moles of each different element are present.
- From this you can work out the ratio of atoms of the different elements in the compound.
- Then the *simplest* whole-number ratio gives you the empirical formula of the compound.

Summary questions

1 What is the percentage mass of hydrogen in hydrogen sulfide, H_2S?
   (A_r values: H = 1, S = 32)

2 Ammonium sulfate, $(NH_4)_2SO_4$, is used as a fertiliser. What is the percentage mass of nitrogen in it?
   (A_r values: H = 1, N = 14, O = 16, S = 32)

3 A compound contains 40% sulfur and 60% oxygen by mass. What is its empirical formula?
   (A_r values: S = 32, O = 16)

4 22.55% of the mass of a sample of phosphorus chloride is phosphorus. What is the empirical formula of this phosphorus chloride?
   (A_r values: P = 31, Cl = 35.5)

5 10.8 g of aluminium react exactly with 9.6 g of oxygen. What is the empirical formula of the compound formed?
   (A_r values: Al = 27, O = 16)

Key points

- The relative atomic masses of the elements in a compound and its formula can be used to work out its percentage composition.

- We can calculate empirical formulae given the masses or percentage composition of elements present.

C2.3 Chemical equations

Learning objectives

After this topic, you should know:

- what happens to the atoms in a chemical reaction

- how the mass of reactants compares with the mass of products in a chemical reaction

- how to write balanced symbol equations, including state symbols, to represent reactions.

Chemical equations show the **reactants** (the substances we start with) and the **products** (the new substances made) in a reaction.

We can represent the test for hydrogen gas using a **word equation**:

$$\text{hydrogen} + \text{oxygen} \rightarrow \text{water}$$
$$\text{(reactants)} \qquad \text{(product)}$$

In chemical reactions the atoms get rearranged. Now you can investigate what happens to the mass of reactants compared with mass of products in a reaction.

Using **symbol equations** helps us to see how much of each substance is involved in a reaction.

For example, calcium carbonate decomposes (breaks down) on heating. We can show the reaction using a symbol equation like this:

$$CaCO_3 \rightarrow CaO + CO_2$$

This equation is **balanced** – there is the same number of each type of atom on both sides of the equation. This is very important, because atoms cannot be created or destroyed in a chemical reaction. This also means that:

The total mass of the products formed in a reaction is equal to the total mass of the reactants.

We can check if an equation is balanced by counting the number of each type of atom on either side of the equation. If the numbers are equal, then the equation is balanced.

We can also add **state symbols** to a balanced symbol equation to give extra information. The state symbols used are:

- (s) for solids
- (l) for liquids
- (g) for gases
- (aq) for substances dissolved in water, i.e. **aqueous solutions**.

So the balanced symbol equation, including state symbols, for the decomposition of calcium carbonate is:

$$CaCO_3(s) \rightarrow CaO(s) + CO_2(g)$$

links

For more information on the decomposition of calcium carbonate, see 6.4 'Metal carbonates'.

Practical

Investigating the mass of reactants and products

You are given solutions of lead nitrate (toxic) and potassium iodide.

Wearing chemical splashproof eye protection, add a small volume of each solution together in a test tube.

- What do you see happen?

The formula of lead nitrate is $Pb(NO_3)_2$ and of potassium iodide is KI.

The precipitate (a solid formed in the reaction between two solutions) is lead iodide, PbI_2 (which is toxic).

- Predict a word equation and a balanced symbol equation, including state symbols, for the reaction.
- How do you think that the mass of reactants compare with the mass of the products?

Now plan an experiment to test your answer to this question. Your teacher must check your plan before you start the practical work. Wash your hands after the experiment.

Making an equation balance

In the case of hydrogen reacting with oxygen it is not so easy to balance the equation. First of all we write the formula of each reactant and product:

$$H_2 + O_2 \rightarrow H_2O$$

Counting the atoms on either side of the equation we see that we have:

Reactants
2 H atoms, 2 O atoms

Products
2 H atoms, 1 O atoms

So we need another oxygen atom on the product side of the equation. We can't simply change the formula of H_2O to H_2O_2. (H_2O_2 – hydrogen peroxide – is a bleaching agent which is certainly not suitable to drink!) But we can have **2 water molecules** in the reaction – this is shown in a symbol equation as:

$$H_2 + O_2 \rightarrow 2H_2O$$

Counting the atoms on either side of the equation again we get:

Reactants
2 H atoms, 2 O atoms

Products
4 H atoms, 2 O atoms

Although the oxygen atoms are balanced, we now need two more hydrogen atoms on the reactant side. We do this by putting 2 in front of H_2:

$$2H_2 + O_2 \rightarrow 2H_2O$$

Now we have:

Reactants
4 H atoms, 2 O atoms

Products
4 H atoms, 2 O atoms

… and the equation is balanced.

H₂ + O₂ reactants
H₂O products (not enough O atoms)
Not balanced

H₂ + O₂ (not enough H atoms)
2H₂O
Still not balanced!

2H₂ + O₂
2H₂O
Balanced at last!

Maths skills

Look at the chemical equation on the previous page. We can work out the mass of $CaCO_3$, CaO or CO_2 given the masses of the other two compounds.

Because the total mass of the products formed in a reaction is equal to the total mass of the reactants, we can write:

$$CaCO_3 \rightarrow CaO + CO_2$$
$$\text{Mass} = \quad a \quad = \quad b \; + \; c$$

So if the mass of CaO formed is 2.8 g (b above) and the mass of CO_2 is 2.2 g (c above); the mass of $CaCO_3$ (a) that we start with must be 2.8 + 2.2 (b + c) which equals **5.0 g**.

Rearranging the equation for a, b and c we get a – c = b.

So if the reaction started with 100 tonnes of $CaCO_3$ (a) and it gave off 44 tonnes of CO_2 (c).

Then the mass of CaO (b) made is 100 – 44 (a – c) = **56 tonnes**.

Summary questions

1 a Why must all symbol equations be balanced?
  b Balance this equation: $H_2 + Cl_2 \rightarrow HCl$

2 a A mass of 33.6 g of magnesium carbonate ($MgCO_3$) completely decomposes when it is heated. It made 16.0 g of magnesium oxide (MgO). What mass of carbon dioxide (CO_2) is produced in this reaction?
  b Write a word equation and a balanced symbol equation, including state symbols, to show the reaction in part **a**.

3 Balance these symbol equations:
  a $KNO_3 \rightarrow KNO_2 + O_2$ b $Li + O_2 \rightarrow Li_2O$ c $Fe + O_2 \rightarrow Fe_2O_3$

4 Sodium metal, Na, reacts with water to form a solution of sodium hydroxide, NaOH, and gives off hydrogen gas, H_2.
  Write a balanced symbol equation, including state symbols, for this reaction.

Key points

● No new atoms are ever created or destroyed in a chemical reaction:

  The total mass of reactants = the total mass of products.

● There is the same number of each type of atom on each side of a balanced symbol equation.

● We can include state symbols to give extra information in balanced symbol equations. These are (s) for solids, (l) for liquids, (g) for gases and (aq) for aqueous solutions.

C2.4 | Equations and calculations

Learning objectives

After this topic, you should know:

- what balanced symbol equations tell us about chemical reactions

- how to use balanced symbol equations to calculate masses of reactants and products.

Chemical equations can be very useful. When we want to know how much of each substance is involved in a chemical reaction, we can use the balanced symbol equation.

Think about what happens when hydrogen molecules (H_2) react with chlorine molecules (Cl_2). The reaction makes hydrogen chloride molecules (HCl):

$$H_2 + Cl_2 \rightarrow HCl \text{ (not balanced)}$$

This equation shows the reactants and the product – but it is not balanced.

Here is the balanced equation:

$$H_2 + Cl_2 \rightarrow 2HCl$$

This balanced equation tells us that '1 hydrogen molecule reacts with 1 chlorine molecule to make 2 hydrogen chloride molecules'. But the balanced equation also tells us the number of moles of each substance involved. So our balanced equation also tells us that '1 mole of hydrogen molecules reacts with 1 mole of chlorine molecules to make 2 moles of hydrogen chloride molecules'.

1 hydrogen molecule	1 chlorine molecule	2 hydrogen chloride molecules
H_2	$+$ Cl_2	$\longrightarrow$ $2\,HCl$
1 mole of hydrogen molecules	1 mole of chlorine molecules	2 moles of hydrogen chloride molecules

Using balanced equations to work out reacting masses

This balanced equation above is really useful, because we can use it to work out what mass of hydrogen and chlorine react together. We can also calculate how much hydrogen chloride is made.

To do this, we need to know that the A_r for hydrogen is 1 and the A_r for chlorine is 35.5:

A_r of hydrogen = 1   ... so mass of 1 mole of H_2 = $2 \times 1 = 2\,g$
A_r of chlorine = 35.5   ... so mass of 1 mole of Cl_2 = $2 \times 35.5 = 71\,g$
M_r of HCl = $(1 + 35.5) = 36.5$ ... so mass of 1 mole of HCl = $36.5\,g$

Our balanced equation tells us that 1 mole of hydrogen reacts with 1 mole of chlorine to give 2 moles of HCl. So turning this into masses we get:

$$
\begin{aligned}
\text{1 mole of hydrogen} &= 1 \times 2\,g &= \mathbf{2\,g} \\
\text{1 mole of chlorine} &= 1 \times 71\,g &= \mathbf{71\,g} \\
\text{2 moles of HCl} &= 2 \times 36.5\,g &= \mathbf{73\,g}
\end{aligned}
$$

Calculations

These calculations are important when we want to know the mass of chemicals that react together. For example, sodium hydroxide reacts with chlorine gas to make bleach.

Here is the balanced symbol equation for the reaction:

$$2NaOH + Cl_2 \rightarrow NaOCl + NaCl + H_2O$$
sodium hydroxide   chlorine   bleach   salt   water

This reaction happens when chlorine gas is bubbled through a solution of sodium hydroxide.

If we have a solution containing 100 g of sodium hydroxide, how much chlorine gas do we need to convert it to bleach? Too much, and some chlorine will be wasted. Too little, and not all of the sodium hydroxide will react.

(A_r values: H = 1, O = 16, Na = 23 and Cl = 35.5)

Mass of 1 mole of	
NaOH	**Cl_2**
= 23 + 16 + 1 = 40	= 35.5 × 2 = 71

The table shows that 1 mole of sodium hydroxide has a mass of 40 g.

So 100 g of sodium hydroxide is $\frac{100}{40} = 2.5$ moles.

The balanced symbol equation tells us that for every 2 moles of sodium hydroxide we need 1 mole of chlorine to react with it.

So we need $\frac{2.5}{2} = 1.25$ moles of chlorine.

The table shows that 1 mole of chlorine has a mass of 71 g.

So we will need 1.25 × 71 = **88.75 g** of chlorine to react with 100 g of sodium hydroxide.

Summary questions

1 '2HCl' can have two meanings. What are they?

2 Magnesium burns in oxygen with a bright white flame:

$$2Mg(s) + O_2(g) \rightarrow 2MgO(s)$$

What mass of oxygen will react exactly with 6.0 g of magnesium? (A_r values: O = 16, Mg = 24)

3 a An aqueous solution of hydrogen peroxide, H_2O_2, decomposes to form water and oxygen gas. Write a balanced symbol equation, including state symbols, for this reaction.
   b When hydrogen peroxide decomposes, what mass of hydrogen peroxide is needed in solution to produce 1.6 g of oxygen gas? (A_r values: H = 1, O = 16)

4 When a small lump of calcium metal, Ca, is added to water it reacts giving off hydrogen gas. A solution of calcium hydroxide, $Ca(OH)_2$, is also formed in the reaction. (A_r values: Ca = 40, O = 16, H = 1)
   a Write a balanced symbol equation, including state symbols, for the reaction.
   b Calculate how much calcium metal must be added to an excess of water to produce 3.7 g of calcium hydroxide in solution.

Key points

- Balanced symbol equations tell us the number of moles of substances involved in a chemical reaction.

- We can use balanced symbol equations to calculate the masses of reactants and products in a chemical reaction.

C2.5 | Reversible reactions

Learning objectives

After this topic, you should know:

- what a reversible reaction is

- how we can represent reversible reactions.

Figure 1 Indicators undergo reversible reactions, changing colour to show us whether solutions are acidic or alkaline

In most chemical reactions, the reactants react completely to form the products. We show this by using an arrow pointing *from* the reactants *to* the products:

$$A + B \rightarrow C + D$$
$$\text{reactants} \quad \text{products}$$

But in some reactions the products can react together to make the original reactants again. We call this a **reversible reaction**.

A reversible reaction can go in both directions so we use two 'half-arrows' in the equation. One arrow points in the forwards direction and one backwards:

$$A + B \rightleftharpoons C + D$$

We still call the substances on the left-hand side of the equation as we look at it the 'reactants' and those on the right-hand side the 'products'. So it is important that you write down the equation of the reversible reaction you are referring to when you use the words 'reactants' and 'products'. If the equation is written as:

$$C + D \rightleftharpoons A + B$$

the reactants are C and D, and the products are A and B!

Examples of reversible reactions

Have you ever tried to neutralise an alkaline solution with an acid? It is very difficult to get a solution which is exactly neutral. You can use an indicator to tell when just the right amount of acid has been added. An indicator forms compounds that are different colours in acidic solutions and in alkaline solutions.

Litmus is a complex molecule. We will represent it as HLit (where H is hydrogen). HLit is red. If you add alkali, HLit turns into the Lit^- ion by losing an H^+ ion. Lit^- is blue. If you then add more acid, blue Lit^- changes back to red HLit and so on.

$$HLit(aq) \rightleftharpoons H^+(aq) + Lit^-(aq)$$
$$\text{Red litmus} \qquad\qquad \text{Blue litmus}$$

Practical

Changing colours

Use litmus solution, dilute hydrochloric acid and dilute sodium hydroxide solution to show the reversible reaction described here.

- Explain the changes you see when adding acid and alkali to litmus.

Safety: Wear eye protection.

Other reversible reactions involve salts and their water of crystallisation. For example:

$$\begin{array}{ccc} CuSO_4.5H_2O & \rightleftharpoons & CuSO_4 \quad + 5H_2O \\ \text{hydrated} & \rightleftharpoons & \text{anhydrous} \quad + \text{water} \\ \text{copper(II) sulfate (blue)} & & \text{copper(II) sulfate (white)} \end{array}$$

Practical

Heating ammonium chloride

Gently heat a small amount of ammonium chloride (harmful) in a test tube with a loose plug of mineral wool. Use test tube holders or clamp the test tube at an angle. Make sure you warm the bottom of the tube.

- What do you see happen inside the test tube?
- Explain the changes.

Safety: Wear eye protection. Take care if you are asthmatic.

When we heat ammonium chloride a reversible reaction takes place.

Ammonium chloride breaks down on heating. It forms ammonia gas and hydrogen chloride gas. This is an example of thermal decomposition:

$$\text{ammonium chloride} \xrightarrow{\text{heat}} \text{ammonia} + \text{hydrogen chloride}$$
$$NH_4Cl(s) \longrightarrow NH_3(g) + HCl(g)$$

The two hot gases rise up the test tube. When they cool down near the mouth of the tube they react with each other (see Figure 2). The gases re-form ammonium chloride again. The white ammonium chloride solid forms on the inside of the glass:

$$\text{ammonia} + \text{hydrogen chloride} \longrightarrow \text{ammonium chloride}$$
$$NH_3(g) + HCl(g) \longrightarrow NH_4Cl(s)$$

We can show the reversible reaction as:

$$\text{ammonium chloride} \rightleftharpoons \text{ammonia} + \text{hydrogen chloride}$$
$$NH_4Cl(s) \rightleftharpoons NH_3(g) + HCl(g)$$

links

For more about reversible reactions, see 12.3 'Energy and reversible reactions'.

Figure 2 An example of a reversible reaction – heating ammonium chloride

Summary questions

1 What do chemists mean by the term 'a *reversible* chemical reaction'?

2 Phenolphthalein is an indicator. It is colourless in acid and pure water but is pink-purple in alkali. In a demonstration a teacher started with a beaker containing a mixture of water and phenolphthalein. In two other beakers she had different volumes of acid and alkali. The acid and alkali had the same concentration.
   She then poured the mixture into the beaker containing 2 cm³ of sodium hydroxide solution. Finally she poured the mixture into a third beaker with 5 cm³ of hydrochloric acid in it.
   Describe what you would observe happening in the demonstration.

3 We can represent the phenolphthalein indicator in question **2** as HPhe. Assuming it behaves like litmus, write a balanced symbol equation to show its reversible reaction in acid and alkali. Show the colour of HPhe and Phe⁻ under their formulae in your equation.

4 Thermochromic materials change colours at different temperatures. The change is reversible. Give a use or potential use for thermochromic materials in the home.

5 Find out about two reversible reactions that can be used to test for the presence of water. Give the positive result for each test, including a balanced symbol equation.

Key points

- In a reversible reaction the products of the reaction can react to make the original reactants.

- We can show a reversible reaction using the $\rightleftharpoons$ sign.

C2.6 The yield of a chemical reaction

Learning objectives

After this topic, you should know:

- what is meant by the yield of a chemical reaction
- what factors can affect the yield
- how to calculate the percentage yield of a chemical reaction.

Many of the substances that we use every day have to be made from other chemicals. This may involve using complex chemical reactions. Examples include the plastics and composites used in your phones and computers, the ink in your pen or printer, and the artificial fibres in your clothes. All of these are made using chemical reactions.

Imagine a reaction: A + 2B → C

If we need 1000 kg of C, we can work out how much A and B we need. All we need to know is the relative formula masses of A, B and C and the balanced symbol equation.

A + 2B ⟶ C
(reactants)   (product)

If we carry out the reaction, it is unlikely that we will get as much of C as we worked out. This is because our calculations assumed that all of the reactants A and B would be turned into product C. We call the amount of product that a chemical reaction produces its **yield**.

It is useful to think about reactions in terms of their **percentage yield**. This compares the amount of product that the reaction *really* produces with the maximum amount that it could *possibly* produce, predicted from the balanced equation:

$$\text{Percentage yield} = \frac{\text{amount of product produced}}{\text{maxmimum amount of product possible}} \times 100\%$$

Calculating percentage yield

An industrial example

Limestone is made mainly of calcium carbonate. Crushed lumps of limestone are heated in a rotating lime kiln. The calcium carbonate decomposes to make calcium oxide, and carbon dioxide gas is given off. A company processes 200 tonnes of limestone a day. It collects 98 tonnes of calcium oxide, the useful product. What is the percentage yield of the reaction in the kiln, assuming limestone contains only calcium carbonate?
(A_r values: Ca = 40, C = 12, O = 16)

$$\text{calcium carbonate} \rightarrow \text{calcium oxide} + \text{carbon dioxide}$$
$$CaCO_3(s) \quad \rightarrow \quad CaO(s) \quad + \quad CO_2(g)$$

Work out the relative formula masses of $CaCO_3$ and CaO.

$$M_r \text{ of } CaCO_3 = 40 + 12 + (16 \times 3) = 100$$
$$M_r \text{ of } CaO \quad = 40 + 16 \qquad \quad = 56$$

So the balanced symbol equation tells us that:

100 tonnes of $CaCO_3$ could make 56 tonnes of CaO, assuming a 100% yield.

Therefore 200 tonnes of $CaCO_3$ could make a maximum of (56 × 2) tonnes of CaO = 112 tonnes.

So   percentage yield $= \dfrac{\text{amount of product produced}}{\text{maximum amount of product possible}} \times 100\%$

$$= \frac{98}{112} \times 100 = \textbf{87.5\%}$$

We can explain this yield as some of the limestone is lost as dust in the crushing process and in the rotating kiln. There will also be some other mineral compounds in the limestone. It is not 100% calcium carbonate as we assumed in our calculation.

Very few chemical reactions have a yield of 100% because:
- The reaction may be reversible (so as products form they react to re-form the reactants again).
- Some reactants may react to give unexpected or unwanted products in alternative reactions.
- Some of the product may be lost in handling or left behind in the apparatus.
- The reactants may not be pure.
- Some of the desired product may be lost during separation from the reaction mixture.

Sustainable production

Chemical companies use reactions to make products they sell. Ideally, they want to use reactions with high yields (that also happen at a reasonable rate). Making a product more efficiently means making less waste. As much product as possible should be made from the reactants.

Chemical factories (or plants) are designed by chemical engineers. They design a plant to work as safely and economically as possible. It should waste as little energy and raw materials as possible. This helps the company to make money. It is better for the environment too as it conserves our limited resources. It also reduces the pollution we get whenever we use fossil fuels as sources of energy.

∞ links

For information about using balanced symbol equations to predict reacting masses, look back to 2.4 'Equations and calculations'.

Summary questions

1 Explain generally why it is good for the environment if industry finds ways to make products using high yield reactions and processes that waste as little energy as possible.

2 List the factors that can affect the percentage yield of a reaction.

3 If the percentage yield for a reaction is 100%, 60 g of reactant A would make 80 g of product C. How much of reactant A is needed to make 80 g of product C if the percentage yield of the reaction is only 75%?

4 Ammonia gas (NH_3) is made by heating the gases nitrogen and hydrogen under pressure in the presence of an iron catalyst:

$$N_2(g) + 3H_2(g) \rightleftharpoons 2NH_3(g)$$

If 7.0 g of nitrogen are reacted with excess hydrogen and 1.8 g of ammonia is collected, what is the percentage yield?

5 Sodium hydrogencarbonate, $NaHCO_3$, can be converted into sodium carbonate, Na_2CO_3, by heating. This is a thermal decomposition reaction in which water vapour and carbon dioxide are also products of the reaction. A student started with 16.8 g of sodium hydrogencarbonate and collected 9.20 g of sodium carbonate.
  a Write a balanced symbol equation for the thermal decomposition of sodium hydrogencarbonate.
  b What percentage yield did the student obtain?

Key points

- The yield of a chemical reaction describes how much product is made.
- The percentage yield of a chemical reaction tells us how much product is made compared with the maximum amount that could be made (100%).
- Factors affecting the yield of a chemical reaction include product being left behind in the apparatus, reversible reactions not going to completion, some reactants may produce unexpected reactions, and losses in separating the products from the reaction mixture.

Summary questions

1 Calculate the mass of 1 mole of each of the following compounds:

a H_2S

b SO_2

c C_2H_4

d NaOH

e Na_2CO_3

f $Al_2(SO_4)_3$

g $NaAl(OH)_4$

(A_r values: H = 1, C = 12, O = 16, Na = 23, Al = 27, S = 32)

2 How many moles of:

a Ag atoms are there in 27 g of silver,

b Fe atoms are there in 0.056 g of iron,

c P_4 molecules are there in 6.2 g of phosphorus?

(A_r values: P = 31, Fe = 56, Ag = 108)

3 a The chemical formula of ethane is C_2H_6. Work out the percentage by mass of carbon in ethane.

b Work out the mass of hydrogen present in 3.8 g of ethane.

(A_r values: H = 1, C = 12)

4 When aluminium reacts with bromine, 4.05 g of aluminium reacts with 36.0 g of bromine. What is the empirical formula of aluminium bromide?

(A_r values: Al = 27, Br = 80)

5 Balance the following symbol equations:

a $Na + Cl_2 \rightarrow NaCl$

b $Al + O_2 \rightarrow Al_2O_3$

c $Al(OH)_3 \rightarrow Al_2O_3 + H_2O$

d $Ba(NO_3)_2 \rightarrow BaO + NO_2 + O_2$

e $C_4H_{10} + O_2 \rightarrow CO_2 + H_2O$

6 In a lime kiln, calcium carbonate is decomposed to calcium oxide:

$$CaCO_3 \rightarrow CaO + CO_2$$

1500 tonnes of calcium carbonate gave 804 tonnes of calcium oxide. Calculate the percentage yield for the process.

(A_r values: C = 12, O = 16, Ca = 40)

7 a Ethene gas (C_2H_4) reacting with steam (H_2O) to form ethanol gas (C_2H_5OH) is a reversible reaction. Write the balanced symbol equation for this reaction, including state symbols.

b If 14.00 g of ethene reacts with excess steam to produce 17.25 g of ethanol, what is the percentage yield of the reaction?

8 Sulfur is mined in Poland and is brought to Britain in ships. The sulfur is used to make sulfuric acid. Sulfur is burned in air to produce sulfur dioxide. Sulfur dioxide and air are passed over a heated catalyst to produce sulfur trioxide. Water can be added to sulfur trioxide to produce sulfuric acid.

The reactions are:

$$S + O_2 \rightarrow SO_2$$
$$2SO_2 + O_2 \rightleftharpoons 2SO_3$$
$$SO_3 + H_2O \rightarrow H_2SO_4$$

(A_r values: H = 1, O = 16, S = 32)

a How many moles of sulfuric acid could be produced from one mole of sulfur?

b Calculate the maximum mass of sulfuric acid that can be produced from 64 kg of sulfur.

c In an industrial process the mass of sulfuric acid that was produced from 64.00 kg of sulfur was 188.16 kg. Use your answer to part **b** to calculate the percentage yield of this process.

d Suggest two reasons why the yield of the industrial process was less than the maximum yield.

AQA Examination-style questions

1 Use the relative atomic masses in the periodic table in the following calculations.

a What is the relative formula mass of O_2? (1)

b What is the relative formula mass of $Ca(OH)_2$? (1)

c How many moles of sodium hydroxide are there in 20 g of $NaOH$? (2)

d What mass of ammonium nitrate is present in 2 mol of NH_4NO_3? (2)

2 The element bromine is formed in the following reaction.

$$HBr + H_2SO_4 \rightarrow H_2O + Br_2 + SO_2$$

a Write a balanced equation for this reaction. (1)

b The formula of a bromine compound formerly used in agriculture is CH_3Br.

What is the percentage by mass of bromine in this compound? (2)

c Another bromine compound contains 15.2% sodium and 53.0% bromine by mass. The remainder is oxygen.

Calculate the empirical formula of this compound. (4)

3 An experiment was carried out to investigate the reduction of an oxide of copper.

Oxide of copper in a dish — Excess hydrogen is burning here
Hydrogen gas
Heat

a The diagram shows the hydrogen burning at the end of the tube.

What would be the risk if the hydrogen were not burned at the end of the tube? (1)

b A student observed some drops of a colourless liquid inside the tube shortly after starting to heat.

What is the liquid? Outline the reaction in which it formed. (2)

c Describe how you could be certain that all the oxide had completely changed into copper. (2)

d A student recorded the following results:

mass of oxide before heating = 5.72 g
mass of copper formed   = 5.08 g

i Calculate the mass of oxygen in the oxide. (1)

ii Calculate the amount, in moles, of oxygen in the oxide. (1)

iii Calculate the amount, in moles, of copper formed. (1)

iv Calculate the empirical formula of the oxide. (2)

4 Some ammonium chloride was heated in a test tube as shown in the diagram.

White solid
Ammonium chloride
HEAT

a When the ammonium chloride is heated gently it decomposes according to this equation:

$$NH_4Cl \rightarrow NH_3 + HCl$$

The diagram shows that a white solid forms near the open end of the tube.

i Name the two gases in the tube between the ammonium chloride and the white solid. (2)

ii Suggest what the white solid is. (1)

iii Deduce the equation to show its formation. (1)

b A student heated the tube strongly and did not observe the formation of the white solid.

Suggest an explanation for this. (1)

5 A reaction used in industry to manufacture methanol is

$$CO + 2H_2 \rightleftharpoons CH_3OH$$

A chemist investigated this reaction under different conditions, starting with 56 g of carbon monoxide.

a What mass of hydrogen is needed to completely react with this mass of carbon monoxide? (2)

b What is the maximum mass of methanol that can be obtained from this mass of carbon monoxide? (2)

c In one experiment the chemist obtained 16 g of methanol.

Calculate the percentage yield of methanol in this experiment. (2)

C3.1

Atoms into ions

Learning objectives

After this topic, you should know:

- what a chemical compound is

- how elements form compounds

- how atoms can form either positive or negative ions

- how the elements in Group 1 bond with the elements in Group 7.

You already know that we can mix two substances together without either of them changing. For example, we can mix sand and salt together and then separate them again. No change will have taken place. But in chemical reactions the situation is very different.

When the atoms of two or more elements react they make a compound.

A compound contains two or more elements which are chemically combined.

The compound formed is different from the elements and we cannot get the elements back again easily. We can also react compounds together to form other compounds. However, the reaction of elements is easier to understand as a starting point.

Figure 1 The difference between mixing and reacting. Separating mixtures is usually quite easy, but separating the elements from compounds once they have reacted can be difficult.

The atoms of the noble gases, in Group 0 of the periodic table, have an arrangement of electrons that make them stable and unreactive. However, most atoms do not have this electronic structure. When atoms react they take part in changes which give them a stable arrangement of electrons. They may do this by either:

- sharing electrons, which we call **covalent bonding**
- transferring electrons, which we call **ionic bonding**.

Losing electrons to form positive ions

In ionic bonding the atoms involved lose or gain electrons to form charged particles called ions. The ions have the electronic structure of a noble gas. So, for example, if sodium (2,8,1), from Group 1 in the periodic table, loses one electron, it is left with the stable electronic structure of neon (2,8).

Figure 2 A positive sodium ion (Na^+) is formed when a sodium atom loses an electron during ionic bonding

However, it is also left with one more proton in its nucleus than there are electrons around the nucleus. The proton has a positive charge so the sodium atom has now become a positively charged ion. The sodium ion has a single positive charge. We write the formula of a sodium ion as Na$^+$. The electronic structure of the Na$^+$ ion is 2,8. This is shown in Figure 2.

Gaining electrons to form negative ions

When non-metals react with metals, the non-metal atoms gain electrons to achieve a stable noble gas structure. Chlorine, for example, has the electronic structure 2,8,7. It is in Group 7 of the periodic table. By gaining a single electron, it gets the stable electronic structure of argon (2,8,8).

In this case, there is now one more electron than there are positive protons in the nucleus. So the chlorine atom becomes a negatively charged ion. This carries a single negative charge. We write the formula of the chloride ion as Cl$^-$. Its electronic structure is 2,8,8. This is shown in Figure 3.

Representing ionic bonding

Metal atoms, which tend to lose electrons, react with non-metal atoms, which tend to gain electrons. So when sodium reacts with chlorine, each sodium atom loses an electron and each chlorine atom gains an electron. They both form stable ions. The electrostatic attraction between the oppositely charged Na$^+$ ions and Cl$^-$ ions is called ionic bonding.

We can show what happens in a diagram. The electrons of one atom are represented by dots, and the electrons of the other atom are represented by crosses. This is shown in Figure 4.

Chlorine
2,8,7

Cl$^-$
2,8,8

Figure 3 A negative chloride ion (Cl$^-$) is formed when a chlorine atom gains an electron during ionic bonding

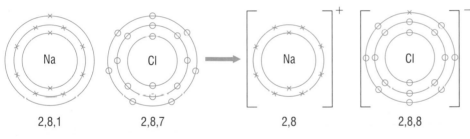

2,8,1   2,8,7   2,8   2,8,8

NaCl (Na$^+$Cl$^-$)

Figure 4 The formation of sodium chloride (NaCl) – an example of ion formation by transferring an electron

Summary questions

1 **a** When atoms bond together by *sharing* electrons, what type of bond is formed?

   b When ions bond together as a result of *gaining* or *losing* electrons, what type of bond is this?

2 Explain how and why atoms of Group 1 and Group 7 elements react with each other, in terms of their electronic structures.

3 Write electron structures to show the ions that would be formed when the following atoms are involved in ionic bonding. For each one, state how many electrons have been lost or gained and show the charge on the ions formed.
   a aluminium (Al)   **b** fluorine (F)
   c potassium (K)   **d** oxygen (O)

Key points

- Elements react together to form compounds by gaining or losing electrons or by sharing electrons.

- The elements in Group 1 react with the elements in Group 7. As they react, atoms of Group 1 elements can each lose one electron to gain the stable electronic structure of a noble gas. This electron can be given to an atom from Group 7, which then also achieves the stable electronic structure of a noble gas.

C3.2

Ionic bonding

You have seen how positive and negative ions form during some reactions. Ionic compounds are usually formed when metals react with non-metals. It is the metals that form positive ions and the non-metals that form negative ions.

The ions formed are held next to each other by very strong forces of attraction between the oppositely charged ions. This electrostatic force of attraction, which acts in all directions, is called ionic bonding.

The ionic bonds between the charged particles result in an arrangement of ions that we call a giant structure (or a **giant lattice**). If we could stand among the ions they would seem to go on in all directions forever.

Ions and the periodic table

We have seen how atoms in Group 1 of the periodic table have 1 electron in their outermost shell (or highest energy level) and form 1+ ions. Group 7 atoms have 7 electrons in their outermost shell and form 1– ions. The group number gives us the number of electrons in the outermost shell. So how does the group number relate to the charges on the ions formed from atoms?

Sometimes the atoms reacting need to gain or lose two electrons to gain the stable electronic structure of a noble gas. An example is when magnesium (2,8,2), from Group 2, reacts with oxygen (2,6), from Group 6. When these two elements react they form magnesium oxide (MgO). This is made up of magnesium ions with a double positive charge (Mg^{2+}) and oxide ions with a double negative charge (O^{2-}).

So we can say that when atoms form **ionic** bonds, atoms from:
● Group 1 form 1+ ions
● Group 2 form 2+ ions
● Group 3 form 3+ ions, when they form ions as opposed to sharing electrons
● Group 4 do not form ions (apart from tin and lead at the bottom of the group)
● Group 5 form 3– ions, when they form ions as opposed to sharing electrons
● Group 6 form 2– ions, when they form ions as opposed to sharing electrons
● Group 7 form 1– ions, when they form ions as opposed to sharing electrons
● Group 0 never form ions in compounds.

Figure 1 shows how the electrons are transferred between a magnesium atom and an oxygen atom.

2,8,2   2,6   2,8   **MgO**   2,8

Figure 1 When magnesium oxide (MgO) is formed, the reacting magnesium atoms lose two electrons and the oxygen atoms gain two electrons

Another example of an ionic compound is calcium chloride. Each calcium atom (2,8,8,2) needs to lose two electrons but each chlorine atom (2,8,7) needs to gain only one electron. This means that two chlorine atoms react with every one calcium atom to form calcium chloride. So the formula of calcium chloride is $CaCl_2$.

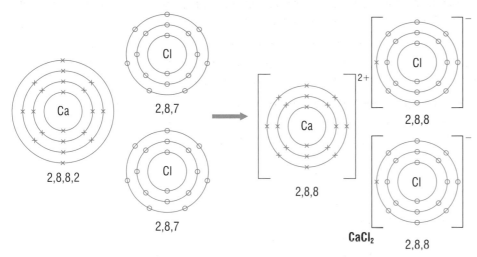

Figure 2 The formation of calcium chloride ($CaCl_2$)

Notice that the charges in the formula of an ionic compound cancel each other out as the overall charge on the compound is zero. So aluminium oxide, made up of aluminium ions, Al^{3+}, and oxide ions, O^{2-}, has the formula Al_2O_3 (total charges of 6+ on the aluminium ions cancelling out 6– on the oxide ions).

Summary questions

1 **a** Copy and complete the table:

Atomic number	Atom	Electronic structure of atom	Ion	Electronic structure of ion
9	F			2,8
3		2,1	Li^+	
16	S		S^{2-}	
20		2,8,8,2		

2 Why do metal atoms form positively charged ions and non-metal atoms form negatively charged ions?

3 Think of rules to follow to remember the charge on any ions formed by elements in:
   a Groups 1, 2 and 3
   b Groups 5, 6 and 7.

4 **a** Explain why potassium bromide is KBr but potassium oxide is K_2O.
   b Explain why magnesium oxide is MgO but magnesium chloride is $MgCl_2$.

5 Draw diagrams to show how you would expect the following elements to form ions together:
   a potassium and oxygen
   b aluminium and fluorine.

Key points

- Ionic compounds are held together by strong forces of attraction between their oppositely charged ions. This is called ionic bonding.

- Besides the elements in Groups 1 and 7, other elements that can form ionic compounds include those from Groups 2 and 6.

C3.3 Giant ionic structures

Learning objectives

After this topic, you should know:

- why ionic compounds have high melting points

- why ionic compounds conduct electricity when we melt them or dissolve them in water.

We have already seen that an ionic compound consists of a giant structure of ions arranged in a lattice. The attractive electrostatic forces between the oppositely charged ions act in all directions and are very strong. This holds the ions in the lattice together very tightly. Look at Figure 1.

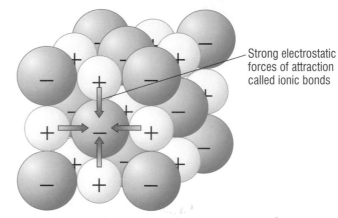

Strong electrostatic forces of attraction called ionic bonds

Figure 1 The attractive forces between the oppositely charged ions in an ionic compound are very strong. The regular arrangement of ions in the giant lattice enables ionic compounds to form crystals.

⬭ links

For more information on the movement and arrangement of particles in solids and liquids, look back to 1.1 'States of matter'.

It takes a lot of energy to break up a giant ionic lattice. There are lots of strong ionic bonds to break. To separate the ions we have to overcome all those electrostatic forces of attraction acting in all directions. This means that ionic compounds have high melting points and boiling points.

Once we have supplied enough energy to separate the ions from the lattice, they are free to move around. That's when the ionic solid melts and becomes a liquid. The ions are free to move anywhere in this liquid. They are attracted to oppositely charged electrodes dipping in the molten compound. Therefore, they can carry their electrical charge through the liquid (see Figure 2). A solid ionic compound cannot conduct electricity because its ions are held in fixed positions in the lattice. They cannot move around. They can only vibrate 'on the spot' when in the solid state.

Examiner's tip

Remember that every ionic compound has a giant structure. The oppositely charged ions in these structures are held together by strong electrostatic forces of attraction. These act in all directions.

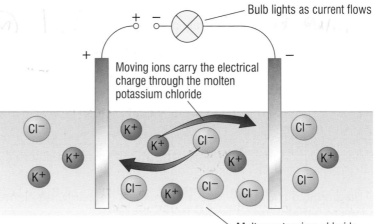

Bulb lights as current flows

Moving ions carry the electrical charge through the molten potassium chloride

Molten potassium chloride

Figure 2 Because the ions are free to move, a molten ionic compound can conduct electricity

Many ionic compounds will dissolve in water. When we dissolve an ionic compound in water, the lattice is split up by the water molecules. Then the ions are free to move around in the solution formed. They can carry their charge to oppositely charged electrodes in the solution. Just as molten ionic compounds will conduct electricity, solutions of ionic compounds will also conduct electricity. The ions are able to move to an oppositely charged electrode dipped in the solution.

Figure 3 Ionic compounds do not conduct electricity in the solid state but do when molten or when dissolved in water

Ionic solid	Molten ionic compound	Ionic compound in solution
Ions are fixed in a giant lattice. They vibrate but cannot move around – it does not conduct electricity.	High temperature provides enough energy to overcome the many strong attractive forces between ions. Ions are free to move around within the molten compound – it does conduct electricity.	Water molecules separate ions from the lattice. Ions are free to move around within the solution – it does conduct electricity.

Practical

Testing conductivity

Using a circuit as shown in Figure 2, dip a pair of electrodes into a 1 cm depth of sodium chloride crystals. What happens?

Now slowly add water.
● What happens to the bulb?

Repeat the experiment using potassium chloride.
● Explain your observations.

Summary questions

1 Explain why ionic compounds have high melting points.

2 Explain why ionic compounds conduct electricity only when they are molten or dissolved in water.

3 Why is seawater a better conductor of electricity than water from a freshwater lake?

4 Which of these ions will move to the positive electrode and which will move to the negative electrode in a circuit as shown in Figure 2?
lithium ions, chloride ions, bromide ions, calcium ions, sodium ions, zinc ions, oxide ions, iodide ions, barium ions

5 Predict which of these two ionic compounds has the higher melting point – sodium oxide or aluminium oxide. Explain your reasoning.

Key points

● It takes a lot of energy to break the many strong ionic bonds that hold a giant ionic lattice together. So, ionic compounds have high melting points. They are all solids at room temperature.

● Ionic compounds will conduct electricity when we melt them or dissolve them in water. That's because their ions can then move freely around and can carry charge through the liquid.

C3.4

Covalent bonding

Reactions between metals and non-metals usually result in compounds with ionic bonding. However, many more compounds are formed in a very different way. When non-metals react together their atoms share pairs of electrons to form molecules. We call this covalent bonding.

Figure 1 Most of the molecules in substances which make up living things are held together by covalent bonds between non-metal atoms

Simple molecules

The atoms of non-metals generally need to gain electrons to achieve stable electron structures. When they react together neither atom can give away electrons. So they get the electronic structure of a noble gas by sharing electrons. The atoms in the molecules are then held together by the shared pairs of electrons. We call these strong bonds between the atoms **covalent bonds**.

Figure 2 Atoms of hydrogen and oxygen join together to form stable molecules. The atoms in H_2 and O_2 molecules are held together by strong covalent bonds.

Sometimes in covalent bonding each atom has the same number of electrons to share. But this is not always the case. Sometimes the atoms of one element will need several electrons, while those of the other element only needs one more electron for each atom to get a stable electron structure. In this case, more atoms become involved in forming the molecule, such as in water, H_2O, and methane, CH_4 (see Figure 3).

Figure 3 The principles of covalent bonding remain the same however many atoms are involved

We can represent the covalent bonds in substances such as water, ammonia and methane in a number of ways. Each way represents the same thing. The method chosen depends on what we want to show.

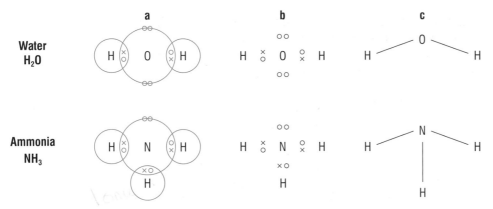

Water
H_2O

Ammonia
NH_3

Figure 4 We can represent a covalent compound by showing **a** the highest energy levels (or outer shells), **b** the outer electrons in a dot and cross diagram or **c** the number of covalent bonds. Double bonds are shown by two lines e.g. O=O in an oxygen molecule.

Giant covalent structures

Many substances containing covalent bonds consist of small molecules, for example, H_2O. However, some covalently bonded substances are very different. They have giant structures where huge numbers of atoms are held together by a network of covalent bonds. These are sometimes referred to as macromolecules.

Diamond has a giant covalent structure. In diamond, each carbon atom forms four covalent bonds with its neighbours. This results in a rigid giant covalent lattice.

Figure 5 Diamonds owe their hardness to the way the carbon atoms are arranged in a giant covalent structure

⬯⬯ links

For more information about diamond, see 3.6 'Giant covalent structures'.

Summary questions

1 Which of these compounds will contain covalent bonds? How did you decide?

   hydrogen iodide, iron(II) chloride, lithium oxide, sulfur dioxide, nitrogen(III) chloride, magnesium nitride

2 Draw diagrams, showing all the electrons, to represent the covalent bonding between the following atoms.
   a two hydrogen atoms
   b two chlorine atoms
   c a hydrogen atom and a fluorine atom

3 Draw dot and cross diagrams to show the covalent bonds when:
   a a phosphorus atom bonds with three hydrogen atoms
   b a carbon atom bonds with two oxygen atoms.

4 Which noble gas electron structures do the atoms in a molecule of hydrogen chloride attain?

5 A covalent bond consists of a pair of electrons which occupy a space mainly between the nuclei of the two atoms bonded together. Explain how this pair of electrons bonds the atoms to each other. (Hint: think of the electrostatic forces of attraction between oppositely charged particles.)

Key points

- Covalent bonds are formed when atoms of non-metals share pairs of electrons with each other.

- Each shared pair of electrons is a covalent bond.

- Many substances containing covalent bonds consist of simple molecules, but some have giant covalent structures.

C3.5

Simple molecules

Learning objectives

After this topic, you should know:

- why substances made of simple molecules have low melting points and boiling points

- why these substances do not conduct electricity.

Many substances made up of simple covalently-bonded molecules have low melting points and boiling points. Look at the graph in Figure 1.

This means that many substances made up of simple molecules are liquids or gases at room temperature. Others are solids with quite low melting points, such as iodine (I_2) and sulfur (S_8).

Figure 1 Substances made of simple molecules usually have low melting points and boiling points

Intermolecular forces

Covalent bonds are very strong. So the atoms within each molecule are held very tightly together. However, each molecule tends to be quite separate from its neighbouring molecules. The force of attraction between the individual molecules in a covalent substance is relatively small. We say that there are weak **intermolecular forces** between molecules. Overcoming these forces does not take much energy.

Look at the molecules in a sample of chlorine gas (Figure 2).

Figure 2 Covalent bonds and the weak forces between molecules in chlorine gas. It is the weak intermolecular forces that are overcome when substances made of simple molecules melt or boil. The covalent bonds are not broken.

We have seen that ionic compounds will conduct electricity when they are liquids. But although a substance that is made up of simple molecules may be a liquid at room temperature, it will not conduct electricity. Look at the demonstration below.

Examiner's tip

Although the covalent bonds in molecules are strong, the forces between molecules are weak.

Demonstration

Conductivity

● What happens?

+ –
Bulb does not light as no current flows

+

–

Ethanol (C_2H_5OH) liquid

Uncharged molecules do not carry charge between the electrodes

Figure 3 Compounds made of simple molecules do not conduct electricity

Safety: Ethanol is highly flammable so no naked flames.

There is no overall charge on the simple molecules in a compound like ethanol. So their neutral molecules cannot carry electrical charge. This makes it impossible for substances made up of simple molecules to conduct electricity.

⊂⊃ **links**

For information on ionic compounds conducting electricity, look back at 3.3 'Giant ionic structures'.

Summary questions

1 What do we mean by 'intermolecular forces'?

2 Which of the following substances will be held together by weak intermolecular forces?
   a aluminium oxide, aluminium, oxygen
   b magnesium chloride, magnesium, chlorine
   c hydrogen sulfide, hydrogen, sulfur

3 a Diamond has a very high melting point. Explain why.
   b Nitrogen gas has a very strong triple covalent bond holding the nitrogen atoms together in diatomic molecules. Explain its boiling point of –196 °C.

4 A compound called sulfur hexafluoride (SF_6) is used to stop sparks forming inside electrical switches designed to control large currents. Explain why the properties of this compound make it particularly useful in electrical switches.

5 Explain why the melting point of hydrogen chloride is –115 °C, whereas sodium chloride's melting point is 801 °C.

Key points

● Substances made up of simple molecules have low melting points and boiling points.

● The forces between simple molecules are weak. These weak intermolecular forces explain why substances made of simple molecules have low melting points and boiling points.

● Simple molecules have no overall charge, so they cannot carry electrical charge. Therefore, substances made of simple molecules do not conduct electricity.

C3.6

Giant covalent structures

Learning objectives

After this topic, you should know:

● the general properties of substances with giant covalent structures

● why diamond is hard and graphite is slippery

● why graphite can conduct electricity

● what fullerenes are made of and some of their uses.

Figure 2 Hard, shiny and transparent – diamonds make beautiful jewellery

Examiner's tip

Giant covalent structures are held together by covalent bonds throughout the lattice.

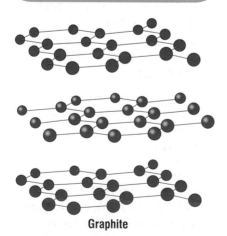

Graphite

Figure 3 The giant structure of graphite. When you write with a pencil, some layers of carbon atoms slide off the 'lead' and are left on the paper.

Most covalently-bonded substances are made up of individual molecules. However, a few form very different structures. These do not have relatively small numbers of atoms arranged in simple molecules. They form huge networks of atoms held together by covalent bonds in **giant covalent structures**. They are sometimes called **macromolecules**.

Substances such as diamond, graphite and silicon dioxide (silica) have giant covalent structures.

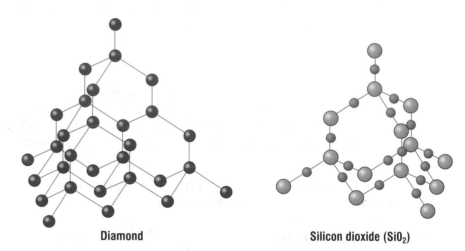

Diamond　　　　　**Silicon dioxide (SiO$_2$)**

Figure 1 The structures of diamond and silicon dioxide (silica) continue on in all directions

All the atoms in these giant lattices are held in position by strong covalent bonds, as in diamond and silicon dioxide shown above. This gives them some very special properties. They have very high melting points and boiling points and are insoluble in water. Apart from graphite, they are hard and do not conduct electricity. Diamond is exceptionally hard and boils at 4827 °C. All its carbon atoms each form four strong covalent bonds, arranged in a perfectly symmetrical giant lattice.

We don't always find carbon as diamonds. Another form is graphite (well known for its use in pencil 'lead'). In graphite, carbon atoms are only bonded to three other carbon atoms. They form hexagons which are arranged in giant layers. There are no covalent bonds between the layers. So the layers can slide over each other easily. It's a bit like playing cards sliding off a pack of cards. This makes graphite a soft material that feels slippery.

??? Did you know …?

Diamond is the hardest natural substance that we know. Artificial diamonds can be made by heating pure carbon to very high temperatures under enormous pressures. 'Industrial diamonds' made like this are embedded in the drill bits used by oil companies when drilling for oil.

Bonding in graphite

The carbon atoms in graphite's layers are arranged in hexagons so each carbon atom forms three strong covalent bonds (see Figure 3). Carbon atoms have four electrons in their outer shell available for bonding. This leaves one spare outer electron on each carbon atom.

This electron is free to move along the layers of carbon atoms. We call the free electrons found in graphite **delocalised electrons**. They behave rather like the electrons in a metallic structure.

These free electrons allow graphite to conduct electricity. Diamond – and most other covalently-bonded substances – cannot conduct electricity. This is because their atoms have no free electrons as all the outer shell electrons are involved in covalent bonding.

Fullerenes

Apart from diamond and graphite, there are other structures that carbon atoms can form. In these structures the carbon atoms join together to make large cages which can have all sorts of shapes. Chemists have made shapes looking like balls, onions, tubes, doughnuts, corkscrews and cones! They are based on *hexagonal rings of carbon atoms*.

Chemists discovered carbon's ability to behave like this in 1985. We call the large carbon molecules containing these cage-like structures **fullerenes**. Scientists can now place other molecules inside these carbon cages. This has exciting possibilities, including the delivery of drugs to specific parts of the body. They are sure to become very important in nanoscience applications, for example as catalysts and lubricants.

Figure 4 The first fullerene to be discovered contained 60 carbon atoms, but chemists can now make giant fullerenes which contain many thousands of carbon atoms

links

For information about delocalised electrons, look at 7.6 'Bonding in metals'.

links

For more information on nanoscience, see 3.7 'Nanoscience'.

Key points

- Some covalently-bonded substances have giant structures. These substances have very high melting points and boiling points.

- Graphite contains giant layers of covalently bonded carbon atoms. However, there are no covalent bonds between the layers. This means they can slide over each other, making graphite soft and slippery. The carbon atoms in diamond have a rigid giant covalent structure, making it a very hard substance.

- Graphite can conduct electricity because of the delocalised electrons along its layers.

- As well as diamond and graphite, carbon also exists as fullerenes which can form large cage-like structures and tubes, based on hexagonal rings of carbon atoms.

Summary questions

1 a Name three forms of the element carbon.
  b Find out what chemists call different forms of the same element in the same state.

2 List the general properties of a substance with a typical giant covalent structure.

3 a State a possible medical application of fullerene cages.
  b Find out why chemists called a molecule of the new form of carbon discovered in 1985 a 'buckyball', and why related molecules became known as fullerenes.

4 Graphite is sometimes used to reduce the friction between two surfaces that are rubbing together. Explain how it does this.

5 Explain in detail why graphite can conduct electricity but diamond cannot.

C3.7

Nanoscience

Did you know ...?

A pin-head measures about 1 million nanometres, and a human hair is about 80 000 nm wide.

Figure 1 Nanoparticles will save many people from damaged skin and cancers caused by too much UV light

Figure 2 Nanoparticles in cosmetic products can work deeper in the skin

Nanoscience is a new and exciting area of science. 'Nano' is a prefix like 'milli' or 'mega'. While 'milli' means 'one-thousandth', 'nano' means 'one thousand-millionth'.

$$1 \text{ nanometre (1 nm)} = 1 \times 10^{-9} \text{ metres}$$
$$(= 0.000\,000\,001 \text{ m or a billionth of a metre})$$

So nanoscience is the science of really tiny things. We are dealing with structures that are just a few hundred atoms in size or even smaller (between 1 and 100 nm in size).

We now know that materials behave very differently at a very tiny scale. Nanoparticles are so tiny that they have a huge surface area for a small volume of material. When we arrange atoms and molecules on a nanoscale, their properties can be truly remarkable.

Nanoscience at work

Here are some uses of nanoscience.

● Glass can be coated with titanium oxide nanoparticles. Sunshine triggers a chemical reaction which breaks down dirt that lands on the window. When it rains the water spreads evenly over the surface of the glass, washing off the broken down dirt.

● Titanium oxide and zinc oxide nanoparticles are also used in modern sunscreens. Scientists can coat nanoparticles of the metal oxide with a coating of silica. The thickness of the silica coating can be adjusted at an atomic level. These coated nanoparticles seem more effective at blocking the Sun's rays than conventional UV absorbers.

● The cosmetics industry is one of the biggest users of this new technology. The nanoparticles in face creams are absorbed deeper into the skin. They are also used in sun tan creams and deodorants.

The delivery of active ingredients in cosmetics can also be applied to medicines. The latest techniques being developed use nanocages of gold to deliver drugs where they need to go in the body. Researchers have found that the tiny gold particles can be injected and absorbed by tumours. Tumours have thin, leaky blood vessels with holes large enough for the gold nanoparticles to pass into. However, they can't get into healthy blood vessels. When a laser is directed at the tumour the gold nanoparticles absorb energy and warm up. The temperature of the tumour increases enough to change the properties of its proteins but barely warms the surrounding tissue. This destroys the tumour cells without damaging healthy cells.

There is potential to use the gold nanocages to carry cancer-fighting drugs to the tumour at the same time. The carbon nanocages we met in topic 3.6 can also be used to deliver drugs in the body. Incredibly strong, yet light, nanotubes are already being used to reinforce materials (see Figure 3). The new materials are finding uses in sport, such as making very strong but light tennis racquets.

Silver nanoparticles are antibacterial. They are used inside fridges to inhibit the growth of microorganisms. The silver particles also act against viruses and fungi. They are put in the sprays used to clean operating theatres in hospitals.

Future developments?

Nanotubes are now being developed that can be used as nanowires. This will make it possible to construct incredibly small electronic circuits. Nanotubes can be used to make highly sensitive selective sensors. For example, nanotube sensors have been made that can detect tiny traces of a gas present in the breath of asthmatics before an attack. This will let patients monitor and treat their own condition without having to visit hospital to use expensive machines.

Nanowires would also help to make computers with vastly improved memory capacities and speeds.

Scientists in the US Army are developing nanotech suits – thin, or even spray-on, uniforms which are flexible and tough enough to withstand bullets and blasts. The uniforms would receive aerial views of the battlefield from satellites, transmitted directly to the soldier's brain. There would also be a built-in air conditioning system to keep the body temperature normal. Inside the suit there would be a full range of nanobiosensors that could send medical data back to a medical team.

Possible risks

The large surface area of nanoparticles would make them very effective as catalysts. However, their large surface area also makes them dangerous. If a spark is made by accident, they may cause a violent explosion.

If nanoparticles are used more and more there is also going to be more risk of them finding their way into the air around us. Breathing in tiny particles could damage the lungs. Nanoparticles could enter the bloodstream this way, or from their use in cosmetics, with unpredictable effects. More research needs to be done to find out their effects on health and the environment.

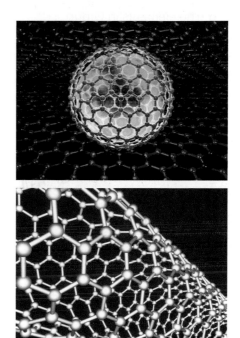

Figure 3 Nanocages can carry drugs inside them and nanotubes can reinforce materials

Summary questions

1 What do we mean by 'nanoscience'?

2 Give two uses of silver nanoparticles.

3 a Give an advantage of using nanoparticles as catalysts.
  b Why are some people concerned about the use of nanoparticles as catalysts?

4 a Give two uses of nanoscience in cosmetic products for the skin.
  b How can nanoscience possibly help to fight cancers?

5 In his book *Engines of Creation* K. Eric Drexler speculates that one day we may invent a nanomachine that can reproduce itself. Then the world could be overrun by so-called 'grey goo'. Some people are so worried they have called for a halt in nanoscience research. What are your views?

Key points

- Nanoscience is the study of small particles that are between 1 and 100 nanometres in size.

- Nanoparticles behave differently from the materials they are made from on a large scale.

- New developments in nanoscience are very exciting but will need more research into possible issues that might arise from their increased use.

Summary questions

1 Write a number to fill in the blanks in **a** to **e**:

a The elements in Group .... in the periodic table all form ions with a charge of 1+.

b The elements in Group .... in the periodic table all form ions with a charge of 2+.

c The elements in Group .... in the periodic table all form ions with a charge of 1–.

d The elements in Group .... in the periodic table all form ions with a charge of 2–.

e The elements in Group 4 in the periodic table have atoms which can form .... covalent bonds.

2 This table contains data about some different substances:

Substance	Melting point (°C)	Boiling point (°C)	Electrical conductor
ammonia	−78	−33	solid – poor
			liquid – poor
magnesium oxide	2852	3600	solid – poor
			liquid – good
lithium chloride	605	1340	solid – poor
			liquid – good
silicon dioxide	1610	2230	solid – poor
			liquid – poor
hydrogen bromide	−88	−67	solid – poor
			liquid – poor
graphite	3652	4827	solid – good
			liquid – good

a Make a table with the following headings:

Giant covalent, Giant ionic, Simple molecules

Now write the name of each substance above in the correct column.

b Which substances are gases at 25 °C?

c One of these substances behaves in a surprising way. Which one and why?

d Draw a diagram to show the electron structures of a lithium atom and a chlorine atom and their ions in lithium chloride. (Atomic number of Li = 3, Cl = 17)

3 a Which of the following substances will have covalent bonding?

hydrogen iodide
chlorine(VII) oxide
silver chloride
phosphorus(V) fluoride
calcium bromide
silver nitrate

b Explain how you decided on your answers in part **a**.

c What type of bonding will the remaining substances in the list have?

d What is the formula of:

i hydrogen iodide

ii calcium bromide?

4 Copy and complete the following table with the formula of each ionic compound formed.
(The first one is done for you.)

	chloride, Cl^-	oxide, O^{2-}	sulfate, SO_4^{2-}	phosphate(V), PO_4^{3-}
potassium, K^+	KCl			
magnesium, Mg^{2+}				
iron(III), Fe^{3+}				

5 Draw a diagram which shows the bonding in:

a hydrogen, H_2

b carbon dioxide, CO_2.

AQA Examination-style questions

1 Lithium and oxygen combine to form lithium oxide, an ionic compound.

The diagrams show the electronic structures of a lithium and oxygen atom.

a Describe, in terms of electrons, what happens when a lithium atom combines with an oxygen atom. (3)

b The electronic structures of lithium and oxygen can be shown as follows:

Li 2,1   O 2,6

Write the charge of each of the ions formed in lithium oxide. (2)

c Explain why lithium oxide has a high melting point. (2)

d Explain why lithium oxide does not conduct electricity when solid but does when molten. (2)

2 Hydrogen and fluorine atoms combine to form the compound hydrogen fluoride.

The diagrams show the electronic structures of a hydrogen and a fluorine atom.

a Draw a diagram to show how the electrons are arranged in a hydrogen fluoride molecule. (2)

b What is the name of the bond in a hydrogen fluoride molecule? (1)

c The bond in a hydrogen fluoride molecule is strong.

Explain why hydrogen fluoride is a gas at room temperature. (2)

d Hydrogen bromide has the same type of bonding as hydrogen fluoride.

A bond in a molecule can be represented by a straight line.

Show the hydrogen bromide molecule in this way. (1)

3 Silicon dioxide has a giant structure.

a Explain why silicon dioxide has a very high melting point. (3)

b Explain why molten silicon dioxide does not conduct electricity. (2)

4 Fullerenes and nanoscience may become more important in the future.

a One type of fullerene exists as molecules containing sixty atoms.

State the element in this molecule and how the atoms are arranged. (2)

b Suggest one use of fullerenes in medicine. (1)

c What is the size of a structure called a nanoparticle? (1)

d Suggest a property of nanoparticles that makes them suitable as catalysts. (1)

C4.1 Gases in the atmosphere

Learning objectives

After this topic, you should know:

- the main gases in the atmosphere and their relative proportions

- the names of other gases found in smaller proportions

- how the gases in air can be separated.

The Earth's atmosphere

By 200 million years ago the proportions of gases in the Earth's **atmosphere** had stabilised. These were much the same as they are today, with nitrogen making up almost four-fifths (78%) of the air and oxygen just over one-fifth (21%). Both these main gases are made up of diatomic molecules, N_2 and O_2.

Look at the percentage of gases in the atmosphere today in the pie chart in Figure 1.

- Nitrogen 78%
- Oxygen 21%
- Argon 0.9%
- Carbon dioxide 0.04%
- Trace amounts of other gases

Figure 1 The relative proportions of nitrogen, oxygen and other gases in the Earth's atmosphere

∞ **links**

For more information about air pollution, look at 9.3 'Burning fuels'.

There are also small percentages of pollutant gases, such as carbon monoxide, sulfur dioxide and oxides of nitrogen, in the air, as well as varying proportions of water vapour.

Separating the gases in air

In industry the gases in air are separated by the fractional distillation of liquid air.

Fractional distillation is a process in which liquids with different boiling points are separated. So first we have to get air cold enough for it to condense into a liquid. It has to be cooled to a temperature below −200 °C.

In industry they do this in a two-stage process. Firstly, they compress the air to about 150 times atmospheric pressure. This actually warms the air up. So it is cooled down to normal temperatures by passing the air over pipes carrying cold water.

The second stage provides the main cooling, which takes place when the pressure is released. As this happens, the air is allowed to expand rapidly. This is similar to what happens in an aerosol can when pressure is released as the aerosol is sprayed. The temperature drops far enough for even the gases in air to condense to liquids. The carbon dioxide and water can be removed easily from the mixture before fractional distillation takes place as they are solids at this low temperature.

Here are the boiling points of the main substances left in the liquid air mixture passed into the fractionating column:

Nitrogen (N_2); boiling point is −196 °C,

Argon (Ar); boiling point is −186 °C,

Oxygen (O_2); boiling point is −183 °C.

The column is colder at the top than the bottom and at −196°C nitrogen boils off first. It is passed out of the top of the tall fractionating column as nitrogen gas.

At −185°C in the fractionating column the oxygen is still cold enough to be a liquid, as it boils at −183°C. So the oxygen can be separated off as a liquid from the bottom of the column. The small amount of argon can be collected from the column below the nitrogen outlet but above the oxygen.

Figure 2 Biological samples are preserved in liquid nitrogen until they are needed

Examiner's tip

In a fractionating column the individual gases can be separated because of their different boiling points. You do not need to memorise the boiling points of the gases – these will be provided in the question if they are needed.

Liquid nitrogen is used to cool things down to very low temperatures. At these temperatures most things solidify. It is used to store sperm in hospitals to help in fertility treatment.

Nitrogen gas is very unreactive so we use it in sealed food packaging to stop food going off. It is also used on oil tankers when the oil is pumped ashore to reduce the risk of explosion. In industry, nitrogen gas is used to make ammonia which we convert into fertilisers.

Oxygen is used to help people breathe, often at the scene of an accident or in hospital. It is also used to help things react. Examples include high temperature welding and in the steel-making process.

Figure 3 Fractional distillation of liquid air

∞ links

For information on how a fractionating column is used to separate crude oil into fractions, look at 9.2 'Fractional distillation'.

Summary questions

1 Copy and complete the table showing the proportion of gases in the Earth's atmosphere today.

Nitrogen	Oxygen	Argon	Carbon dioxide	Other gases
%	%	%	%	%

2 a Which technique is used to separate the main gases in liquid air?
   b How can water and carbon dioxide be removed from the air before the gases enter the fractionating column?
   c Look at the boiling points of nitrogen, argon and oxygen:

Gas	Nitrogen	Argon	Oxygen
Boiling point/°C	−196	−186	−183

   i Which gas will boil off first if liquid air at −200°C is allowed to warm up?
   ii Which gas will remain in the liquid state at −185°C?

3 a Nitrogen gas and oxygen gas exist as diatomic molecules. What does this mean?
   b Argon exists as a monatomic gas. What does this mean and why does it happen?

4 Explain why the percentages of gases in the air will vary slightly in different places.

Key points

- The main gases in the Earth's atmosphere are oxygen and nitrogen.

- About four-fifths (78%) of the atmosphere is nitrogen, and about one-fifth (21%) is oxygen.

- The main gases in the air can be separated by fractional distillation. These gases are used in industry as useful raw materials.

C4.2

Oxygen and oxides

Learning objectives

After this topic, you should know:

- what is formed when elements burn in air
- how oxides can be classified as acidic or basic
- the test for oxygen gas
- how to define oxidation and reduction in terms of oxygen gain or loss.

The reactive gas in the air is oxygen. When any substance burns, it reacts with the oxygen gas in air to form compounds called oxides.

Practical

Burning elements in oxygen

Your teacher can show you some elements burning in oxygen gas.

The oxygen can be prepared from hydrogen peroxide solution, using a manganese(IV) oxide catalyst. Gas jars of oxygen can be collected over water.

The elements to be burned are ignited on a combustion spoon, then plunged into a gas jar of oxygen.

- Draw a table to record your observations.

Also try the test for oxygen gas: **a glowing splint will relight in oxygen**. **Safety:** Wear your eye protection.

The elements burn more vigorously in pure oxygen than in air, which only contains 21% oxygen.

The metallic elements burn to form solid oxides. For example:

$$2Mg(s) + O_2(g) \rightarrow 2MgO(s)$$
$$4Li(s) + O_2(g) \rightarrow 2Li_2O(s)$$

When non-metallic elements burn they often form oxides which are produced as gases. For example:

$$C(s) + O_2(g) \rightarrow CO_2(g)$$
$$S(s) + O_2(g) \rightarrow SO_2(g)$$

These reactions with oxygen to form oxides are known as combustion reactions. They are examples of **oxidation**, in which oxygen is added to an element.

Other reactions, in which oxygen is removed from an oxide, are known as **reduction**. This is important in the extraction of metals from their ores.

Basic and acidic oxides

Practical

Testing the pH of oxides

Collect 2 cm³ of each oxide solution in separate test tubes.

Add 3 drops of universal indicator solution to each oxide solution.

Suitable oxide solutions can be made from nitrogen(IV) oxide, sodium oxide, potassium oxide, phosphorus(V) oxide, calcium oxide, sulfur dioxide and carbon dioxide. Some of these may be corrosive and/or toxic.

Record your results in a table.

- Which compounds in the table are metal oxides?
- What do you notice about your results for the metal oxides?
- What can you say about your results for the non-metal oxides?

Safety: Wear eye protection. Warn asthmatics not to breathe in gas.

Figure 1 Sodium burns in oxygen to give sodium oxide, seen as a white smoke

⊂⊃ links

For more information about chemical reactions involved in burning compounds, look at 9.3 'Burning fuels'.

⊂⊃ links

For more information on the reduction of metal oxides, look at 7.3 'Extracting metals'.

Metal oxides

If a metal oxide dissolves in water, it makes an alkaline solution. For example,

sodium oxide + water → sodium hydroxide

$$Na_2O(s) + H_2O(l) → 2NaOH(aq)$$

an alkaline solution

Some metal oxides do not dissolve in water. Copper(II) oxide is insoluble. These metal oxides test neutral with universal indicator. However, they do react with acid. Insoluble metal oxides (or hydroxides) are called **bases**.

Some metal oxides are called **amphoteric**, such as lead(II) oxide (PbO) and aluminium oxide (Al_2O_3). Amphoteric oxides behave like both acids and bases. They do not dissolve in water so we cannot test the pH of solutions formed. However, they do react and dissolve in acids, thus behaving like a base, but they also react and dissolve in alkalis, thus behaving like an acid.

Non-metal oxides

Most non-metal oxides dissolve in water to form **acids**. For example,

carbon dioxide + water → carbonic acid

$$CO_2(g) + H_2O(l) → H_2CO_3(aq)$$

In general we can say:

Metal oxides are basic. Non-metal oxides are acidic.

N.B. Some oxides, such as water (H_2O) and carbon monoxide (CO) are neutral.

Figure 2 In general, metal oxides are basic and the soluble ones (usually oxides of Group 1 and 2 metals) form alkalis when added to water

---

Summary questions

1 Write word equations and balanced symbol equations, including state symbols, for the reactions of the following elements with oxygen gas:

  a carbon   **b** hydrogen   **c** calcium   **d** iron

2 A student tested the pH of solutions after mixing some oxides with water. These are her results:

Unknown oxides	pH of solution
A	14
B	3
C	11
D	7 (insoluble)
E	2

  a Which oxides are definitely oxides of metallic elements? Explain your answer and say which part of the periodic table the metals are likely to be from.

  b Which oxide might be a metallic oxide?

  c Which oxides are oxides of non-metallic elements? How can you tell?

3 Lithium oxide dissolves in water to form a solution, like the other Group 1 oxides.

  a Write a balanced symbol equation, including state symbols, for this reaction.

  b Predict the pH of the solution formed.

4 Look at this reaction between magnesium powder and copper oxide. The reaction mixture was heated on a tin lid inside a fume cupboard:

$$Mg(s) + CuO(s) → MgO(s) + Cu(s)$$

Explain which substance is oxidised and which is reduced in this reaction.

Key points

- Oxygen is the reactive gas in air. It reacts with substances to form oxides.

- Metallic elements form basic oxides. If they dissolve in water, their solutions will be alkaline.

- Non-metallic elements form oxides which dissolve in water to form acidic solutions.

- Amphoteric oxides react like both acids and bases.

- Oxidation can be thought of as the addition of oxygen. The removal of oxygen from a compound is called reduction.

C4.3

Water treatment

Learning objectives

After this topic, you should know:

● how we can make water safe to drink

● why chlorine and fluoride are added to water.

Figure 1 Many people claim that water filters like these improve the taste of water and ensure it is safe to drink

∞ links

For more information about the uses of nanoscience, look back to 3.7 'Nanoscience'.

Figure 2 Mineral waters contain dissolved minerals, which is what gives them their taste and 'character'

Water is a vital and useful resource. We use it in industry as an important raw material, solvent and coolant. Other uses of water are for washing and cleaning – and of course, for drinking. Providing people with clean drinking water is a major issue all over the world.

Water from natural sources contains dissolved minerals (salts) and microbes. These both have to be reduced to meet strict safety standards. The best sources contain low levels of minerals and microbes to start with. When we take water from rivers and reservoirs we need to treat it to make it safe to drink. This treatment involves techniques, such as:

– passing the untreated water through filter beds made of sand to remove solid particles, and

– the addition of chlorine to sterilise the water by killing microbes.

Some people also choose to use filter jugs in their homes. These usually have a top part into which you put tap water. As the water goes from the top part of the jug to the lower part, it passes through a filter cartridge. This often contains activated carbon, an **ion-exchange resin** and silver.

● The carbon in the filter reduces the levels of chlorine left in the water, as well as pesticides and other organic impurities in the water.

● The ion-exchange resin removes calcium, magnesium, lead, copper and aluminium ions.

● Some filters may also contain silver. Silver nanoparticles discourage the growth of bacteria within the filter.

In most jugs the filter cartridge needs to be changed every few weeks.

Pure water

Water from any source, even seawater, can be made pure by distilling it, i.e. boiling, followed by condensation of the steam. We can test for pure water by measuring its boiling point; pure water boils at 100.°C. However, distillation is an expensive process because of the energy costs involved in heating large volumes of water. Nonetheless, in some countries with few sources of natural freshwater, seawater is converted into usable water for homes and industry. The process is called **desalination**. The seawater undergoes distillation at an industrial plant, but at reduced pressure to lower the boiling point and save energy. However, it is still an expensive method to purify water. Desalination is used in the Middle East in some oil-rich nations and on some islands with no natural sources of water apart from occasional rainwater.

Fluoride in water

You probably know that most toothpastes contain fluoride. It is added to protect your teeth from decay. Some places also have fluoride added to their water supply. So, if you drink tap water you get a small dose of fluoride, whether you want it or not.

There is a debate about whether fluoride should be added to public water supplies. There are lots of arguments for and against it. These arguments are often based on research that gets criticised because it doesn't control the different variables well enough.

We can't really set up a 'fair test' to compare areas where the water is fluoridated with areas where no fluoride is added. There are many other factors that may vary between the people living in these different test areas. Increasing the size of the samples and matching groups is the best we can do to get higher quality data. Here are some of the arguments for and against fluoridation:

For fluoridation of water	Against fluoridation of water
Some areas have had fluoridated water for about 50 years now and nobody has proved that there are any harmful effects – that is, apart from fluorosis (see right).	What happens to your teeth reflects what's happening to your bones. Fluorosis is a condition caused when children take too much fluoride. White streaks or tips appear on their teeth. These are deposits of calcium fluoride. They are porous and can become stained. Fluorosis could be a sign of other changes in bones. Some studies have linked **excess** fluoride to weakening of bones (increased number of fractures) and bone cancer.
The effect of fluoridation in the latest studies show about a 30 per cent reduction in cavities on teeth. This is not as good as studies in the 1960s. Then they showed that you were five times more likely to have tooth decay if your water was not fluoridated. However, this is because the bacteria that cause tooth decay are dying out because of the success of fluoridation.	The benefit of fluoridation for teeth is not significant (accounting for less than one filling saved per person). So why should we take any risks with our health? Toothpastes and dental care have improved since the 1960s. The claims of huge benefits of fluoridation were not really proved then, so we don't need it now.
We need fluoridation to protect the teeth of those people who do not have good dental hygiene habits and who don't visit their dentist regularly.	It is ethically wrong to give people treatments that they have not consented to. People have a right to choose.
The bacteria associated with tooth decay also cause some types of heart disease, so fluoridation will protect us from that.	Some studies show that excess fluoride affects the brain, producing learning difficulties. It has also been associated with Alzheimer's disease in older people.
The fluoride is only added in tiny amounts (1 part per million) anyway.	You can't ensure that people stick to set safe limits of fluoride because you can't control people's intakes.

Summary questions

1 Water that looks colourless and clear may not be fit to drink. How could the water be treated to make it safe to drink?

2 a How can you convert water from a natural source into pure water?
  b How can you test that the water is pure?
  c Why aren't anhydrous copper sulfate or blue cobalt chloride used to test the purity of water?

3 Explain why bottles of water sold in the supermarket should not be described as 'pure' water.

4 Write two letters to your water supplier who is planning to add fluoride to your water supply, one in support of the plans and the other against them.

5 If you were setting up a study of the effects of fluoridation, how would you go about it? How would you make your investigation as repeatable, reproducible and valid as possible? What groups of people would you compare? How could you gain the information you need to set up matching groups in different areas?

Key points

- Water for drinking should contain only low levels of dissolved substances and microbes.

- Water is made fit to drink by passing it through filter beds to remove solids and adding chlorine (sterilising) to reduce the number of microbes.

- We can make pure water by distillation but this requires large amounts of energy, which makes it expensive.

C4.4 | Rusting

Learning objectives

After this topic, you should know:

- the conditions needed for iron to rust

- how to protect iron from rusting.

Figure 1 Rusting stops machines working properly

The corrosion of iron is called **rusting.** The rusting of iron costs us millions of pounds every year.

Rust forms on the surface of iron (or most steels). Unfortunately, this rust is a soft, crumbly substance.

It soon flakes off, exposing fresh iron, so that more iron can rust.

Practical

What causes iron to rust?

Set up the test tubes as shown.

Tube A tests to see if air alone will make iron rust.
Tube B tests to see if water alone will make iron rust.
Tube C tests to see if air and water will make iron rust.

Figure 2 Investigating the conditions needed for iron to rust

Leave the tubes for a week.

- What do you observe in each test tube?

This experiment shows that ***both air and water*** are needed for iron to rust.

Rust is a form of iron(III) oxide. It has water loosely bonded to it. It is called **hydrated iron(III) oxide**.

We can show the reaction as:

$$\text{iron} + \text{oxygen} + \text{water} \rightarrow \text{hydrated iron(III) oxide}$$

Preventing rust

We know that air and water are needed for iron to rust. Therefore, if we can keep these away from iron, it can't rust.

We can do this by coating the iron or steel with:

- paint
- oil or grease
- plastic
- a less reactive metal, or
- a more reactive metal.

Practical

How to prevent iron rusting

Set up the test tubes as shown:

The rust indicator turns blue at the first signs of rust.

Look at your test tubes every few minutes.
- Which method is best at preventing rust?
- Explain why we set up a control experiment.

| Greased nail | Painted nail | Nail wrapped in zinc | Nail in copper | Nail in tin | Nail in magnesium | Control experiment |

Figure 3 Investigating the effectiveness of ways to prevent rusting using ferroxyl indicator to show when rusting starts

Most methods for preventing rust rely on keeping the iron away from air and water. A complete barrier is placed around the iron, usually as a protective coating on its surface. The iron will rust if there is even a tiny gap in the coating. Then the rust soon spreads under the coating.

However, this does not happen if you use a more reactive metal. Even if the coating is scratched, the iron does not rust. Zinc is often used to protect iron. We say that the iron is **galvanised**. The zinc is *more reactive* than the iron. Therefore, any water or oxygen reacts with the zinc rather than the iron. This is called **sacrificial protection**. The zinc sacrifices itself to protect the iron.

Magnesium or aluminium can also be used instead of zinc to sacrificially protect iron. Sacrificial protection is used in harsh conditions, such as when the iron is in contact with seawater, which accelerates rusting. Examples are bars of zinc connected to the legs of an iron pier or a ship's hull. The method is also used to protect underground pipes which can be attached to the sacrificial metal by wires. The bars of metal need replacing eventually.

Sacrificial protection is also used where the coating is likely to be scratched, such as when emptying commercial wheelie bins. You can clearly see the coating of zinc metal on these bins and on some lamp posts.

Figure 4 The zinc coating will protect this bin even when it gets scratched

Summary questions

1 How could you show in an experiment that *both* **air (oxygen)** *and* **water** are needed for iron to rust? Explain in detail how the experimental conditions are established.

2 a What is the chemical name for rust?
  b Find out why it is difficult to write a chemical formula for rust.

3 a List five ways to prevent iron rusting.
  b *Explain* which method is best to protect:
    i   a bicycle chain   ii railings
    iii a gas pipeline along the seabed.

4 Plan an investigation you could do in the lab:
  a to show that iron rusts faster in seawater than in freshwater
  b to find out how the concentration of salt (sodium chloride) in water affects the rate of corrosion of iron.

Key points

- Both air (oxygen) and water are needed for iron to rust.
- Providing a barrier between iron and any air (oxygen) and water protects the iron from rusting.
- Sacrificial protection provides protection against rusting even when the iron is exposed to air and water. The iron needs to be attached to a more reactive metal (zinc, magnesium or aluminium).

Summary questions

1 a Explain why heated chemical elements react more vigorously in oxygen gas than in air.

b Write balanced symbol equations for the following reactions between oxygen and:
  i barium (Ba), forming barium oxide (BaO)
  ii nitrogen (N_2), forming nitrogen(II) oxide (NO)
  iii sulfur (S), forming sulfur dioxide
  iv lithium (Li), forming lithium oxide (Li_2O)

c Explain the pH of the solution formed when lithium oxide (Li_2O) reacts with water. Include a balanced symbol equation, with state symbols, in your answer.

2 The gases oxygen, nitrogen and argon can be separated from the air. Carbon dioxide and water vapour are removed from air, which is then cooled to −200 °C. The liquid obtained is a mixture of oxygen, nitrogen and argon. The table shows the boiling points of these gases.

Element	Boiling point in °C
argon	−186
nitrogen	−196
oxygen	−183

a Explain how oxygen and nitrogen can be separated. Make sure you include the name of the process in your answer.

b Five gases are named in this question. Write down:
  i the chemical formula of each one
  ii which gases are elements and which are compounds.

3 In some hot countries getting sufficient freshwater is difficult. However, some have large coastlines and so have plenty of seawater available. Here they construct desalination plants – see the photo to the right. These use a process called 'flash distillation' to turn the salty water into drinking water. Inside the desalination plant, seawater is boiled under reduced pressure, then the water vapour given off is cooled and condensed.

a Why is the pressure reduced before boiling the seawater? How does this keep costs down?

b Rusting of the steel vessels and pipework in the desalination plant is a big problem. Why?

An alternative process uses 'reverse osmosis' to remove the salts from seawater. This passes seawater through a membrane. The latest membranes can remove 98 per cent of the salts from seawater.

c Why is reverse osmosis a better option than flash distillation for obtaining drinking water?

4 The rusting of iron costs society a huge amount of money every year.

The experiment below shows an investigation into the factors that are needed for iron to rust.

a Which test tube shows an iron nail in contact with:
  i only air
  ii water and air
  iii only water?

b Why is the water in Tube B boiled?

c Explain why the nail in Tube A is suspended on cotton wool above the calcium chloride in the bottom of the tube.

d What will be the conclusion drawn from this experiment?

e Car owners who live near the coast often complain that their cars have more problems with rust than those in other places.

  Which chemical compound causes their cars to rust more quickly?

f Describe a simple experiment that you could do to show that the substance in part **e** makes an iron nail rust more quickly.

g Explain the method used to prevent rusting in:
  i cogs in a machine
  ii food cans
  iii underground pipes.

AQA Examination-style questions

1 Argon, nitrogen and oxygen are elements obtained from the air by fractional distillation.

  a List the three elements in order, starting with the most abundant. (1)

  b Which two gases in the air are removed before fractional distillation? (2)

  c What property of the gases in air allows them to be separated in this way? (1)

  d Outline how air is fractionally distilled. (3)

2 When some elements are heated in air, they burn to form oxides.

  a **i** State two observations you could make when magnesium burns in oxygen. (2)

    ii Write a symbol equation for the reaction that occurs. (2)

  b Sulfur dioxide forms when sulfur burns in air.

    The magnesium oxide formed in **a** and the sulfur dioxide were added to separate samples of water. A piece of litmus paper was placed in each sample.

    i Write a symbol equation for each of the reactions that occurs with water. (2)

    ii State the colour of the litmus in each sample. (2)

    iii State what these colours show about each of the oxides. (2)

  c Aluminium oxide does not react with water and is classified differently.

    i State the class of oxides to which aluminium oxide belongs. (1)

    ii Name two types of compound that aluminium oxide reacts with. (2)

3 Water is treated in many ways to purify it and to make it suitable for drinking.

  a **i** Describe a chemical test to show that a liquid contains water. (2)

    ii Describe a physical test to show that a sample of water is pure. (2)

  b Although tap water is safe to drink, some people use filters to remove some of the dissolved substances before they drink it.

    State one substance used in such a filter and give one example of a substance removed. (2)

  c Some drinking water supplies are fluoridated.

    i What is the main reason for fluoridation? (1)

    ii State one argument used against fluoridation. (1)

4 Objects made from iron can rust.

  a **i** State the name of the main compound in rust. (1)

    ii Name the two substances needed for iron to rust. (2)

  b Iron objects are often prevented from rusting by coating with a layer of oil or paint. The disadvantage of this is that the protection is lost when the layer comes off.

    The advantage of using zinc instead of oil or paint is that the protection continues even when some of the layer comes off.

    i Name this method of protection. (1)

    ii Explain why the protection continues when some of the zinc comes off. (2)

C5.1

The periodic table

Learning objectives

After this topic, you should know:

- how atomic structure is linked to the periodic table

- why the noble gases are so unreactive.

The periodic table was first developed by a Russian chemist called Dmitri Mendeleev and published in 1869. He put elements in order of their atomic masses and started new rows to produce groups of similar elements. The word 'periodic' means repeated at regular intervals.

However, not all elements fit in with the pattern. For example, argon atoms have a greater average mass than potassium atoms. Ordering by atomic mass would result in argon (a **noble gas**) being in the same group as reactive metals such as sodium and lithium, and would group potassium (an extremely reactive metal) with the unreactive noble gases. So argon must be put before potassium in the periodic table to maintain the periodic pattern, even though the average mass of its atoms is heavier than that of potassium's atoms. Look at Figure 1 to check this out.

At the start of the 20th century scientists began to find out more about the structure of the atom. Only then could they solve this problem of certain elements breaking the periodic pattern. We now arrange the elements *in order of their atomic (proton) number*. This puts them all in exactly the right place in the periodic table. It arranges the elements so that they line up in groups (vertical columns) with similar properties.

Electronic structures and the periodic table

The periodic table also gives us an important summary of the electronic structures of all the elements. Elements in the same group of the periodic table react in similar ways because their atoms have the same number of electrons in the highest occupied energy level (outer shell). We saw in Chapter 3 how it is these outer electrons that are transferred or shared when atoms combine with each other.

Also:

the group number in the periodic table tells us the number of electrons in the outermost shell (highest occupied energy level) of an atom.

For example, all the atoms of Group 2 elements have 2 electrons in their outermost shell (highest energy level) and those in Group 6 have 6 electrons in their outermost shell.

We also saw in Chapter 3 how atoms transfer or share electrons when bonding in order to attain the stable electronic structures of the noble gases. Look at the Group 0 noble gases, shaded purple in Figure 1. You can see how atoms of elements in Group 6 and 7 can gain electrons to form negative ions. These then have the electronic structure of the noble gas at the end of their row (called a period). Elements in Groups 1, 2 or 3 lose electrons and their positive ions attain the electronic structure of the noble gas at the end of the period one row above them.

The atoms of noble gases have 8 electrons in their outermost shell, making the atoms very stable. The exception is the first of the noble gases, helium, which has just 2 electrons, but this complete first shell is also a very stable electronic structure.

The stable electronic structures of the noble gases explains why they exist as single atoms. They are monatomic gases. They have no tendency to react to form molecules. However, chemists have managed to make a few compounds of the larger noble gases. These contain the most reactive non-metallic elements, fluorine and oxygen, for instance in the compounds XeF_6 and XeO_4.

Figure 1 The modern periodic table. The upper number on the left of a symbol is the element's relative atomic mass. The lower number is its atomic number (or proton number) – the number of protons in the nucleus. The elements are arranged in order of atomic number.

Key

Reactive metals These metals react vigorously with other elements like oxygen or chlorine, and with water. They are all soft – some of them can even be cut with a knife, like cheese!

Transition elements This group contains the elements that most people probably think of when the word 'metal' is mentioned, like iron, copper, silver and gold. These metals are not usually very reactive – some, like silver and gold, are very unreactive.

Non-metals These elements have low melting and boiling points, and many are liquids or gases at room temperature and pressure.

Noble gases These (non-metal) elements are very unreactive, and it is very difficult to get them to combine with other elements.

Examiner's tip

Metals react by losing electrons. Non-metals react with metals by gaining electrons.

Summary questions

1 a What does 'periodic' mean in the term 'periodic table'?
  b In the periodic table, what is:
   i a group   ii a period?

2 In the periodic table, how does the number of metallic elements compare with the number of non-metal elements?

3 Explain why elements in many groups of the periodic table have similar chemical properties.

4 How many electrons do atoms of the following elements have in their highest energy level (outermost shell)?
   a beryllium, Be   b boron, B   c potassium, K   d helium, He
   e argon, Ar   f radium, Ra   g radon, Rn   h iodine, I

5 Why are the noble gases so unreactive?

Key points

● The atomic (proton) number of an element determines its position in the periodic table.

● The number of electrons in the outermost shell (highest energy level) of an atom determines its chemical properties.

● The group number in the periodic table equals the number of electrons in the outermost shell.

● The noble gases in Group 0 are unreactive because of their very stable electron arrangements.

C5.2

Group 1 – the alkali metals

Learning objectives

After this topic, you should know:

● how the Group 1 elements behave

● how the properties of the Group 1 elements change going down the group.

We call the first group (Group 1), on the left-hand side of the periodic table, the **alkali metals**. This group consists of the metals lithium (Li), sodium (Na), potassium (K), rubidium (Rb), caesium (Cs) and francium (Fr). You will probably only see the first three of these as the others are too reactive to use in schools.

Properties of the alkali metals

All the alkali metals are very reactive. They have to be stored in oil (see Figure 2). This stops them reacting with oxygen in the air. Their reactivity increases as we go down the group. So lithium is the least reactive alkali metal and francium is the most reactive.

All the alkali metals have a very low density compared with other metals. In fact lithium, sodium and potassium all float on water. The alkali metals are also all very soft. They can be cut with a knife. They have a silvery, shiny surface when we first cut them. However, this quickly goes dull as the metals react with oxygen in the air. This forms a layer of oxide on the shiny surface.

The properties of this unusual group of metals result from their electronic structure. The atoms of alkali metals all have one electron in their outermost shell (highest energy level). This gives them similar properties. It also makes them very reactive. That's because they need to lose just one electron to get a stable (noble gas) electronic structure.

They react with non-metals, losing their single outer electron. They form a metal ion carrying a 1+ charge, for example, Na^+ and K^+. They always form ionic compounds.

Figure 1 The alkali metals (Group 1)

Melting points and boiling points

The Group 1 metals melt and boil at relatively low temperatures for metals. Going down the group, the melting points and boiling points get lower and lower. In fact, caesium turns into a liquid at just 29 °C.

Reaction with water

When we add lithium, sodium or potassium to water the metal floats on the water, moving around and fizzing. The fizzing happens because the metal reacts with the water to form hydrogen gas. Potassium reacts so vigorously with the water that the hydrogen produced catches fire. It burns with a lilac flame.

The reaction between an alkali metal and water also produces a metal hydroxide, hence the name 'alkali metals'.

The hydroxides of the alkali metals are all soluble in water. The solution is colourless with a high pH. (**Universal indicator** turns purple.)

sodium + water → sodium hydroxide + hydrogen
$$2Na(s) + 2H_2O(l) \rightarrow 2NaOH(aq) + H_2(g)$$

potassium + water → potassium hydroxide + hydrogen
$$2K(s) + 2H_2O(l) \rightarrow 2KOH(aq) + H_2(g)$$

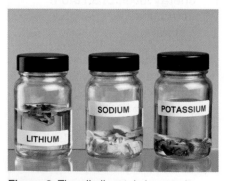

Figure 2 The alkali metals have to be stored in oil

Demonstration

Reactions of alkali metals with water

The reaction of the alkali metals with water can be demonstrated by dropping a small piece of the metal into a trough of water. This must be done with great care. The reactions are vigorous, releasing a lot of energy. Hydrogen gas is also given off.

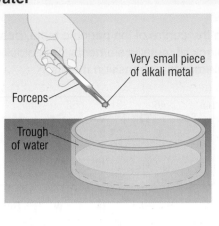

- Describe your observations in detail.

Safety: Wear your safety goggles when watching this demonstration.

Other reactions

The alkali metals also react vigorously with non-metals such as chlorine gas. They produce metal chlorides, which are white solids. Their chlorides all dissolve readily in water to form colourless solutions.

The reactions get more and more vigorous as we go down the group. That's because it becomes easier to lose the single electron in the outer shell to form ions with a 1+ charge.

$$\text{sodium} + \text{chlorine} \rightarrow \text{sodium chloride}$$
$$2Na(s) + Cl_2(g) \rightarrow 2NaCl(s)$$

They react in a similar way with fluorine, bromine and iodine.

All of these ionic compounds of the alkali metals and non-metals are also white and dissolve easily in water. The solutions formed are all colourless.

⚭ links

For further information on reactivity within groups, look at 5.5 'Explaining trends'.

Figure 3 Lithium, sodium and potassium reacting with water (the lithium is on the left of the trough, the potassium has burning hydrogen above it, and the sodium is the molten silvery ball on the right)

Key points

- The elements in Group 1 of the periodic table are called the alkali metals.

- Their melting points and boiling points decrease going down the group.

- The metals all react with water to produce hydrogen and an alkaline solution containing the metal hydroxide.

- They form 1+ ions in reactions to make ionic compounds. These are generally white and dissolve in water, giving colourless solutions.

- The reactivity of the alkali metals increases going down the group.

Summary questions

1 Why are the alkali metals stored under oil?

2 What is the trend in the melting points of the alkali metals as their atomic number increases?

3 Explain why the alkali metals form ions with a 1+ charge.

4 Caesium is near the bottom of Group 1 in the periodic table.
What do you think would happen if it was dropped into water? Include an explanation of your observations and a balanced symbol equation with state symbols in your answer.

5 Write a balanced symbol equation, including state symbols, for the reaction of caesium (Cs) with:
   a iodine
   b bromine.

C5.3   The transition elements

In the centre of the periodic table, between Groups 2 and 3, there is a large block of metallic elements. This block, shown below, contains the **transition elements** or transition metals.

45 Sc 21	48 **Ti** 22	51 V 23	52 **Cr** 24	55 **Mn** 25	56 **Fe** 26	59 **Co** 27	59 **Ni** 28	63 **Cu** 29	64 **Zn** 30
89 Y 39	91 Zr 40	93 Nb 41	96 Mo 42	99 Tc 43	101 Ru 44	103 Rh 45	106 Pd 46	108 **Ag** 47	112 Cd 48
	178 Hf 72	181 Ta 73	184 **W** 74	186 Re 75	190 Os 76	192 Ir 77	195 **Pt** 78	197 **Au** 79	201 **Hg** 80

Figure 1 The transition elements. The more common metals are shown in bold type.

Physical properties

The transition elements have the properties of 'typical' metals. Their metallic bonding and giant structures explain most of their properties.

Transition elements:

- are good conductors of electricity and heat
- are hard and strong
- have high densities
- have high melting points (with the exception of mercury, which is a liquid at room temperature).

The transition elements have very high melting points compared with those of the alkali metals in Group 1 (see Figure 2). They are also harder, stronger and much denser.

Figure 2 The melting points of the transition elements are much higher than those of the Group 1 elements

Chemical properties

The transition elements are much less reactive than the metals in Group 1. This means they do not react as readily with oxygen or water as the alkali metals do. So if they corrode, they do so very slowly. Together with their physical properties, this makes the transition elements very useful as structural materials.

Compounds of transition elements

Many of the transition elements form coloured compounds. These include some very common compounds that we use in the laboratory. For example, copper(II) sulfate is blue (from the copper ions, Cu^{2+}).

Figure 3 Compounds of transition elements are coloured (as opposed to the mainly white compounds of the alkali metals). The colours of many minerals, rocks and gemstones are due to transition element ions. The reddish-brown colour in a rock is often due to iron ions, Fe^{3+}. The blue colour of sapphires and the green of emeralds are both due to transition element ions in the structures of their crystals.

Notice that the name of a compound containing a transition element usually includes a Roman number. For example, you will have seen copper(II) sulfate or iron(III) oxide.

This is because transition elements can form more than one ion. For example, iron may exist as Fe^{2+} or Fe^{3+}. Copper can form Cu^+ and Cu^{2+}, and chromium Cr^{2+} and Cr^{3+}. Compounds of these ions are different colours. For example, iron(II) ions (Fe^{2+}) give compounds a green colour, but iron(III) ions (Fe^{3+}) give a reddish-brown colour.

Transition elements and their compounds are also very important in the chemical industry as catalysts. For example, nickel is used as a catalyst in the manufacture of margarine.

Summary questions

1 **a** List the properties of a typical transition element.
  b How is mercury unlike a typical transition metal?

2 Write down the name of the following compounds of transition elements:
  a $FeCl_2$ **b** Cr_2O_3

3 Copper (Cu) can form ions that carry a 1+ or a 2+ charge. Write down the name and formula of each compound copper can form with oxygen.

4 Find out the name and formula of the transition metal compound used as a catalyst in the manufacture of sulfuric acid.

C5.4

Group 7 – the halogens

Figure 1 The Group 7 elements

Properties of the halogens

The Group 7 elements are called the **halogens**. They are a group of poisonous non-metals that have coloured vapours. They have fairly typical properties of non-metals.

● They have low melting points and boiling points. Their melting points and boiling points increase going down the group (see Figure 2).

● They are also poor conductors of heat and electricity.

As elements, the halogens all exist as molecules made up of pairs of atoms. The atoms in each pair are joined to each other by a covalent bond.

	F—F (F_2)	Cl—Cl (Cl_2)	Br—Br (Br_2)	I—I (I_2)
Melting point (°C)	−220	−101	−7	114
Boiling point (°C)	−188	−35	59	184

Figure 2 The halogens all form molecules made up of a pair of atoms, joined by a covalent bond. We call this type of molecule a diatomic molecule.

Reactions of the halogens

The electronic structure of the halogens determines the way they react with other elements. They all have seven electrons in their outermost shell (highest energy level). So they need to gain just one more electron to achieve the stable electronic structure of a noble gas. This means that the halogens take part in both ionic and covalent bonding.

	How the halogens react with hydrogen
$F_2(g) + H_2(g) \rightarrow 2HF(g)$	Explosive even at −200 °C and in the dark
$Cl_2(g) + H_2(g) \rightarrow 2HCl(g)$	Explosive in sunlight / slow in the dark
$Br_2(g) + H_2(g) \rightarrow 2HBr(g)$	300 °C + platinum catalyst
$I_2(g) + H_2(g) \rightleftharpoons 2HI(g)$	300 °C + platinum catalyst (very slow, reversible)

Look at the table of reactions of the halogens with hydrogen gas. It shows a general trend that we find in Group 7 – **the elements get less reactive going down the group**.

The halogens also all react with metals. They gain a single electron to give them a stable arrangement of electrons. They form ions with a 1− charge, e.g. F^-, Cl^-, Br^-. Examples of their ionic compounds include sodium chloride, NaCl, and iron(III) bromide, $FeBr_3$.

Look at the diagram of the ions in calcium chloride, $CaCl_2$, below:

  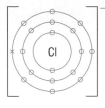

When a halogen reacts with another non-metal, the atoms of the halogen **share electrons** with the atoms of the other element. This gives the atoms of both elements the stable electronic structure of one of the noble gases. Therefore, the compounds of halogens with non-metals contain covalent bonds.

Look at the **dot and cross diagram** of hydrogen chloride, HCl, below, showing only the outer shell electrons:

(Note that the circles need not be shown in dot and cross diagrams.)

Displacement reactions between halogens

We can use a more reactive halogen to displace a less reactive halogen from solutions of its salts.

Bromine displaces iodine from solution because it is more reactive than iodine. Chlorine will displace both iodine and bromine.

For example, chlorine will displace bromine:

chlorine + potassium bromide → potassium chloride + bromine
$$Cl_2(aq) + 2KBr(aq) \rightarrow 2KCl(aq) + Br_2(aq)$$

Obviously fluorine, the most reactive of the halogens, would displace all of the others. However, it reacts so violently with water that we cannot carry out reactions in aqueous solutions.

Practical

Displacement reactions

Add bromine water to potassium iodide solution in a test tube. Then try some other combinations of solutions of halogens and potassium halides.

● Record your results in a table.

● Explain your observations.

Safety: Wear chemical splash proof eye protection. Chlorine and bromine are toxic.

Summary questions

1 In the Group 7 elements, what is the trend going down the group in:
   a their melting points   b their reactivity?

2 a Using the data in the table in Figure 2, give the state of each Group 7 element at 20 °C.
   b What is the general name given to the Group 7 elements?

3 a Show the ions in lithium fluoride, LiF, in a diagram showing all the electrons.
   b Draw a dot and cross diagram, showing only the outer shell electrons, of a molecule of hydrogen iodide.

4 a Write a word equation for the reaction of lithium with bromine.
   b Write a word equation for the reaction of bromine water with potassium iodide solution.

5 Write a balanced symbol equation, including state symbols, for the reaction of:
   a sodium metal with iodine vapour
   b chlorine water with sodium iodide solution.

Key points

● The halogens all form ions with a single negative charge in their ionic compounds with metals.

● The halogens form covalent compounds by sharing electrons with other non-metals.

● A more reactive halogen can displace a less reactive halogen from a solution of one of its salts.

● The reactivity of the halogens decreases going down the group.

C5.5

Explaining trends

Learning objectives

After this topic, you should know:

- the trends in reactivity in Group 1 and Group 7

- how electronic structure can explain trends in reactivity in these groups.

As we saw in 5.2, the Group 1 elements get more reactive going down the group:

Li
Na
K   getting *more* reactive
Rb
Cs ▼

The opposite trend is observed in the Group 7 elements (see 5.4):

F
Cl
Br   getting *less* reactive
I
At ▼

We can explain these trends by looking at the electronic structures and how the atoms tend to lose or gain electrons in their reactions.

Reactivity within groups

As we go down a group the number of shells occupied by electrons increases, by one extra electron shell per period, and the atoms get bigger.

This has two effects:

- larger atoms lose electrons more easily going down a group
- larger atoms gain electrons less easily going down a group.

This happens because the outer electrons are further away from the attractive force of the nucleus. Not only that, the inner shells 'screen' or 'shield' the outer electrons from the positive charge in the nucleus. We can see this effect with the alkali metals and the halogens. Remember that the atoms of alkali metals tend to lose electrons when they form chemical bonds. On the other hand, the atoms of the halogens tend to gain electrons.

Explaining the trend in Group 1

Reactivity increases going down Group 1 because the atoms get bigger so the single electron in the outermost shell (highest energy level) is attracted less strongly to the positive nucleus. The electrostatic attraction gets weaker because the distance between the outer electron and the nucleus increases.

Also the outer electron experiences a shielding effect from inner shells of electrons. This reduces the attraction between the oppositely charged outer electron and the nucleus.

The size of the positive charge on the nucleus does become larger as we go down a group, as more protons are added. This suggests that the attraction for the outer electron should get stronger. However, the greater distance and the shielding effect of inner electrons outweigh the increasing nuclear charge. So the change from Li to Li^+ takes more energy than Na changing to Na^+.

Therefore in Group 1, the outer electron gets easier to remove going down the group and the elements get more and more reactive.

This electron is easier to remove than the outer electron in a lithium atom

Li atom

Na atom

Figure 1 Sodium's outer electron is further from the nuclear charge and is shielded by more inner shell electrons than lithium's outer electron

Explaining the trend in Group 7

Reactivity decreases going down Group 7. To explain this, we consider the same factors we looked at with the alkali metals:

- the size of the atom,
- the shielding effect of inner electrons, and
- the nuclear charge.

When Group 7 elements react, their atoms gain an electron into their outermost shell (highest energy level). Going down the group, the outermost shell gets further away from the attractive force of the nucleus so it is harder to attract and gain an incoming electron.

The outer shell will also be shielded by more inner electrons, again reducing the attraction of the nucleus for an incoming electron.

The effect of the increased nuclear charge going down the group (which helps atoms gain an incoming electron) is outweighed by the effect of increased distance and shielding by more inner electrons. So iodine is less reactive than fluorine. The attraction for the incoming electron when F changes to F^- is much greater than when I changes to I^-.

An incoming electron experiences more attraction going into the outer shell of F compared to Cl

F atom

Cl atom

Figure 2 F forms F^- more readily than Cl forms Cl^-

Key points

- We can explain trends in reactivity as we go down a group in terms of the attraction between electrons in the outermost shell and the nucleus.

- This electrostatic attraction depends on:
  - the distance between the outermost electrons and the nucleus
  - the number of occupied inner shells (energy levels) of electrons, which provide a shielding effect.

- In deciding how easy it is for atoms to lose or gain electrons from their outermost shell, these two factors outweigh the increased nuclear charge, due to extra protons in the nucleus, going down a group.

Summary questions

1 Which one of these atoms will have electrons in its outermost shell (highest energy level) which experience the greatest attractive force between themselves and the nucleus?

   Helium   Lithium   Fluorine   Potassium   Argon

   Explain your answer.

2 Explain why potassium is more reactive than lithium.

3 Explain why fluorine is more reactive than bromine.

4 Predict the difference in reactivity, giving reasons, seen in:
   a Group 2, between magnesium and calcium
   b Group 6, between oxygen and sulfur.

Summary questions

1 a Where in the periodic table do we find:
  i the halogens
  ii the noble gases
  iii the alkali metals
  iv the transition elements?

b In which groups would you find the four elements described in **i**, **ii**, **iii** and **iv** below?
  i This is a dense metal with a high melting point. It reacts only very slowly with water but will react when heated with steam.
  ii This is a metal that can be cut with a knife and is stored under oil. It reacts violently with water and forms ions with a 1+ charge.
  iii This is a very unreactive, monatomic gas.
  iv This toxic gas is the most reactive of the all the non-metallic elements. It forms ions with a 1− charge and will also form covalent compounds.

2 Astatine (At) is a halogen whose atomic number is 85. It lies at the bottom of Group 7.

a How many electrons occupy its outermost shell (highest energy level)? How did you figure out the answer?

b Predict the state of astatine at 20 °C.

c For the compound *sodium astatide*, predict:
  i its type of bonding
  ii its colour
  iii its chemical formula
  iv the balanced symbol equation for its formation from its elements
  v whether or not you would see signs of a reaction if a solution of sodium astatide was mixed with chlorine water. Explain how you arrived at your answer.

3 Rubidium (Rb) is in Group 1 of the periodic table, lying directly beneath potassium.

a Predict the physical properties of rubidium, to include:
  i its hardness
  ii its electrical conductivity
  iii its melting point.

b i What will be the charge on a rubidium ion?
  ii Copy and complete the table below:

Rubidium compound	Chemical formula
rubidium iodide	
rubidium fluoride	
rubidium hydroxide	

  iii What is the colour of the rubidium compounds in the table in part **iii**? Comment on their solubility in water.

c Write down word equations and balanced symbol equations, including state symbols, for the following reactions:
  i rubidium and water
  ii rubidium and chlorine.

d Will the reactions of rubidium in part **c** be more or less vigorous than the same reactions using potassium? Explain your answer by comparing the electronic structures of the two elements.

4 Draw dot and cross diagrams to show the bonding in the following substances. (Draw only the outer shell electrons.)

a i hydrogen bromide
  ii iodine

b Draw a diagram showing all the electrons in lithium chloride.

5 Copper is a typical transition element. Sodium is a Group 1 element.

a i How would you be able to tell which compound was which if you were given unlabelled samples of copper(II) sulfate and sodium sulfate?
  ii Why does copper in copper(II) sulfate have a Roman numeral after its name but sodium in sodium sulfate does not?

b How do the physical properties of copper differ from those of sodium?

c How does the reactivity of copper compare with that of sodium? Use a test with water to illustrate your answer.

AQA Examination-style questions

1 The metals in Group 1 of the periodic table are chemically very reactive but have physical properties very different from most other metals.

a State two physical properties whose values are much lower for Group 1 metals than for most other metals. (2)

b A small piece of lithium is added to a large trough of water. A similar piece of potassium is added to a different trough of water. A reaction occurs in both troughs.

  i State two observations that could be made in the lithium reaction. (2)

  ii State two observations that could be made in the potassium reaction that would **not** be made in the lithium reaction. (2)

  iii A piece of litmus paper was dipped in the solution formed in the lithium reaction. State and explain the final colour of the litmus. (2)

  iv Write a symbol equation for the reaction between potassium and water. (2)

c Lithium and potassium also react with chlorine. Potassium reacts more vigorously than lithium. The electronic structures of the metals are

Li 2,1   K 2,8,8,1

Use these electronic structures to explain why potassium reacts more vigorously than lithium. (4)

2 The elements in the centre of the periodic table are called transition elements and they have several properties in common with each other.

a One property is the formation of ions with different charges.

State the formula of the metal ion in $FeCl_2$ and in $FeCl_3$ (2)

b Another property is the formation of coloured compounds.

State the colour of $Fe(OH)_2$ and of $Fe(OH)_3$ (2)

c The name of the compound manganese(IV) oxide contains the Roman numeral with a value of 4.

  i What does this numeral indicate about the manganese in this compound? (1)

  ii Manganese(IV) oxide speeds up the decomposition of hydrogen peroxide. What name is used for compounds that speed up reactions but remain chemically unchanged at the end of the reaction? (1)

3 The elements in Group 7 of the periodic table are called halogens. They form salts called halides.

a Write a symbol equation for the salt formed when calcium reacts with chlorine. (2)

b When a halogen is added to a solution of a halide a displacement reaction sometimes occurs.

Complete the following word equations with the names of the products where a reaction occurs. If no reaction occurs, write "no reaction".

  i iodine + lithium bromide → .... (1)

  ii chlorine + sodium bromide → .... (1)

  iii bromine + potassium iodide → .... (1)

c Fluorine is more reactive than chlorine. The electronic structures of these halogens are:

F 2,7   Cl 2,8,7

Use these electronic structures to explain why fluorine reacts more vigorously than chlorine. (3)

C6.1

Acids and alkalis

After this topic, you should know:

● why solutions are acidic or alkaline

● what bases and alkalis are

● how we measure acidity.

Figure 1 Acids and bases are all around us, in many of the things we buy at the shops, in our schools and factories – and in our bodies too

Acids and bases are an important part of our understanding of chemistry. They play an important part inside us and all other living things.

What are acids and bases?

When we dissolve a substance in water we make an aqueous solution. Whether the solution formed is acidic, alkaline or neutral depends on which substance we have dissolved.

● Soluble hydroxides are called **alkalis**. Their solutions are alkaline. An example is sodium hydroxide solution.

● **Bases**, which include alkalis, are substances that can neutralise acids. Metal oxides and metal hydroxides are bases. Examples include iron oxide and copper hydroxide.

● **Acids** include citric acid, sulfuric acid and ethanoic acid. All acids taste very sour, although many acids are far too dangerous to put in your mouth. Ethanoic acid (in vinegar) and citric acid (in citrus fruit and fizzy drinks) are acids that are edible.

● Pure water is **neutral**.

One acid that we use in science labs is hydrochloric acid. This is formed when the gas hydrogen chloride (HCl) dissolves in water:

$$HCl(g) \xrightarrow{\text{water}} H^+(aq) + Cl^-(aq)$$

All acids form H^+ ions when we add them to water. It is these $H^+(aq)$ ions that make a solution acidic.

Because alkalis are bases that dissolve in water and form solutions, they are the bases we often use in experiments. Sodium hydroxide solution is often found in school labs. We get sodium hydroxide solution when we dissolve solid sodium hydroxide in water:

$$NaOH(s) \xrightarrow{\text{water}} Na^+(aq) + OH^-(aq)$$

All alkalis form hydroxide ions (OH^-) when we add them to water. It is these aqueous hydroxide ions, $OH^-(aq)$, that make a solution alkaline.

Measuring acidity or alkalinity

Indicators are substances which change colour when we add them to acids and alkalis. Litmus paper is a well-known indicator, but there are many more.

We use the **pH scale** to show how acidic or alkaline a solution is. The scale runs from 0 (most acidic) to 14 (most alkaline). We can use universal indicator (UI) to find the pH of a solution. It is a special indicator made from a number of dyes. It turns a range of colours as the pH changes. Anything in the middle of the pH scale (pH 7) is neutral, i.e. neither acidic nor alkaline.

Maths skills

We can use the mathematical symbols '>' (read as 'is greater than') and '<' ('is less than') when interpreting pH values.

We can say:

$$pH < 7 \text{ indicates an acidic solution.}$$

i.e. pH values less than 7 are acidic.

$$pH > 7 \text{ indicates an alkaline solution.}$$

i.e. pH values greater than 7 are alkaline.

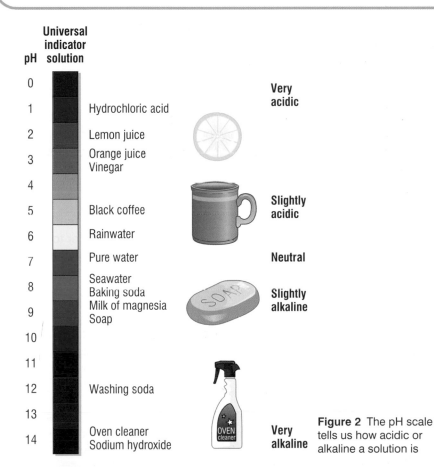

Figure 2 The pH scale tells us how acidic or alkaline a solution is

Practical

Which is the most alkaline cleaning product?

Compare the alkalinity of various cleaning products.

You can test washing-up liquids, shampoos, soaps, hand-washing liquids, washing powders/liquids and dishwasher powders/tablets.

You could use a pH sensor and data logger to collect your data.

- What are the advantages of using a pH sensor instead of universal indicator solution or paper?

Safety: Wear chemical splash proof eye protection and disposable gloves.

Summary questions

1 a What distinguishes alkalis from other bases?
  b What do all alkalis have in common?
  c Show the change that happens when potassium hydroxide (KOH) dissolves in water using an equation, including state symbols.

2 a What ions do all acids produce in aqueous solution?
  b Show the change that happens when hydroiodic acid (HI) dissolves in water, including state symbols.

3 How could you use universal indicator paper as a way of distinguishing between distilled water, sodium hydroxide solution and ethanoic acid solution?

4 Which would be the more accurate way of finding the pH of a solution, using universal indicator paper or a pH sensor and datalogger? Why?

Key points

- Acids are substances which produce $H^+(aq)$ ions when we add them to water.

- Bases are substances that will neutralise acids.

- An alkali is a soluble hydroxide. Alkalis produce $OH^-(aq)$ ions when we add them to water.

- We can use the pH scale to show how acidic or alkaline a solution is.

Making salts from metals or insoluble bases

Learning objectives

After this topic, you should know:

- the products made when acids react with metals

- the products made when acids react with bases

- how to prepare crystals of salts from their solutions.

Acids + metals

A **salt** is a compound formed when the hydrogen in an acid is wholly or partially replaced by a metal or ammonium ions. One way we can make salts is by reacting acids directly with metals. This is only possible if the metal is more reactive than hydrogen. If it is, then the metal will react with an acid to form a salt plus hydrogen gas:

$$\text{acid} \quad + \quad \text{metal} \quad \rightarrow \quad \text{a salt} \quad + \text{hydrogen}$$
$$2HCl(aq) \quad + \quad Mg(s) \quad \rightarrow \quad MgCl_2(aq) \quad + \quad H_2(g)$$

hydrochloric acid + magnesium → magnesium chloride + hydrogen

N.B. If the metal is very reactive, the reaction with acid is too violent to carry out safely. So metals such as sodium or potassium are never added to acid.

Crystals of a salt (magnesium chloride in the equation above) can be obtained from the solution. Some of the water is evaporated off from the solution until the point of crystallisation. At this point, the solution becomes saturated and crystals will appear at the edge of a salt solution being heated in an evaporating dish. This point can also be tested by dipping a glass rod into the hot salt solution, removing it and seeing if crystals form on the solution left on the rod as it cools down. The salt solution should then be left at room temperature for the remaining water to evaporate off slowly in order to prepare the best samples of salt crystals. Wear eye protection in case the solution 'spits'.

Acid + insoluble base

When we react an acid with a base, a salt and water is formed.

The general equation which describes this **neutralisation** reaction is:

acid + base → a salt + water

The salt that we make depends on the metal or the base that we use, as well as the acid. So bases that contain sodium ions will always make sodium salts. Those that contain potassium ions will always make potassium salts.

In terms of the acid used:

- the salts formed when we neutralise hydrochloric acid (HCl) are always **chlorides** (containing Cl^- ions)

- sulfuric acid (H_2SO_4) always makes salts which are **sulfates** (containing SO_4^{2-} ions)

- nitric acid (HNO_3) always makes **nitrates** (containing NO_3^- ions).

The oxide of a transition metal, such as iron(III) oxide, is an example of a base that we can use to make a salt in this way:

$$\text{acid} \quad + \quad \text{base} \quad \rightarrow \quad \text{a salt} \quad + \quad \text{water}$$
$$\textbf{6HCl(aq)} \quad + \quad \textbf{Fe}_2\textbf{O}_3\textbf{(s)} \quad \rightarrow \quad \textbf{2FeCl}_3\textbf{(aq)} \quad + \textbf{3H}_2\textbf{O(l)}$$

hydrochloric acid + solid iron(III) oxide → iron(III) chloride solution + water

links

For more information on neutralisation reactions, see 6.3 'Neutralisation, precipitation and making salts'.

Practical

Making a copper salt

We can make copper sulfate crystals from copper(II) oxide (an insoluble base) and sulfuric acid. The equation for the reaction is:

acid + base → a salt + water

$$H_2SO_4(aq) + CuO(s) \rightarrow CuSO_4(aq) + H_2O(l)$$

sulfuric acid + copper(II) oxide → copper(II) sulfate + water

1 Add insoluble copper oxide to sulfuric acid and stir. Warm gently on a tripod and gauze (do not boil).

Warm gently

2 The solution turns blue as the reaction occurs, showing that copper sulfate is being formed. Excess black copper oxide can be seen.

3 When the reaction is complete, filter the solution to remove excess copper oxide

4 Copper(II) sulfate solution — Boiling water — HEAT

We can evaporate the water so that crystals of copper sulfate start to form. Stop heating when you see the first crystals appear at the edge of the solution. Then leave for the rest of the water to evaporate off slowly. This will give you larger crystals.

● What does the copper sulfate look like? Draw a diagram if necessary.

Safety: Wear eye protection. Chemicals in this practical are harmful.

Summary questions

1 Write the general word equation for the reaction between an acid and:
   a a base   **b** a metal.

2 Describe in detail how you could prepare a sample of copper sulfate crystals from its solution.

3 **a** Why can't copper sulfate be prepared by adding copper metal to dilute sulfuric acid?
   b Why is potassium chloride never prepared by reacting potassium metal and dilute hydrochloric acid together?

4 Write balanced symbol equations, including state symbols, for the following reactions:
   a magnesium + hydrochloric acid
   b lithium oxide (in excess) + sulfuric acid

Key points

● A salt is a compound formed when the hydrogen in an acid is wholly or partially replaced by metal or ammonium ions.

● When we react an acid with a base a neutralisation reaction occurs.

● The reaction between an acid and a base produces a salt and water.

● Salts can also be made by reacting a suitable metal with an acid. This reaction produces hydrogen gas as well as a salt. A sample of the salt made can then be crystallised out of solution by evaporating off the water.

71

C6.3

Neutralisation, precipitation and making salts

Learning objectives

After this topic, you should know:

- the ionic equation to describe neutralisation
- how to prepare salts from an acid and an alkali
- how to prepare insoluble salts.

There are two other important ways of making salts from solutions.

- We can react an acid and an alkali together to form a soluble salt.
- We can make an *insoluble* salt by reacting solutions of two soluble salts together.

Acid + alkali

When an acid reacts with an alkali, a neutralisation reaction takes place.

Hydrochloric acid reacting with sodium hydroxide solution is an example:

$$\text{acid} \quad + \quad \text{alkali} \quad \rightarrow \quad \text{a salt} \quad + \text{ water}$$
$$\textbf{HCl(aq)} \quad + \quad \textbf{NaOH(aq)} \quad \rightarrow \quad \textbf{NaCl(aq)} \quad + \textbf{H}_2\textbf{O(l)}$$
hydrochloric acid + sodium hydroxide solution → sodium chloride + water

We can think about neutralisation in terms of $H^+(aq)$ ions reacting with $OH^-(aq)$ ions. They react to form water and this can be shown in an ionic equation. An ionic equation just shows the ions, as well as atoms and molecules, that change in a chemical reaction and the products they form:

$$H^+(aq) + OH^-(aq) \rightarrow H_2O(l)$$

We can make ammonium salts, as well as metal salts, by reacting an acid with an alkali. Ammonia reacts with water to form a weakly alkaline solution:

$$NH_3(aq) + H_2O(l) \rightleftharpoons NH_4^+(aq) + OH^-(aq)$$

Ammonia solution reacts with an acid (for example, nitric acid):

$$\text{acid} \quad + \quad \text{ammonia solution} \quad \rightarrow \text{an ammonium salt} + \text{ water}$$
$$\textbf{HNO}_3\textbf{(aq)} + \textbf{NH}_4^+\textbf{(aq)} + \textbf{OH}^-\textbf{(aq)} \rightarrow \quad \textbf{NH}_4\textbf{NO}_3\textbf{(aq)} \quad + \textbf{H}_2\textbf{O(l)}$$
nitric acid + ammonia solution → ammonium nitrate + water

Ammonium nitrate contains a high proportion of nitrogen, and it is very soluble in water. This makes it ideal as a source of nitrogen for plants to take up through their roots. It replaces the nitrogen taken up from the soil by plants as they grow (see Figure 1).

When we react an acid with an alkali we need to be able to tell when the acid and alkali have completely reacted. It is not obvious by just observing the reaction – so we use an indicator to help.

Ammonium salts are made by adding ammonia solution to an acid until there is a small excess of ammonia. We can detect the excess ammonia by using universal indicator paper which will turn blue. We then crystallise the ammonium salt from its solution. The excess ammonia evaporates off.

Making insoluble salts

We can sometimes make salts by combining two solutions that contain different soluble salts. When the soluble salts react to make an insoluble salt, we call the reaction a precipitation reaction. That's because the insoluble solid formed in the reaction mixture is called a **precipitate**.

$$\textbf{Pb(NO}_3\textbf{)}_2\textbf{(aq)} + \quad \textbf{2KI(aq)} \quad \rightarrow \quad \textbf{PbI}_2\textbf{(s)} \quad + \quad \textbf{2KNO}_3\textbf{(aq)}$$
lead nitrate + potassium iodide → lead iodide + potassium nitrate
solution   solution   precipitate   solution

AMMONIUM NITRATE
BASED FERTILIZER
34,4% N

TOTAL NITROGEN (N)	34,4%
NITRIC NITROGEN (N)	17,2%
AMMONIACAL NITROGEN (N)	17,2%

500 KG NET

UN 2067

EC FERTILIZER
MADE IN RUSSIA
JSC "CHEREPOVETSKY AZOT"
162600, RUSSIA, VOLOGDA REG., CHEREPOV
SEVERNOYE SHOSSE, 36

Figure 1 Ammonium nitrate (NH$_4$NO$_3$) made from ammonia and nitric acid is used as a fertiliser

Each of the reactant solutions contains one of the ions that make up the insoluble salt. In this case, they are lead ions in lead nitrate and iodide ions in potassium iodide. Lead iodide forms a yellow precipitate that we can filter off from the solution.

Practical

Making an insoluble salt

Potassium iodide solution

Lead nitrate solution

1
We add potassium iodide solution to lead nitrate solution and stir

2
The precipitate of lead iodide that forms is filtered off from the solution

3
The precipitate is washed with distilled water and dried

We can make the salt lead iodide from lead nitrate solution and potassium iodide solution. The equation for the reaction is shown at the bottom of the previous page.

● Why is the precipitate of lead iodide washed with distilled water?

Safety: Wear chemical splash proof eye protection. Lead compounds are toxic.

Summary questions

1 **a** Write down a general equation for the neutralisation reaction between an acid and an alkali.
   b Write an ionic equation to show what happens in this neutralisation reaction.

2 **a** Name the salt made when ammonia solution neutralises dilute nitric acid.
   b Why is this salt important?
   c Work out the percentage of nitrogen in this salt. Show your working out. (A_r values: H = 1, N = 14, O = 16)
   d Write a balanced symbol equation for the reaction to make this salt.

3 Write balanced symbol equations, including state symbols, and a method to show how to make lithium chloride (a soluble salt – look ahead to 6.5 for help if necessary).

4 Lead chloride, $PbCl_2$, is an insoluble salt.
   a Suggest a method to prepare a sample of lead chloride. (Hint: all nitrates are soluble in water.)
   b Write balanced symbol equations, including state symbols, for the reaction used in part **a**.
   c What type of bonding will be present in the lead chloride?

5 A chemical factory produces aqueous chromium(III) ions as a by-product. Suggest how the chemical company can remove the chromium ions from the wastewater before it is discharged from the factory.

Using precipitation

We use precipitation reactions to remove pollutants from the wastewater produced by factories. The effluent must be treated before it is discharged into rivers and the sea.

Precipitation is used in the removal of metal ions from industrial wastewater. By raising the pH of the water, we can make insoluble metal hydroxides precipitate out. This produces a sludge which we can easily remove from the solution.

The cleaned-up water can then be discharged safely into a river or the sea.

Precipitation can be also used to remove unwanted ions from drinking water.

Figure 2 Water treatment plants use chemical treatments, such as adding lime, to precipitate out metal compounds which can then be removed by filtering

Key points

● An indicator is needed when a soluble salt is prepared by reacting an alkali with an acid.

● Insoluble salts can be made by reacting two solutions to produce a precipitate.

● Precipitation is an important way of removing some metal ions from industrial wastewater.

C6.4

Metal carbonates

Learning objectives

After this topic, you should know:

- what happens when dilute acid is added to a metal carbonate

- how the test for carbon dioxide gas works

- what happens in the thermal decomposition of metal carbonates

- some uses of limestone.

Buildings and statues made of limestone suffer badly from damage by acid rain. You might have noticed statues where the fine features have been lost. Limestone, which is quarried from the ground, is mostly calcium carbonate. This reacts with acid, giving off carbon dioxide gas in the reaction.

Metal carbonates react with acids to give a salt, water and carbon dioxide. For calcium carbonate the reaction with hydrochloric acid is:

$$\text{calcium carbonate} + \text{hydrochloric acid} \rightarrow \text{calcium chloride} + \text{water} + \text{carbon dioxide}$$

The balanced symbol equation, including state symbols, is:

$$CaCO_3(s) + 2HCl(aq) \rightarrow CaCl_2(aq) + H_2O(l) + CO_2(g)$$

Powdered limestone is used to raise the pH of acidic soils or lakes affected by acid rain, making use of the reaction between calcium carbonate and acid.

Testing for carbon dioxide

You can use a simple test to verify that the gas given off is carbon dioxide. Carbon dioxide turns **limewater** solution cloudy. The test works as follows:

- Limewater is a solution of calcium hydroxide. It is alkaline.

- Carbon dioxide is a weakly acidic gas so it reacts with the alkaline limewater.

- In this reaction tiny solid particles of insoluble calcium carbonate are formed as a precipitate.

- The reaction is:

$$\text{calcium hydroxide} + \text{carbon dioxide} \rightarrow \text{calcium carbonate} + \text{water}$$
$$\text{(limewater)} \qquad\qquad\qquad\qquad \text{(an insoluble white precipitate)}$$
$$Ca(OH)_2(aq) + CO_2(g) \rightarrow CaCO_3(s) + H_2O(l)$$

- This precipitate of calcium carbonate makes the limewater turn cloudy. That's because light can no longer pass through the solution with the particles of white solid calcium carbonate suspended in it.

Figure 1 Limestone, made up mainly of calcium carbonate, is attacked and damaged by acids

?? Did you know ... ?

Sculptures from the Parthenon (a temple), built by the ancient Greeks in Athens, have had to be removed and replaced by copies to avoid any more damage from acid pollution from vehicle exhausts.

Practical

Acid plus metal carbonates

Set up the apparatus as shown.

Try the test with some other carbonates, such as those of magnesium, copper, zinc and sodium.

Record your observations.

- What conclusion can you draw?

Safety: Wear eye protection. Some of the chemicals are harmful.

Thermal decomposition of carbonates

The calcium carbonate in limestone decomposes when we heat it. The reaction produces calcium oxide and carbon dioxide:

$$CaCO_3(s) \rightarrow CaO(s) + CO_2(g)$$
$$\text{(lime or quicklime)}$$

This reaction takes place in industry in a lime kiln. The calcium oxide made can be reacted with water to make a cheap alkali, calcium hydroxide. The thermal decomposition reaction shown above is also important when limestone is used in making **cement** and glass, as well as in the extraction of iron in a blast furnace.

So do other metal carbonates also decompose when we heat them?

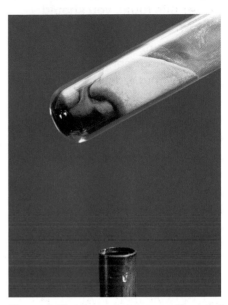

Figure 2 The thermal decomposition of copper(II) carbonate

Practical

Investigating carbonates

You can investigate the thermal decomposition of carbonates by heating samples in a Bunsen flame. You will have samples of the carbonates listed below.

Powdered carbonate samples: sodium carbonate, potassium carbonate, calcium carbonate, magnesium carbonate, zinc carbonate, copper carbonate

● What observations might tell you if a sample decomposes when you heat it?

● How could you test any gas given off?

Safety: It is important to remove the delivery tube from the limewater before you stop heating the carbonate. If you don't, the cold limewater will be 'sucked back' into the hot boiling tube causing it to smash.
You must wear eye protection when doing this practical.
Some chemicals will be harmful.

Investigations like this show that many metal carbonates decompose when they are heated in a Bunsen flame. They form the metal oxide and carbon dioxide – just as calcium carbonate does. Sodium and potassium carbonate do not decompose at the temperature of the Bunsen flame. They need a higher temperature.

Magnesium carbonate decomposes like this:

$$MgCO_3(s) \rightarrow MgO(s) + CO_2(g)$$

Summary questions

1 Give a general word equation for: **a** the reaction of a metal carbonate plus an acid; **b** the thermal decomposition of a metal carbonate.

2 Write a word equation plus a balanced symbol equation, including state symbols, for the reaction of sodium carbonate powder with dilute hydrochloric acid.

3 Copper(II) carbonate, $CuCO_3$, undergoes thermal decomposition. Write the balanced symbol equation, including state symbols, for this reaction.

4 Write the balanced symbol equation for the reaction of copper carbonate with dilute nitric acid.

5 Explain in detail why limewater turns cloudy in the test for carbon dioxide.

Key points

● Carbonates react with dilute acid to form a salt, water and carbon dioxide.

● Limewater turns cloudy in the test for carbon dioxide gas. A precipitate of insoluble calcium carbonate causes the cloudiness.

● Metal carbonates decompose on heating to form the metal oxide and carbon dioxide.

● Limestone, containing mainly calcium carbonate ($CaCO_3$), is quarried and can be used as a building material, or powdered and used to control acidity in the soil. It can also be used in the manufacture of cement, glass and iron, as well as producing calcium oxide (lime) when heated.

C6.5

Titrations

Learning objectives

After this topic, you should know:

- how to measure accurately the amount of acid and alkali that react together completely

- how to determine when the reaction is complete.

⚬⚬ **links**

For information about strong and weak acids see 11.3 'Carboxylic acids and esters'.

⚬⚬ **links**

For more information on neutralisation reactions, look back at 6.2 'Making salts from metals or insoluble bases' and 6.3 'Neutralisation, precipitation and making salts'.

Examiner's tip

We use a pipette to measure out a fixed volume of solution. We use a burette to measure the volume of the solution added.

An acid and an alkali (a soluble base) react together and neutralise each other. They form a salt (plus water) in the process.

Suppose we mix a strong acid and a strong alkali. The solution made will be neutral only if we add exactly the right quantities of acid and alkali.

If we start off with more acid than alkali, then the alkali will be neutralised. However, the solution left after the reaction will be acidic, not neutral. That's because some acid will be left over. We say that the acid is *in excess*. If we have more alkali than acid to begin with, then all the acid will be neutralised and the solution left will be alkaline.

We can measure the exact volumes of acid and alkali needed to react with each other using a technique called **titration**. The point at which the acid and alkali have reacted completely is called the **end point** of the reaction. We judge when the end point is reached by using an acid/base indicator.

Practical

Carrying out a titration

In this experiment you can carry out a titration. You will find out how much acid is needed to completely react with an alkali:

1 Measure a known volume of alkali into a conical flask using a volumetric **pipette**. Before doing this, you should first wash the pipette with distilled water, and then with some of the alkali.

Pipette filler

Pipette

Figure 1 A volumetric pipette and pipette filler. Fill the pipette until the bottom of the meniscus (curved surface of the solution) coincides with the mark. Allow the liquid to run out of the pipette and touch the tip on the side of the flask to drain out the solution. It is normal for a tiny amount of solution to remain in the pipette.

2 Now add a few drops of acid/base indicator to the solution in the flask and swirl.

3 Pour the acid you are going to use into a **burette**. This is a long tube with a tap on one end. The tube has markings on it to enable you to measure volumes accurately (often to the nearest $0.05\,cm^3$). Before doing this, you should first wash the burette with distilled water, and then with some of the acid.

4 Record the reading on the burette. Then open the tap to release a small amount of acid into the flask. Swirl the flask to make sure that the two solutions are mixed.

Figure 2 A burette – use the bottom of the meniscus to read the scale. The reading here is 0.65 cm³.

5 Keep on repeating step 4 until the indicator in the flask changes colour. This shows when the alkali in the flask has completely reacted with the acid added from the burette. Record the reading on the burette and work out the volume of acid run into the flask. (On your first go at doing this you will probably run too much acid into the flask, so treat this as a rough estimate of how much acid is needed.)

6 Repeat the whole process at least three times. Discard any anomalous results. Then calculate an average value to give the most accurate results possible. Alternatively, repeat the titration until you get two consecutive identical results.

7 Now you can use your results to calculate the concentration of the alkali.

Safety: Wear eye protection. Chemicals in this practical may be harmful or irritant.

⊂⊃ **links**

For more information on calculations, see 6.6 'Titration calculations'.

Summary questions

1 What word do we use for a set of repeat readings with a very narrow range? (Hint: see page 197 in the 'Experimental data handling' section.)

2 a What word is used for the curved surface of a liquid in a measuring cylinder?
  b i Name two measuring instruments used to measure volumes of liquid in a titration.
    ii What is the correct way to read the volume from the level of liquid in one of these measuring instruments.

3 a Describe how to carry out a titration between dilute nitric acid of known concentration and sodium hydroxide solution of unknown concentration.
  b Write a balanced symbol equation, including state symbols, for the reaction in part **a**.

4 a Name two acid/base indicators that can be used in the titration between dilute hydrochloric acid and sodium hydroxide solution.
  b Explain what makes a good indicator for a titration between an acid and an alkali.

Key points

● Titration is used to measure accurately how much acid and alkali react together completely.

● The point at which an acid–alkali reaction is complete is called the end point of the reaction.

● We use an acid/base indicator to show the end point of the reaction between an acid and an alkali.

C6.6 Titration calculations

Learning objectives

After this topic, you should know:

- how to calculate concentrations from reacting volumes of solutions
- how to calculate the amount of acid or alkali needed in a neutralisation reaction.

Calculating concentrations

The concentration of a solute in a solution is the number of moles of solute dissolved in one cubic decimetre of solution. We write these units as **moles per decimetre cubed** or **mol/dm³** for short. So if we know the mass of solute dissolved in a certain volume of solution, we can work out its concentration.

As an example, imagine that we make a solution of sodium hydroxide in water. We dissolve exactly 40 g of sodium hydroxide to make exactly 1 dm³ of solution. We know how to work out the mass of 1 mole of sodium hydroxide (NaOH). We add up the relative atomic masses of sodium, oxygen and hydrogen:

$$23 \, (\text{Na}) + 16 \, (\text{O}) + 1 \, (\text{H}) = 40 \, \text{g} = \text{mass of 1 mole of NaOH}$$

Therefore we know that the solution contains 1 mole of sodium hydroxide in 1 dm³ of solution. So the concentration of sodium hydroxide in the solution is 1 mol/dm³. See Worked example 1.

Sometimes we know the concentration of a solution and need to work out the mass of solute in a certain volume. See Worked example 2.

Maths skills

Worked example 1

But what if we use 20 g of sodium hydroxide to make 200 cm³ of solution instead of 40 g in 1 dm³? (Remember that 1 dm³ = 1000 cm³.)

Solution

To find the concentration of the solution we must work out how much sodium hydroxide there would be if we had 1000 cm³ (1 dm³) of the solution.

20 g of NaOH are dissolved in 200 cm³ of solution, so

$\dfrac{20}{200}$ g of NaOH would be dissolved in 1 cm³ of solution, and

$\dfrac{20}{200} \times 1000$ g = **100 g** of NaOH would be dissolved in 1000 cm³ of solution.

The mass of 1 mole of NaOH is 40 g, so

$$100 \, \text{g of NaOH is } 100 \div 40 \, \text{moles} = \textbf{2.5 moles}.$$

2.5 moles of NaOH are dissolved in 1 dm³ of solution. So the concentration of NaOH in the solution is **2.5 mol/dm³**.

Worked example 2

What mass of potassium sulfate, K_2SO_4, is there in 25 cm³ of a 2.0 mol/dm³ solution?

Solution

In 1 dm³ of solution there would be 2 moles of K_2SO_4

The mass of 1 mole of K_2SO_4 is $(2 \times 39) + 32 + (4 \times 16)$ g = 174 g, so in 1000 cm³ of solution there would be $(174 \times 2) = 348$ g of K_2SO_4, and in 1 cm³ of solution there are $\dfrac{348}{1000}$ g of K_2SO_4

So in 25 cm³ of solution there are $\dfrac{348}{1000} \times 25$ g of K_2SO_4 = **8.7 g** of K_2SO_4

There is **8.7 g of K_2SO_4** in 25 cm³ of 2.0 mol/dm³ potassium sulfate solution.

Titration calculations

In a titration we always have one solution with a concentration which we know accurately. We can put this in the burette. Then we can place the other solution, with an unknown concentration, in a conical flask. We do this using a volumetric pipette. This ensures we know the volume of this solution accurately. The result from the titration is used to calculate the number of moles of the substance in the solution in the conical flask. See Worked example 3.

Maths skills

Worked example 3

A student put $25.0\,cm^3$ of sodium hydroxide solution of unknown concentration into a conical flask using a volumetric pipette. The sodium hydroxide reacted with exactly $20.0\,cm^3$ of $0.50\,mol/dm^3$ sulfuric acid added from a burette. What was the concentration of the sodium hydroxide solution in mol/dm^3?

Solution

The equation for this reaction is:

$$2NaOH(aq) + H_2SO_4(aq) \rightarrow Na_2SO_4(aq) + 2H_2O(l)$$

This equation tells us that 2 moles of NaOH reacts with 1 mole of H_2SO_4.

The concentration of the H_2SO_4 is $0.50\,mol/dm^3$, so

   0.50 moles of H_2SO_4 are dissolved in $1000\,cm^3$ of acid, and

   $\dfrac{0.50}{1000}$ moles of H_2SO_4 are dissolved in $1\,cm^3$ of acid, therefore

   $\dfrac{0.50}{1000} \times 20.0$ moles of H_2SO_4 are dissolved in $20.0\,cm^3$ of acid.

So there are 0.010 moles of H_2SO_4 dissolved in $20.0\,cm^3$ of acid.

The equation for the reaction tells us that 0.010 moles of H_2SO_4 will react with exactly 2×0.010 moles of NaOH. This means that there must have been 0.020 moles of NaOH in the $25.0\,cm^3$ of solution in the conical flask. To calculate the concentration of NaOH in the solution in the flask we need to calculate the number of moles of NaOH in $1\,dm^3$ ($1000\,cm^3$) of solution.

0.020 moles of NaOH are dissolved in $25.0\,cm^3$ of solution, so

$\dfrac{0.020}{25}$ moles of NaOH are dissolved in $1\,cm^3$ of solution, and there will be

$\dfrac{0.020}{25} \times 1000 = 0.80$ moles of NaOH in $1000\,cm^3$ of solution.

The concentration of the sodium hydroxide solution is $0.80\,mol/dm^3$.

Summary questions

In a titration, a $12.5\,cm^3$ sample of nitric acid (HNO_3) reacted exactly with $10.0\,cm^3$ of $0.40\,mol/dm^3$ potassium hydroxide solution. Answer questions 1 to 4 below:

1 Write down a balanced symbol equation, including state symbols, for this reaction.

2 Calculate the number of moles of potassium hydroxide used.

3 How many moles of nitric acid react?

4 Calculate the concentration of the nitric acid.

Key points

- To calculate the concentration of a solution, given the mass of solute in a certain volume:

  1 Calculate the mass (in grams) of solute in $1\,cm^3$ of solution.
  2 Calculate the mass (in grams) of solute in $1000\,cm^3$ of solution.
  3 Convert the mass (in grams) to moles.

- To calculate the mass of solute in a certain volume of solution of known concentration:

  1 Calculate the mass (in grams) of the solute there is in $1\,dm^3$ ($1000\,cm^3$) of solution.
  2 Calculate the mass (in grams) of solute in $1\,cm^3$ of solution.
  3 Calculate the mass (in grams) of solute there is in the given volume of the solution.

Summary questions

1 Nickel(II) sulfate crystals can be made from an insoluble oxide base and sulfuric acid.

a i Name the insoluble base that can be used to make nickel(II) sulfate.

ii Write a balanced symbol equation, including state symbols, to show the reaction.

iii What type of reaction is shown in the equation?

b Describe how you could obtain crystals of nickel(II) sulfate from the reaction in **a ii**.

2 Write balanced symbol equations, including state symbols, to describe the reactions below. (Each reaction forms a salt.)

a Lithium hydroxide solution (in excess) and dilute sulfuric acid.

b Iron(III) oxide (an insoluble base) and dilute nitric acid.

c Zinc metal and dilute hydrochloric acid.

d Barium nitrate solution and potassium sulfate solution (this reaction produces an insoluble salt).

3 a What is the chemical formula of calcium carbonate – the main compound in limestone.

b Calcium carbonate reacts with dilute hydrochloric acid, giving off a gas.

i Write a balanced symbol equation, including state symbols, for this reaction.

ii Draw a diagram of the apparatus you would use to give a positive test for the gas given off.

iii Write a word equation and a balanced symbol equation for the change that happens in a positive test for the gas in part **ii**.

c This is a lime kiln for roasting limestone:

Air + carbon dioxide · Kiln rotates · Hot air in · Limestone in · Temperature *increases* as the limestone travels through the kiln · Calcium oxide out

i Write a word equation and a balanced symbol equation, including state symbols, for the reaction in the lime kiln.

ii What do we call the type of reaction that takes place in a lime kiln?

iii What mass of the gas would be produced if 12.5 tonnes of limestone was roasted in a lime kiln, assuming all the limestone was composed of calcium carbonate and there was 100% conversion to calcium oxide?
(A_r values: Ca = 40; O = 16; C = 12)

iv State three uses of limestone not mentioned in this question.

4 A student placed 12.5 cm³ of potassium hydroxide solution of an unknown concentration into a conical flask using a volumetric pipette. The potassium hydroxide reacted with exactly 20.0 cm³ of 0.50 mol/dm³ hydrochloric acid which was added from a burette.

Dilute hydrochloric acid

Potassium hydroxide solution

a Write the balanced symbol equation, including state symbols, for this reaction.

b i How many moles of hydrochloric acid are there in 20.0 cm³ of 0.50 mol/dm³ hydrochloric acid?

ii How many moles of potassium hydroxide will this react with?

c What is the concentration of the potassium hydroxide solution:

i in moles per dm³?

ii in grams per dm³?
(A_r values: K = 39; O = 16; H = 1)

AQA Examination-style questions

1 Three solutions are made by dissolving equal amounts of compounds in water. The pH values of these solutions are 2, 7, and 12.

Solution 1 contains hydrochloric acid
Solution 2 contains sodium chloride
Solution 3 contains sodium hydroxide

  a Write the appropriate pH value for each solution shown above. (1)

  b Name one indicator that could be used to identify each solution and explain why it is better than using litmus. (2)

  c Solution 4 has a pH value of 9. Solution 5 has a pH value of 11.

    Which solution contains more H^+ ions? (1)

2 One way to prepare soluble salts involves adding a metal or a metal compound to a dilute acid.

  a Complete the following word equations that show the reactions used to make three salts.
    i magnesium + hydrochloric acid →
    ii zinc oxide + nitric acid →
    iii copper(II) carbonate + sulfuric acid → (6)

  b What would you observe in reactions **i** and **iii** but not in reaction **ii**? (1)

  c Why should an excess of metal or metal compound be used in each case? (1)

  d After each reaction is complete, filtration is used.
    i State the name of the substance in solution when reaction **i** is filtered. (1)
    ii What does the residue in reaction **ii** contain? (1)
    iii What is the colour of the filtrate in reaction **iii**? (1)

  e The method used for all the reactions above produces a dilute solution of the salt. Describe how crystallisation is used to obtain a pure dry sample of the salt produced in reaction **iii**. (4)

3 Insoluble salts are made by the precipitation method.

  a The word equation for a reaction used to make an insoluble salt is

    magnesium chloride + sodium fluoride → magnesium fluoride + sodium chloride

    Write a symbol equation, including state symbols, for this reaction. (3)

  b i Name two compounds that could be used to make the insoluble salt lead sulfate. (2)
    ii When lead sulfate is made the reaction mixture is filtered. Lead sulfate is in the residue.
    Why should the residue be washed with distilled water before it is dried? (1)

4 The symbol equation for a reaction used to make potassium nitrate is

$$KOH + HNO_3 \rightarrow KNO_3 + H_2O$$

  a What is the simplest ionic equation for this reaction? (1)

  b In an experiment used to make potassium nitrate, it was found that $27.80\,cm^3$ of nitric acid was needed to neutralise $25.00\,cm^3$ of potassium hydroxide solution.
    i Which reactant solution is more concentrated? Give a reason for your choice. (2)
    ii Name the pieces of equipment used to measure the volume of each reactant. (2)

  c In another experiment to make potassium nitrate by the same method, a student recorded these volumes, in cm^3, of nitric acid added:

    26.85   27.20   26.10   26.20

    i State which volumes should be used to calculate the average volume of nitric acid added. (1)
    ii Calculate the average volume of nitric acid added. (2)

  d A student recorded the following information from a titration.

    Volume of $0.120\,moles/dm^3$ KOH(aq) = $25.00\,cm^3$
    Volume of HNO_3(aq) = $28.50\,cm^3$
    Calculate the concentration of nitric acid. (2)

C7.1 | The reactivity series

Learning objectives

After this topic, you should know:

- what the reactivity series is

- how some common metals react with water and with dilute acid.

Metals are important in all our lives. For example in transport we use metals to make bicycles, cars, ships, trains and aeroplanes. In this chapter we will look at the chemistry involved in getting these metals from their raw materials, **ores**. Ores are rocks from which it is economical to extract the metals that they contain. With new techniques, we can now extract metals from rock once thought of as waste.

Most metals in ores are chemically bonded to other elements in compounds. So, how can we extract the metals from their ores? To answer this we must understand the **reactivity series** of metals. The reactivity series is a list of metals in order of their reactivity, with the most reactive metals at the top and the least reactive ones at the bottom (see Table 1 on the right).

Practical

Predicting reactions

Calcium is a metal that is more reactive than magnesium, but less reactive than lithium.

- Predict what you will see when a piece of calcium is added to a beaker of water and name any products that might be formed.

Try out the reaction in a large beaker (or trough) of water. Have an inverted test tube full of water ready to collect any gas given off and test the solution left with universal indicator paper. Test if the gas collected is hydrogen, using a lighted spill.

- Evaluate your prediction by comparing your observations with your ideas before trying out the experiment.

- Write a word and balanced symbol equation for the reaction between calcium and water.

Safety: Do not touch calcium metal or the solution formed in the reaction. Wear eye protection. Calcium is highly flammable.

Metals plus water

We can start putting the metals in order of reactivity by looking at their reactions with water. Most metals don't react vigorously with water. Metals such as copper, which does not react at all with water, can be used to make water pipes. However, there is a great range in reactivity between different metals. For example, you have seen how the alkali metals in Group 1 react with water in Topic 5.2. They react vigorously, giving off hydrogen gas and leaving alkaline solutions. The reactivity increases going down Group 1, so of the metals you observed the order of reactivity is **1** potassium (most reactive), **2** sodium and **3** lithium.

Magnesium lies somewhere between lithium and copper in the reactivity series. If magnesium is left in a beaker of water, it takes several days to collect enough gas to test with a lighted spill. The resulting 'pop' shows that the gas is hydrogen.

Although magnesium reacts very slowly with water, we can speed up the reaction by heating and reacting the metal with steam.

Demonstration

Magnesium and steam

Watch your teacher demonstrate the reaction below:

Ceramic wool soaked in water (to make steam)   Magnesium

You can light the hydrogen gas given off

Heat

- Describe what happens as the magnesium reacts with the steam.
- Which gas burns off at the end of the tube?
- The white solid left in the test tube is magnesium oxide (MgO). Write a word equation and a balanced symbol equation, including state symbols, for the reaction of magnesium and steam.

Metals plus dilute acid

You have now seen how a range of metals react with water, and that we can use our observations of these reactions to place the metals into an order of reactivity. However, where the reactions are very slow, the task of ordering the metals is difficult. With these metals we can look at their reactions with dilute acid to arrive at an order of reactivity.

Here is a table that summarises the reactions of some important metals with water and dilute acid:

Order of reactivity	Reaction with water	Reaction with dilute acid
potassium	fizz, giving off hydrogen, leaving an alkaline solution of metal hydroxide	explode
sodium		
lithium		
calcium		fizz, giving off hydrogen and forming a salt
magnesium	react with steam, giving off hydrogen and forming the metal oxide	
aluminium		
zinc		
iron		
tin	slight reaction with steam	react slowly with warm acid
lead		
copper	no reaction, even with steam	no reaction
silver		
gold		

Table 1 The reactivity series

Note: Aluminium is protected by a layer of aluminium oxide so will not undergo the reactions above unless the oxide layer is removed. That's why this fairly reactive metal can be used outside, for example in sliding patio doors, without corroding.

For more about the reaction of metals with dilute acid, look back to 6.2 'Making salts from metals or insoluble bases'.

Practical

Metals and acid

You are given coarse-grained filings of the metals copper, aluminium, zinc, iron and magnesium to put into an order of reactivity according to their reactions with dilute hydrochloric acid.

Plan a test to put the metals in order of reactivity based on your observations. Your plan should include the quantities of reactants you intend to use. (You will have access to a balance and measuring cylinders.)

Let your teacher check your plan before you start your tests.

- Give a brief outline of your method, including how you will make it as fair a test as possible.
- Record your results in a suitable table.
- Put the metals in order of reactivity according to your observations.
- Identify any hazards.

links

For more about the reaction of metals with dilute acid, look back to 6.2 'Making salts from metals or insoluble bases'.

Summary questions

1 Write the word equation and balanced symbol equation, including state symbols, for the reaction between:
   a lithium and water
   b zinc and steam.

2 A student added a piece of magnesium ribbon to dilute sulfuric acid.
   a List three ways she could tell that a chemical reaction was taking place.
   b Write down the general equation that describes the reaction between a metal and an acid.
   c Write the word equation and balanced symbol equation, including state symbols, for the reaction between magnesium and dilute sulfuric acid.

3 Explain these facts in terms of chemical reactivity:
   a Gold, silver and platinum are used to make jewellery.
   b Potassium, lithium and sodium are stored in jars of oil.
   c Food cans are plated with tin, but not zinc.

4 Explain why aluminium can be used outdoors, e.g. as window frames, even though it is quite high in the reactivity series.

Key points

- The metals can be placed in order of reactivity by their reactions with water and dilute acid.
- Hydrogen gas is given off if metals react with water or dilute acids. The gas 'pops' with a lighted spill.

C7.2 Displacement reactions

Learning objectives

After this topic, you should know:

- how displacement reactions take place

- the position of hydrogen and carbon in the reactivity series

- the definitions of reduction and oxidation in terms of electron transfer.

Magnesium + Copper sulfate

Magnesium sulfate + copper

Figure 1 Magnesium displaces copper from copper(II) sulfate solution

Practical

Displacing a metal from solution

Set up the test tube as shown:

Zinc

Lead nitrate solution

Leave the tube until you see metal crystals on the surface of the zinc sheet.

- What do the crystals look like?
- Explain what happens.

Safety: Lead compounds are toxic. Wear chemical splash proof eye protection.

We have now seen how to use the reactions of metals with water and dilute acid to get an order of reactivity. We can also judge reactivity by putting the metals 'into competition' with each other. One metal starts off as the element and the other metal as an ion in a solution of one of its salts. For example, we might have magnesium metal, Mg(s), and copper(II) ions, Cu^{2+}(aq), in a solution of copper(II) sulfate.

A more reactive metal will displace a less reactive metal from an aqueous solution of one of its salts.

In this case, magnesium is more reactive than copper. Therefore the copper ions will be displaced from solution to form copper metal, Cu(s). In this reaction, the magnesium metal forms aqueous magnesium ions, Mg^{2+}(aq), and dissolves into the solution. This is a **displacement reaction**.

The word equation is:

magnesium + copper(II) sulfate → magnesium sulfate + copper

The balanced symbol equation is:

$$Mg(s) + CuSO_4(aq) \rightarrow MgSO_4(aq) + Cu(s)$$

The **ionic equation** (showing only the atoms and ions that change in the reaction):

$$Mg(s) + Cu^{2+}(aq) \rightarrow Mg^{2+}(aq) + Cu(s)$$

This shows that magnesium atoms have a greater tendency to form positive ions than copper atoms.

Zinc is more reactive than lead – it is higher up the reactivity series. Therefore, zinc displaces lead from its solution:

zinc + lead nitrate → zinc nitrate + lead
$$Zn(s) + Pb(NO_3)_2(aq) \rightarrow Zn(NO_3)_2(aq) + Pb(s)$$

We see the lead metal forming as crystals on the zinc.

Practical

Predicting reactions

Copy and fill in the table below.

Solution / Metal	Magnesium	Copper	Zinc	Iron
Magnesium sulfate	✗			
Copper sulfate		✗		
Zinc sulfate			✗	
Iron sulfate				✗

Predict which will react (enter a tick in the table), and which won't (enter a cross).

Try out the reactions on a spotting tile.

Safety: Wear eye protection. Some chemicals are harmful.

Hydrogen and carbon in the reactivity series

We can include the non-metals hydrogen and carbon in the reactivity series using displacement reactions. We can think of the metal plus acid reactions as displacement of hydrogen ions, $H^+(aq)$, from solution. Copper cannot displace the hydrogen from an acid, whereas lead can. So hydrogen is positioned between copper and lead. Carbon can be used in the extraction of metals from their oxides (another type of displacement reaction). However, it can only do this for metals below aluminium in the reactivity series. It does not displace aluminium from aluminium oxide, but can displace zinc from zinc oxide. So carbon is placed between aluminium and zinc in the series.

Oxidation and reduction

We have seen in Topic 4.2 that oxidation can be defined as the chemical addition of oxygen, and reduction as the removal of oxygen. A wider definition involves the transfer of electrons rather than oxygen atoms.

Oxidation is the loss of electrons.   **Reduction is the gain of electrons.**

We can apply these definitions to displacement reactions in solution. Take as an example, the displacement of copper by iron. This reaction is used in industry to extract copper metal from copper sulfate solution. The iron added to the copper sulfate solution is cheap scrap iron (see 7.4 'Extracting copper'):

$$Fe(s) + Cu^{2+}(aq) \rightarrow Fe^{2+}(aq) + Cu(s)$$

We can consider what happens to each reactant in the ionic equation above:

$$Fe(s) \rightarrow Fe^{2+}(aq) + 2e^-$$

Iron atoms lose two electrons to form iron(II) ions. This is oxidation (the loss of electrons). We say that iron atoms have been oxidised.

These two electrons from iron are gained by the copper(II) ions as they form copper atoms:

$$Cu^{2+}(aq) + 2e^- \rightarrow Cu(s)$$

This is reduction (the gain of electrons). The copper(II) ions have been reduced.

This is why these displacement reactions are also known as redox reactions (**red**uction-**ox**idation).

Summary questions

1 Which of the following pairs of metals and solutions will result in a reaction? If a reaction is predicted, write a balanced symbol equation, including state symbols.
   a iron + zinc sulfate   **b** zinc + copper sulfate
   c magnesium + iron(II) chloride
2 Explain why carbon can be used to reduce zinc oxide but not magnesium oxide.
3 Hydrogen gas is used in the reduction of tungsten oxide, WO_3, to extract tungsten metal.
   a What does this tell you about the position of tungsten in the reactivity series?
   b Write a balanced symbol equation for the reduction of tungsten oxide by hydrogen.
4 **a** Write the ionic equation, including state symbols, for the reaction between zinc and iron(II) sulfate.
   b Explain in terms of the transfer of electrons which species is oxidised and which is reduced in the reaction.

Key points

- A more reactive metal will displace a less reactive metal from its aqueous solution.
- The non-metals hydrogen and carbon can be given positions in the reactivity series on the basis of displacement reactions.
- Oxidation is the loss of electrons.
- Reduction is the gain of electrons.

C7.3 Extracting metals

Learning objectives

After this topic, you should know:

● where metals come from

● how metals can be extracted from their ores.

Figure 1 The Angel of the North stands 20 metres tall. It is made of steel which contains a small amount of copper.

Potassium — **Most reactive**

Sodium

Calcium

Magnesium

Aluminium

(Carbon)

Zinc

Iron

Tin

Lead

Copper

Silver

Gold

Platinum — **Least reactive**

Figure 2 This reactivity series shows the position of the non-metal carbon in the series

Metals have been important to people for thousands of years. You can follow the course of history by the materials people used. Starting from the Stone Age, we go to the Bronze Age (copper/tin) and then on to the Iron Age.

Where do we get metals from?

Metals are found in the Earth's crust. We find most metals combined chemically with other chemical elements, often with oxygen or sulfur. This means that the metal must be chemically separated from its compounds before it can be used.

When there is enough of a metal or metal compound in a rock to make it worth extracting the metal, we call the rock a **metal ore**. Ores are mined from the ground. Some need to be concentrated before the metal is extracted and purified. For example, copper ores are ground up into a powder. Then they are mixed with water and a chemical that makes the copper compound repel water. Air is then bubbled through the mixture and the copper compound floats on top as a froth. The rocky bits sink and the concentrated copper compound is scraped off the top. It is then ready to have its copper extracted.

Whether it is worth extracting a particular metal depends on:

● how easy it is to extract it from its ore

● how much metal the ore contains.

These two factors can change over time. For example, a new, cheaper method might be discovered for extracting a metal. We might also discover a new way to extract a metal efficiently from rock which contains only small amounts of a metal ore. An ore that was once thought of as 'low grade' could then become an economic source of a metal.

A few metals, such as gold and silver, are so unreactive that they are found in the Earth as the metals (elements) themselves. We say that they exist in their native state.

Sometimes a nugget of gold is so large it can simply be picked up. At other times tiny flakes have to be physically separated from sand and rocks by panning.

?? Did you know ...?

Gold in Wales is found in seams, just like coal – although not as thick, unfortunately! Gold jewellery was worn by early Welsh princes as a badge of rank. Welsh gold has been used in modern times to make the wedding rings of royal brides.

Figure 3 Panning for gold. Mud and stones are washed away while the dense gold remains in the pan.

How do we extract metals?

The way that we extract a metal depends on its place in the reactivity series. The reactivity series lists the metals in order of their reactivity (see Figure 2 which includes the non-metal carbon). As we have seen in 7.2, a more reactive metal will displace a less reactive metal from its compounds. Carbon (a non-metal) will also displace less reactive metals from their oxides. We use carbon to extract some metals from their ores in industry.

We can find many metals, such as copper, lead, iron and zinc, combined with oxygen as metal oxides. Because carbon is more reactive than each of these metals, we can use carbon to extract the metals from their oxides.

We must heat the metal oxide with carbon. The carbon removes the oxygen from the metal oxide to form carbon dioxide. The metal is also formed, as the element:

$$\text{metal oxide} + \text{carbon} \rightarrow \text{metal} + \text{carbon dioxide}$$

For example:

$$\text{lead oxide} + \text{carbon} \xrightarrow{\text{heat}} \text{lead} + \text{carbon dioxide}$$
$$2PbO(s) + C(s) \longrightarrow 2Pb(l) + CO_2(g)$$

The removal of oxygen from a compound is called chemical reduction. You can see how iron(III) oxide is reduced to extract iron on page 98.

The metals that are more reactive than carbon are not extracted from their ores by reduction with carbon. Instead they are extracted by **electrolysis** of the molten metal compound (see Chapter 14).

Summary questions

1 Define the term 'metal ore'.

2 Why is gold found as the metal rather than combined with other elements in compounds?

3 Platinum is found native. What does this tell you about its reactivity? Give a use of platinum that depends on this chemical property.

4 Zinc oxide (ZnO) can be reduced to zinc by heating it in a furnace with carbon. Carbon monoxide (CO) gas is given off in the reaction. The zinc formed is molten at the temperature in the furnace.
   a Write a word equation for the reduction of zinc oxide by carbon in the furnace.
   b Now write a balanced symbol equation, including state symbols, for the reaction in part a.

5 Lead is often found in the ore called galena which contains lead sulfide (PbS). Before reduction with carbon, the lead sulfide must be converted into lead oxide (PbO) by roasting the ore. This reaction with oxygen from the air also produces sulfur dioxide gas.
   a Write a word equation for the roasting of lead sulfide.
   b Now write a balanced symbol equation, including state symbols, for the reaction in part a.
   c Lead oxide is reduced by heating with carbon. Write a balanced symbol equation for this reaction, assuming carbon dioxide is one of the products.

C7.4 Extracting copper

Learning objectives

After this topic, you should know:

- how copper is obtained from copper-rich ores
- the methods used to obtain copper from low-grade ores
- how copper is purified.

Figure 1 Mining copper ores can leave huge scars on the landscape. This is called open-cast mining. About 90% of copper comes from open-cast mines. Our supplies of copper-rich ores are a limited resource.

Extracting copper from copper-rich ores

We extract most of our copper from **copper-rich ores**. These are a limited resource and are in danger of running out.

There are two main methods used to obtain the copper metal from the ore.

- In one method we use sulfuric acid to produce copper sulfate solution, before extracting the copper metal.
- The other process is called **smelting** (roasting). We heat copper ore very strongly in a furnace with air to produce crude copper metal.

For example, copper can be found in an ore called chalcocite. This contains copper(I) sulfide, Cu_2S. If we roast the copper(I) sulfide in air, it decomposes to give copper metal:

$$\text{copper(I) sulfide} + \text{oxygen} \rightarrow \text{copper} + \text{sulfur dioxide}$$
$$Cu_2S(s) \quad + \quad O_2(g) \rightarrow 2Cu(s) + \quad SO_2(g)$$

Care has to be taken to avoid letting sulfur dioxide gas into the atmosphere. This gas causes acid rain. So chimneys are fitted with basic 'scrubbers' to neutralise the acidic gas or it is used to make sulfuric acid.

Then we use the impure copper as the positive electrode in electrolysis cells to make pure copper. About 80% of copper is still produced by smelting. Smelting and purifying copper ore uses huge amounts of heat and electricity. This costs a lot of money and will cause pollution in the environment.

Practical

Extracting copper from malachite

Malachite is a copper ore containing copper carbonate (harmful). To extract the copper we first heat the copper carbonate in a boiling tube. **Thermal decomposition** takes place. Copper oxide is left in the tube.

- Which gas is given off?

We then add dilute sulfuric acid to the copper oxide (harmful). Stopper and shake the tube. This makes copper sulfate solution (harmful). Filter off any excess black copper oxide in the solution.

To extract the copper metal, either:

1 Put an iron nail into the copper sulfate solution (harmful). What happens to the iron nail?

or;

2 Collect some extra copper sulfate solution (harmful) and place it in a small beaker. Set up the circuit as shown in Figure 2. Turn the power on until you see copper metal collecting. Which electrode – the positive or the negative – does the copper metal form on?

Safety: Wear eye protection. Chemicals used in this practical are harmful.

Carbon electrodes

Copper sulfate solution

Figure 2 Extracting copper metal using electrolysis. In industry, copper electrodes are used to obtain very pure copper metal at the negative electrode.

Metal ions are always positively charged. Therefore, in electrolysis they are attracted to the negative electrode. So, metals are always deposited at the negative electrode. In industry the electrolysis is carried out in many cells running at once. This method gives the very pure copper needed to make electrical wiring. Electrolysis is also used to purify the impure copper extracted by smelting. In the industrial process, the electrolysis cells use copper electrodes.

Look at Figure 3. We can show what happens with the ionic half equations shown below. At the negative copper electrode (cathode) we get reduction:

$$Cu^{2+}(aq) + 2e^- \rightarrow Cu(s)$$

At the positive copper electrode (anode) we get oxidation:

$$Cu(s) \rightarrow Cu^{2+}(aq) + 2e^-$$

The copper can also be extracted from copper sulfate solution in industry by adding scrap iron. Iron is more reactive than copper, so it can displace copper from its solutions:

$$iron + copper(\text{II}) \text{ sulfate} \rightarrow iron(\text{II}) \text{ sulfate} + copper$$

Extracting copper from low-grade copper ores

Instead of extracting copper from our limited copper-rich ores, scientists are developing new ways to get copper from low-grade ores. This would be uneconomical using traditional methods. We can now use bacteria (**bioleaching**) and even plants (**phytomining**) to help extract copper.

In phytomining, plants can absorb copper ions from low-grade copper ore as they grow. This could be on slag heaps of previously discarded waste from the processing of copper-rich ores. Then the plants are burned and the metals can be extracted from the ash. The copper ions can be 'leached' (dissolved) from the ash by adding sulfuric acid. This makes a solution (leachate) of copper sulfate. Then we can use displacement by scrap iron and electrolysis to extract pure copper metal.

In bioleaching, bacteria feed on low-grade metal ores. By a combination of biological and chemical processes, we can get a solution of copper ions (leachate) from waste copper ore. Once again, we use scrap iron and electrolysis to extract the copper from the leachate.

About 20% of our copper comes from bioleaching. This is likely to increase as sources of copper-rich ores run out. Bioleaching is a slow process so scientists are researching ways to speed it up. At present it can take years to extract 50% of the metal from a low-grade ore.

⟳ links

For information on the half equations at electrodes in electrolysis, see 14.2 'Changes at the electrodes'.

⟳ links

For information on the displacement (redox) reaction between copper ions in solution and iron metal, look back to 7.2 'Displacement reactions'.

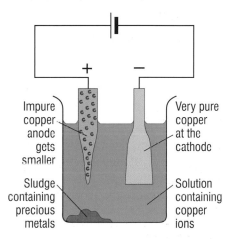

Figure 3 Many of these cells operate at the same time in industry. The cathodes are removed about every two weeks.

Summary questions

1 Why is copper an important metal in our technological society?

2 a Explain briefly two traditional ways of extracting copper metal.
  b State an advantage of extracting copper using bacteria rather than traditional methods.
  c Why can copper occasionally be found native?
  d When copper is purified by electrolysis, which electrode do you think the pure copper collects at? Explain your answer.

3 Write a balanced chemical equation, including state symbols, for the extraction of copper:
  a from copper(II) sulfide by smelting
  b from copper sulfate solution by displacement.

4 a Write ionic half equations for the reactions at each copper electrode in the electrolysis of copper sulfate solution.
  b Explain where reduction and oxidation takes place in the electrolysis cell in part **a**.

5 Explain how copper is extracted by phytomining and why this method will become increasingly important.

Key points

- Most copper is extracted by smelting (roasting) copper-rich ores, although our limited supplies of ores are becoming more scarce.

- Copper can be extracted from copper solutions by electrolysis or by displacement using scrap iron. Electrolysis is also used to purify impure copper, e.g. the copper metal obtained from smelting.

- Scientists are developing ways to extract copper that use low-grade copper ores. Bacteria are used in bioleaching and plants in phytomining.

C7.5 Recycling metals

Learning objectives

After this topic, you should know:

● why we should recycle metals in terms of the Earth's natural resources, the use of energy and the effects on the environment.

∞ **links**

To find out more about the production of aluminium, see 14.3 'The extraction of aluminium'.

??? Did you know ... ?

It has been estimated that aluminium production uses 5% of the electricity generated in the United States.

∞ **links**

For more information on the extraction of iron and production of steel, see 7.9 'Iron and steels', and about the pollution caused by fossil fuels, see 9.3 'Burning fuels'.

Recycling aluminium

In the UK each person uses on average around 8 kg of aluminium every year. This is why it is important to **recycle** aluminium to help conserve the Earth's reserves of aluminium ore. Aluminium is extracted from molten aluminium oxide at high temperatures using electrolysis. The process requires huge amounts of electrical energy. Recycling saves energy, and therefore money, since recycling aluminium does not involve electrolysis. Comparing recycled aluminium with aluminium extracted from its ore, there is a 95% energy saving.

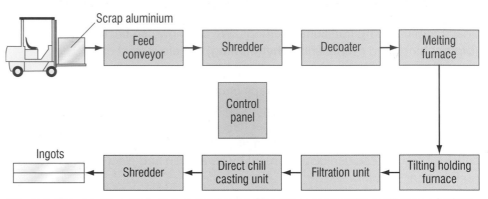

Figure 1 The recycling of aluminium involves melting the scrap metal but still uses a lot less energy than extracting aluminium from its ore, bauxite

Figure 2 Recycling cans saves energy, as well as our limited supplies of metal ores. It also reduces pollution.

Recycling iron and steel

We also recycle iron and steel, for example from the bodywork and engines of scrap cars. 'Tin cans' are another source of scrap iron. These are usually steel cans with a very thin coating of tin to prevent rusting. The cans are easy to separate from other domestic rubbish as they are magnetic.

Using recycled steel saves about 50% of the energy used to extract iron and turn it into steel. Much of the energy in the production of steel from iron ore is supplied by burning fossil fuels, such as natural gas used to heat the air entering a blast furnace. Therefore recycling helps save our dwindling supplies of the **non-renewable** fuels. There are also pollution problems that arise whenever we burn fossil fuels so using less energy helps reduce these effects. The pollutants produced by fossil fuels include sulfur dioxide, carbon dioxide, carbon monoxide, unburnt hydrocarbons and particulates.

Recycling copper

Copper is also recycled but this is difficult as it is often alloyed with other metals, e.g. in brass where copper is mixed with zinc. Therefore, the impure copper from recycling would need to be purified for use in electrical wiring unless it was reclaimed solely from old electricity wires. High quality copper from wires can be recycled by melting and/or re-using it.

However, with a lot of old copper, which is mixed with other metals in alloys, it has to be analysed to find the percentages of each metal present. Then there is the option of just melting the mixture of metals and re-using as the alloy.

With just a few impurities, a copper alloy can be made the anode and purified by electrolysis but if the percentage of copper is low, this method of purification does not work. The percentages of metals might be able to be adjusted to get another useful alloy. Alternatively, more copper can be added to the impure copper by melting them together. This raises the percentage of copper in the alloy so then you can purify it electrically. However, this makes the copper more expensive to recycle.

Figure 3 The recycling of copper is made more difficult by the presence of other metals in copper alloys

Environmental considerations

Recycling metals reduces the need to mine the metal ore and conserves the Earth's limited reserves of metal ores. It also prevents any pollution problems that arise from extracting the metal from its ore. For example, whenever we mine metal ores from the Earth's crust there are consequences for our environment. You have seen that open-cast mining is often used to get copper ore from the ground. The ores of iron and aluminium are also mainly mined like this. Huge pits that scar the landscape are made, creating noise and dust and destroying the habitats of plants and animals. The mines also leave large heaps of waste rock. The water in an area subjected to the mining of metal ores can also be affected. As rain drains through exposed ores and slag heaps of waste, the groundwater can become acidic.

Having mined the ores, then they must be processed to extract the metals. For example, sulfide ores are heated strongly in smelting. Any sulfur dioxide gas that escapes into the air will cause acid rain. In the extraction of iron, carbon dioxide is given off which can contribute to the enhanced greenhouse effect and global warming issues. Reducing these factors are why recycling metals is so important.

Figure 4 Recycling helps to reduce the pollution problems arising from extracting metals

Summary questions

1 What can a mining company do to help the environment when an open-cast mine is no longer economic?

2 Each person in the UK uses about 8 kg of aluminium each year. Recycling 1 kg of aluminium saves about enough energy to run a small electric fire for 14 hours. If you recycle 50% of the aluminium you use in one year, how long could you run a small electric fire on the energy you have saved?

3 Explain why the energy savings are so great when recycling aluminium compared with extracting aluminium from its ore.

4 Explain why it is difficult to recycle some metals, such as copper, and how this can be overcome.

5 Explain how a range of pollution problems are reduced by recycling metals.

Key points

- There are social, economic and environmental issues associated with exploiting metal ores.

- Recycling metals saves energy and our limited, non-renewable metal ores (and fossil fuels). The pollution caused by the mining and extraction of metals is also reduced by recycling.

C7.6 Bonding in metals

Learning objectives

After this topic, you should know:

- how the atoms in metals are arranged
- how the atoms in metals are bonded to each other.

∞ links

For more information on protecting iron from rusting, look back at 4.4 'Rusting'.

Metal crystals

The atoms in metals are built up layer upon layer in a regular pattern (see Figure 1).

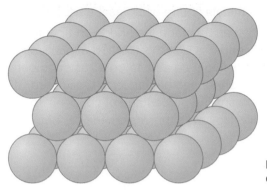

Figure 1 The close-packed arrangement of copper atoms in copper metal

This means that they form crystals, although these are not always obvious to the naked eye. However, sometimes we can see them. You can see zinc crystals on the surface of some steel that has been dipped into molten zinc to prevent it from rusting. This is called galvanised steel. For example, look at the surface of galvanised lamp posts and commercial wheelie bins (see Figure 3).

Figure 3 Metal crystals, such as the zinc ones shown on this galvanised lamp post, give us evidence that metals are made up of atoms arranged in regular patterns

Practical

Growing silver crystals

You can grow crystals of silver metal by suspending a length of copper wire in silver nitrate solution. The crystals of silver will appear on the wire quite quickly. However, for the best results they need to be left for several hours.

- Explain your observations.

Safety: Wear eye protection.

Figure 2 Growing silver crystals

Practical

Survey of metallic crystals

Take a look around your school or college to see if you can find any galvanised steel. See if you can spot the metal crystals. You can also look for crystals on brass fittings that have been left outside and not polished.

Metallic bonding

Metals are another example of giant structures. You can think of a metal as a lattice of positively charged ions. The metal ions are arranged in regular layers, one on top of another.

The outer electrons from each metal atom can easily move throughout the giant structure. The outer electrons (in the highest occupied energy level) form a 'sea' of free-moving electrons surrounding the positively charged metal ions. Strong electrostatic attraction between the negatively charged electrons and positively charged ions bonds the metal ions to each other.

The electrons in the 'sea' of free-moving electrons are called delocalised electrons. They are no longer linked with any particular metal ion in the giant metallic structure. These delocalised electrons help us explain the properties of metals. (See 7.7 'Giant metallic structures'.)

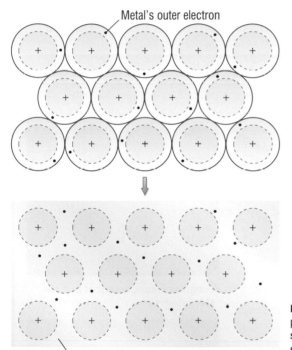

Metal's outer electron

The 'sea' of delocalised electrons

Figure 4 A metal consists of positively charged metal ions surrounded by a 'sea' of delocalised electrons. This diagram shows us a model of metallic bonding.

∞ **links**

For more information about the properties of metals, see 7.7 'Giant metallic structures'.

Summary questions

1 What can we deduce about the arrangement of the particles in a metal from the fact that metals form crystals?

2 a Why are the particles that make up a metal described as positively charged ions?

   b What are delocalised electrons?

3 Use the theory of metallic bonding to explain the bonding in magnesium metal. Make sure you mention delocalised electrons. (The atomic number of magnesium is 12.)

4 Using a model to explain metallic bonding, delocalised electrons could be thought of as a 'glue'.
   Explain why thinking of delocalised electrons in a metal as a glue is a useful model but one which has a major drawback.

Key points

- The atoms in metals are closely packed together and arranged in regular layers.

- We can think of metallic bonding as positively charged metal ions which are held together by electrons from the outermost shell of each metal atom. These delocalised electrons are free to move throughout the giant metallic lattice.

C7.7 Giant metallic structures

Learning objectives

After this topic, you should know:

- why metals can be bent and shaped without breaking
- why alloys are harder than pure metals
- why metals conduct electricity and heat
- what 'shape memory alloys' are.

We can hammer and bend metals into different shapes, and draw them out into wires. This is because the layers of atoms in a pure metal are able to slide easily over each other.

The atoms in a pure metal, such as iron, are held together in a giant metallic structure. The atoms are arranged in closely-packed layers. This regular arrangement allows the atoms to slide over one another quite easily. This is why pure iron is relatively soft and easily shaped.

Alloys are usually mixtures of metals. However, most steels contain iron with controlled amounts of carbon, a non-metal, mixed in its structure. The carbon atoms are a different size to the iron atoms. This makes it more difficult for the layers in the metal's giant structure to slide over each other. So, alloys are harder than the pure metals used to make them. This is shown in Figure 2.

Figure 1 Drawing copper out into wires depends on being able to make the layers of metal atoms slide easily over each other, without breaking the metal

Practical

Making models of metals

Figure 3 Making a bubble raft to model the structure of a metal

We can make a model of the structure of a metal by blowing small bubbles of gas on the surface of soap solution to represent atoms.

- Why are models useful in science?

A regular arrangement of bubble 'atoms'

A larger bubble 'atom' disrupts the regular arrangement around it

Iron

Alloy

Figure 2 The atoms in pure iron are arranged in layers which can easily slide over each other. In alloys the layers cannot slide so easily because atoms of other elements distort the layers.

- Metal cooking utensils are used all over the world, because metals are good conductors of heat.
- Wherever we generate electricity, it passes through metal wires (usually made of copper) to get to where it is needed because metals are also good conductors of electricity.

Explaining the properties of metals

The positive ions in a metal's giant structure are held together by a sea of delocalised electrons. These electrons are a bit like 'glue'. Their negative charge between the positively charged ions holds the metal ions in position.

However, unlike glue, the electrons are able to move throughout the whole giant lattice. Because they can move around and hold the metal ions together at the same time, the delocalised electrons enable the lattice to distort. When struck, the metal atoms can slip past one another without breaking up the metal's structure.

Metals are good conductors of heat and electricity because the delocalised electrons can readily flow through the giant metallic lattice. The electrical current and heat energy are transferred quickly through the metal by the free-moving electrons.

⚮ links

For more about the bonding in metals, look back at 7.6 'Bonding in metals'.

Figure 4 Metals are essential in our lives – the delocalised electrons mean that they are good conductors of both heat and electricity

Shape memory alloys

Some alloys have a very special property. Like all metals they can be bent (or **deformed**) into different shapes. The difference comes when you heat them up and they return to their original shape automatically. We call these metals **shape memory alloys**, which describes the way they behave. They seem to 'remember' their original shape!

We can use the properties of shape memory alloys in many ways, for example in health-care. Doctors treating a badly broken bone can use alloys to hold the bones in place while they heal. They cool the alloy before it is wrapped around the broken bone. When it heats up again the alloy goes back to its original shape. This pulls the bones together and holds them in place while they heal.

Dentists can also make braces to pull teeth into the right position using this technique (see Figure 5).

Figure 5 This dental brace pulls the teeth into the right position as it warms up. It is made of a shape memory alloy called nitinol. It is an alloy of nickel and titanium.

Summary questions

1 a Why can metals be bent, shaped and pulled out into wires when forces are applied?
   b Find out the word used to describe a material, such as a metal, that can be:
      i hammered into shapes   ii drawn out into wire.

2 a Use your knowledge of metal structures to explain why alloying a metal can make the metal harder.
   b What is a shape memory alloy?

3 Explain how a dental brace made out of nitinol is more effective than a brace made out of a traditional alloy.

4 Explain why metals are good conductors of heat and electricity in terms of their structure and bonding.

Key points

- We can bend and shape metals because the layers of atoms (or positively charged ions) in a giant metallic structure can slide over each other.

- Alloys are harder than pure metals because the regular layers in a pure metal are distorted by differently-sized atoms in an alloy.

- Delocalised electrons in metals enable electricity and heat to pass through a metal easily.

- If a shape memory alloy is deformed, it can return to its original shape on heating.

C7.8 | Useful metals

Transition metals

In the centre of the periodic table there is a large block of metallic elements. Most are called transition metals and have similar properties. Like all metals, the transition metals are very good conductors of electricity and heat. They are strong but can also be bent or hammered into useful shapes.

Figure 1 The transition metals are found in the yellow block of the periodic table shown here

The properties of the transition metals mean that we can use them in many different ways. You will find them in buildings and in cars, trains and other types of transport. Their strength makes them useful as building materials. We use them in heating systems and for electrical wiring because heat energy and electricity pass through them easily.

Copper is a very useful transition metal. It can be bent but is still hard enough for plumbers to use as water tanks or pipes and it does not react with water. Copper also conducts electricity and heat very well. So it is ideal where we need:

- pipes that will carry water, or
- wires that will conduct electricity.

Figure 2 Copper is particularly useful because it is such a good conductor of electricity

🔗 **links**

For more information of the transition metals, look back to 5.3 'The transition elements'.

Figure 3 Transition metals are used in many different ways because of their useful properties

Copper alloys

Bronze was probably the first alloy made by humans, about 5500 years ago. It is usually made by mixing copper with tin. We use it to make ship's propellers because of its toughness and resistance to corrosion.

We make brass by alloying copper with zinc. Brass is much harder than copper but it is workable. It can be hammered into sheets and pressed into intricate shapes. This property is used to make musical instruments, such as trumpets.

Aluminium alloys

Aluminium has a low density for a metal. It can be alloyed with a wide range of other elements. There are over 300 alloys of aluminium available. These alloys have very different properties. We can use 'light-weight', but strong, aluminium alloys to build aircraft while others can be used as armour plating on tanks and other military vehicles.

Gold alloys

As with copper and iron, we can make gold and aluminium harder by adding other elements. We usually alloy gold with copper when we use it in jewellery. Pure gold wears away more easily than its alloy with copper. By varying the proportions of the two metals we also get different shades of 'gold' objects.

Figure 4 The Statue of Liberty in New York contains over 80 tonnes of copper

Figure 5 Alloying with copper makes gold more hardwearing. This is especially important in wedding rings, which many married people wear most of the time.

Summary questions

1 a Write a list of the properties of a typical transition metal.
  b Where in the periodic table do we find the transition metals?
  c Which metal mentioned on this page is **NOT** a transition metal?

2 a Why is copper metal used so much in plumbing?
  b Why is gold alloyed with copper in many wedding rings?

3 Silver and gold are transition metals that are better conductors of electricity than copper. Why do we use copper to make electric cables instead of either of these metals?

4 Why are aluminium alloys used extensively in the aircraft industry?

5 Explain in detail why copper alloys are more suitable for making coins than pure copper metal.

Key points

- The transition metals are found in the central block of elements in the periodic table.

- Transition metals have properties that make them useful for building and making things. For example, copper is used in wiring because of its high electrical conductivity.

- Copper, gold and aluminium are all alloyed with other metals to make them harder.

C7.9

Iron and steels

Learning objectives

After this topic, you should know:

- how iron ore is reduced

- why iron directly from a blast furnace is not very useful

- how iron from a blast furnace is changed to make it more useful

- the main types and uses of steels.

⊂⊃ links

For more about extracting metals using carbon, look back to 7.3 'Extracting metals'.

Figure 1 The iron which has just come out of a blast furnace contains about 96% iron. The main impurity is carbon.

Examiner's tip

You need to know how the hardness of steels is related to their carbon content.

Iron ore contains iron combined with oxygen in iron(III) oxide along with rocky impurities. Iron is less reactive than carbon. So, we can extract iron by using carbon to remove oxygen from the iron(III) oxide in the ore. We extract iron in a **blast furnace**. The raw materials fed into the furnace, which is run continuously, are:

- iron ore (called haematite),
- coke (a cheap form of carbon made from coal)
- air, and
- limestone (used to remove impurities by reacting with them to form slag).

Some of the iron(III) oxide reacts with carbon. The carbon reduces iron(III) oxide, forming molten iron and carbon dioxide gas. This is one of the reduction reactions which takes place in a blast furnace. It is called a 'blast furnace' because high temperatures are generated inside the furnace by blasts of hot air, containing oxygen, which reacts with the coke (carbon) – a bit like in a giant barbecue:

$$\text{carbon} + \text{oxygen} \rightarrow \text{carbon dioxide}$$
$$C(s) + O_2(g) \rightarrow CO_2(g)$$

However, the main reducing agent in a blast furnace is not carbon but carbon monoxide gas. This is made from the carbon dioxide passing over hot coke (carbon):

$$\text{carbon dioxide} + \text{carbon} \rightarrow \text{carbon monoxide}$$
$$CO_2(g) + C(s) \rightarrow 2CO(g)$$

The carbon monoxide then reduces the iron(III) oxide:

$$\text{iron(III) oxide} + \text{carbon monoxide} \rightarrow \text{iron} + \text{carbon dioxide}$$
$$Fe_2O_3(s) + 3CO(g) \rightarrow 2Fe(l) + 3CO_2(g)$$

The molten iron is tapped off from the bottom of the furnace.

Iron straight from the blast furnace has limited uses. It contains about 96% iron and contains impurities, mainly carbon. This makes the iron brittle, although it is very hard and can't be easily compressed. When molten it can be run into moulds and cast into different shapes. This **cast iron** is used to make wood-burning stoves, man-hole covers on roads, and engines. Despite being brittle, cast iron can withstand high forces of compression without breaking; hence its use in man-hole covers.

We can treat the iron from the blast furnace to remove some of the carbon.

Removing all the carbon and other impurities from cast iron gives us pure iron. This is relatively soft and easily-shaped. However, it is too soft for most uses. If we want to make iron really useful we have to make sure that it contains tiny amounts of other elements. These include carbon and metals, such as nickel and chromium. We call a metal that is mixed with other elements an alloy.

Steels

Steels are alloys of iron. By adding elements in carefully controlled amounts, we can change the properties of the steels.

Steel is not a single substance. Like all alloys, it is a mixture. There are lots of different types of steel. All of them are alloys of iron with carbon and/or other elements.

Carbon steels

The simplest steels are the **carbon steels**. We make these by removing most of the carbon from cast iron, just leaving small amounts of carbon (from 0.03% to 1.5%). These are the cheapest steels to make. We use them in many products, such as the bodies of cars, knives, machinery, ships, containers and structural steel for buildings.

Often these carbon steels have small amounts of other elements in them as well. High carbon steel, with a relatively high carbon content, is very strong but brittle. On the other hand, low carbon steel is soft and easily shaped. It is not as strong, but is much less likely to shatter on impact with a hard object.

Mild steel is one type of low carbon steel. It contains less than 0.1% carbon. It is very easily pressed into shapes. This makes it particularly useful in mass production, such as making car bodies.

Alloy steels

Low-alloy steels are more expensive than carbon steels because they contain between 1% and 5% of other metals. Each of these metals produces a steel that is well-suited for a particular use.

Even more expensive are the **high-alloy steels**. These contain a much higher percentage of other metals. The chromium–nickel steels are known as **stainless steels**. We use them to make cooking utensils and cutlery. They are also used to make chemical reaction vessels. That's because they combine hardness and strength with great resistance to corrosion. Unlike most other steels, they do not rust!

Figure 2 Low carbon steel called mild steel is easily pressed into shapes

Figure 3 The properties of alloy steels make them ideal for use in bridges

Figure 4 The resistance of stainless steels to rusting make them ideal for making utensils and cutlery

Did you know ... ?

We use nickel–steel alloys to build long-span bridges, bicycle chains and military armour-plating. That's because they are very resistant to stretching forces. Tungsten steel operates well under very hot conditions so it is used to make high-speed tools such as drill bits.

Summary questions

1 a Why is iron from a blast furnace very brittle?
   b How does cast iron differ from pure iron in its composition and properties?
   c Give one use of cast iron which relies on its high strength in compression.

2 a Name the raw materials used in a blast furnace for the extraction of iron.
   b Name the main reducing agent in the blast furnace and write a balanced symbol equation for its formation. Include state symbols.
   c A small amount of iron(III) oxide is reduced by solid carbon in the blast furnace. Write a word equation and a balanced symbol equation with state symbols for this reaction.
   d Explain why carbon monoxide, as opposed to solid carbon, reduces most of the iron(III) oxide in the blast furnace.

3 Make a table to summarise the main useful properties of low carbon steel, high carbon steel and chromium–nickel steel.

4 a Why are surgical instruments made from steel containing chromium and nickel?
   b Explain which type of steel is used to make:
      i car bodies   ii railway tracks.

Key points

- We extract iron from iron ore by reducing it using carbon in a blast furnace. The main reducing agent is carbon monoxide gas.

- Pure iron is too soft for it to be very useful.

- Carefully controlled quantities of carbon and other elements are added to iron to make steel alloys with different properties.

- Important examples of steels are:
  – low carbon steels which are easily shaped,
  – high carbon steels which are very hard,
  – stainless steels which are resistant to corrosion.

Summary questions

1 Imagine that a new metal, given the symbol X, has been discovered. It lies between calcium and magnesium in the reactivity series.

   a Describe its reaction when heated in steam and give a word equation and a balanced symbol equation, including state symbols. (Metal X forms 2+ ions)

   b Describe the reaction of X with dilute sulfuric acid and give word and symbol equations.

   c Why can't you be sure how X will react with cold water?

   d X is added to a solution of copper(II) nitrate.
     i Explain what you would expect to see happen, including a balanced symbol equation with state symbols.
     ii Write an ionic equation showing what happens in the change.
     iii Explain which species is oxidised and which is reduced, using ionic half equations.

   e Another new metal, Y, does not react with water or steam, but there is a slight reaction with warm dilute acid.
     i Where would you place metal Y in the reactivity series?
     ii Explain what you would expect to happen if metal Y was added to magnesium sulfate solution.

2 Decide which of the pairs below will react. If they do react, complete the word equations and balanced symbol equations, including state symbols:

   a carbon + copper(II) oxide

   b iron + zinc nitrate

   c iron + magnesium oxide

   d magnesium + copper(II) sulfate

3 The reaction between aluminium powder and iron(III) oxide is used in the rail industry.

   a i Write a word equation and a balanced symbol equation for the reaction that takes place.
     ii What do we call this type of reaction?

   b Compare the reaction described above with the reaction you would expect to see between powdered aluminium and copper(II) oxide.

   c Predict what would happen if we heat a mixture of aluminium oxide and iron.

   d Explain why the uses of aluminium metal are surprising given its position in the reactivity series.

4 a What name is given to the method of extracting copper from an ore:
     i using bacteria
     ii using plants
     iii using heat
     iv using electricity?

   b Which methods in part **a** are being developed to extract copper from low-grade copper ores?

5 Choose from this list to name the metal described in **a** to **f**.

   nitinol chromium gold aluminium copper magnesium

   a A precious metal, often alloyed with copper to make it more hard-wearing.

   b A shape memory metal used to make dental braces.

   c A low density metal used to make alloys for the aircraft industry.

   d A metal that is extracted from its leachate using scrap iron.

   e A metal that reacts very slowly with cold water but reacts vigorously when heated in steam, forming a white basic oxide.

   f A metal that is alloyed with nickel and iron in stainless steel.

6 Iron is extracted from iron ore in a blast furnace.

In a blast furnace, limestone is used to remove impurities. The calcium carbonate in limestone decomposes at the high temperatures in the furnace. The basic product formed then reacts with rocky impurities such as silicon dioxide, SiO_2. The molten slag formed (calcium silicate, $CaSiO_3$) is tapped off from above the molten iron near the bottom of the furnace and used to make roads and building blocks.

Write a balanced symbol equation for:

   a the breakdown of calcium carbonate in the blast furnace

   b the formation of slag.

AQA Examination-style questions

1 One way to compare the reactivities of metals is to add them to acids. Some students added samples of five metals to separate tubes containing dilute hydrochloric acid. The teacher provided the metal labelled X. The amount of metal was the same in each experiment.

a To make the comparison fair, some other factors should be the same in each experiment.

i State **two** properties/factors applying to the acid that should be the same. (2)

ii State **one** other factor applying to the metal that should be the same. (1)

b The students recorded their observations in a table.

Metal	Observation
copper	nothing happened
iron	very few bubbles
magnesium	very large numbers of bubbles
X	very few bubbles
zinc	quite a lot of bubbles

i Which metal in the table is the most reactive? (1)

ii Why is it not possible to deduce that iron is the least reactive metal in the table? (1)

c The teacher suggested that a better method to compare the reactivities of the metals is to see how long it takes to collect a certain volume of the gas formed.

Name **two** pieces of apparatus needed in the suggested method. (2)

2 The reactivities of metals can be compared by using displacement reactions.

a A more reactive metal will displace a less reactive metal from its salt in solution. An equation for a displacement reaction is

zinc + copper(II) sulfate → zinc sulfate + copper

Write a symbol equation for this reaction. (2)

b The equation for another displacement reaction is

$Fe + CuCl_2 \rightarrow FeCl_2 + Cu$

Write the simplest ionic equation for this reaction. (1)

c The reaction in **b** is a redox reaction.

i State the meaning of the term redox. (1)

ii State and explain, in terms of redox and electrons, what happens to the iron in this reaction. (2)

d The reactions between carbon and metal oxides are also examples of displacement reactions. Both carbon and hydrogen can be included in the reactivity series of metals.

i Suggest the product formed from carbon in the reaction with zinc oxide. (1)

ii Arrange the elements hydrogen, carbon and zinc in order of reactivity, starting with the most reactive. Give reasons for your choice. (3)

3 Copper is a useful metal.

a Some copper is extracted by phytomining.

Outline this process and state why it has become more important. (4)

b The diagram represents the structure of copper.

i Use this diagram to explain why copper can be easily shaped. (2)

ii Explain why copper is a good conductor of electricity. (2)

c Pure copper is very soft and is made harder by adding other metals.

i What name is used for a mixture of metals? (1)

ii Explain how the other metals make copper harder. (2)

C8.1

How fast?

The rate of a chemical reaction tells us how fast reactants turn into products. In our bodies, there are lots of reactions taking place all the time. They happen at the correct rate to supply our cells with what they need, whenever required.

Reaction rate is also very important in the chemical industry. Any industrial process has to make money by producing useful products. This means the right amount of product needed must be made as cheaply as possible. If it takes too long to produce, it will be hard to make a profit when it is sold. The rate of the reaction must be fast enough to make it quickly but safely.

How can we find out the rate of reactions?

Reactions happen at all sorts of different rates. Some are really fast, such as the combustion of chemicals inside a firework exploding. Others are very slow, such as an old piece of iron rusting.

There are two ways we can work out the rate of a chemical reaction. We can find out how quickly:

- the reactants are used up as they make products, or
- the products of the reaction are made.

Here are three ways we can make these kinds of measurement in experiments.

Practical

Measuring the decreasing mass of a reaction mixture

We can measure the rate at which the *mass* of a reaction mixture changes if the reaction gives off a gas. As the reaction takes place, the mass of the reaction mixture decreases. We can measure and record the mass at time intervals which we decide.

Some balances can be attached to a computer to monitor the loss in mass continuously.

- Why is the cotton wool placed in the neck of the conical flask?
- How would the line on the graph differ if you plot 'Loss in mass' on the vertical axis?

Safety: Wear eye protection. Hydrochloric acid 5M – irritant.

Practical

Measuring the increasing volume of gas given off

If a reaction produces a gas, we can use the gas to find out the rate of reaction. We do this by collecting the gas and measuring the volume given off at time intervals.

● What are the sources of error when measuring the volume of gas?

Safety: Wear eye protection.

Practical

Measuring the decreasing light passing through a solution

Some reactions in solution make a suspension of an insoluble solid (precipitate). This makes the solution go cloudy. We can use this to measure the rate at which the precipitate appears.

The reaction is set up in a flask. Under the flask, we put a piece of paper marked with a cross. Then we can record the time taken for the cross to disappear. The shorter the time, the faster the reaction rate.

Or we can use a light sensor and data logger. Then we measure the amount of light passing through the solution over time, as the graph shows.

● What are the advantages of using a light sensor rather than the 'disappearing cross' method?

We can summarise these methods of working out the rate of a reaction using this equation:

$$\text{Average rate of reaction} = \frac{\text{amount of reactant used or amount of product formed}}{\text{time}}$$

Summary questions

1 a Write a word equation and a balanced symbol equation, including state symbols, for the reaction taking place in the practical box on the previous page.
 b In the same experiment, there were some marble chips left when the fizzing stopped. Why was no more gas given off?
 c How can you tell from a graph of the experimental results when the reaction had finished?

2 Sketch graphs to show the results of:
 a i measuring the mass of products formed in a reaction over time
  ii measuring the mass of reactants remaining in a reaction over time.
 b What does the slope of the line at any particular time on the graphs in part **a** tell us about the reaction?

Key points

● We can find out the rate of a chemical reaction by following the amount of reactants used up over time.

● Alternatively, we can find out the rate of reaction by following the amount of products made over time.

● The slope of the line at any given time on the graphs drawn from such experiments tells us the rate of reaction at that time. The steeper the slope, the faster the reaction.

C8.2 Collision theory and surface area

Learning objectives

After this topic, you should know:

- the factors that can affect the rate of a chemical reaction

- collision theory

- how to use collision theory to explain the effect of surface area on reaction rate.

Figure 1 There is no doubt that the chemicals in these fireworks have reacted. But how can we explain what happens in a chemical reaction?

Figure 2 Cooking – an excellent example of controlling reaction rates!

In everyday life we often control the rates of chemical reactions without thinking about it. For example, cooking cakes in an oven or revving up a car engine. In chemistry we need to know what affects the rate of reactions. We also need to explain why each factor affects the rate of a reaction.

There are four main factors which affect the rate of chemical reactions:

- temperature
- surface area
- concentration of solutions or pressure of gases
- presence of a catalyst.

Reactions can only take place when the particles (atoms, ions or molecules) of reactants come together. But the reacting particles don't just have to bump into each other. They also need to collide with enough energy to cause a reaction to take place. This is known as **collision theory**.

The minimum amount of energy that particles must have before they can react is called the **activation energy**.

So reactions are more likely to happen between reactant particles if we:

- increase the frequency of reacting particles colliding with each other
- increase the energy they have when they collide.

If we increase the chance of particles reacting, we will also increase the rate of reaction.

Surface area and reaction rate

Imagine lighting a campfire. It is not a good idea to pile large logs together and try to set them alight. You use small pieces of wood to begin with. Doing this increases the surface area of the wood. This results in more wood being exposed to react with oxygen in the air.

When a solid reacts in a solution, the size of the pieces of solid affects the rate of the reaction. The particles inside a large lump of solid are not in contact with the reactant particles in the solution, so they can't react. The particles inside the solid have to wait for the particles on the surface to react first before they have a chance to react.

In smaller lumps, or in a powder, each tiny piece of solid is surrounded by solution. Many more particles of the solid are exposed to attack at a given time. This means that reactions can take place much more quickly.

Practical

Which burns faster?

Using tongs, try igniting a 2 cm length of magnesium ribbon and time how long it takes to burn.

Take a small spatula tip of magnesium powder and sprinkle it into the Bunsen flame.

- Write a balanced symbol equation, including state symbols, for the reaction.
- Explain your observations.

Safety: Make sure you have a heatproof mat under the Bunsen burner and you must wear eye protection.

Practical

Investigating the effect of surface area

In this investigation you will be measuring the mass lost against time for different sizes of marble (calcium carbonate) chips. You need at least two different sizes of marble chips in order to vary the surface area.

- What variables should you control to make this a fair test?
- Why does this method of finding out the rate of reaction work?
- Use the data collected to draw a graph. Explain what the graph shows. (A data logger would help to plot a graph of the results.)

Safety: Wear eye protection.

Summary questions

1 List the factors that can affect the rate of a chemical reaction.

2 **a** Draw a diagram to explain why it is easier for an iron nail that has been cut into small pieces to rust than for a whole iron nail to rust under the same conditions.
   b Why is the term 'under the same conditions' used in part **a**?

3 Explain why the idea of 'activation energy' is an important part of the collision theory used to explain rates of reaction.

4 Explain why the acid in your stomach can help you digest your food more quickly if you chew it well before you swallow it.

Examiner's tip

Particles collide all the time, but only some collisions lead to reactions.

Increasing the number of collisions in a certain time and the energy of collisions produces faster rates of reaction.

Larger surface area does not result in collisions with more energy but does increase the frequency of collisions.

Key points

- Particles must collide, with a certain minimum amount of energy, before they can react.

- The minimum amount of energy that particles must have in order to react is called the activation energy of a reaction.

- The rate of a chemical reaction increases if the surface area of any solid reactants is increased. This increases the frequency of collisions between reacting particles.

C8.3 The effect of temperature

Learning objectives

After this topic, you should know:

- how increasing the temperature affects the rate of reactions

- how to use collision theory to explain this effect.

Figure 1 Lowering the temperature will slow down the reactions that make foods go off

Figure 2 Moving faster means it's more likely that you'll bump into someone else – and the collision will be harder too!

When we increase the temperature, it increases the rate of reaction. We can use fridges and freezers to reduce the temperature and slow down the rate of reactions. When food goes off it is because of chemical reactions, so reducing the temperature slows down these unwanted reactions.

Collision theory tells us why raising the temperature increases the rate of a reaction. There are two reasons:

- particles collide more often
- particles collide with more energy.

Particles collide more frequently

When we heat up a substance, energy is transferred to its particles. In solutions and in gases, this means that the particles move around faster. And when particles move around faster they collide more often. Imagine a lot of people walking around in the school playground blindfolded. They may bump into each other occasionally. However, if they start running around, they will bump into each other much more often.

When particles collide more frequently, there are more chances for them to react. This increases the rate of reaction.

Particles collide with more energy

Particles that are moving around more quickly have more energy. This means that any collisions they have are much more energetic. It's like two people colliding when they're running rather than when they are walking.

When we increase the temperature of a reacting mixture, a higher proportion of the collisions will result in a reaction taking place. This is because a higher proportion of particles have energy greater than the activation energy. **This second factor has a greater effect on rate than the increased frequency of collisions.**

Around room temperature, if we increase the temperature of a reaction by 10 °C the rate of the reaction will roughly double.

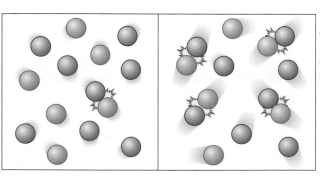

Figure 3 More frequent collisions, with more energy – both of these factors lead to the increase in the rate of a chemical reaction that is caused by increasing the temperature

Practical

The effect of temperature on rate of reaction

Time how long it takes for the cross to disappear when viewed from above

Sodium thiosulfate solution and dilute hydrochloric acid

When we react sodium thiosulfate solution and hydrochloric acid it makes sulfur. The sulfur is insoluble in water. This makes the solution go cloudy. We can record the length of time it takes for the solution to go cloudy at different temperatures.

- How could you vary the temperature? Check your idea with your teacher before starting.
- Which variables do you have to control to make this a fair test?
- Why is it difficult to get accurate timings by eye in this investigation?
- How can you improve the **precision** of the data you collect?

Safety: Wear eye protection. Take care if you are an asthmatic. Do not exceed 50 °C.

Maths skills

The effect of temperature on the rate of reaction

As one goes up, the other comes down

In the experiment opposite we can measure the time for an X to disappear as a precipitate forms.

This means that the longer the time, the slower the rate of reaction. There is an inverse relationship between time and rate. So as time increases, rate decreases.

We say the rate is proportional to 1/time (also written as time^{-1}). Therefore, we can plot a graph of temperature against 1/time to investigate the effect of temperature on rate of reaction.

The results of an investigation like this can be plotted on a graph (see right).

The graph shows how the time for the solution to go cloudy changes with temperature.

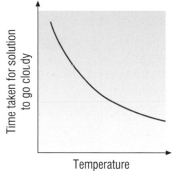

Time taken for solution to go cloudy

Temperature

Summary questions

1 a Why does increasing the temperature increase the rate of a reaction?
  b By how much does a 10 °C rise in temperature increase reaction rate at room temperature?

2 Look at the experiment in the Practical box above.
  a Why does the solution turn cloudy?
  b Describe what happens to the time it takes the solution to go cloudy as the temperature increases.
  c Explain your answer to part b in detail using collision theory.

3 Water in a pressure cooker boils at a much higher temperature than water in a saucepan because it is under pressure. Explain why food takes longer to cook in a pan than it does in a pressure cooker.

Key points

- Reactions happen more quickly as the temperature increases.

- Increasing the temperature increases the rate of reaction because particles collide more frequently and more energetically. More of the collisions result in a reaction because a higher proportion of particles have energy greater than the activation energy.

C8.4

The effect of concentration or pressure

Learning objectives

After this topic, you should know:

- how, and why, increasing the concentration of reactants in solutions affects the rate of reaction

- how, and why, increasing the pressure of reacting gases affects the rate of reaction.

Figure 1 Limestone statues are damaged by acid rain. This damage happens more quickly as the concentration of the acids in rainwater increases.

Some of our most beautiful buildings are made of limestone or marble. These buildings have stood for centuries. However, they are now crumbling away at a greater rate than before. This is because both limestone and marble are mainly calcium carbonate. This reacts with acids, leaving the stone soft and crumbly. The rate of this reaction has speeded up because the concentration of acids in rainwater has increased.

Increasing the concentration of reactants in a solution increases the rate of reaction because there are more particles of the reactants moving around in the same volume of solution. The more 'crowded' together the reactant particles are, the more likely it is that they will collide. So the more frequent collisions result in a faster reaction.

Increasing the pressure of reacting gases has the same effect. Increased pressure squashes the gas particles more closely together. We have more particles of gas in a given space. This increases the chance that they will collide and react. So, increasing the pressure produces more frequent collisions which speeds up the rate of the reaction.

Low concentration/ low pressure

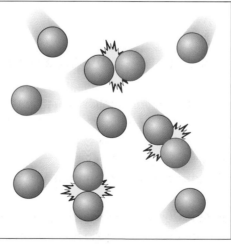

High concentration/ high pressure

Figure 2 Increasing concentration and pressure both mean that particles are closer together. This increases the frequency of collisions between particles, so the reaction rate increases.

Practical

Investigating the effect of concentration on rate of reaction

We can investigate the effect of changing concentration by reacting marble chips with different concentrations of hydrochloric acid:

$$CaCO_3(s) + 2HCl(aq) \rightarrow CaCl_2(aq) + CO_2(g) + H_2O(l)$$

We can find the rate of reaction by plotting the mass of the reaction mixture over time. The mass will decrease as carbon dioxide gas is given off in the reaction.

● How do you make this a fair test?
● What conclusion can you draw from your results?

Safety: Wear eye protection.

Examiner's tip

Increasing concentration or pressure does not increase the energy with which the particles collide. However, it does increase the frequency of collisions.

If we plot the results of an investigation like the one above on a graph they look like the graph on the right.

The graph shows how the mass of the reaction mixture decreases over time at three different concentrations.

Summary questions

1 Look at the graph on the right.
   a Which line on the graph shows the fastest reaction? How can you tell from the data displayed?
   b Why is the cotton wool bung used in the Practical box above?
   c The electric balance used in the experiment needs a high resolution. What does this mean?

2 You could also follow the reaction in the Practical box above by measuring the volume of gas given off over time. Sketch a graph of volume of gas against time for three different concentrations. Label the three lines as high, medium and low concentration.

3 Explain why the concentration of a gas is proportional to its pressure in terms of its particles.

4 Acidic cleaners are designed to remove limescale (calcium carbonate) when they are used neat, i.e. undiluted. They do not work as well when they are diluted. Using your knowledge of collision theory, explain why this is.

Key points

● Increasing the concentration of reactants in solutions increases the frequency of collisions between particles, and so increases the rate of reaction.

● Increasing the pressure of reacting gases also increases the frequency of collisions and so increases the rate of reaction.

C8.5   The effect of catalysts

Learning objectives

After this topic, you should know:

- what a catalyst is
- why catalysts are important in industry.

Figure 1 Catalysts are all around us, in the natural world and in industry. The catalysts in living things are called enzymes. Our planet would be very different without catalysts.

Sometimes a reaction might only work if we use very high temperatures or pressures. This can cost industry a lot of money. However, we can speed up some reactions by using **catalysts**.

A catalyst is a substance which increases the rate of a reaction. However, it is not changed chemically itself at the end of the reaction. A catalyst is not used up in the reaction so it can be used over and over again.

We need different catalysts for different reactions. Many of the catalysts we use in industry involve transition metals. Examples include iron, used to make ammonia, and platinum, used to make nitric acid. We normally use catalysts in the form of powders, pellets or fine gauzes. This gives them the biggest possible surface area and makes them as effective as possible as the reactions they catalyse often involve gases reacting on their surfaces.

Figure 2 The transition metals platinum and palladium are used in the **catalytic converters** in cars

Advantages of catalysts in industry

Catalysts are often very expensive precious metals. Gold, platinum and palladium are all costly but are the most effective catalysts for particular reactions. But it is often cheaper to use a catalyst than to pay for the extra energy needed without one. To get the same rate of reaction without a catalyst would require higher temperatures and/or pressures.

So catalysts save money and help the environment. That's because using high temperatures and pressures often involves burning fossil fuels. So operating at lower temperatures and pressures conserves these non-renewable resources. It also stops more carbon dioxide entering the atmosphere, helping to combat climate change.

Not only does a catalyst speed up a reaction, but it also does not get used up in the reaction, so a tiny amount of catalyst can be used to speed up a reaction over and over again.

Practical

Investigating catalysis

Rubber tubing

Gas syringe

Hydrogen peroxide solution and catalyst

We can investigate the effect of different catalysts on the rate of a reaction. We will look at hydrogen peroxide solution decomposing:

$$2H_2O_2(aq) \rightarrow 2H_2O(l) + O_2(g)$$

The reaction produces oxygen gas. We can collect this in a gas syringe using the apparatus shown above.

We can investigate the effect of many different substances on the rate of this reaction. Examples include manganese(IV) oxide, MnO_2, and potassium iodide, KI.

● State the independent variable in this investigation.

A table of the time taken to produce a certain volume of oxygen can then tell us which catalyst makes the reaction go fastest.

● What type of graph would you use to show the results of your investigation? Why?

Safety: Wear eye protection. If the syringe is glass take care to not expel piston. Manganese(IV) oxide is harmful.

??? Did you know ... ?

The catalysts used in chemical plants eventually become 'poisoned' so that they don't work any more. This happens because impurities in the reaction mixture combine with the catalyst and stop it working properly.

Examiner's tip

Catalysts change only the rate of reactions. They do not change the products.

Summary questions

1 How is a catalyst affected by a chemical reaction it speeds up?

2 Solid catalysts used in chemical processes are often shaped as tiny beads or cylinders with holes through them. Why are they made in these shapes?

3 Why is the number of moles of catalyst needed to speed up a chemical reaction very small compared with the number of moles of reactants?

4 Do some research to find out four industrial processes that make products using catalysts. Write a word equation for each reaction and name the catalyst used.

5 Explain why catalysts are so useful in the chemical industry.

Key points

● A catalyst speeds up the rate of a chemical reaction but is not used up itself during the reaction. It remains chemically unchanged.

● Different catalysts are needed for different reactions.

● Catalysts are used whenever possible in industry to increase rates of reaction and reduce energy costs.

Summary questions

1 A student investigated the reaction between magnesium and dilute hydrochloric acid. He started by reacting a piece of magnesium ribbon in 1.0 mol/dm³ hydrochloric acid.

a Describe **one** method the student could use to measure the rate of this reaction.

b Suggest **three** ways in which the student could increase the rate of this reaction.

c i The student decided to investigate the effect of **temperature** on rate of reaction. Write an outline plan of how he should set up his investigation.

ii What would you expect the student to find out from the data he collected?

iii Explain the expected pattern in his results using collision theory.

2 Two students investigated the reaction of some marble chips with dilute nitric acid.

Time (minutes)	Investigation A Mass of gas produced (g)	Investigation B Mass of gas produced (g)
0.0	0.00	0.00
0.5	0.56	0.28
1.0	0.73	0.36
1.5	0.80	0.39
2.0	0.82	0.41
2.5	0.82	0.41

a Which gas was produced in the reaction? What is the test for this gas?

b i Marble chips contain calcium carbonate. Write a word equation for the reaction investigated.

ii Now write a balanced symbol equation, including state symbols, for the reaction.

c The students were investigating the effect of concentration on rate of reaction. How do you think the students got the data for their table above?

d Plot a graph of these results, with time on the *x*-axis.

e After 30 seconds, how does the rate of reaction in Investigation B compare with the rate of reaction in Investigation A?

f How does the final mass of gas produced in Investigation B compare with that produced in Investigation A?

g From the results, what can you say about the initial concentration of the acids in Investigations A and B?

h Explain the data obtained using collision theory.

3 A pair of students are studying the effect of surface area on rate of reaction. They use zinc foil reacting with dilute sulfuric acid.

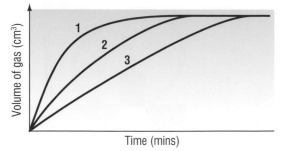

a What did the students investigating the reaction have to do to make it a *fair test*?

b Which gas was given off in the reaction? How could you test for this gas?

c Write a balanced symbol equation, including state symbols, for the reaction under investigation.

d Which line (1, 2 or 3) shows results for the zinc with the largest surface area (given the same mass of zinc in each test)?

e Which sized pieces of zinc would react most slowly?

f The students doing the experiments also tried reacting the same mass of *powdered* zinc with the acid. What would their results look like on the graph above?

g Use collision theory to explain the results in this investigation.

4 a Define the word catalyst.

b Hydrogen peroxide (H_2O_2) solution decomposes to form water and oxygen gas. Write a balanced symbol equation, including state symbols, for this reaction.

c The reaction is catalysed by some metal oxides. You are provided with oxides of copper, lead, manganese and iron. Describe how you can test which is the best catalyst for the decomposition of hydrogen peroxide, collecting quantitative (measured) data to support your conclusion.

d How can you get a pure dry sample of the metal oxides from the mixture left at the end of the reaction?

AQA Examination-style questions

1 Some students investigated the reaction between calcium carbonate and nitric acid. They used this apparatus to collect the gas given off when dilute nitric acid was added to marble chips of different sizes.

Measuring cylinder

50 cm³ of dilute nitric acid

Marble chips

They recorded the volume of gas every 10 seconds until no more gas was collected.

The graph of their results is shown below.

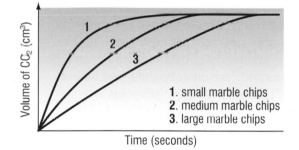

Volume of CO₂ (cm³)

Time (seconds)

1. small marble chips
2. medium marble chips
3. large marble chips

a The students all used the same mass of marble chips.

State two other factors that should have been kept constant to ensure a fair test. (2)

b Reaction 1 was the fastest of the three reactions. State how the graph shows this. (2)

c Why do small marble chips react faster than large marble chips? (1)

d Another group of students investigated the same reaction using equal masses of medium marble chips but using different concentrations of dilute nitric acid in each experiment. Student 1 used the original nitric acid. The other students added water to decrease the concentrations of the acid in their experiments. They recorded the time taken to collect 100 cm³ of gas.

The table shows their results.

Student	Acid concentration	Time in seconds
1	100%	11
2	80%	16
3	60%	22
4	40%	32
5	20%	61

i Suggest which student's recorded results are least likely to be accurate. Give a reason for your choice. (2)

ii One student calculated the rate of reaction using the expression

$$\text{rate} = \frac{1}{\text{time}}$$

What is the rate of the experiment carried out by student 1? (2)

iii Another student plotted a graph of rate against concentration. She drew a straight line of best fit through the origin.

State the relationship between rate and concentration shown by this line. (2)

iv Explain why the rate of student 2's reaction was double that of student 4's reaction. (3)

2 The reaction between sodium thiosulfate and hydrochloric acid can be used to investigate reaction rates. The equation for the reaction is

$$Na_2S_2O_3 + 2HCl \rightarrow 2NaCl + H_2O + SO_2 + S$$

a i Identify the product that is used in measuring the rate, giving a reason for your choice. (2)

ii Identify the product that is an environmental problem and state what the problem is. (2)

b Some students measured the rate of this reaction in a series of experiments. All the experiments were done in the same way, except that the temperatures were different. The students noticed that the rate was a lot faster at higher temperatures.

One student suggested that this was because there were more frequent collisions between the particles.

i Why do the particles collide more frequently? (1)

ii What is the other reason why the rate is faster at higher temperatures? (1)

3 Many reactions in industry are carried out at high temperatures and using catalysts.

a What is a catalyst? (2)

b Some expensive metals, such as platinum, are used as catalysts.

Explain why it is worthwhile to use expensive metals as catalysts. (1)

c Platinum is used as a catalyst in car exhausts.

Suggest why it is used in thin layers rather than as lumps. (1)

C9.1 Hydrocarbons

Learning objectives

After this topic, you should know:

- what crude oil is made up of
- what alkanes are
- how to represent alkanes.

Figure 1 The price of nearly everything we buy is affected by oil because the cost of moving goods to the shops affects the price we pay for them

So far, some of the 21st Century's most important chemicals come from crude oil. These chemicals play a major part in our lives. We use them as fuels to run our cars, to warm our homes and to make electricity.

Fuels are important because they keep us warm and on the move. So when oil prices rise, it affects us all. Countries that produce crude oil can affect the whole world economy by the price they charge for their oil.

Crude oil

Crude oil is a dark, smelly liquid. It is a **mixture** of many different chemical compounds. A mixture contains two or more elements or compounds that are not chemically combined together. Nearly all of the compounds in crude oil are compounds containing only hydrogen and carbon atoms. We call these compounds **hydrocarbons**.

Crude oil straight from the ground is not much use. There are too many substances in it, all with different boiling points. Before we can use crude oil, we must separate it into different substances with similar boiling points. These are known as **fractions**. Because the properties of substances do not change when they are mixed (as opposed to reacted), we can separate mixtures of substances in crude oil by **distillation**. Distillation separates liquids with different boiling points.

Demonstration

Distillation of crude oil

Mixtures of liquids can be separated using distillation. This can be done in the lab on a small scale. We heat the crude oil mixture so that it boils. The different fractions vaporise between different ranges of temperature. We can collect the vapours by cooling and condensing them.

Figure 2 The distillation of crude oil in the lab

- What colour are the first few drops of liquid collected?

Alkanes

Most of the hydrocarbons in crude oil are **alkanes**. You can see some examples of alkane molecules in Figure 3. Notice how all their names end in '–ane'. The first part of their names tells you how many carbon atoms are in their molecules.

| Methane | Ethane | Propane | Butane |

Figure 3 We can represent alkanes like this, showing all of the atoms in the molecule. They are called displayed formulae. The line drawn between two atoms in a molecule, as shown above, represents a single covalent bond.

Look at the formulae of the first five alkane molecules below:

$$CH_4 \text{ (methane)}$$

$$C_2H_6 \text{ (ethane)}$$

$$C_3H_8 \text{ (propane)}$$

$$C_4H_{10} \text{ (butane)}$$

$$C_5H_{12} \text{ (pentane)}$$

Can you see a pattern in the formulae of the alkanes? We can write the general formula for alkane molecules like this:

$$C_nH_{(2n + 2)}$$

This means that 'for every n carbon atoms there are $(2n + 2)$ hydrogen atoms' in an alkane molecule. For example, if an alkane molecule contains 12 carbon atoms its formula will be $C_{12}H_{26}$.

We describe alkanes as **saturated hydrocarbons**. All the carbon–carbon bonds are single covalent bonds. This means that they contain as many hydrogen atoms as possible in each molecule. No more hydrogen atoms can be added.

links

For information on covalent bonding, look back at 3.4 'Covalent bonding'.

Summary questions

1 a What is crude oil?
  b Why is oil so important to society?
  c Why can we separate crude oil using distillation?

2 We drill crude oil from beneath the ground or seabed. Why is this crude oil not very useful as a product itself?

3 a Write the general formula of the alkanes.
  b Write the formulae of the alkanes which have 6 to 10 carbon atoms. Then find out their names.

4 a Draw the displayed formula of octane, whose molecules have 8 carbon atoms.
  b How many hydrogen atoms are there in an alkane molecule which has 22 carbon atoms?
  c How many carbon atoms are there in an alkane molecule which has 32 hydrogen atoms?
  d Why are alkanes described as 'saturated hydrocarbons'?

Key points

- Crude oil is a mixture of many different compounds.

- Most of the compounds in crude oil are hydrocarbons – they contain only hydrogen and carbon atoms.

- Alkanes are saturated hydrocarbons. They contain as many hydrogen atoms as possible in their molecules.

- The general formula of an alkane is:
  $$C_nH_{(2n + 2)}$$

C9.2 Fractional distillation

The properties of hydrocarbons

Hydrocarbon molecules can be very different. Some are quite small, with relatively few carbon atoms in short chains. These short-chain molecules make up the hydrocarbons that tend to be most useful. These hydrocarbons make good fuels as they ignite easily and burn well, with less smoky flames than hydrocarbons made up of larger molecules. They are very **flammable** (see Figure 1 below). Other hydrocarbons have lots of carbon atoms in their molecules, and may have branches or side-chains.

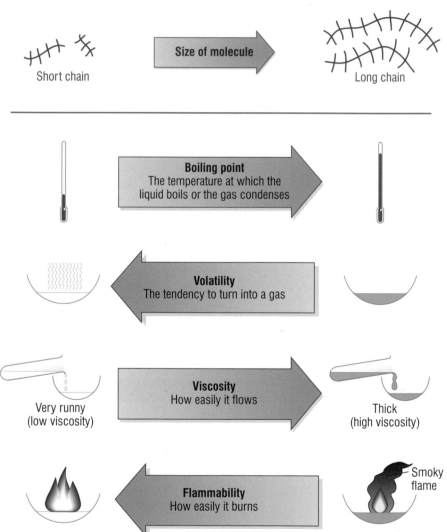

Figure 1 The properties of hydrocarbons depend on the chain-length of their molecules

Fractional distillation of crude oil

We separate out crude oil into hydrocarbons with similar boiling points, called fractions. This process is called **fractional distillation**. Each hydrocarbon fraction contains molecules with similar numbers of carbon atoms. Each of these fractions boils at a different temperature range because of the different sizes of the molecules in it.

Refinery/petroleum gas
(short-chain hydrocarbons
and low boiling point
alkanes, used as fuel)

50°C

Gasoline/petrol
(used for fuel in car engines)

Kerosene
(used for aircraft fuel)

Diesel oil/gas oil
(used as fuel in diesel
engines and as boiler fuel)

The oil is vaporised
before it goes into
the tower

350°C

Residue
(very thick, sticky mixture
of long-chain hydrocarbons,
used in making roads and
flat roofs)

Figure 2 We use fractional distillation to separate the mixture of hydrocarbons in crude oil into fractions. Each fraction contains hydrocarbons with similar boiling points.

Crude oil is heated and fed in near the bottom of a tall tower (a fractionating column) as hot vapour. The column is kept very hot at the bottom and much cooler at the top. The temperature decreases going up the column. The gases condense when they reach the temperature of their boiling points. The different fractions are collected as liquids at different levels. The fractions are collected from the column in a continuous process.

Hydrocarbons with the smallest molecules have the lowest boiling points. They are collected at the cool top of the column. At the bottom of the column, the fractions have high boiling points. They cool to form very thick liquids or solids at room temperature.

Once collected, the fractions need more processing before they can be used.

Figure 3 An oil refinery at night

Summary questions

1 a How does the size of a hydrocarbon molecule affect:
  i the boiling point
  ii the volatility
  iii the viscosity (thickness) of a hydrocarbon?
 b A hydrocarbon catches fire very easily. Is it likely to have molecules with long hydrocarbon chains or short ones? Will it give off lots of black smoke when it burns?

2 Make a table to summarise how the properties of hydrocarbons depend on the size of their molecules.

3 Explain the steps involved in the fractional distillation of crude oil.

Key points

- We separate crude oil into fractions using fractional distillation.

- The properties of each fraction depend on the size of the hydrocarbon molecules in it.

- Lighter fractions make better fuels as they ignite more easily and burn well, with cleaner (less smoky) flames.

C9.3 Burning fuels

After this topic, you should know:

- the products of combustion when we burn fuels in a good supply of air, or in a limited supply of air
- the pollutants produced when we burn fuels.

The lighter fractions from crude oil are very useful as fuels. When hydrocarbons burn in plenty of air they release lots of energy.

For example, when propane burns:

$$\text{propane} + \text{oxygen} \rightarrow \text{carbon dioxide} + \text{water}$$
$$C_3H_8 + 5O_2 \rightarrow 3CO_2 + 4H_2O$$

The carbon and hydrogen in the fuel are **oxidised** completely when they burn like this. Remember that one definition of 'oxidation' means adding oxygen in a chemical reaction. The products of complete combustion are carbon dioxide and water.

Figure 1 On a cold day we can often see the water produced when fossil fuels burn

Practical

Products of combustion

We can test the products given off when a hydrocarbon burns as shown in Figure 2.

Figure 2 Testing the products formed when a hydrocarbon burns

- What happens to the limewater? Which gas is given off?
- What happens in the U-tube? Which substance is present?

Safety: Wear eye protection. Handle cobalt chloride papers as little as possible.

Pollution from fuels

All fossil fuels – oil, coal and natural gas – produce carbon dioxide and water when they burn in plenty of air. But as well as hydrocarbons, these fuels also contain other substances. Impurities containing sulfur found in fuels cause us major problems.

All fossil fuels contain at least some sulfur. This reacts with oxygen when we burn the fuel. It forms a gas called **sulfur dioxide**. This acidic gas is toxic. This is bad for the environment, as it is a cause of acid rain which damages trees, as well as killing animal life in lakes. The sulfur impurities can be removed from a fuel *before* the fuel is burned. This happens in petrol and diesel for cars. In power stations, sulfur dioxide is also removed from the waste or 'flue' gases by reacting it with basic calcium oxide or calcium hydroxide.

When we burn fuels in a car engine, even more pollution can be produced.

- When we burn any fuel containing carbon, it makes carbon dioxide. Carbon dioxide is the main greenhouse gas in the air. It absorbs energy released as radiation from the surface of the Earth. Most scientists think that this is causing **climate change**, which affects temperatures around the world and might result in more severe weather events and the flooding of low-lying land as sea levels rise.

- When there is not enough oxygen inside an engine, we get **incomplete** (or partial) **combustion**. Instead of all the carbon in the fuel turning into carbon dioxide, we also get **carbon monoxide** gas (CO) formed. Carbon monoxide is a toxic gas. It is colourless and odourless. Your red blood cells pick up this gas and carry it around in your blood instead of oxygen.

- The high temperature inside an engine also allows the nitrogen and oxygen in the air to react together. This reaction makes **nitrogen oxides**. These are toxic and can trigger some people's asthma. They also cause acid rain.

- Diesel engines burn hydrocarbons with bigger molecules than petrol engines. When these large molecules react with oxygen in an engine they do not always burn completely. Tiny solid particles containing carbon and unburnt hydrocarbons are produced. These **particulates** get carried into the air. They travel into the upper atmosphere, reflecting sunlight back into space, causing **global dimming**. Scientists also think that they may damage the cells in our lungs and even cause cancer.

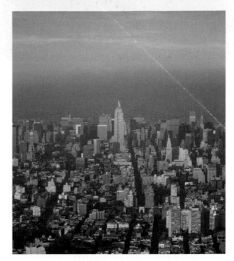

Figure 3 A combination of many cars in a small area and the right weather conditions can cause smog to be formed. This is a mixture of SMoke and fOG.

Key points

- When we burn hydrocarbon fuels in plenty of air the carbon and hydrogen in the fuel are completely oxidised. They produce carbon dioxide and water.

- Sulfur impurities in fuels burn to form sulfur dioxide, which can cause acid rain. Sulfur can be removed from fuels before we burn them or sulfur dioxide can be removed from flue gas.

- Changing the conditions in which we burn hydrocarbon fuels can change the products made.

- In insufficient oxygen, we get poisonous carbon monoxide gas formed. We can also get particulates of carbon (soot) and unburnt hydrocarbons, especially if the fuel is diesel. They can cause global dimming.

- At the high temperatures in engines, nitrogen from the air reacts with oxygen to form oxides of nitrogen. These cause breathing problems and can also cause acid rain.

Summary questions

1. a What are the products of the complete combustion of a hydrocarbon?
   b When fossil fuels burn, which element present in impurities can produce sulfur dioxide?

2. a Which pollution problem does sulfur dioxide gas contribute to?
   b Which other non-metal oxides released from cars also cause this pollution problem?

3. Explain how **a** sulfur dioxide, **b** nitrogen oxides, and **c** particulates, are produced when fuels burn in vehicles.

4. a Natural gas is mainly methane (CH_4). Write a balanced symbol equation, including state symbols, for the complete combustion of methane.
   b When natural gas burns in a faulty gas heater it can produce carbon monoxide (and water). Write a balanced symbol equation, including state symbols, to show this reaction.
   c Why is carbon monoxide dangerous?

C9.4

Alternative fuels

Learning objectives

After this topic, you should know:

- what biofuels are

- the advantages and disadvantages of using biofuels

- the potential of using hydrogen as a fuel.

Biofuels

Biofuels are fuels that are made from plant or animal products. Examples are **biodiesel**, which is made from oils extracted from plants, and biogas, which is generated from animal waste. Biofuels will become more and more important as our supplies of crude oil diminish.

Figure 1 This coach runs on biodiesel

Advantages of biodiesel and other biofuels

There are advantages in using biodiesel and other biofuels as a fuel.

- Biodiesel is much less harmful to animals and plants if it is spilled than the diesel we get from crude oil.

- When we burn biodiesel in an engine it burns much more cleanly, reducing the particulates emitted. It also makes very little sulfur dioxide.

- As non-renewable fossil fuels, such as crude oil, run out, their price will increase and biofuels will become cheaper to use.

- Another really big advantage over fossil fuels is the fact that the crops used to make biofuels absorb carbon dioxide gas as they grow. So biofuels from plants are in theory 'CO_2 neutral'. That means the amount of carbon dioxide given off when it burns is balanced by the amount absorbed as the plants it is made from grow. Therefore, biofuels make little contribution to the carbon dioxide in our atmosphere.

However, we can't claim that all biofuels make a *zero* contribution to carbon dioxide emissions. We should really take into account the CO_2 released when:

- – fertilising and harvesting the crops
- – extracting and processing the biofuel
- – transporting the plant material and biofuel.

Plants absorb CO_2 as they grow

Converted to biodiesel

CO_2

CO_2 produced as biodiesel is burned

Figure 2 Cars that run on biodiesel produce very little CO_2 overall, as CO_2 is absorbed by the plants used to make the biofuel

Disadvantages of biofuels

There are also disadvantages in using biofuels.

- The use of large areas of farmland to produce biofuel instead of food could pose problems. If we start to rely on oil-producing crops for our fuel, farmers will turn land once used for food crops to land for growing biofuel crops.

- This could result in famine in poorer countries if the price of staple food crops rises as demand overtakes supply. Forests, which absorb lots of carbon dioxide, might also be cleared to grow the biofuel crops if they get more popular.

- People are also worried about endangered species because of the destruction of their habitats, such as tropical forests, cleared to grow biofuel crops.

Using ethanol as a biofuel

Another biofuel is ethanol. It can be made by fermenting sugar solution, extracted from sugar beet or sugar cane, using yeast. The **fermentation** is a slow batch process that takes place in large vats, at temperatures between 20 °C and 35 °C. The ethanol is then distilled from the aqueous solution for use as a biofuel.

$$\text{glucose} \rightarrow \text{ethanol} + \text{carbon dioxide}$$
$$C_6H_{12}O_6(aq) \rightarrow 2C_2H_5OH(aq) + 2CO_2(g)$$

As with other biofuels, the ethanol gives off carbon dioxide (a greenhouse gas) when it burns:

$$C_2H_5OH(l) + 3O_2(g) \rightarrow 2CO_2(g) + 3H_2O(g)$$

However, this should be balanced against the sugar cane absorbing CO_2 gas during photosynthesis.

Hydrogen – a fuel for the future

Scientists are very interested in developing hydrogen as a fuel. It burns well with a very clean flame as there is no carbon in the fuel:

$$\text{hydrogen} + \text{oxygen} \rightarrow \text{water}$$
$$2H_2(g) + O_2(g) \rightarrow 2H_2O(g)$$

As you can see in the equation, water is the only product in the combustion of hydrogen. There are no pollutants made when hydrogen burns and no extra carbon dioxide is added to the air. Not only that, water is potentially a huge natural source of hydrogen. The hydrogen can be obtained from water by electrolysis. But the electricity must be supplied by a renewable energy source if we want to conserve fossil fuels and control carbon dioxide emissions.

However, there are problems to solve before hydrogen becomes a common fuel. When mixed with air and ignited it is explosive. So there are safety concerns in case of leaks, or accidents, in vehicles powered by hydrogen. Vehicles normally run on liquid fuels but hydrogen is a gas. Therefore, it takes up a much larger volume than liquid fuels so storage becomes an issue. We can use high-pressure cylinders but these also have safety problems in crashes.

A more efficient use of the energy from oxidising hydrogen is in a fuel cell. These cells are fed with hydrogen and oxygen, which react to produce water. Most of the energy released in the reaction is transferred directly to electrical energy. This can be used to run a vehicle. However, we still need a constant supply of hydrogen to run the fuel cell.

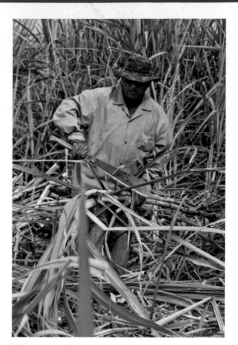

Figure 3 Ethanol can be made from sugar cane

⚭ links

For more information on ethanol, see 11.2 'Properties and uses of alcohols'.

Key points

- Biofuels are a renewable source of energy that could be used to replace some fossil fuels.

- Biodiesel can be made from vegetable oils.

- There are advantages, and some disadvantages, in using biofuels.

- Ethanol is also a biofuel as it can be made from the sugar in plants.

- Hydrogen is a potential fuel for the future.

Summary questions

1 Why is burning ethanol a better choice of fuel than petrol if we want to reduce carbon dioxide emissions?

2 Explain where the energy in biodiesel comes from.

3 a Explain why hydrogen is potentially a pollution-free fuel. Include a balanced symbol equation in your answer.

   b Explain two problems that have to be overcome before hydrogen is used as an everyday fuel.

Summary questions

1 a i Complete this general formula for the alkanes:

$$C_nH?$$

ii What is the formula of the alkane with 18 carbon atoms?

iii What is the formula of the alkane with 18 hydrogen atoms?

b Look at the boiling points in this table below:

Alkane	Number of carbon atoms	Boiling point in °C
methane	1	−161
ethane	2	−88
propane	3	−42
butane	4	−0.5
pentane	5	
hexane	6	69

Draw a graph of the alkanes' boiling points (vertical axis) against the number of carbon atoms (horizontal axis).

c What is the general pattern you see from your graph?

d Use your graph to predict the boiling point of pentane.

2 a The alkanes are all 'saturated hydrocarbons'.
i What is a hydrocarbon?
ii What does saturated mean when describing an alkane?

b i Give the name and formula of this alkane:

```
    H   H   H
    |   |   |
H—C—C—C—H
    |   |   |
    H   H   H
```

ii What do the letters represent in this displayed formula?

iii What do the lines between the letters represent?

3 One alkane, A, has a boiling point of 344 °C and another, B, has a boiling point of 126 °C.

a Which one will be collected nearer the top of a fractionating column in an oil refinery? Explain your choice.

b Which one will be the better fuel? Explain your choice.

c State the differences you would expect between A and B in terms of their:
i viscosity
ii volatility.

4 a What problem is associated with the increased levels of carbon dioxide gas in the atmosphere?

b i What gas is given off from fossil fuel power stations that can cause acid rain?
ii Give **two** ways of stopping this acidic gas getting into the atmosphere.
iii Name the other cause of acid rain which comes from car engines and how it arises.

5 Two students are testing the products formed when ethanol burns. They set up the experiment below:

a Why do they put ice around the U-tube?

b How can they test for the substance formed in the U-tube?

c Explain what happens to the limewater.

d There is a small amount of carbon dioxide in the air. How can they show that the carbon dioxide they test for is not just the result of the carbon dioxide in the air?

e Write a word equation and balanced symbol equation for the complete combustion of ethanol.

f The students wanted to test the products of combustion of a hydrocarbon. Wax is made of hydrocarbons. How would the students change their experiment to carry out this test?

g Write a word equation and balanced symbol equation for the complete combustion of propane gas.

h Propane is used in portable gas heaters but there must be good ventilation in the room. Which toxic gas will be produced when the propane burns if there is a poor supply of air in the room?

6 a Which one of these fuels could be termed a 'biofuel'? Explain your choice.

Hydrogen   Butane   Ethanol   Diesel   Petrol

b Explain what is meant by the statement 'Biodiesel is potentially CO_2 neutral'.

c Why is the use of hydrogen as a fuel one way to tackle the problem of climate change?

d State **two** problems with the use of hydrogen as a fuel.

e Write a word equation and a balanced symbol equation to show the combustion of hydrogen.

f What piece of equipment can turn energy from the reaction in part **e** into electrical energy?

AQA Examination-style questions

1 Crude oil is a mixture of many compounds, most of which are saturated hydrocarbons. Most of these hydrocarbons are alkanes.

  a **i** What is a hydrocarbon? (2)

     ii What is the meaning of *saturated*? (1)

  b The formulae of the first two alkanes are CH_4 and C_2H_6

    i What is the general formula of the alkanes? (1)

    ii What is the molecular formula of the alkane with three carbon atoms in each molecule? (1)

    iii Draw the displayed formula of the alkane with four carbon atoms in each molecule. (1)

  c The compounds in crude oil are separated into fractions by fractional distillation. This process involves converting most of the crude oil into vapour, and then cooling it. The fraction that reaches the top of the fractionating column contains the smallest molecules.

    i Name the changes of state involved in this process of fractional distillation. (2)

    ii State two properties of the liquid fraction that leaves the column near the lowest part. (2)

2 Many of the smaller molecules obtained from crude oil are used as fuels.

  a Name the two products of complete combustion of a hydrocarbon fuel. (2)

  b Write the symbol equation for the complete combustion of methane. (2)

  c If there is not enough oxygen, then a hydrocarbon may undergo incomplete combustion.

    Name one solid product and one gaseous product that could form by incomplete combustion. (2)

  d The combustion of hydrocarbon fuels can produce small amounts of oxides of nitrogen.

    i What condition is needed for oxides of nitrogen to form? (1)

    ii What is the main environmental problem caused by oxides of nitrogen? (1)

  e Hydrocarbon fuels may contain small amounts of sulfur, which can release sulfur dioxide into the atmosphere during combustion.

    i What is done to prevent the emission of sulfur dioxide from a car exhaust? (1)

    ii What is done to prevent the emission of sulfur dioxide from a power station? (1)

3 Alternative fuels are increasingly used to replace fuels obtained from crude oil. Biofuels are one type of alternative fuel.

  a One common biofuel that has been used for many centuries is wood.

    Why is wood described as a biofuel? (1)

  b Ethanol is another biofuel.

    State the main source of ethanol and name the method used to convert it into ethanol. (2)

  c **i** State one reason why biofuels are being increasingly used. (1)

    ii State the main disadvantages of using large areas of land for biofuel production. (1)

  d Hydrogen is another alternative fuel.

    i State why the combustion of hydrogen is less likely to cause climate change than burning a hydrocarbon fuel. (1)

    ii State two problems in using hydrogen as a fuel in cars. (2)

C10.1

Cracking hydrocarbons

Learning objectives

After this topic, you should know:

- how smaller, more useful hydrocarbon molecules are made from larger, less useful ones in crude oil

- what alkenes are and how they differ from alkanes.

Figure 1 In an oil refinery, huge crackers like this are used to break down large hydrocarbon molecules into smaller ones

Figure 3 A molecule of ethene (C_2H_4) and a molecule of propene (C_3H_6). These are both alkenes – each molecule has a carbon–carbon double bond in it.

Some of the heavier fractions that we get from the fractional distillation of crude oil are not very useful. The hydrocarbons in them are made up of large molecules. They are thick liquids or solids with high boiling points. They are difficult to vaporise and do not burn easily – so they are poor fuels. Yet the main demand from crude oil is for fuels. Fortunately these large hydrocarbon molecules can be broken down in a process we call **cracking**.

The process takes place at an oil refinery in a steel vessel called a cracker. In the cracker, a heavy fraction distilled from crude oil is heated to vaporise the hydrocarbons. The vapour is then either passed over a hot catalyst or mixed with steam and heated to a high temperature. The hydrocarbons are cracked as thermal decomposition reactions take place. The large molecules split apart to form smaller, more useful ones.

An example of cracking

Decane, $C_{10}H_{22}$, is a medium-sized alkane molecule. When we heat it to 500 °C with a catalyst it breaks down. One of the molecules produced is pentane, which is used in petrol.

Figure 2 Pentane (C_5H_{12}) can be used as a fuel. This is the displayed formula of pentane.

We also get propene and ethene, which we can use to produce other chemicals.

$$C_{10}H_{22} \xrightarrow{\text{500 °C + catalyst}} C_5H_{12} + C_3H_6 + C_2H_4$$
$$\text{decane} \qquad\qquad\qquad \text{pentane} \quad \text{propene} \quad \text{ethene}$$

This reaction is an example of thermal decomposition.

Notice how this cracking reaction produces different types of molecules. One of the molecules is pentane. The first part of its name tells us that it has five carbon atoms (*pent-*). The last part of its name (*-ane*) shows that it is an alkane. Like all other alkanes, pentane is a saturated hydrocarbon. Its molecules have as much hydrogen as possible in them.

The other molecules in this reaction have names that end slightly differently. They end in *-ene*. We call this type of molecule an **alkene**. The different ending tells us that these molecules are **unsaturated**. Unsaturated compounds contain at least one **double bond** between their carbon atoms. Look at Figure 3. You can see that these alkenes have one C=C double covalent bond and have the general formula $\mathbf{C_nH_{2n}}$.

A simple experiment like the one on the next page shows that alkenes burn (but not as well as equivalent small alkanes which are used as fuels). Alkenes also react with bromine water, which is orange in colour. The products of this reaction are colourless so we have a good test to see if a compound contains a C=C double bond:

**Positive test for an unsaturated hydrocarbon –
orange bromine water turns colourless.**

Practical

Cracking

Medicinal paraffin is a mixture of hydrocarbon molecules. You can crack it by heating it and passing the vapour over hot pieces of broken pot. The broken pot acts as a catalyst.

● Why must you remove the end of the delivery tube from the water before you stop heating?

If you carry out this practical, collect at least two test tubes of gas. Test one by putting a lighted splint into it. Test the other by shaking it with a few drops of bromine water (harmful).

● Record your observations.

Safety: Avoid cold water being sucked back into the hot tube by removing the delivery tube from the water trough before you stop heating. Wear eye protection. Some gases collected may be harmful or even toxic.

Making ethanol from ethene (hydration)

Ethanol for industrial use as a fuel or solvent can be made from ethene gas instead of by fermentation. Ethene is the main by-product made in cracking. Ethene gas can react with steam to make ethanol.

$$\text{ethene} + \text{steam} \underset{}{\overset{\text{catalyst}}{\rightleftharpoons}} \text{ethanol}$$
$$C_2H_4 + H_2O \rightleftharpoons C_2H_5OH$$

This reaction is called **hydration**. The reaction requires energy to heat the gases and to generate a high pressure. The reaction is reversible so ethanol can break down back into ethene and steam. So unreacted ethene and steam are recycled over the catalyst.

∞ links

For more information on fermentation to make ethanol, look back to 9.4 'Alternative fuels'.

Summary questions

1 a Why is cracking so important?
  b How can large hydrocarbon molecules be cracked in an oil refinery?

2 Cracking a hydrocarbon makes two new hydrocarbons, A and B. When bromine water is added to A, nothing happens. Bromine water added to B turns from an orange solution to colourless.
  a i Which hydrocarbon, A or B, is unsaturated?
    ii What is an 'unsaturated' hydrocarbon?
    iii What do we call the type of unsaturated hydrocarbon formed in cracking?
  b i Which hydrocarbon, A or B, is used as a fuel?
    ii What do we call the type of saturated hydrocarbon formed in cracking?
  c What type of reaction is cracking an example of?

3 An alkene molecule with one double bond contains 12 carbon atoms. How many hydrogen atoms does it have? Write down its formula.

4 Dodecane (an alkane with 12 carbon atoms) can be cracked into octane (with 8 carbon atoms) and ethene. Write a balanced symbol equation for this reaction.

Key points

● We can split large hydrocarbon molecules up into smaller molecules by passing the vapours over a hot catalyst or by mixing them with steam and heating them to a very high temperature.

● Cracking produces saturated hydrocarbons which are used as fuels and unsaturated hydrocarbons (called alkenes).

● Alkenes (and other unsaturated compounds containing carbon–carbon double bonds) react with yellow-orange bromine water, turning it colourless.

C10.2 Making polymers from alkenes

Learning objectives

After this topic, you should know:

● how monomers make polymers

● how alkenes undergo polymerisation reactions

● how to represent polymerisation reactions by an equation.

Figure 1 All of these products were manufactured using chemicals originating from crude oil

The fractional distillation of crude oil and cracking produces a large range of hydrocarbons. These are very important to our way of life. Crude oil-based products are all around us. It is difficult to imagine life without them.

Hydrocarbons are our main fuels. We use them in our transport and at home to cook and for heating. We also use them to generate electricity in oil-fired and gas-fired power stations.

Then there are the chemicals we make from crude oil. We use them to make things ranging from cosmetics to explosives. But one of the most important ways that we use chemicals from crude oil is to make plastics.

Plastics

Plastics are made up of huge molecules made from lots of small molecules joined together. We call the small molecules **monomers**. We call the huge molecules they make **polymers**. (*Mono* means 'one' and *poly* means 'many'). We can make different types of plastics, which can have very different properties, by using different monomers.

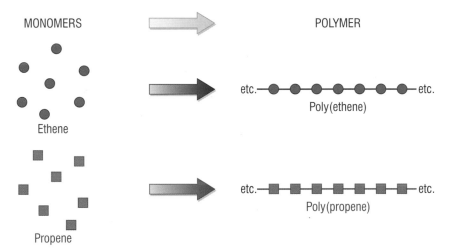

Figure 2 Polymers are made from many smaller molecules called monomers

Ethene (C_2H_4) is the smallest unsaturated hydrocarbon molecule. We can turn it into a polymer known as poly(ethene) or polythene. Poly(ethene) is a really useful plastic as it is easy to shape, strong and transparent (unless we add colouring material to it). 'Plastic' carrier bags, some drinks bottles, dustbins, washing-up bowls and clingfilm are all examples of uses of poly(ethene).

Propene (C_3H_6) is another alkene. We can also make polymers with propene as the monomer. The polymer formed is called poly(propene). It forms a very strong, tough plastic. We can use it to make many things, including carpets, milk crates and ropes.

Figure 3 Polymers produced from compounds derived from crude oil are all around us and are part of our everyday lives

How do monomers join together?

When alkene molecules join together, the double bond between the carbon atoms in each molecule 'opens up'. It is replaced by single bonds as thousands of molecules join together. The reaction is called **polymerisation**.

Ethene monomers   Poly(ethene)

We can also write this more simply as:

where n is a large number

Many single ethene monomers | Long chain of poly(ethene)

Activity

Modelling polymerisation

Use a molecular model kit to show how ethene molecules polymerise to form poly(ethene).

Make sure you can see how the equation shown above represents the polymerisation reaction you have modelled.

● Describe what happens to the bonds in the reaction.
● Think up a model to demonstrate the polymerisation of ethene, using people in your class as monomers.

Then evaluate the ideas of other groups.

Examiner's tip

The C=C double bond in ethene (an alkene) makes it much more reactive than ethane (an alkane).

Summary questions

1 **a** Define a monomer and a polymer.
   b What do we call the reaction between a large number of monomers?
   c Write an equation to represent the formation of poly(ethene) from ethene.
   d State **two** uses of poly(ethene).

2 Why is ethene the smallest possible alkene molecule whereas methane is the smallest alkane?

3 **a** Draw the displayed formula of a propene molecule, showing all its bonds.
   b Draw a diagram to show how propene molecules join together to form poly(propene).
   c State **two** uses of poly(propene).
   d Explain the polymerisation reaction in part **b**.

Key points

● Plastics are made of polymers.

● Polymers are large molecules made when many monomers (small, reactive molecules) join together.

● The reaction between monomers to form a polymer is called polymerisation.

C10.3 The properties of polymers

Learning objectives

After this topic, you should know:

- that the properties of polymers depend on their monomers

- that changing reaction conditions can modify the polymers made

- the differences between thermosetting and thermosoftening polymers.

As you know, we can make **polymers** from chemicals derived from crude oil. Small molecules called monomers join together to make much bigger molecules called polymers. As the monomers join together they produce a tangled web of very long chain molecules. Poly(ethene) is an example.

The properties of a polymer depend on:
- the monomers used to make it, and
- the conditions chosen to carry out the reaction.

Different monomers

Polymer chains can be made from many different monomers. The monomers chosen make a big difference to the properties of the polymer made. Consider the properties of the polymers in the bag in Figure 1 and the electrical socket in Figure 4.

Different reaction conditions

There are two types of poly(ethene). One is called high density (HD) and the other low density (LD) poly(ethene). Both are made from ethene monomers but they are formed under different reaction conditions.

- Using very high pressures and a trace of oxygen, ethene forms LD poly(ethene). The polymer chains are randomly branched and they can't pack closely together, hence its lower density.

- Using a catalyst at 50 °C and a slightly raised pressure, ethene makes HD poly(ethene). This is made up of straighter poly(ethene) chains. They can pack more closely together than branched chains, hence its higher density. The HD poly(ethene) also has a higher softening temperature and is stronger than LD poly(ethene).

Figure 1 The forces between the molecules in poly(ethene) are relatively weak as there are no strong covalent bonds (cross links) between the molecules. This means that this plastic softens fairly easily when heated.

LD poly(ethene) or LDPE

Polymer chains

HD poly(ethene) or HDPE

Figure 2 The branched chains of LD poly(ethene) cannot pack as tightly together as the straighter chains in HD poly(ethene), giving the polymers different properties

Thermosoftening and thermosetting polymers

We can classify polymers by looking at what happens to them when they are heated. Some will soften quite easily. They will reset when they cool down. These are called **thermosoftening polymers**. They are made up of individual polymer chains that are tangled together.

Other polymers do not melt when we heat them. These are called **thermosetting polymers**. These have strong covalent bonds forming 'cross links' between their polymer chains. (See Figure 3.)

The tangled web of polymer chains are relatively easy to separate

Thermosoftening polymer

Chains fixed together by strong covalent bonds – this is called **cross linking**

Thermosetting polymer

Figure 3 Extensive cross linking by covalent bonds between polymer chains makes a thermosetting plastic that is heat-resistant and rigid

Bonding in and between polymer chains

The atoms in polymer chains are held together by very strong covalent bonds. This is true for all plastics. But the size of the forces *between* polymer molecules in different plastics can be very different.

In thermosoftening polymers the forces between the polymer chains are weak. When we heat the polymer, these weak intermolecular forces are broken. The polymer becomes soft. When the polymer cools down, the intermolecular forces bring the polymer molecules back together. Then the polymer hardens again. This type of polymer can be remoulded.

However, thermosetting polymers are different. Their monomers make covalent bonds between the polymer chains when they are first heated in order to shape them. These covalent bonds are strong, and they stop the polymer from softening. The covalent 'cross links' between chains do not allow them to separate. Even if heated strongly, the polymer will still not soften. Eventually, the polymer will char at high enough temperatures.

Figure 4 Electrical sockets are made out of thermosetting polymers. If the plug or wires get hot, the socket will not soften.

Summary questions

1 a How are the polymer chains arranged in a thermosoftening polymer?
  b i What is the difference between the structures of a thermosoftening and a thermosetting polymer?
    ii Give two differences in the properties of the two types of polymer.

2 Why do we use thermosetting rather than thermosoftening polymers to make the handles of pans?

3 Polymer A starts to soften at 100 °C while polymer B softens at 50 °C. Polymer C resists heat but eventually starts to char if heated to very high temperatures.
  Explain this using ideas about intermolecular forces.

4 There are two types of poly(ethene), high density (HD) and low density (LD) poly(ethene).
  a What is varied in order to produce the different types of poly(ethene)?
  b Which statement is true?
    HDPE is a thermosetting polymer and LDPE is thermosoftening polymer.
    Both HDPE and LDPE are thermosoftening polymers.
  c Explain the differing densities of HDPE and LDPE in terms of their structures.

Key points

- Monomers affect the properties of the polymers that they produce.

- Changing reaction conditions can also change the properties of the polymer that is produced.

- Thermosoftening polymers will soften or melt easily when heated because their intermolecular forces are relatively weak. Thermosetting polymers will not soften because of their 'cross linking' but will eventually char if heated very strongly.

C10.4

New and useful polymers

Figure 1 A sticking plaster is often needed when we cut ourselves but taking the plaster off can be painful too

Chemists can design new polymers to make materials with special properties to do particular jobs. Medicine is one area where we are beginning to see big benefits from these 'polymers made to order'.

New polymer materials will eventually take over from the current metal fillings for teeth, which contain mercury. Working with the toxic mercury every day is a potential hazard to dental workers.

Other developments include:

- new softer linings for dentures (false teeth)
- new packaging materials
- implants that can slowly release drugs into a patient.

Light-sensitive plasters

We all know how uncomfortable pulling a plaster off your skin can be. But for some of us taking off a plaster is really painful. Both very old and very young people have quite fragile skin. But now a group of chemists has made a plaster where the 'stickiness' can be switched off before the plaster is removed. The plaster uses a light-sensitive polymer (see Figure 2 below).

1 The plaster is put on just like any normal plaster.

2 To remove the plaster, the top layer is peeled away from the lower layer which stays stuck to the skin.

3 Once the lower layer is exposed to the light, the adhesive becomes less sticky, making it easy to peel off your skin.

Figure 2 This plaster uses a light-sensitive polymer

Hydrogels

Hydrogels are polymer chains with a few cross-linking units between chains. This makes a matrix (framework) that can trap water. These hydrogels are used as wound dressings. They let the body heal in moist, sterile conditions. This makes them useful for treating burns.

The latest 'soft' contact lenses are also made from hydrogels. To change the properties of hydrogels, scientists can vary the amount of water in their matrix structure.

Practical

Evaluating plastics

Plan an investigation to compare and evaluate the suitability of different plastics for a particular use.

For example, you might look at treated and untreated fabrics for waterproofing and 'breatheability' (gas permeability), or different types of packaging.

Shape memory polymers

A new 'shape memory polymer' is being developed for surgeons which will make stitching in awkward places easier. When a shape memory polymer is used to stitch a wound loosely, the temperature of the body makes the thread tighten and close the wound, applying just the right amount of force.

This is an example of a '**smart polymer**', i.e. one that changes in response to changes in its surroundings. In this case a change in temperature causes the polymer to change its shape. Later, after the wound is healed, the polymer is designed to dissolve and is harmlessly absorbed by the body. So, there will be no need to go back to hospital to have the stitches out.

Figure 3 A shape memory polymer uses the temperature of the body to make the thread tighten and close the wound

New uses for old polymers

The bottles that we buy fizzy drinks in are a good example of using a plastic because of its properties. These bottles are made out of a plastic called PET.

The polymer it is made from is ideal for making drinks bottles. It produces a plastic that is very strong and tough, and which can be made transparent. The bottles made from this plastic are much lighter than glass bottles. This means that they cost less to transport and are easier for us to carry around.

The PET from recycled bottles is used to make polyester fibres for clothing, such as fleece jackets, and the filling for duvet covers. School uniforms and football shirts are now also made from recycled drinks bottles.

Did you know ... ?

PET is an abbreviation for poly(ethene terephthalate). It takes 5 two-litre PET lemonade bottles to make one T-shirt.

Summary questions

1 a What do we mean by:
    i a 'designer polymer'
    ii a 'smart polymer'?
  b i Why is PET used to make drinks bottles?
    ii State **two** uses of recycled PET.
    iii Is PET a thermosetting polymer or a thermosoftening polymer? How did you decide?

2 a What is a hydrogel?
  b Give **two** uses of hydrogels.

3 Explain how a light-sensitive plaster works.

4 Explain how stitches made from smart polymers work.

Key points

- New polymers are being developed all the time. They are designed to have properties that make them specially suited for certain uses.

- Smart polymers may have their properties changed by light, temperature or by other changes in their surroundings.

- We are now recycling more plastics and finding new uses for them.

C10.5

Plastic waste

Learning objectives

After this topic, you should know:

- the problems caused by the disposal of plastics
- what biodegradable polymers are
- how polymers can be made biodegradable.

One of the problems with plastics is what to do with them when we've finished with them. Too much ends up as rubbish in our streets. Even the beaches in the most remote parts of the world can be polluted with the eyesore of plastic waste. Wildlife can also get trapped in the waste or eat the plastics and die.

Not only that, just think of all the plastic packaging that goes in the bin after shopping. Most of it ends up as rubbish in landfill sites. Other landfill rubbish rots away quite quickly as microorganisms in the soil break it down. However, many waste polymers last for hundreds of years before they are broken down completely, taking up valuable space in our landfill sites. So, what was a useful property during the working life of the plastic (its lack of reactivity) becomes a disadvantage in a landfill site.

Figure 1 Finding space to dump and bury our waste is becoming a big problem

Biodegradable polymers

Scientists are working to solve the problems of plastic waste. We are now making more plastics that do rot away in the soil when we dump them. The polymers in these plastics are called **biodegradable**. They can be broken down by microorganisms.

Scientists have found different ways to speed up the decomposition:

- One way uses granules of cornstarch built into a plastic. The microorganisms in soil feed on the starch. This breaks the plastic up into small pieces more quickly.
- Other types of polymer have been developed that are made from plant products.

A polymer called PLA, poly(lactic acid), can be made from cornstarch. The polymer is totally biodegradable. It is used in food packaging. However, it cannot be put in a microwave, which limits its use in ready-meal packaging.

We can also make plastic carrier bags using PLA. In carrier bags the PLA is mixed with a traditional polymer. This makes sure the bag is strong enough but will still biodegrade a lot more quickly.

Using polymers such as PLA also helps preserve our supplies of crude oil. Remember that crude oil is the raw material for many traditional polymers, such as poly(ethene).

Figure 2 The breakdown of a biodegradable polymer. PLA can be designed to break down in a few months.

Disadvantages of biodegradable polymers

The use of a food crop like corn to make polymers can raise the same issues as biofuels. Farmers who sell their crops to be turned into fuel and plastics could cause higher food prices. The lack of basic food supplies could result in starvation in developing countries. Another problem is the destruction of tropical forests to create more farmland. This will destroy the habitats of wildlife and could affect climate change.

Other degradable polymers used for bags will break down in light. However, they will not decompose when buried in a landfill site. One of the best solutions is to reuse the same plastic carrier bags over and over again.

Summary questions

1 Why are waste plastics proving to be a problem for us?

2 Explain what we mean by a 'biodegradable' polymer.

3 a Why are plastics whose raw materials are plants becoming more popular?
  b PLA is a biodegradable plastic. What is its monomer?

4 Non-biodegradable polymers such as poly(ethene) can be made to decompose more quickly by mixing with additives. These enable the polymer chain to be broken down by reacting with oxygen.
  a Why might this be a waste of money if the plastic is buried and compressed under other waste in a landfill site?
  b What could be a disadvantage of using this type of degradable plastic?
  c Explain how cornstarch can play a role in helping to solve the problems of plastic waste.

Practical

Investigating cornstarch

Cornstarch can be fermented to make the starting material for PLA. However, cornstarch itself also has some interesting properties. You can make your own plastic material directly from cornstarch.

● Investigate how varying the proportions of cornstarch and water affect the product.

Safety: Be aware of allergies and sensitisation.

links

For information on the issues of using biofuels, look back at 9.4 'Alternative fuels'.

Key points

● Non-biodegradable polymers cause unsightly rubbish, can harm wildlife and take up space in landfill sites.

● Biodegradable polymers are decomposed by the action of microorganisms in soil.

● Making plastics with starch granules in their structure help the microorganisms break down a polymer.

● We can make biodegradable polymers from plant material such as cornstarch.

Summary questions

1 Propene is a hydrocarbon molecule containing three carbon atoms and six hydrogen atoms.

a What is the chemical formula of propene?

b Draw the displayed formula of propene, showing all its bonds.

c Is propene a saturated molecule or an unsaturated molecule? Explain your answer.

d You are given two unlabelled test tubes. One test tube contains propane gas, while the other test tube contains propene gas.
Explain how you could test which tube contains which gas, stating clearly the results obtained in each case.

e Propene molecules will react together to form long chains.
  i What do we call this type of reaction?
  ii Name the product of the reaction.
  iii What is the general name given to the many propene molecules that react together?
  iv Compare the properties of the reactants to those of the product.

2 Give a symbol equation to show the reaction of ethene to make poly(ethene).

3 a Write a word equation and a balanced symbol equation, including state symbols, for the reaction between ethene and steam.

b If 56 tonnes of ethene reacted with excess steam, and 69 tonnes of ethanol were collected, what is the percentage yield of ethanol?
(A_r values: H = 1, C = 12, O = 16)

c Give an advantage and a disadvantage of making ethanol from ethene compared with making it from sugar obtained from plant material.

4 Chemists have developed special waterproof materials made from polymers. It is easy to make plastic material that is waterproof but they tend to make the wearer hot and sweaty. However, we now have polymer materials that have pores 2000 times smaller than a drop of water. However, the tiny pores are 700 times larger than a water molecule.

a Explain why these materials are described as 'breathable'.

b Would you describe the 'breathable' polymer material as a smart polymer? Explain your answer.

5 Read the following information then answer the questions.

New biodegradable polymers are now being developed. They use normal crops as their starting material. They do not use up our decreasing supplies of crude oil. The crop is fermented with microorganisms which make a polymer called PHB, poly(hydroxybutyrate). In America, scientists have used genetic engineering to grow plants which make PHB themselves. They are continuing their research to increase the yield of the polymer in crops such as potatoes.

Look at this cycle for the plastic PHB:

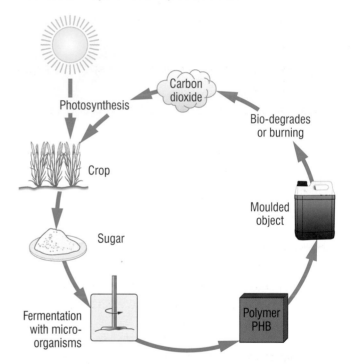

a Why might people object to the crops that make PHB directly?

b Does the use of PHB increase the amount of carbon dioxide in the air? Explain your answer.

c Why is it difficult to say whether PHB made directly by plants will be cheaper than the PHB shown in the cycle?

AQA Examination-style questions

1 The fractions from crude oil that contain the biggest molecules have few uses. Cracking converts them into more useful substances, including alkenes.

a Describe the conditions used in two different types of cracking. (4)

b Unlike alkanes, alkenes are *unsaturated*.
i What feature is present in an alkene but not in an alkane? (1)
ii Give the displayed formula of the simplest alkene. (1)
iii Propene has the molecular formula C_3H_6.

Deduce the molecular formula of the alkene with four carbon atoms in each molecule. (1)

c Complete this equation for a cracking reaction.

$C_{12}H_{26} \rightarrow C_8H_{18} +$ ----------- (1)

d Alkanes and alkenes can be distinguished by a simple chemical test.

State the reagent used and the result with each type of compound. (3)

e The traditional way to make ethanol is by fermentation.

State how it is made using one of the products of cracking. (3)

2 Most alkenes are used to make polymers.

a State two features of polymer molecules that alkenes do not have. (2)

b Poly(ethene) is made in two forms, depending on the conditions used for polymerisation. These are described as LD and HD forms.
i State the meanings of the terms LD and HD. (1)
ii Both forms are described as *thermosoftening*. What is the meaning of this term? (1)

c Another type of polymer is described as thermosetting.
i How does a thermosetting polymer behave when heated? (1)
ii Describe how the bonding in a thermosetting polymer differs from the bonding in a thermosoftening polymer. (2)

d Some polymers are *biodegradable*.

State the meaning of this term and one advantage of these polymers over non-biodegradable polymers. (2)

3 A manufacturer plans to produce objects made from two new polymers. Polymer 1 needs to withstand heat without changing shape. Polymer 2 needs to be able to change shape but does not need to withstand heat.

The diagrams show two types of polymer.

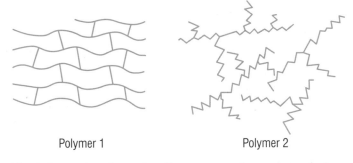

Polymer 1   Polymer 2

Use information from the diagrams and your knowledge and understanding of polymers to identify the types of polymer that could be used as Polymer 1 and Polymer 2. You should support your choices by referring to the properties, structure and bonding in polymers.

Marks awarded for this answer will be determined by the quality of communication as well as the standard of the scientific response.

Structures of alcohols, carboxylic acids and esters

Learning objectives

After this topic, you should know:

- the names and formulae of the first three alcohols, carboxylic acids and esters

- how to represent the structures of alcohols, carboxylic acids and esters.

?? Did you know ...?

Not all carbon compounds are classified as organic compounds. The oxides of carbon and compounds containing carbonate and hydrogencarbonate ions are classed as inorganic compounds.

⬭ links

For more information on the use of ethanol as a biofuel, look back at 9.4 'Alternative fuels'.

Examiner's tip

If you draw displayed formulae, make sure you show all the bonds, including those in the functional group (as lines between atoms) and all the atoms (as their chemical symbols).

The substances that form the basis of all living things, including ourselves, are organic compounds. Organic molecules all contain carbon atoms. The carbon atoms tend to form the 'backbone' of organic molecules.

You have already met some organic compounds in Chapters 9 and 10. You will probably recall how we draw molecules of alkanes and alkenes (see Figure 1):

Figure 1 The structures of the smallest alkane and alkene molecules. The lines between atoms represent covalent bonds. Notice the double bonds in ethene and propene. This type of 2D drawing to show the structure of a molecule is called a 'displayed formula'.

Both alkanes and alkenes are made of only carbon and hydrogen atoms. However, there are many more 'families' of organic compounds that also contain a few other types of atom.

In this chapter you will learn about some organic compounds made up of carbon, hydrogen and oxygen. The three 'families' you will look at are called alcohols, carboxylic acids and esters.

Alcohols

You have also met a member of the alcohol 'family' before. This was ethanol, which can be used as a biofuel. So what is an alcohol?

Imagine removing an H atom from an alkane molecule and replacing it with an O–H group. This would give us an alcohol molecule. The –OH group of atoms is an example of a **functional group**.

A functional group gives a 'family' of organic compounds their characteristic reactions. A 'family' of compounds with the same functional group is called a **homologous series**.

You need to know the first three members of the homologous series of alcohols:

Figure 2 The structures and names of the first three alcohol molecules. We name alcohols from the alkane with the same number of carbon atoms. Just take the 'e' from the end of the alkane's name and replace it with 'ol'.

If you were asked for the formula of ethanol, you might count the atoms in a molecule and write C_2H_6O. This is correct but chemists can give more information in a **structural formula**. This doesn't show all the bonds, as in a displayed formula, but shows what is bonded to each carbon atom. So for ethanol, a chemist will often show its formula as CH_3CH_2OH (often shortened to C_2H_5OH). Can you see how this relates to the structure of ethanol shown in Figure 2?

Carboxylic acids

You will certainly know of one carboxylic acid. Ethanoic acid is the main acid in vinegar. All carboxylic acids contain the –COOH functional group. Look at the first three members of the homologous series of carboxylic acids below:

Methanoic acid   Ethanoic acid   Propanoic acid

Figure 3 The structures and names of the first three carboxylic acid molecules

We show the structural formula of each of the carboxylic acids in Figure 3 as HCOOH, CH_3COOH and CH_3CH_2COOH (or C_2H_5COOH).

Esters

Esters are closely related to carboxylic acids. If we replace the H atom in the –COOH group by a hydrocarbon (alkyl) group, such as $-CH_3$ or $-C_2H_5$, we get an ester. Here is the ester called ethyl ethanoate:

Ethyl ethanoate

Figure 5 The structure of the ester ethyl ethanoate

An ester's structural formula always has the –COO– functional group in it. The structural formula of ethyl ethanoate is $CH_3COOCH_2CH_3$ (or $CH_3COOC_2H_5$).

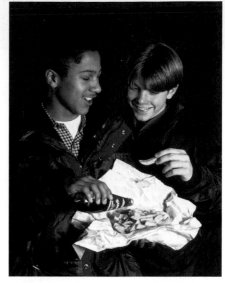

Figure 4 Vinegar contains less than 10 per cent ethanoic acid in an aqueous solution but the acid provides the characteristic sharp taste and smell

∞ links

For information about the homologous series of carboxylic acids and esters, see 11.3 'Carboxylic acids and esters'.

Summary questions

1 Which homologous series do the following compounds belong to?
   a $CH_3COOCH_2CH_2CH_3$
   b $CH_3CH_2CH_2CH_2CH_2CH_2OH$
   c $CH_3CH_2CH_2CH_2COOH$

2 Name the following compounds:
   a $CH_3CH_2CH_2OH$
   b $CH_3COOC_2H_5$
   c HCOOH

3 Draw a displayed formula, showing all the bonds, in:
   a ethanol
   b ethyl ethanoate
   c butanoic acid, which contains 4 carbon atoms.

Key points

- The homologous series of alcohols contain the –OH functional group.

- The homologous series of carboxylic acids contain the –COOH functional group.

- The homologous series of esters contain the –COO– functional group.

C11.2 Properties and uses of alcohols

∞ links

For more information on how ethanol is manufactured by fermentation, look back to 9.4 'Alternative fuels', and from ethene in 10.1 'Cracking hydrocarbons'.

Figure 1 Alcohols are used as solvents in perfumes

Alcohols, especially ethanol, are commonly used in everyday products. Ethanol is the main alcohol in alcoholic drinks. It is made by fermenting sugars from plant material and is becoming an important alternative fuel to petrol and diesel. Ethanol can also be made in industry from ethene and steam in the presence of a catalyst.

Alcohols dissolve many of the same substances as water. In fact the alcohols with smaller molecules mix very well with water, giving neutral solutions. The alcohols can also dissolve many other organic compounds. This property makes them useful as solvents. For example, we can remove ink stains from permanent marker pens using methylated spirits.

Methylated spirits ('meths') is mainly ethanol but has the more toxic methanol mixed with it. It also has a purple dye and other substances added to make it unpleasant to drink. Alcohols are also used as solvents in products such as perfumes, aftershaves and mouthwashes.

Reactions of alcohols

Practical/Demonstration

Comparing the reactions of methanol, ethanol and propanol

a Ignite and observe the flame in three spirit burners – one containing methanol, one ethanol and the other propanol.
   Compare the three combustion reactions.

b Watch your teacher add a small piece of sodium metal to each of the alcohols.
   Compare the reactions. Which gas is given off?

c Watch your teacher boil some of each alcohol with acidified potassium dichromate(VI) solution.
   What do you see happen in each reaction?

Safety: Ethanol is highly flammable and harmful. Methanol is highly flammable and toxic. Propanol is highly flammable and irritant. No naked flames. Wear chemical splash proof eye protection.

Combustion

The use of ethanol (and also methanol) as fuels shows that the alcohols are flammable. Ethanol is used in spirit burners and can be used as a biofuel in cars. It burns with a 'clean' blue flame:

$$\text{ethanol} + \text{oxygen} \rightarrow \text{carbon dioxide} + \text{water}$$
$$C_2H_5OH + 3O_2 \rightarrow 2CO_2 + 3H_2O$$

??? Did you know ... ?

Ethanol is the main solvent in many perfumes but a key ingredient in some perfumes is octanol. It evaporates more slowly and so holds the perfume on the skin for longer.

Reaction with sodium

The alcohols react in a similar way to water when sodium metal is added. The sodium effervesces (gives off bubbles of gas), producing hydrogen gas, and gets smaller and smaller as it forms a solution of sodium ethoxide in ethanol. Their reactions are not as vigorous as the reaction we observe between sodium and water. For example, with ethanol:

$$\text{sodium} + \text{ethanol} \rightarrow \text{sodium ethoxide} + \text{hydrogen}$$
$$2Na + 2C_2H_5OH \rightarrow 2C_2H_5ONa + H_2$$

Oxidation

Combustion is one way to oxidise an alcohol. However, when we use chemical oxidising agents, such as potassium dichromate(VI), we get different products. An alcohol is oxidised to a carboxylic acid when boiled with acidified potassium dichromate(VI) solution. So ethanol can be oxidised to ethanoic acid:

$$\text{ethanol} + \text{oxygen atoms from oxidising agent} \rightarrow \text{ethanoic acid} + \text{water}$$
$$C_2H_5OH + 2[O] \rightarrow CH_3COOH + H_2O$$

The same reaction takes place if ethanol is left exposed to air. Microbes in the air produce ethanoic acid from the ethanol. That's why bottles of beer or wine taste and smell like vinegar when they are left open for too long.

Figure 2 Alcohols are flammable. They produce carbon dioxide and water in their combustion reactions.

Practical

Oxidation by microbes in air

Add 5 cm³ of ethanol to 50 cm³ of water in a conical flask, mix and test the pH of the solution formed.

Then mix 5 cm³ of ethanol with 50 cm³ of water in a second conical flask but this time seal the flask with a stopper.

Leave both solutions for a few weeks, swirling occasionally.

- What happens to the pH of the solutions?
- Explain your observations.

Safety: Ethanol is highly flammable and harmful.

Summary questions

1 Give the name and structural formula of the main alcohol in alcoholic drinks.

2 List the main uses of alcohols.

3 a Write a word equation and a balanced symbol equation for the reaction between sodium metal and methanol.

   b Name and give the structural formula of the acidic product formed when methanol is boiled with acidified potassium dichromate(VI), a chemical oxidising agent.

   c Write a word equation and a balanced symbol equation for the complete combustion of methanol.

4 Methanol, ethanol and propanol are all liquids at room temperature. Plan an investigation to see which alcohol – methanol, ethanol or propanol – releases most energy per gram when it burns.

Key points

- Alcohols are used as solvents and fuels, and ethanol is the main alcohol in alcoholic drinks.

- Alcohols burn in air, forming carbon dioxide and water.

- With sodium metal, alcohols react to form a solution, and hydrogen gas is given off.

- Ethanol can be oxidised to ethanoic acid, either by chemical oxidising agents or by the action of microbes in the air. Ethanoic acid is the main acid in vinegar.

C11.3 — Carboxylic acids and esters

Learning objectives

After this topic, you should know:

- how to recognise carboxylic acids from their properties
- some uses of carboxylic acids and esters
- why carboxylic acids are described as weak acids
- how to make esters.

⬭ links
For more information on the structure of carboxylic acids, look back to 11.1 'Structures of alcohols, carboxylic acids and esters'.

Figure 2 Testing the pH of a solution using a pH sensor

⬭ links
Look back to Chapter 6 to see the typical reactions of acids.

You have already learned about the structure of carboxylic acids. The most well-known carboxylic acid is ethanoic acid.

Ethanoic acid

Figure 1 Ethanoic acid, CH_3COOH, is the main acid in vinegar. Its old name was 'acetic acid'. Carboxylic acids are also used to make polyester fibres.

Carboxylic acids, as their name suggests, form acidic solutions when they dissolve in water. You can look at one of their reactions in the practical opposite.

Carboxylic acids have the typical reactions of all acids. For example, reaction with a metal carbonate forms a salt, water and carbon dioxide. In the practical opposite:

ethanoic acid + sodium carbonate → sodium ethanoate + water + carbon dioxide

$$2CH_3COOH(aq) + Na_2CO_3(s) \rightarrow 2CH_3COONa(aq) + H_2O(l) + CO_2(g)$$

Why are carboxylic acids called 'weak acids'?

You will see in the practical opposite how CO_2 gas is given off more slowly when a metal carbonate reacts with a carboxylic acid as compared with hydrochloric acid of the same concentration. Carboxylic acids are called **weak** acids, as opposed to **strong** acids such as hydrochloric acid.

The pH of a $0.1\,mol/dm^3$ solution of hydrochloric acid (a strong acid) is 1.0. Yet a $0.1\,mol/dm^3$ solution of ethanoic acid (a weak acid) has a pH of only 2.9. The solution of ethanoic acid is not as acidic even though the two solutions have the same concentration. Why is this?

Acids must dissolve in water before they show their acidic properties. That is because in water all acids ionise (split up). Their molecules split up to form $H^+(aq)$ ions and negative ions. It is the $H^+(aq)$ ions that all acidic solutions have in common. For example, in hydrochloric acid, the HCl molecules all ionise in water:

$$HCl(aq) \xrightarrow{\text{water}} H^+(aq) + Cl^-(aq)$$

We say that strong acids ionise *completely* in solution. However, in weak acids most of the molecules stay as they are. Only some will ionise in their solutions. A position of **equilibrium** is reached in which both molecules and ions are present. So, in ethanoic acid we get:

$$CH_3COOH(aq) \underset{}{\overset{\text{water}}{\rightleftharpoons}} CH_3COO^-(aq) + H^+(aq)$$

ethanoic acid   ethanoate ions   hydrogen ions

Therefore, given two aqueous solutions of equal concentration, the strong acid will have a higher concentration of $H^+(aq)$ ions than the solution of the weak acid. So, a weak acid has a higher pH (and hence reacts more slowly with a metal carbonate).

Making esters

Carboxylic acids also react with alcohols to make esters. Water is also formed in this reversible reaction. A strong acid, usually sulfuric acid, is used as a catalyst. For example:

$$\text{ethanoic acid} + \text{ethanol} \underset{\text{catalyst}}{\overset{\text{sulfuric acid}}{\rightleftharpoons}} \text{ethyl ethanoate} + \text{water}$$
$$CH_3COOH + C_2H_5OH \rightleftharpoons CH_3COOC_2H_5 + H_2O$$

In general:

$$\textbf{carboxylic acid} + \textbf{alcohol} \underset{\text{catalyst}}{\overset{\text{strong acid}}{\rightleftharpoons}} \textbf{ester} + \textbf{water}$$

Here is another example:

ethanoic acid + **methanol** ⇌ **methyl ethanoate** + water

$$\text{ethanoic acid} + \text{methanol} \underset{\text{catalyst}}{\overset{\text{sulfuric acid}}{\rightleftharpoons}} \text{methyl ethanoate} + \text{water}$$
$$CH_3COOH + CH_3OH \rightleftharpoons CH_3COOCH_3 + H_2O$$

Another example is:

$$\text{propanoic acid} + \text{ethanol} \underset{\text{catalyst}}{\overset{\text{sulfuric acid}}{\rightleftharpoons}} \text{ethyl propanoate} + \text{water}$$
$$C_2H_5COOH + C_2H_5OH \rightleftharpoons C_2H_5COOC_2H_5 + H_2O$$

The esters formed have distinctive smells. They are volatile (evaporate easily). Many smell sweet and fruity. This makes them ideal to use in perfumes and food flavourings.

Summary questions

1 Look at the three organic molecules **A**, **B** and **C** below:

Answer these questions about **A**, **B** and **C**:

a Which one is a carboxylic acid?

b Which one is an alcohol?

c Which homologous series of organic compounds does **B** belong to?

d Which of the compounds can be represented as the structural formula $CH_3CH_2COOCH_2CH_2CH_2CH_3$?

e Using a structural formula as shown in part **d**, give the structural formulae of the other two compounds.

2 a i Describe what you would **see** happen if a small piece of sodium metal was dropped into a beaker containing some ethanol.

ii Name the gas given off in this reaction.

iii Name the sodium compound formed in the reaction.

iv The sodium in the compound formed is present as ions. Give the formula of a sodium ion.

v Write a balanced symbol equation for the reaction of sodium with ethanol.

b Using your knowledge of the periodic table and trends in reactivity, suggest how ethanol's reaction with lithium metal would differ from its reaction with sodium.

3 a Draw the displayed formula of methanoic acid, showing all the atoms and bonds.

b i Some potassium carbonate powder is dropped into a test tube of a solution of methanoic acid. How would you positively identify the gas given off? Include a labelled diagram of the apparatus you could use.

ii Write a word equation and balanced symbol equation for the reaction.

c i Which aqueous solution of the following would you expect to have the highest pH value if they all had the same concentration?
   A hydrochloric acid
   B sulfuric acid
   C methanoic acid
   D nitric acid
   E ethanol

ii Which of the five solutions listed above would have the second highest pH value? Explain your choice.

4 a What is the name of this compound?

b Name the carboxylic acid and alcohol used to make the compound in part **a** and give one use for each.

c Write a word equation and a balanced symbol equation, showing how this compound can be made. Include the name of the catalyst.

d The compound shown in part **a** is volatile. What does this mean?

e Name the carboxylic acid and the alcohol we would use to make methyl propanoate.

5 Describe how you could distinguish between samples of propanol, propanoic acid and ethyl ethanoate using simple experimental tests. Give the results of any tests suggested.

6 You are given a $0.5\,mol/dm^3$ solution of nitric acid, and a $0.5\,mol/dm^3$ solution of methanoic acid.

a What does 'a $0.5\,mol/dm^3$ solution' mean?

b What can you predict about the relative pH values of the two solutions?

c Explain in detail your answer to part **b**, including equations to show the ionisation of nitric acid and methanoic acid in aqueous solution.

AQA Examination-style questions

1 Ethanol is often known as alcohol, but is just one member of a homologous series of alcohols. Methanol and propanol are two other members of the same homologous series.

a State two features that members of a homologous series have in common. (2)

b i What is the molecular formula of methanol? (1)
  ii Draw the displayed formula of propanol. (1)

c A small piece of sodium is added to a beaker containing methanol.

  Describe two observations you could make. (2)

d A sample of propanol burns completely in air.

  Name the products formed. (2)

e Ethanol burns completely in air in an oxidation reaction.

  Write a balanced symbol equation for this reaction. (2)

f Ethanol can also be oxidised by microbial action.
  i What is the organic product of this reaction? (1)
  ii What is the common name of the solution containing this organic product? (1)

2 Carboxylic acids are compounds in a homologous series.

Like alcohols they dissolve in water to form colourless solutions.

a A student was given separate solutions of ethanol and ethanoic acid.

  Describe how these could be distinguished by adding sodium carbonate. Include one observation for each compound. (2)

b The student was given separate solutions of ethanoic acid and nitric acid with the same concentration.

  These solutions can be distinguished by using a pH meter.

  Choose a possible pH value for each solution.
  i The pH value of ethanoic acid is   1 5 7 9 13   (1)
  ii The pH value of nitric acid is   1 5 7 9 13   (1)

c The student was shown these equations:

$$CH_3COOH \rightleftharpoons CH_3COO^- + H^+$$
$$HNO_3 \rightarrow H^+ + NO_3^-$$

  Explain how the arrows show that ethanoic acid is weaker than nitric acid. (2)

3 Esters are organic compounds formed in the reaction between an alcohol and a carboxylic acid. A reaction of this type is known as esterification.

a An example of an esterification reaction is shown by this equation:

$$HCOOH + CH_3CH_2CH_2OH \rightleftharpoons HCOOCH_2CH_2CH_3 + H_2O$$

  i Name the two reactants. (2)
  ii Draw the displayed formula of the ester. (1)

b What is the name of the ester made from ethanol and ethanoic acid? (1)

c State two uses for esters. (2)

Exothermic and endothermic reactions

Figure 1 When a fuel burns in oxygen, energy is transferred to the surroundings. We usually don't need a thermometer to know that there is a temperature change!

⚭ links

For more information about enthalpy changes and how we represent them, see 12.6 'Energy level diagrams'.

Whenever chemical reactions take place, energy is always transferred as chemical bonds are broken and new ones are made.

Some reactions transfer energy **from** the reacting chemicals **to** their surroundings. We call these **exothermic** reactions. The energy transferred from the reacting chemicals often heats up the surroundings. This means that we can measure a rise in temperature as the reaction happens.

Some reactions transfer energy **from** the surroundings **to** the reacting chemicals. We call these **endothermic** reactions. As they take in energy from their surroundings, these reactions cause a drop in temperature as they happen.

Exothermic reactions

Burning fuels are an obvious example of exothermic reactions. For example, when methane (in natural gas) burns it gets oxidised and releases energy.

Neutralisation reactions between acids and alkalis are also exothermic. We can easily measure the rise in temperature using simple apparatus (see the experiment on the next page).

Scientists use the term 'enthalpy change' to describe the transfer of energy in chemical reactions at constant pressure. As the reactions we carry out in the lab are at constant pressure, the energy we are considering in these reactions is enthalpy, symbol H. Any temperature change we measure when a reaction takes place is a result of enthalpy changes between the reactants and products of the reaction. The enthalpy change is given the symbol ΔH. The products of exothermic reactions have less enthalpy content than the reactants so numerical values, measured in kilojoules per mole, are given a negative sign. For example:

$$CH_4(g) + 2O_2(g) \rightarrow CO_2(g) + 2H_2O(l) \quad \Delta H = -890 \, kJ/mol$$

Figure 2 All warm-blooded animals rely on exothermic reactions in **respiration** to keep their body temperatures steady

Endothermic reactions

Endothermic reactions are much less common than exothermic ones.

Thermal decomposition reactions are endothermic. An example is the decomposition of calcium carbonate. When heated, it forms calcium oxide and carbon dioxide. This reaction only takes place if we keep heating the calcium carbonate strongly. The calcium carbonate needs to absorb energy from the surroundings to be broken down.

The products have more enthalpy content than the reactants in endothermic reactions, so numerical values are given a positive sign. For example:

$$CaCO_3(s) \rightarrow CaO(s) + CO_2(g) \quad \Delta H = +178\,kJ/mol$$

Figure 3 When you eat sherbet you can feel an endothermic reaction. Sherbet dissolving in the water in your mouth takes in energy. It provides a slight cooling effect.

Practical

Investigating energy changes

We can use very simple apparatus to investigate the energy changes in reactions. Often we don't need to use anything more complicated than a styrofoam cup and a thermometer.

The thermometer is used to measure the temperature change which takes place during the reaction.

Chemicals are mixed in the cup. The insulation reduces the rate at which energy can enter or leave the contents of the cup.

Styrofoam cup

- State two ways in which you could make the data you collect more accurate.

Safety: Wear eye protection.

Summary questions

1. **a** What do we call a reaction that releases energy to its surroundings?
   b What do we call a reaction that absorbs energy from its surroundings?
   c Give **two** examples of exothermic reactions.
   d Give an example of an endothermic reaction.

2. Potassium nitrate dissolving in water is an endothermic process. Explain what you would feel if you held a beaker of water in your hand as you stirred in potassium nitrate.

3. Two solutions are added together and the temperature changes from 19 °C to 27 °C. Explain what you can say about the enthalpy change in this reaction, including the sign given to ΔH.

4. The enthalpy change for the thermal decomposition of 16.8 g of magnesium carbonate is +23.4 kJ. (A_r values: C = 12, O = 16, Mg = 24)
   a Write a balanced symbol equation, including state symbols, for the reaction.
   b Calculate the value of ΔH for the thermal decomposition in kilojoules per mole.

Key points

- Energy may be transferred to or from the reacting substances in a chemical reaction.

- A reaction in which energy is transferred from the reacting substances to their surroundings is called an exothermic reaction.

- In exothermic reactions, the change in enthalpy, ΔH, has a negative value.

- A reaction in which energy is transferred to the reacting substances from their surroundings is called an endothermic reaction.

- In endothermic reactions, the change in enthalpy, ΔH, has a positive value.

C12.2

Using energy transfers from reactions

Learning objectives

After this topic, you should know:

- how we can make use of the energy from exothermic reactions

- how we can use the cooling effect of endothermic reactions.

Warming up

Chemical hand and body warmers can be very useful. These products use exothermic reactions to warm you up. People can take hand warmers to places they know will get very cold. For example, spectators at outdoor sporting events in winter can warm their hands up. People usually use the body warmers to help ease aches and pains.

Some hand warmers can only be used once. An example of this type uses the energy released in the oxidation of iron. Iron turns into hydrated iron(III) oxide in an exothermic reaction. The reaction is similar to rusting. Sodium chloride (common salt) is used as a catalyst. This type of hand warmer is disposable. It can be used only once but it lasts for hours.

Other hand warmers can be reused many times. These are based on the formation of crystals from solutions of a salt. The salt used is often sodium ethanoate. A supersaturated solution is prepared. We do this by dissolving as much of the salt as possible in hot water. The solution is then allowed to cool.

A small metal disc in the plastic pack is used to start the exothermic change. When you press this a few times small particles of metal are scraped off. These 'seed' (or start off) the crystallisation. The crystals spread throughout the solution, releasing energy in an exothermic change. They work for about 30 minutes.

To reuse the warmer, you simply put the solid pack into boiling water to re-dissolve the crystals. When cool, the pack is ready to activate again.

Exothermic reactions are also used in self-heating cans (see Figure 2). The reaction used to release the energy is usually:

$$\text{calcium oxide} + \text{water} \rightarrow \text{calcium hydroxide}$$

You press a button in the base of the can. This breaks a seal and lets the water and calcium oxide mix. Coffee is available in these self-heating cans.

Development took years and cost millions of pounds. Even then, over a third of the can was taken up with the reactants to release energy. Also, in some early versions, the temperature of the coffee did not rise high enough in cold conditions.

Figure 1 Here is a hand warmer based on the recrystallisation of sodium ethanoate

Activity

Hot food

Mountaineers and explorers can take 'self-heating' foods with them on their journeys. One example uses the energy released when calcium oxide reacts with water to heat the food.

Design a self-heating, disposable food container for stew.

- Draw a labelled diagram of your container and explain how it works.
- What are the safety issues involved in using your product?

Cooling down

Endothermic processes can be used to cool things down. For example, chemical cold packs usually contain ammonium nitrate and water. When ammonium nitrate dissolves it absorbs energy from its surroundings, making them colder. These cold packs are used as emergency treatment for sports injuries. The coldness reduces swelling and numbs pain.

The ammonium nitrate and water (sometimes present in a gel) are kept separate in the pack. When squeezed or struck the bag inside the water pack breaks releasing ammonium nitrate. The instant cold packs work for about 20 minutes.

They can only be used once but are ideal where there is no ice available to treat a knock or strain.

The same endothermic change can also be used to chill cans of drinks.

Figure 2 Development of this self-heating can in the USA took about 10 years

Figure 3 Instant cold packs can be applied as soon as an injury occurs to minimise damage

Summary questions

1 a Describe the chemical reaction which takes place in a disposable hand warmer.
  b Describe how a re-usable hand warmer works.
  c Give an advantage and a disadvantage of each type of hand warmer.
  d Name **one** use of an exothermic reaction in the food industry.

2 a Give **two** uses of endothermic changes.
  b Which endothermic change is often used in cold packs?
  c The solid used in cold packs is often ammonium nitrate.
    i Give the formula of ammonium nitrate.
    ii State another use of ammonium nitrate.

3 a Which solid is usually used in the base of self-heating coffee cans?
  b Write a balanced symbol equation, including state symbols, for the reaction of water with the solid in part **a**.
  c Why is it essential that the coffee stays out of contact with the solid in part **a**?

Key points

- Exothermic changes can be used in hand warmers and self-heating cans. Crystallisation of a supersaturated solution is used in reusable warmers. However, disposable, one-off warmers can give off heat for longer.

- Endothermic changes can be used in instant cold packs for sports injuries.

C12.3 Energy and reversible reactions

Learning objectives

After this topic, you should know:

- what happens in the energy transfers in reversible reactions.

Energy changes are involved in reversible reactions too. Let's consider an example.

Figure 1 shows a reversible reaction where A and B react to form C and D. The products of this reaction (C and D) can also react to form A and B again.

If the reaction **releases** energy when it goes in this direction ...

$$A+B \quad \rightleftharpoons \quad C+D$$

... it will **absorb** exactly the same amount of energy when it goes in this direction

Figure 1 A reversible reaction

If the reaction between A and B is exothermic, energy will be released when the reaction forms C and D.

If C and D then react to make A and B again, the reaction must be endothermic. What's more, it must absorb exactly the same amount of energy as it released when C and D were formed from A and B.

Energy cannot be created or destroyed in a chemical reaction. The amount of energy released when we go in one direction in a reversible reaction must be exactly the same as the energy absorbed when we go in the opposite direction.

We can see how this works if we look at what happens when we heat blue copper(II) sulfate crystals. The crystals contain water as part of the lattice formed when the copper(II) sulfate crystallised. We say that the copper sulfate is **hydrated**. Heating the copper(II) sulfate drives off the water from the crystals, producing white **anhydrous** ('without water') copper(II) sulfate. This is an endothermic reaction.

$$\begin{array}{ccc}
CuSO_4 \cdot 5H_2O & \rightleftharpoons & CuSO_4 & + 5H_2O \\
\text{hydrated} & & \text{anhydrous} & + \text{water} \\
\text{copper(II) sulfate (blue)} & & \text{copper(II) sulfate (white)} &
\end{array}$$

When we add water to anhydrous copper(II) sulfate we form hydrated copper(II) sulfate. The colour change in the reaction, from white to blue, is a useful test for the presence of water. The reaction in this direction is exothermic. In fact, so much energy may be produced that we may see steam rising as the water boils.

Figure 2 Hydrated copper(II) sulfate and white anhydrous copper(II) sulfate

Practical

Energy changes in a reversible reaction

Figure 3 Heating hydrated copper(II) sulfate

Gently heat a few copper(II) sulfate crystals in a test tube. Observe the changes. When the crystals are completely white allow the tube to cool to room temperature (this takes several minutes). Add two or three drops of water from a dropper and observe the changes. Carefully feel the bottom of the test tube.

● Explain the changes you have observed.

You can repeat this with the same solid, as it is a reversible reaction, or try with other hydrated crystals, such as cobalt(II) chloride. Some are not so colourful but the changes are similar.

Safety: Wear eye protection. Avoid skin contact with cobalt(II) chloride (toxic). Copper salts are harmful.

We can soak filter paper in cobalt(II) chloride solution and allow it to dry in an oven. The blue paper that is produced is called cobalt(II) chloride paper. The paper turns pale pink when water is added to the paper, and so can be used as an indicator for water.

Figure 4 Blue cobalt(II) chloride paper turns pink when water is added

Summary questions

1 a How does the enthalpy change for a reversible reaction in one direction compare with the energy change for the reaction in the opposite direction?
  b What can anhydrous copper(II) sulfate be used to test for?
  c Why does blue cobalt(II) chloride turn pink if left out in the open air?
  d When water is added to blue cobalt(II) chloride is energy released or absorbed?

2 A reversible reaction gives out 50 kilojoules (kJ) of energy in the forward reaction. In this reaction W and X react to give Y and Z.
  a Write an equation to show the reversible reaction.
  b What can you say about the energy transfer in the reverse reaction?

3 Blue cobalt(II) chloride crystals turn pink when they become damp. The formula for the two forms can be written as $CoCl_2.2H_2O$ and $CoCl_2.6H_2O$.
  a How many moles of water will combine with 1 mole of $CoCl_2.2H_2O$?
  b Write a balanced chemical equation for the reaction, which is reversible.
  c How can pink cobalt(II) chloride crystals be changed back to blue cobalt(II) chloride crystals?

Key points

● In reversible reactions, one reaction is exothermic and the other is endothermic.

● In any reversible reaction, the amount of energy released when the reaction goes in one direction is exactly equal to the energy absorbed when the reaction goes in the opposite direction.

Comparing the energy released by fuels

Learning objectives

After this topic, you should know:

- how to measure the energy released by different fuels
- the units of energy.

Figure 1 The energy released by fuels and foods when they burn can be compared using a simple calorimeter. The energy content of food is sometimes given in units called calories. However, the joule is the usual scientific unit of energy.

Thermometer

Metal can containing water (calorimeter)

Crisp

⚬⚬ links

For more information on exothermic reactions, look back at 12.1 'Exothermic and endothermic reactions'.

We have already seen that exothermic reactions release energy. When we burn a fuel, we use this energy to keep ourselves warm or we use it for transport.

Not all fuels release the same amount of energy when they burn. Some combustion reactions are more exothermic than others. It is often very important to know how much energy a fuel releases when it burns. In a school chemistry lab it is very difficult to measure accurately the energy released by fuels when they burn.

The actual amount of energy released by a burning fuel in an experiment is related to the rise in temperature of the water in a calorimeter (a glass or metal container). The larger the rise in temperature, the more energy has been released (see Figure 1).

🖩 *Maths skills*

Calculating the energy released

There is an equation we can use to work out the energy released, measured in joules (J):

$$\frac{\text{energy}}{\text{released}} = \frac{\text{mass of water}}{\text{heated}} \times \frac{\text{specific heat capacity}}{\text{of water}} \times \frac{\text{rise in}}{\text{temperature}}$$

This is sometimes written as:

$$Q = mc\,\Delta T$$

Where:

Q is the energy released by the fuel

m is the mass of water heated in the calorimeter (1 cm³ of water has a mass of 1 g)

c is the specific heat capacity of water (this is the amount of energy needed to raise 1 g of water by 1 °C)

ΔT is the rise in temperature (i.e. the final temperature of the water minus the initial temperature).

Here is an example of how to do the calculation:

Worked example

In an experiment, a burning fuel raised the temperature of 50 cm³ of water from 16 °C to 41 °C. How much energy was released by the fuel? (4.2 J of energy raises the temperature of 1 g of water by 1 °C)

Write down the data given:

Mass of water heated in the calorimeter = 50 g
Specific heat capacity of water = 4.2 J/g °C
Rise in temperature of the water = 41 °C − 16 °C = 25 °C

Now use the data in the $Q = mc\,\Delta T$ equation (which will always be provided for you in the exam):

$$Q = mc\,\Delta T$$
$$Q = 50 \times 4.2 \times 25\,\text{J}$$
$$Q = \textbf{5250 J (or 5.25 kJ)}$$

It is useful to be able to compare the energy content of different fuels. Their combustion data is given as the number of joules (or kilojoules) of energy released per gram or per mole of fuel burned.

In the previous experiment, the fuel was weighed before and after burning. It was found that the mass had decreased by 0.2 g. So the energy given out in the experiment will be multiplied by the number of 0.2 g there are in 1 g.

$$\text{energy released per gram} = 5.25 \times \frac{1}{0.2} \text{kJ/g}$$
$$= \textbf{26.25 kJ/g}$$

Suppose we know that the relative formula mass of the fuel is 46. We can now also work out the energy released per mole. One mole of the fuel has a mass of 46 g. So the energy given out in the experiment will be multiplied by the number of 0.2 g there are in 46 g:

$$\text{energy released per mole} = 5.25 \times \frac{46}{0.2} \text{kJ/mol}$$
$$= \textbf{1207.5 kJ/mol}$$

And as it is an exothermic reaction we can write:

$$\Delta H = \textbf{-1207.5 kJ/mol}$$

Examiner's tip

Measurements using simple calorimeters are not accurate because of energy losses, but they can be used to compare the amounts of energy released.

Summary questions

1 A simple calorimeter was used to compare the energy released by three different fuels. The results were as follows:

	Mass of fuel burned (g)	Volume of water (cm³)	Initial temperature (°C)	Final temperature (°C)
Fuel A	0.24	160	18.0	28.0
Fuel B	0.18	100	18.0	26.0
Fuel C	0.27	150	18.0	27.0

a Using the equation $Q = mc\Delta T$, calculate the energy released by each fuel in the three tests. (4.2 J of energy raises the temperature of 1 g of water by 1 °C.)

b Calculate the energy released per gram for each fuel.

c Arrange the fuels in order of the amount of energy they release per gram.

d The relative formula mass of Fuel A is 48, Fuel B is 42 and Fuel C is 58.
What is the energy released by Fuels A, B and C in kilojoules per mole (kJ/mol)?

e Now arrange the fuels in order of the amount of energy they release per mole.

f Comment on the accuracy of the figures for the amount of energy released per mole of fuel burned that were calculated in part d.

Key points

● When fuels and food react with oxygen, energy is released in an exothermic reaction. The unit of energy is the joule (but calories are still sometimes used for the energy content of foods).

● A simple calorimeter can be used to compare the energy released by different fuels or different foods in a school chemistry lab.

● We can use the equation $Q = mc\Delta T$ to calculate the amount of energy transferred from a burning fuel or food to the water in a calorimeter.

C12.5 Energy transfers in solutions

Learning objectives

After this topic, you should know:

- how to measure the energy change for a reaction that takes place in solution.

You can use a simple calorimeter to measure temperature changes in reactions involving solutions. A polystyrene cup and a thermometer can monitor reactions in solution.

The thermometer is used to measure the temperature change which takes place during the reaction.

The temperature change in reactions such as those when solids are added to aqueous solutions can be measured, e.g. in displacement or neutralisation reactions. The insulated cup reduces the rate of energy transfer to or from the surroundings.

Polystyrene cup

Figure 1 A simple calorimeter used to measure energy changes in solution. Polystyrene is a good thermal insulator, which helps to reduce energy transfer through the sides of the container during reactions. A lid on the calorimeter reduces energy transfer to the surroundings even further.

However, we have now seen how we can calculate actual energy changes using:

$$Q = mc\,\Delta T$$

In words:

$$\text{energy released} = \text{mass of water heated} \times \text{specific heat capacity of water} \times \text{change in temperature}$$

In these calculations we will assume that the solutions behave like water. So 1 cm³ of solution has a mass of 1 g. We also assume solutions have a specific heat capacity of 4.2 J/g °C. Therefore 4.2 J of energy raises the temperature of 1 g of solution by 1 °C. Look at the worked example opposite.

Examiner's tip

You do not have to learn the equation $Q = mc\,\Delta T$

In the exam this equation will be provided for you, but you should know how to use it.

Practical

Measuring energy changes in reactions

We can use a simple polystyrene calorimeter to work out the energy changes in the following:

- iron filings + copper sulfate solution (a displacement reaction)
- magnesium ribbon + dilute hydrochloric acid
- sodium hydroxide solution + dilute hydrochloric acid (a neutralisation reaction)
- dissolving potassium nitrate, anhydrous copper sulfate, and other salts in water.

Safety: Wear eye protection. Copper sulfate is harmful. Sodium hydroxide, if equal to or less than 0.4 m, is irritant. Potassium nitrate is oxidising. Dilute hydrochloric acid is an irritant.

Maths skills

Worked example

A simple calorimeter is used to measure the energy change in the reaction:

$$A + B \rightarrow C$$

$60\,cm^3$ of a solution containing 0.1 moles of A is mixed with $40\,cm^3$ of a solution containing 0.1 moles of B. The temperature of the two solutions before mixing is 19.6 °C. After mixing them, the maximum temperature reached is 26.1 °C.

Step 1 – calculate the temperature change:

$$\text{temperature change} = 26.1\,°C - 19.6\,°C$$
$$= 6.5\,°C$$

Step 2 – calculate the energy change:

$$Q = mc\,\Delta T$$

The mass of solution heated up in the reaction is $60\,g + 40\,g = 100\,g$

$$\text{energy change} = 100\,g \times 4.2\,J/g\,°C \times 6.5\,°C$$
$$= 2730\,J$$
$$= 2.73\,kJ$$

This is the energy change when 0.1 moles of reactants A and B are mixed. So when 1 mole of reactants are mixed there will be ten times as much energy released (1 mole is 10 × 0.1 moles)

$$= 2.73\,kJ \times 10$$
$$= 27.3\,kJ$$

So this experiment gives the energy change for the reaction:

$$A + B \rightarrow C$$

as 27.3 kJ/mol.

The temperature rises so the reaction is exothermic. Therefore:

$$\Delta H = -27.3\,kJ/mol$$

Summary questions

1 Why is polystyrene a good material for a simple calorimeter used for measuring temperature changes of reactions in solution?

2 A student added $25\,cm^3$ of dilute hydrochloric acid to $25\,cm^3$ of sodium hydroxide solution in a polystyrene calorimeter. She recorded a temperature rise of 5.5 °C. There were 0.050 moles of both the acid and the alkali used in the experiment.
   a Write a balanced symbol equation, including state symbols, for the reaction that takes place.
   b What do we call this type of reaction?
   c Calculate the concentration of the solutions used in this experiment in moles per decimetre cubed (mol/dm^3).
   d Using $Q = mc\,\Delta T$, work out the energy change in her experiment. (Specific heat capacity of the solution is $4.2\,J/g\,°C$.)
   e What would be the change in enthalpy, ΔH, for this reaction in kJ per mole?

Examiner's tip

The energy released by an exothermic reaction heats up the water (and its container). The temperature rise is proportional to the amount of energy released.

Figure 2 Here is the energy level diagram for the reaction A + B → C

∞ links

For more information on energy level diagrams, see 12.6 'Energy level diagrams'.

Key points

- We can calculate the energy change for reactions in solution by measuring the temperature change and using the equation:

$$Q = mc\,\Delta T$$

(The equation will be given in the exam.)

- Neutralisation and displacement reactions are both examples of reactions that we can use this technique for.

C12.6 Energy level diagrams

Learning objectives

After this topic, you should know:

- what energy level diagrams show us
- how catalysts affect the activation energy of a reaction
- the energy changes when bonds are broken
- the energy changes when bonds are made.

We can find out more about what is happening in a particular reaction by looking at its energy level diagram. These diagrams show us the relative amounts of energy contained in the reactants and the products. This energy is measured in kilojoules per mole (kJ/mol).

Exothermic reactions

Figure 1 shows the energy level diagram for an exothermic reaction. The products are at a lower energy level than the reactants. Therefore when the reactants form the products, energy is released.

Figure 1 The energy level diagram for an exothermic reaction

The difference between the energy levels of the reactants and the products is the energy change during the reaction, measured in kJ/mol.

The difference in energy between the products and the reactants is released to the surroundings. Therefore in exothermic reactions the temperature of the surroundings increases. The surroundings get hotter and we give the value of ΔH for the reaction a negative sign.

Endothermic reactions

Figure 2 shows the energy level diagram for an endothermic reaction.

Figure 2 The energy level diagram for an endothermic reaction

Here the products are at a higher energy level than the reactants. As the reactants react to form products, energy is absorbed from the surroundings. The temperature of the surroundings decreases because energy is taken in during the reaction. The surroundings get colder. The products are at a higher energy level than the reactants, and the value of ΔH for the reaction is given a positive sign.

links

For more information about the enthalpy change, ΔH, in chemical reactions, look back at 12.1 'Exothermic and endothermic reactions'.

Activation energy and catalysis

Think back to your work on rates of reaction in Chapter 8; you learned about the collision theory of reactions. This stated that there is a minimum amount of energy needed before colliding particles can react. This energy needed to start a reaction is called the activation energy. We can show this on our energy level diagrams. Look at Figure 3.

Catalysts can increase the rate of a reaction. The way they do this is to provide an alternative pathway to the products, which has a lower activation energy. This means that a higher proportion of reactant particles now have enough energy to react when they collide. This is shown on the energy level diagram in Figure 4.

Figure 3 The minimum amount of energy needed to start a reaction is called its activation energy

Bond breaking and bond making

Think about what happens as a chemical reaction takes place. We can think of the chemical bonds between the atoms or ions in the reactants being broken. Then new chemical bonds can be formed to make the products.

- Energy has to be supplied to break chemical bonds. This means that breaking bonds is an **endothermic** process. Energy is taken in from the surroundings.
- But, when new bonds are formed, energy is released. Making bonds is an **exothermic** process.

Figure 5 Hydrogen and oxygen react to make water. The bonds between hydrogen atoms and between oxygen atoms have to be broken so that bonds between oxygen atoms and hydrogen atoms in water can be formed.

Figure 4 A catalyst provides a different reaction pathway with a lower activation energy, so that a higher proportion of reactant particles have enough energy to react

Summary questions

1 Draw energy level diagrams for the following reactions:
   a $H_2(g) + Cl_2(g) \rightarrow 2HCl(g)$
      ΔH for the reaction is $-184\,kJ/mol$
   b $H_2(g) + I_2(g) \rightarrow 2HI(g)$
      ΔH for the reaction $+26.5\,kJ/mol$

2 a Draw an energy level diagram for an endothermic reaction, $X \rightarrow Y + Z$, including its activation energy.
   b Now show the effect of adding a catalyst on your energy level diagram drawn in part **a**.
   c Explain how a catalyst increases the rate of a reaction.

3 a Explain why bond breaking is an endothermic process.
   b Using a diagram like Figure 5 above, show the bonds being broken and new bonds made in the reaction between methane (CH_4) and oxygen which produces carbon dioxide and water.
   c List the number and type of each bond broken and formed in your answer to part **b**.

Key points

- We can show the relative difference in the energy of reactants and products on energy level diagrams.

- Catalysts lower the activation energy so a greater proportion of reactant particles have enough energy to react.

- Bond breaking is endothermic, whereas bond making is exothermic.

Bond dissociation energy calculations

Learning objectives

After this topic, you should know:

● how the balance between bonds breaking in the reactants and bond making in the products affect the overall energy change of a reaction

● how to use bond dissociation energies to calculate energy changes in reactions.

Making and breaking bonds

There is always a balance between the energy needed to break bonds and the energy released when new bonds are made in a reaction. This is what decides whether the reaction is endothermic or exothermic.

● In some reactions the energy released when new bonds are formed (as the products are made) is more than the energy needed to break the bonds in the reactants. These reactions transfer energy to the surroundings. They are **exothermic**.

● In other reactions the energy needed to break the bonds in the reactants is more than the energy released when new bonds are formed in the products. These reactions transfer energy from the surroundings to the reacting chemicals. They are **endothermic**.

Bond dissociation energy

The energy needed to break the bond between two atoms is called the **bond dissociation energy** for that bond.

Bond dissociation energies are measured in kJ/mol. We can use bond dissociation energies to work out the energy change (ΔH) for many chemical reactions. Before we can do this, we need to have a list of the most common bond dissociation energies:

Bond	Bond dissociation energy (kJ/mol)	Bond	Bond dissociation energy (kJ/mol)
C–C	347	H–Cl	432
C–O	358	H–O	464
C–H	413	H–N	391
C–N	286	H–H	436
C–Cl	346	O=O	498
Cl–Cl	243	N≡N	945

To calculate the energy change for a chemical reaction we need to work out:

1 how much energy is needed to break the chemical bonds in the reactants

2 how much energy is released when the new bonds are formed in the products.

It is very important to remember that the data in the table is the energy required for *breaking* bonds. When we want to know the energy released as these bonds are formed, the amount of energy is the same (see Figure 1).

For example, the bond dissociation energy for a C—C bond is +347 kJ/mol (an endothermic change). This means that the energy released *forming* a C—C bond is –347 kJ/mol (an exothermic change).

Bond breaking

H(g) + H(g)

436 kJ/mol of energy absorbed

H—H(g)

Bond making

H(g) + H(g)

436 kJ/mol of energy released

H—H(g)

Figure 1 Breaking and making a particular bond always involves the same amount of energy, but the change in enthalpy will have opposite signs (+ for bond breaking and – for bond making)

Maths skills

Worked example

Ammonia is made from nitrogen and hydrogen in the Haber process. The balanced symbol equation for this reaction is:

$$N_2(g) + 3H_2(g) \rightleftharpoons 2NH_3(g)$$

Calculate the overall energy change for the forward reaction using bond dissociation energies.

Solution

This equation tells us that we need to break the bonds in 1 mole of nitrogen molecules and 3 moles of hydrogen molecules in this reaction. Look at Figure 2:

Nitrogen molecules are held together by a triple bond (written like this: N≡N). This bond is very strong. Using data from the table, its bond energy is 945 kJ/mol.

Hydrogen molecules are held together by a single bond (written like this: H—H). From the table, the bond energy for this bond is 436 kJ/mol. The energy needed to break 1 mole of N≡N and 3 moles of H—H bonds = 945 + (3 × 436) kJ = **+2253 kJ** (given a plus sign as this is an endothermic process).

When these atoms form ammonia (NH_3), 6 new N—H bonds are made as 2 moles of NH_3 are formed (see Figure 3). The bond energy of the N—H bond is 391 kJ/mol.

Energy released when 6 moles of N—H bonds are made = 6 × 391 kJ = **−2346 kJ** (given a minus sign as this is an exothermic process).

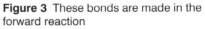

Figure 2 These bonds are broken in the forward reaction

Figure 3 These bonds are made in the forward reaction

Figure 4 shows the overall energy change for the forward reaction, as written.

So *the overall energy change*
= (+2253 kJ) + (−2346 kJ)
= **−93 kJ** (this is the energy *released* in the forward reaction as written above).

Figure 4 The formation of ammonia. The energy released, 93 kJ, is for the formation of 2 moles of ammonia as shown in the balanced equation. So if you wanted to know the energy change for the reaction per mole of ammonia formed, it would release exactly half this, i.e. 46.5 kJ/mol.

Key points

- In chemical reactions, energy must be supplied to break the bonds between atoms in the reactants.

- When new bonds are formed between atoms in a chemical reaction, energy is released.

- In an exothermic reaction, the energy released when new bonds are formed is greater than the energy absorbed when bonds are broken.

- In an endothermic reaction, the energy released when new bonds are formed is less than the energy absorbed when bonds are broken.

- We can calculate the overall energy change in a chemical reaction using bond energies.

Summary questions

1. If the energy required to break bonds is greater than the energy released when bonds are made, will the reaction be exothermic or endothermic?

2. What do we mean by the bond dissociation energy of a chemical bond?

3. Write balanced symbol equations and calculate the energy changes for the following chemical reactions:
   (Use the bond energies supplied in the table on the previous page.)
   a hydrogen + chlorine → hydrogen chloride
   b hydrogen + oxygen → water

Summary questions

1 Two solutions are mixed and react in an endothermic reaction. When the reaction has finished, the reaction mixture is allowed to stand until it has returned to its starting temperature.

a Sketch a graph of temperature (*y*-axis) against time (*x*-axis) to show how the temperature of the reaction mixture changes.

b Label the graph clearly and explain what is happening wherever you have shown that the temperature is changing.

c In the experiment 15 cm³ of one solution was mixed with 25 cm³ of the other solution, and once mixed the temperature fell from 18 °C to 15 °C. Use $Q = mc\Delta T$, where $c = 4.2$ J/g°C (i.e. 4.2 J of energy raises the temperature of 1 g of water by 1 °C), to calculate the energy absorbed in the experiment.

2 a Draw an energy level diagram to show the exothermic reaction between nitric acid and sodium hydroxide, including its activation energy.

b Draw an energy level diagram to show the endothermic change when ammonium nitrate dissolves in water, including its activation energy.

c Show an energy level diagram, including its activation energy, for the exothermic breakdown of hydrogen peroxide into water and oxygen. Then add to your diagram to show what happens when the same reaction is catalysed by manganese(IV) oxide.

3 When we eat sugar we break it down eventually to produce water and carbon dioxide.

a Complete the balanced symbol equation:

$$C_{12}H_{22}O_{11} + O_2 \rightarrow$$

b Why must your body *supply* energy in order to break down a sugar molecule?

c When we break down sugar in our bodies, energy is released. Explain where this energy comes from in terms of the bonds in molecules.

d We can get about 1700 kJ of energy by breaking down 100 g of sugar.
If a heaped teaspoon contains 5 g of sugar, how much energy does this release when broken down by your body?

4 Hydrogen peroxide has the structure H—O—O—H. It decomposes slowly to form water and oxygen.

$$2H_2O_2(aq) \rightarrow 2H_2O(l) + O_2(g)$$

The table shows the bond dissociation energies for different types of bond.

Bond	Bond dissociation energy (kJ/mol)
H—O	464
H—H	436
O—O	144
O=O	498

a Use the bond dissociation energies to calculate the enthalpy change, ΔH, for the decomposition of hydrogen peroxide as shown above.

b Explain the sign (+ or −) in your answer to part **a** in terms of bond breaking and making.

5 Bomb calorimeters are used in research laboratories to calculate the energy in food.

As you can see from this diagram, it is sealed and has its own supply of oxygen. There is a supply of electricity to produce a spark that will ignite the food. The increase in temperature of the water around the bomb is measured.

a Using a bomb calorimeter, a food scientist burned a sample of a sugar. There were 250 cm³ of water in the calorimeter and its temperature went from 18 °C to 44 °C.
Use $Q = mc\Delta T$, where $c = 4.2$ J/g°C (i.e. 4.2 J of energy raises the temperature of 1 g of water by 1 °C), to calculate the energy released by the burning sugar.

b The scientists burned 0.01 moles of the sugar in the bomb calorimeter. How much energy does this sugar release in kJ per mole?

AQA Examination-style questions

1 Most chemical reactions are exothermic. Some are endothermic.

Some equations are shown with a ΔH value.

a i What is the difference between these types of reaction? (2)

ii What is the meaning of ΔH? (1)

iii How can you decide from the ΔH value whether a reaction is exothermic or endothermic? (1)

b The progress of a reaction can be represented on an energy level diagram.

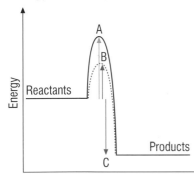

The diagram represents a reaction that can be done with or without a catalyst.

i How can you decide from this diagram that the reaction is exothermic? (1)

ii What name is used for the energies represented by arrows A and B? (1)

iii Why is arrow B shorter than arrow A? (1)

iv What is the enthalpy change for the reaction? (1)

c The following equation represents a reversible reaction.

$A + B \rightleftharpoons C + D \qquad \Delta H = + 31\,kJ/mole$

What is the value of ΔH for the following reaction?

$C + D \rightleftharpoons A + B$ (1)

2 Some students investigated the energy released when a liquid fuel burns.

They used the following apparatus.

100 g of water

HEAT

They obtained these results.

Student	Mass of fuel burned in grams	Start temperature of water in °C	End temperature of water in °C
1	0.32	16.5	29.0
2	0.38	17.0	32.0
3	0.35	18.0	32.5

a i What temperature rise did student 1 obtain? (1)

ii Which student obtained the biggest increase in temperature? (1)

b The amount of heat produced can be calculated using this expression:

$$\text{heat} = \text{mass of water} \times \text{specific heat capacity of water} \times \text{temperature rise}$$

i Use this expression to calculate the heat, in joules, produced in student 3's experiment. Assume that it takes 4.18 J to raise the temperature of 1 g of water by 1 °C. (3)

ii Another student used the same apparatus and obtained a value of 6200 J by burning 0.40 g of fuel.

Calculate the heat produced in kJ/gram. (3)

c Why is the calculated value of heat produced in these experiments much less than the true value? (1)

3 The energy change in a reaction can be calculated using values of bond energy. The combustion of methane can be represented as follows:

$$\underset{\underset{H}{|}}{\overset{\overset{H}{|}}{H-C-H}} + 2\,O{=}O \longrightarrow O{=}C{=}O + 2\,H-O-H$$

Use bond energy values from the table in the calculation.

Bond	Bond energy in kJ/mole	Bond	Bond energy in kJ/mole
C–H	412	C=O	743
O=O	496	H–O	463

a Calculate the energy needed to break the bonds in the reactants. (2)

b Calculate the energy given out when the bonds in the products are formed. (2)

c What is the enthalpy change for the combustion of methane? (1)

C13.1 Chemical equilibrium

Some reactions are reversible. The products formed can react together to make the original reactants again:

$$A + B \rightleftharpoons C + D$$

So what happens when we start with just reactants in a reversible reaction?

1) A+B ⟶   Reactants only at start of reaction

2) A+B ⇌ C+D   Rate of ⟶ much greater than ⟵ at first

3) A+B ⇌ C+D   Rate of ⟵ increases as C+D build up. Rate of ⟶ slows down as reactants get used up

4) A+B ⇌ C+D   Eventually the rates of ⟶ and ⟵ are the same

In a **closed system**, no reactants, products or energy can get in or out. So in a reversible reaction, as the concentration of products builds up, the rate at which they react to re-form reactants increases. As this starts to happen, the rate of the forward reaction is decreasing. That's because the concentration of reactants is decreasing from its original maximum value. Eventually both forward and reverse reactions are going at the same rate, but in opposite directions.

⌷⌷ links

For more information on reversible reactions, look back at 2.5 'Reversible reactions'.

When this happens the reactants are making products at the same rate as the products are making reactants. Overall, there is **no change** in the amount of products and reactants. We say that the reaction has reached **equilibrium**.

At equilibrium, the rate of the forward reaction equals the rate of the reverse reaction. As the forward and reverse reactions are continuously taking place, we sometimes say that there is a state of 'dynamic' equilibrium.

Figure 2 The situation at equilibrium is just like running *up* an escalator which is going down – if you run up as fast as the escalator goes *down*, you will get **nowhere**!

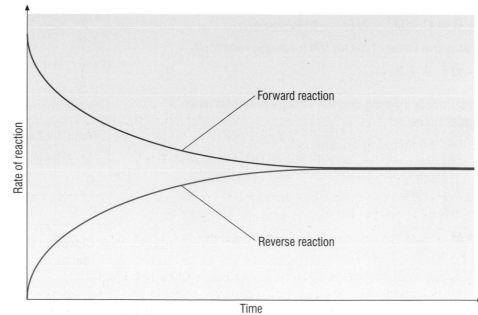

Figure 1 In a reversible reaction at equilibrium, the rate of the forward reaction is the same as the rate of the reverse reaction

One example of a reversible reaction is the reaction between iodine monochloride (ICl) and chlorine gas. Iodine monochloride is a brown liquid, while chlorine is a yellowish green gas. We can react these substances together to make yellow crystals of iodine trichloride (ICl_3).

When there is plenty of chlorine gas the forward reaction makes iodine trichloride crystals, which are quite stable. But, if we lower the concentration of chlorine gas the rate of the forward reaction decreases. The reverse reaction becomes the faster of the two reactions. This starts turning more iodine trichloride back to iodine monochloride and chlorine, until equilibrium is established again.

We can change the relative amounts of the reactants and products in a reacting mixture by changing the conditions. This is very important in the chemical industry. In a process with a reversible reaction, we need conditions that give as much product as possible.

However, there are always other economic and safety factors to consider when chemists manipulate reversible reactions in industry.

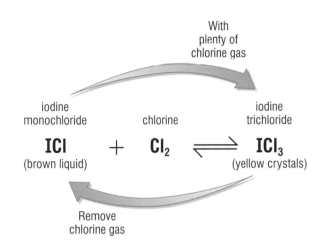

Figure 3 This reacting mixture can be changed by adding or removing chlorine from the mixture

⊂⊃ **links**

For more information about economic and safety issues associated with reversible reactions in industry, see 13.3 'Making ammonia – the Haber process' and 13.4 'The economics of the Haber process'.

Summary questions

1 How does the rate of the reverse reaction compare with the rate of the forward reaction in a reaction at equilibrium?

2 What can we say about the concentration of reactants and products in a reversible reaction at equilibrium?

3 Explain why chemists describe chemical equilibrium as 'dynamic' as opposed to 'static'.

4 An equilibrium mixture is set up in a closed system with iodine monochloride, chlorine gas and iodine trichloride. In order to make more iodine trichloride, would you pump more chlorine gas into the mixture or remove chlorine gas? Explain your answer.

Key points

- In a reversible reaction the products of the reaction can react to re-form the original reactants.

- In a closed system, the rate of the forward and reverse reactions are equal at equilibrium.

- Changing the reaction conditions can change the amounts of products and reactants in a reaction mixture at equilibrium.

C13.2 Altering conditions

Learning objectives

After this topic, you should know:

- how changing the pressure affects reversible reactions involving gases

- how changing the temperature affects reversible reactions.

∞ **links**

For information on the effect of concentration on a reversible reaction, look back at 13.1 'Chemical equilibrium'.

Pressure and equilibrium

We have seen how changing concentration can affect a reversible reaction at equilibrium. In general, we find that the position of equilibrium shifts as if trying to cancel out any change in conditions. Think about increasing the concentration of a reactant. This will cause the position of equilibrium to shift to the right, in favour of the products, in order to reduce the concentration of that reactant. It opposes the change we introduce.

If a reversible reaction involves changing numbers of gas molecules, altering the pressure can also affect the equilibrium mixture. In many reversible reactions, there are more molecules of gas on one side of the equation than on the other. By changing the pressure at which we carry out these reactions, we can change the amount of products that are made. Look at the table below:

If the forward reaction produces *more* molecules of gas …	If the forward reaction produces *fewer* molecules of gas …
… an increase in pressure decreases the amount of products formed.	… an increase in pressure increases the amount of products formed.
… a decrease in pressure increases the amount of products formed.	… a decrease in pressure decreases the amount of products formed.

We can show this in the following reversible reaction:

$$2NO_2(g) \rightleftharpoons N_2O_4(g)$$
$$\text{brown gas} \quad \text{pale yellow gas}$$

In this reaction we can see from the balanced symbol equation that we have:

2 molecules of gas on the left-hand side of the equilibrium equation and
1 molecule of gas on the right-hand side.

Imagine that we increase the pressure in the reaction vessel. The position of equilibrium will shift to reduce the pressure. It will move in favour of the reaction that produces fewer gas molecules. In this case that is to the right, in favour of the forward reaction. So more N_2O_4 gas will be made. The colour of the gaseous mixture will get lighter.

Figure 1 The effect of changing the pressure on $2NO_2(g) \rightleftharpoons N_2O_4(g)$

> ### Examiner's tip
>
> Changing the pressure affects the equilibrium only if there are different numbers of molecules of gases on each side of the balanced equation.

∞ **links**

For information on how changes in pressure are useful in industry, look at 13.3 'Making ammonia – the Haber process' and 13.4 'The economics of the Haber process'.

Energy and equilibrium

When we have a closed system, nothing is added or taken away from the reaction mixture. In a closed system, the relative amounts of the reactants and products in a reversible reaction at equilibrium depend on the temperature.

By changing the temperature, we can plan to get more of the products and less of the reactants. Look at the table below:

If the forward reaction is exothermic …	If the forward reaction is endothermic …
… an increase in temperature decreases the amount of products formed.	… an increase in temperature increases the amount of products formed.
… a decrease in temperature increases the amount of products formed.	… a decrease in temperature decreases the amount of products formed.

We can show this by looking at the reaction involving $NO_2(g)$ and $N_2O_4(g)$ again.

$$2NO_2(g) \rightleftharpoons N_2O_4(g)$$

The forward reaction is exothermic, releasing energy, so the reverse reaction is endothermic, absorbing the same amount of energy.

If we increase the temperature, the equilibrium shifts as if to try to reduce the temperature. The reaction that is endothermic (taking in energy) will cool it down. So in this case the reverse reaction is favoured and more NO_2 is formed.

More NO_2 formed   Heat up $2\ NO_2(g) \rightleftharpoons N_2O_4(g)$ Cool down   More N_2O_4 formed

(Favours endothermic reaction)   (Favours exothermic reaction)

Figure 3 The effect of changing the temperature on $2NO_2(g) \rightleftharpoons N_2O_4(g)$

Summary questions

1 How does increasing the pressure affect the amount of products formed in a reaction that produces a larger volume (more molecules) of gas?

2 Look at the reversible reaction below:

$$H_2O(g) + C(s) \rightleftharpoons CO(g) + H_2(g)$$

The forward reaction is endothermic.
How will the amount of hydrogen gas formed change by increasing the temperature?

3 a Look at Figure 1. How will increasing the pressure affect the colour of a mixture of NO_2 and N_2O_4 gases? Explain your answer.
   b Look at Figure 3 above. What will happen to the colour of a mixture of NO_2 and N_2O_4 gases if we increase the temperature? Explain your answer.

4 Explain what effect increasing the pressure would have on the equilibrium mixture below:

$$H_2(g) + I_2(g) \rightleftharpoons 2HI(g)$$

Exothermic

$2NO_2(g) \rightleftharpoons N_2O_4(g)$

Endothermic

Figure 2 Energy changes in the reversible reaction $2NO_2(g) \rightleftharpoons N_2O_4(g)$

Demonstration

The effect of temperature and pressure on equilibrium

Using a gas syringe, your teacher can show an equilibrium mixture of NO_2 and N_2O_4 gases.

You can see the effect of changing temperature by using warm water and ice.

Pushing and pulling the plunger of the syringe can change the pressure.

● Explain your observations.

Safety: take care if you are asthmatic. The teacher should be wearing chemical splash proof eye protection as gases are 'very toxic'.

Key points

● Pressure can affect reversible reactions involving gases at equilibrium. Increasing the pressure favours the reaction that forms fewer molecules of gas. Decreasing the pressure favours the reaction with the greater number of molecules of gas formed.

● We can change the relative amount of products formed at equilibrium by changing the temperature at which we carry out a reversible reaction.

● Increasing the temperature favours the endothermic reaction. Decreasing the temperature favours the exothermic reaction.

C13.3

Making ammonia – the Haber process

Learning objectives

After this topic, you should know:

- why ammonia is an important product
- how ammonia is manufactured in industry
- how ammonia is made without wasting raw materials.

We need plants for food, and as a way of maintaining oxygen in the air. Plants need nitrogen to grow. Although nitrogen gas makes up nearly 80 per cent of the air, most plants cannot use it directly.

Instead, plants absorb soluble nitrates from the soil through their roots. When we harvest crops the nitrogen in plants is lost. That's because the plants do not die and decompose to replace the nitrogen in the soil. So farmers need to put nitrogen back into the soil for the next year's crops.

Nowadays we usually do this by adding nitrate fertilisers to the soil. We make these fertilisers using a process devised by a German chemist called Fritz Haber.

Figure 1 Plants are surrounded by nitrogen in the air. They cannot use this nitrogen, and rely on soluble nitrates in the soil instead. We supply these by spreading fertiliser on the soil.

The Haber process

The Haber process provides a way of turning nitrogen in the air into ammonia. We can use ammonia in many different ways. The most important of these is to make fertilisers.

The raw materials for the production of ammonia are:
- nitrogen from the air
- hydrogen, which we get mainly from natural gas (which contains methane, CH_4).

The nitrogen and hydrogen are purified. Then they are passed over an iron catalyst at a high temperature (about 450 °C) and a high pressure (about 200 atmospheres). The product of this reversible reaction is ammonia.

- The reaction used in the Haber process is reversible. This means that the ammonia made breaks down again into nitrogen and hydrogen.
- We remove the ammonia by cooling the gases so that the ammonia liquefies. It can then be separated from the unreacted nitrogen gas and hydrogen gas.

① Gas stream containing hydrogen and nitrogen

③ Reaction vessel containing iron catalyst

⑤ Unreacted nitrogen and hydrogen are returned to the reaction vessel via the compressor

Cooling chamber

② The nitrogen/hydrogen mixture is compressed to a pressure of 200 atm and heated to 450 °C

④ The mixture of gases emerging from the reactor is cooled. Ammonia liquefies and is separated.

Figure 2 The Haber process

- The unreacted nitrogen and hydrogen gases are recycled back into the reaction mixture. They are then re-compressed and heated before returning to the reaction vessel. There they have a chance to react again on the surface of the iron catalyst.

$$N_2(g) + 3H_2(g) \underset{\text{catalyst}}{\overset{\text{iron}}{\rightleftharpoons}} 2NH_3(g)$$

We carry out the Haber process in carefully chosen conditions to give a reasonable yield of ammonia as quickly as possible.

 links

For more information about the choice of conditions, see 13.4 'The economics of the Haber process'.

⁇ Did you know ... ?

Fritz Haber's work on the Haber process took place just before the First World War. When the war started, he was involved in the first chemical weapons used in warfare. His wife, also a chemist, opposed his work on chemical weapons. She committed suicide before the war ended.

Summary questions

1 What are the main raw materials used to get the nitrogen gas and hydrogen gas needed for the production of ammonia in industry?

2 a Write a balanced symbol equation, including state symbols, for the production of ammonia in the Haber process.
  b State the conditions chosen for the Haber process, including the catalyst used.

3 a How is ammonia separated from the reaction mixture in the Haber process?
  b What happens to unreacted nitrogen and hydrogen that leaves the reaction vessel?

4 Draw a flowchart to show how the Haber process is used to make ammonia.

Key points

- Ammonia is an important chemical for making other products, including fertilisers.

- Ammonia is made from nitrogen and hydrogen in the Haber process.

- We carry out the Haber process under conditions of about 450 °C and 200 atmospheres pressure, using an iron catalyst.

- Any unreacted nitrogen and hydrogen are recycled back into the reaction vessel in the Haber process.

The economics of the Haber process

Learning objectives

After this topic, you should know:

- why a pressure of about 200 atmospheres is chosen for the Haber process

- why a temperature of about 450 °C is chosen for the Haber process.

The effect of pressure

We have just seen how ammonia is made in the Haber process. Nitrogen and hydrogen react to make ammonia in a reversible reaction:

$$N_2(g) + 3H_2(g) \rightleftharpoons 2NH_3(g)$$

As the balanced equation above shows, there are four molecules of gas on the left-hand side of the equation (N_2 and $3H_2$), but on the right-hand side there are only two molecules of gas ($2NH_3$). This means that the volume of the reactants is greater than the volume of the products. So, an increase in pressure will tend to shift the position of equilibrium to the right, producing more ammonia.

To get the maximum possible yield of ammonia, we need to make the pressure as high as possible. But very high pressures need lots of energy to compress the gases. Very high pressures also need expensive reaction vessels and pipes. They have to be strong enough to withstand very high pressures, otherwise there is always the danger of an explosion. To avoid the higher costs of building a stronger chemical plant, the Haber process uses a pressure of 200 atmospheres. This is a good compromise. This pressure gives a lower yield than it would with even higher pressures but it does reduce the expense and helps produce a reasonable rate of reaction between the gases.

Figure 1 It is very expensive to build chemical plants that operate at very high pressures

The effect of temperature

The effect of temperature on the Haber process is more complicated than the effect of pressure. The forward reaction is exothermic:

$$N_2(g) + 3H_2(g) \rightleftharpoons 2NH_3(g) \quad \Delta H = -93\,kJ = -46.5\,kJ/mol$$

So lowering the temperature would increase the amount of ammonia in the reaction mixture at equilibrium. This happens because the forward reaction to form ammonia releases energy to the surroundings and raises the temperature of the surroundings.

However, at a low temperature, the rate of the reaction would be very slow because the gas molecules would collide less often and less energetically. To make ammonia commercially we must get the reaction to go quickly. We don't want to waste time waiting for the ammonia to be produced.

This is achieved in the Haber process by another compromise. A reasonably high temperature is used to get the reaction going at a reasonable rate, even though this reduces the yield of ammonia. Look at the graph in Figure 2.

Figure 2 The conditions for the Haber process are a compromise between getting a reasonable yield of ammonia and getting the reaction to take place at a fast enough rate

A lower temperature can also reduce the effectiveness of the iron catalyst.

The effect of a catalyst

We also use an iron catalyst to speed up the reaction. A catalyst speeds up the rate of both the forward and reverse reactions by the same amount. Therefore it does not affect the actual yield of ammonia but we do get ammonia produced more quickly, which is an important economic consideration in industry.

Summary questions

1 Explain the effect of increasing the pressure in the Haber process on:
   i the yield of ammonia from the reversible reaction
   ii the rate of production of ammonia.

2 Why is an iron catalyst used in the Haber process?

3 Look at Figure 2.
   a What is the approximate yield of ammonia at a temperature of 500 °C and 400 atmospheres pressure?
   b What is the approximate yield of ammonia at a temperature of 500 °C and 100 atmospheres pressure?
   c What is the approximate yield of ammonia at a temperature of 200 °C and 400 atmospheres pressure?
   d What is the approximate yield of ammonia at a temperature of 200 °C and 100 atmospheres pressure?
   e Given your answers to parts **a**–**d**, explain why the Haber process is carried out at around 200 atmospheres and 450 °C.

Summary questions

1 Here is an example of a reaction mixture in a state of dynamic equilibrium:

$$ICl(l) + Cl_2(g) \rightleftharpoons ICl_3(s)$$
brown liquid   yellow/green gas   yellow solid

The equilibrium can be set up in a glass U-tube:

ICl(l)
Cl₂(g)
ICl₃(s)

a The equilibrium mixture contains the three states of matter. What does this statement mean?

b The pressure inside the U-tube is increased. What happens to the equilibrium mixture? Explain your answer.

c What would happen to the equilibrium mixture if the chlorine gas was allowed to escape? Explain your answer.

2 A chemical reaction can make product C from reactants A and B. Under the reaction conditions, A, B and C are all gases.
A, B and C react in the proportions 1:1:2. The reaction is carried out at 250 °C and 100 atmospheres. The reaction is reversible, and it is endothermic in the forward direction.

a Write a balanced symbol equation, including state symbols, for this reversible reaction.

b How would increasing the pressure affect:
  i the amount of C formed
  ii the rate at which C is formed?

c How would increasing the temperature affect:
  i the amount of C formed
  ii the rate at which C is formed?

3 In the manufacture of sulfuric acid, sulfur dioxide is oxidised to form sulfur trioxide:

$$2SO_2(g) + O_2(g) \rightleftharpoons 2SO_3(g)$$

This reversible reaction is exothermic from left to right. State and explain the effect of each of the following conditions on the rate and yield of this reaction.

a increase in temperature

b increase in pressure

c use of a catalyst.

4 When nitric acid is made in industry, ammonia is oxidised to nitrogen monoxide.

$$4NH_3(g) + 5O_2(g) \rightleftharpoons 4NO(g) + 6H_2O(g)$$

The reaction is exothermic in the forward direction. Ammonia and air, at about 7 atmospheres pressure, is passed over a platinum catalyst at 900 °C.
Explain how changing the conditions used could increase the yield of nitrogen monoxide.

5 The table below gives data on the yield of ammonia at equilibrium in the reversible reaction with nitrogen and hydrogen:

	Ammonia present at equilibrium (%)				
Pressure (atmospheres)	Temperature (°C)				
	100	200	300	400	500
10	88	51	15	4	1
25	92	64	27	9	3
50	94	74	39	15	6
100	97	82	52	25	11
200	98	89	67	39	18
400	99	95	80	55	32
1000	99.9	98	93	80	57

a i What is the effect of increasing the pressure on the yield of ammonia?
  ii What is the effect of increasing the temperature on the yield of ammonia?
  iii Explain how you used the table to judge the effect of changing the temperature and the pressure on the yield of ammonia.

b Explain why the conditions in the Haber process (200 atmospheres pressure and a temperature of 450 °C) are described as a 'compromise'.

c How does the use of an iron catalyst affect the yield of ammonia?

6 Here is the equation for the reaction used in the Haber process:

$$N_2(g) + 3H_2(g) \underset{\text{catalyst}}{\overset{\text{Fe(s)}}{\rightleftharpoons}} 2NH_3(g) \quad \Delta H = -92\,kJ/mol$$

Draw an energy level diagram for this reaction, showing the reaction pathway with and without the use of the iron catalyst.

AQA Examination-style questions

1 If a reversible reaction occurs in a closed container it can reach equilibrium.

  a State two features of a reversible reaction that has reached equilibrium. (2)

  b A gaseous oxide of nitrogen has the formula N_2O_4. It decomposes into another gaseous oxide of nitrogen when it is heated without changing the pressure. This decomposition is endothermic. The progress of this reaction can be checked using the differences in colour.

$$N_2O_4(g) \rightleftharpoons 2NO_2(g)$$
pale yellow   brown

    i How does the colour of the reaction mixture change when the temperature increases? (1)

    ii Explain how the information in the question helps to predict the colour change. (2)

  c A mixture of the two oxides of nitrogen is placed in a gas syringe and the pressure is increased.

    Predict what happens to the colour of the mixture. Explain your answer by reference to the equation in **b**. (3)

2 Ammonia is manufactured by the Haber process. This process is shown in the flow diagram.

  a **i** What is the source of the nitrogen? (1)
    ii What is the source of the hydrogen? (1)

  b State three conditions used in the reactor. (3)

  c What substances are represented by X in the diagram? (1)

  d What condition is used in the separator? (1)

  e Write a symbol equation for the reaction that occurs in the reactor. (2)

3 A company builds a new factory to produce ammonia.

The new factory uses the same process as the old factory but with these changes in conditions:
    the temperature is decreased by 100 °C in the new factory
    the pressure is increased by 100 atmospheres in the new factory

  a Predict how each change affects the yield of ammonia in this reaction in the new factory. Explain your answers. (6)

  b How does the catalyst affect the rate of reaction? (1)

  c Why does the catalyst not affect the yield of the reaction? (2)

C14.1 Electrolysis

Figure 1 The first person to explain electrolysis was Michael Faraday. He worked on this and many other problems in science nearly 200 years ago.

The word electrolysis means 'breaking down using electricity'. In electrolysis we use an electric current to break down an ionic substance. We call the substance that is broken down by electrolysis the **electrolyte**.

To set up an electrical circuit for electrolysis, we have two electrodes which dip into the electrolyte. The electrodes are conducting rods. One of these is connected to the positive terminal of a power supply. This positive electrode is called the **anode**. The other electrode is connected to the negative terminal and is called the **cathode**.

The electrodes are often made of an unreactive (or **inert**) substance. This is often graphite or sometimes platinum. This is so the electrodes do not react with the electrolyte or the products made in electrolysis.

During electrolysis, positively charged ions move to the cathode (negative electrode). At the same time, the negative ions move to the anode (positive electrode).

When the ions reach the electrodes they lose their charge and become elements. Gases may be given off or metals deposited at the electrodes. This depends on the compound used and whether it is molten or dissolved in water.

Demonstration

The electrolysis of molten lead bromide

- This demonstration needs a fume cupboard because bromine is toxic and corrosive.

- When does the bulb light up?

- What is observed at each electrode?

Figure 2 Passing electricity through molten lead bromide. It forms molten lead and brown bromine gas as the electrolyte is broken down by the electricity.

Safety: Warn asthmatics. Wear chemical splash proof eye protection. Lead bromide and bromine are toxic.

Figure 2 above shows how electricity breaks down lead bromide into lead and bromine:

$$\text{lead bromide} \rightarrow \text{lead} + \text{bromine}$$
$$PbBr_2(l) \rightarrow Pb(l) + Br_2(g)$$

Lead bromide is an ionic substance. Ionic substances do not conduct electricity when they are solid as their ions are in fixed positions in their giant lattice. But once we melt them, the ions are free to move around within the liquid and carry their charge towards the electrodes.

The positive lead ions (Pb^{2+}) move towards the cathode (negative electrode). At the same time, the negatively charged bromide ions (Br^-) move towards the anode (positive electrode).

Notice the state symbols in the equation. They tell us that the lead bromide and the lead are molten at the temperature in the dish. The bromine is given off as a gas.

Electrolysis of solutions

Many ionic substances have very high melting points so it takes a lot of energy to melt them and free the ions to move to electrodes in electrolysis. However, some ionic substances dissolve in water and when this happens, the ions also become free to move around.

When electrolysing ionic compounds in solution, and not as molten compounds, it is more difficult to predict what will be formed. This is because water also forms ions so the products at each electrode are not always exactly what we expect (see 14.2 'Changes at the electrodes'). Only metal of very low reactivity, below hydrogen in the reactivity series, are deposited from their aqueous solutions in electrolysis.

When we electrolyse an aqueous solution of copper(II) bromide, copper ions (Cu^{2+}) move to the cathode (negative electrode). The bromide ions (Br^-) move to the anode (positive electrode). Copper(II) bromide is split into its elements at the electrodes (see Figure 3):

$$\text{copper(II) bromide} \rightarrow \text{copper} + \text{bromine}$$
$$CuBr_2(aq) \rightarrow Cu(s) + Br_2(aq)$$

The state symbols in the equation tell us that the copper bromide is dissolved in water, the copper is formed as a solid, and the bromine formed dissolves in the water.

Covalent compounds cannot usually be electrolysed unless they react (or ionise) in water to form ions. For example, acids in water always contain $H^+(aq)$ ions plus negatively charged aqueous ions.

⚭ links

Remind yourself of the relative reactivity of metals and hydrogen in 7.1 'The reactivity series' and 7.2 'Displacement reactions'.

⚭ links

For more information about the effect of water in electrolysis, see 14.2 'Changes at the electrodes' and 14.4 'Electrolysis of brine'.

Bromine   Copper

Copper bromide solution

Figure 3 If we dissolve copper bromide in water, we can decompose it by electrolysis. Copper metal is formed at the cathode (negative electrode). Brown bromine appears in solution around the anode (positive electrode).

Summary questions

1 **a** What is electrolysis?
   b What do we call the substance broken down by electrolysis?
   c What type of bonding is present in compounds that can be electrolysed?

2 Predict the products formed at the cathode and anode when the following compounds are melted and then electrolysed:
   a zinc iodide   **d** sodium oxide
   b lithium bromide   **e** potassium chloride.
   c iron(III) fluoride

3 Write a balanced symbol equation, including state symbols, for the electrolytic decomposition of molten sodium chloride.

4 **a** Which of the following solutions would deposit a metal at the cathode during electrolysis?

   KBr(aq), CaCl₂(aq), FeBr₂(aq), CuCl₂(aq), Na₂SO₄(aq), AgNO₃(aq)

   b How did you decide on your answer to part **a**?

5 Solid ionic substances do not conduct electricity. Using words and diagrams explain why they conduct electricity when molten, or in aqueous solution, but not when solid.

Key points

- Electrolysis breaks down a substance using electricity.

- Ionic compounds can only be electrolysed when they are molten or dissolved in water. That's because their ions are then free to move and carry their charge to the electrodes.

- In electrolysis, positive ions move to the cathode (negative electrode) while negative ions move to the anode (positive electrode).

C14.2

Changes at the electrodes

Learning objectives

After this topic, you should know:

- what happens to the ions during electrolysis
- how we can represent what happens at each electrode
- how water affects the products of electrolysis.

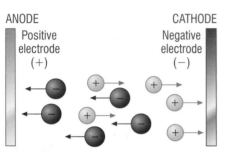

Figure 1 An ion always moves towards the oppositely charged electrode

links

For more information on reduction and oxidation in terms of electron transfer, look back to 7.2 'Displacement reactions'.

Examiner's tip

Oxidation and reduction reactions don't have to involve oxygen. More generally they involve the transfer of electrons. Remember **OILRIG** – **O**xidation **I**s **L**oss (of electrons), **R**eduction **I**s **G**ain (of electrons).

During electrolysis, mobile ions move towards the electrodes. The direction they move in depends on their charge. As we saw in 14.1, positive ions move towards the cathode (negative electrode). Negative ions move towards the anode (positive electrode).

When ions reach an electrode, they either lose or gain electrons, depending on their charge.

Negatively charged ions *lose* electrons to become neutral atoms. Positively charged ions *gain* electrons to become neutral atoms.

The easiest way to think about this is to look at an example.

Think back to the electrolysis of molten lead bromide. The lead ions (Pb^{2+}) move towards the negative electrode. When they get there, each ion gains two electrons to become a neutral lead atom.

Gaining electrons is called **reduction**. We say that the lead ions are **reduced**. 'Reduction' is simply another way of saying 'gaining electrons'.

The negatively charged bromide ions (Br^-) move towards the positive electrode. Once there, each ion loses its one extra electron to become a neutral bromine atom. Two bromine atoms then form a covalent bond to make a bromine molecule, Br_2.

Losing electrons is called **oxidation**. We say that the bromide ions are **oxidised**. 'Oxidation' is another way of saying 'losing electrons'.

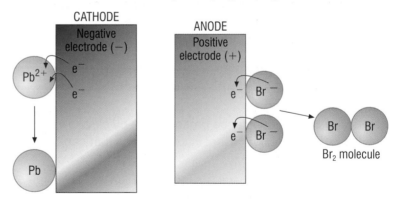

Half equations

We represent what is happening at each electrode using **half equations**.

At the cathode (negative electrode) we get reduction of a positive ion:

$$Pb^{2+} + 2e^- \rightarrow Pb$$

At the anode (positive electrode) we get oxidation of a negative ion:

$$2Br^- \rightarrow Br_2 + 2e^-$$

Sometimes half equations at the anode can show the electrons being removed from negative ions, like this:

$$2Br^- - 2e^- \rightarrow Br_2$$

You can write the half equation for negative ions either way. They both show the same oxidation of the negatively charged ions.

The effect of water

In aqueous solutions, electrolysis is more complex because of the ions formed by water as it ionises:

$$H_2O(l) \rightleftharpoons H^+(aq) + OH^-(aq)$$
$$\text{hydrogen ions} \quad \text{hydroxide ions}$$

There is a rule for working out what will happen. Remember that if two elements can be produced at an electrode, the less reactive element will usually be formed. In solutions, we will usually have positively charged metal ions and H^+ ions (from water) attracted to the cathode (negative electrode).

Look at Figure 2. It shows what happens in the electrolysis of a solution of a potassium compound. Hydrogen is less reactive than potassium, so hydrogen is produced at the cathode rather than potassium.

At cathode (–):

$$2H^+(aq) + 2e^- \rightarrow H_2(g)$$

So what happens at the anode in the electrolysis of aqueous solutions?

Hydroxide ions, $OH^-(aq)$, from water are often discharged. When hydroxide ions are discharged, we see oxygen gas given off at the anode (positive electrode).

At anode (+):

$$4OH^-(aq) \rightarrow 2H_2O(l) + O_2(g) + 4e^-$$

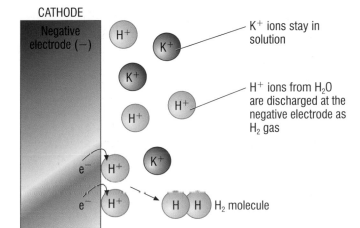

Figure 2 Here is the cathode in the electrolysis of a solution of a potassium compound. Hydrogen is less reactive than potassium, so hydrogen gas is given off at the electrode.

This happens unless the solution contains a reasonably high concentration of a halide ion, i.e. Group 7 ions, such as $Cl^-(aq)$. In this case, the halide ion is discharged and the halogen is formed:

$$2Cl^-(aq) \rightarrow Cl_2(g) + 2e^-$$

So the 'order of discharge' (starting with the easiest) at the anode is:

halide ion > hydroxide > all other negatively charged ions.

Summary questions

1 a i How do negatively charged ions become neutral atoms in electrolysis?
   ii Is this reduction or oxidation of the negatively charged ion?
  b i How do positively charged ions become neutral atoms in electrolysis?
   ii Is this reduction or oxidation of the positively charged ion?

2 Predict what is formed at each electrode in the electrolysis of:
   a molten lithium oxide
   b copper chloride solution
   c sodium sulfate solution.

3 Copy and balance the following half equations where necessary:
   a $Cl^- \rightarrow Cl_2 + e^-$
   b $Br^- \rightarrow Br_2 + e^-$
   c $Mg^{2+} + e^- \rightarrow Mg$
   d $Al^{3+} + e^- \rightarrow Al$
   e $K^+ + e^- \rightarrow K$
   f $H^+ + e^- \rightarrow H_2$
   g $O^{2-} \rightarrow O_2 + e^-$
   h $OH^- \rightarrow O_2 + H_2O + e^-$

Key points

- In electrolysis, the ions move towards the oppositely charged electrodes.

- At the electrodes, negative ions are oxidised (at the anode) while positive ions are reduced (at the cathode).

- When electrolysis happens in aqueous solution, the less reactive element, either hydrogen or the metal, is usually produced at the cathode. At the anode, we often get oxygen gas given off from discharged hydroxide ions produced from water.

C14.3 The extraction of aluminium

After this topic, you should know:

- how aluminium is obtained from aluminium oxide
- why cryolite is used in the process
- what happens at each electrode in the process.

You already know that aluminium is a very important metal. The uses of the metal or its alloys include:

- pans
- overhead power cables
- aeroplanes
- cooking foil
- drink cans
- window and patio door frames
- bicycle frames and car bodies.

Figure 1 Aluminium alloys have a low density but are very strong

Aluminium is quite a reactive metal. It is less reactive than magnesium but more reactive than zinc or iron. Carbon is not reactive enough to use in its extraction so we must use electrolysis. The compound electrolysed is aluminium oxide, Al_2O_3.

We get aluminium oxide from the ore called bauxite. The ore is mined by open cast mining. Bauxite contains mainly aluminium oxide. However, it is mixed with other rocky impurities. So the first step is to separate aluminium oxide from the ore. The impurities contain a lot of iron(III) oxide. This colours the waste solution from the separation process rusty brown. The brown wastewater has to be stored in large lagoons.

Electrolysis of aluminium oxide

To electrolyse the aluminium oxide we must first melt it. This enables the ions to move to the electrodes.

Unfortunately aluminium oxide has a very high melting point of 2050 °C. However, chemists have found a way of saving at least some energy. This is done by mixing the aluminium oxide with molten cryolite. Cryolite is another ionic compound. The molten mixture can be electrolysed at about 850 °C. The electrical energy transferred to the electrolysis cells keeps the mixture molten (see Figure 3).

Extracting aluminium from its ore

BAUXITE

Purified (aluminium oxide is separated from the ore)

ALUMINIUM OXIDE

Extracted (by electrolysis)

ALUMINIUM METAL

Figure 2 Extracting aluminium from its ore. This process requires a lot of energy. The purification of aluminium oxide from the ore makes aluminium hydroxide. This is separated from the impurities but then must be heated to turn it back to pure aluminium oxide. Then even more energy is needed melting and electrolysing the oxide.

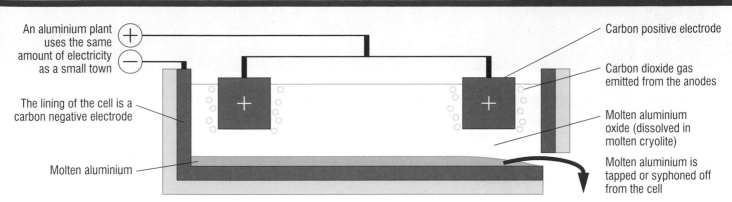

Figure 3 A cell used in the extraction of aluminium by electrolysis

The overall reaction in the electrolysis cell is:

$$\text{aluminium oxide} \xrightarrow{\text{electrolysis}} \text{aluminium} + \text{oxygen}$$
$$2Al_2O_3(l) \longrightarrow 4Al(l) + 3O_2(g)$$

At the cathodes (negative electrodes):

Each aluminium ion (Al^{3+}) gains 3 electrons. The ions turn into aluminium atoms. We say that the Al^{3+} ions are reduced (as they gain electrons) to form Al atoms:

$$Al^{3+}(l) + 3e^- \rightarrow Al(l)$$

The aluminium metal formed is molten at the temperature of the cell and collects at the bottom. It is siphoned or tapped off.

At the anodes (positive electrodes):

Each oxide ion (O^{2-}) loses 2 electrons. The ions turn into oxygen atoms. We say that the O^{2-} ions are oxidised (as they lose electrons) to form oxygen atoms. These bond in pairs to form molecules of oxygen gas (O_2):

$$2O^{2-}(l) \rightarrow O_2(g) + 4e^-$$

The oxygen reacts with the hot carbon anodes, making carbon dioxide gas:

$$C(s) + O_2(g) \rightarrow CO_2(g)$$

So the carbon anodes gradually burn away. They need to be replaced in the cells regularly.

Did you know ...?

Recycling one aluminium can can save enough energy to run a TV for about 3 hours.

Summary questions

1 a Explain why aluminium oxide must be molten for electrolysis to take place?
  b Why is aluminium oxide dissolved in molten cryolite in the extraction of aluminium?

2 Why are the carbon anodes replaced regularly in the industrial electrolysis of aluminium oxide?

3 a Write half equations for the changes at each electrode in the electrolysis of molten aluminium oxide.
  b Explain which ions are oxidised and which ions are reduced in the electrolysis of molten aluminium oxide.

4 a Explain why the extraction of aluminium requires so much energy.
  b Explain why aluminium metal was only discovered in the early 1800s despite it being the most common metallic element in the Earth's crust.

Key points

● Aluminium oxide, from the ore bauxite, is electrolysed in the manufacture of aluminium metal.

● The aluminium oxide is mixed with molten cryolite to lower its melting point.

● Aluminium forms at the cathode (negative electrode) and oxygen forms at the anode (positive electrode).

● The carbon anodes are replaced regularly as they gradually burn away.

C14.4 Electrolysis of brine

Learning objectives

After this topic, you should know:

- what is produced when brine is electrolysed

- how we use these products.

The electrolysis of **brine** (concentrated sodium chloride solution) is a very important industrial process. When we pass an electric current through brine we get three products:

- chlorine gas is produced at the anode (positive electrode)
- hydrogen gas is produced at the cathode (negative electrode)
- sodium hydroxide solution is also formed.

We can summarise the electrolysis of brine as:

$$\text{sodium chloride solution} \xrightarrow{\text{electrolysis}} \text{hydrogen gas} + \text{chlorine gas} + \text{sodium hydroxide solution}$$

At the anode (+):

The negative chloride ions (Cl^-) are attracted to the positive electrode. When they get there, they each lose one electron. The chloride ions are oxidised, as they lose electrons. The chlorine atoms bond together in pairs and are given off as chlorine gas (Cl_2). The half equation at the anode is:

$$2Cl^-(aq) \rightarrow Cl_2(g) + 2e^-$$

[This can also be written as: $2Cl^-(aq) - 2e^- \rightarrow Cl_2(g)$]

At the cathode (–):

There are H^+ ions in brine, formed when water breaks down:

$$H_2O(l) \rightleftharpoons H^+(aq) + OH^-(aq)$$

These positive hydrogen ions are attracted to the negative electrode. The sodium ions (Na^+) are also attracted to the same electrode. But remember in 14.2, we saw what happens when two ions are attracted to an electrode. It is the less reactive element that gets discharged. In this case, hydrogen ions are discharged and sodium ions stay in solution.

When the H^+ ions get to the negative electrode, they each gain one electron. The hydrogen ions are reduced, as they each gain an electron. The hydrogen atoms formed bond together in pairs and are given off as hydrogen gas (H_2). The half equation at the cathode is:

$$2H^+(aq) + 2e^- \rightarrow H_2(g)$$

The remaining solution:

You can test the solution around the cathode (negative electrode) with indicator. It shows that the solution is alkaline. This is because we can think of brine as containing aqueous ions of Na^+ and Cl^- (from salt) and H^+ and OH^- (from water). The $Cl^-(aq)$ and $H^+(aq)$ ions are removed during electrolysis. So this leaves a solution containing $Na^+(aq)$ and $OH^-(aq)$ ions, i.e. a solution of sodium hydroxide, $NaOH(aq)$.

Look at the way we can electrolyse brine in industry in Figure 1.

Figure 1 In industry, brine can be electrolysed in a cell in which the two electrodes are separated by a porous membrane. This is called a diaphragm cell.

Practical

Electrolysing brine in the lab

Turn off the electricity once the tubes are nearly full of gas to avoid inhaling chlorine gas (toxic).

● How can you positively test for the gases collected?

Test the solution near the cathode (negative electrode) with universal indicator solution.

● What does the indicator tell us?

Safety: Wear eye protection. Do not smell the gas.

Chlorine gas   Hydrogen gas

Sodium chloride solution

+   −

+ Carbon rod as positive electrode (+)   Carbon rod as negative electrode (−) −

⊂⊃ **links**

For information about what happens when two ions are attracted to an electrode, look back to 14.2 'Changes at the electrodes'.

Using chlorine

We can react chlorine with the sodium hydroxide produced in the electrolysis of brine. This makes a solution of bleach. Bleach is very good at killing bacteria.

Chlorine is also important in making many other disinfectants, as well as plastics such as PVC.

Using hydrogen

The hydrogen that we make by electrolysing brine is particularly pure. This makes it very useful in the food industry. We make margarine by reacting hydrogen with vegetable oils.

Using sodium hydroxide

The sodium hydroxide from the electrolysis of brine is an important alkali in industry. It is used to make soap and paper, as well as bleach (see above).

Figure 2 The chlorine made when we electrolyse brine is used to kill bacteria in drinking water, and also in swimming pools

Summary questions

1 **a** What are the **three** products made when we electrolyse brine?
   b What are they used for?

2 For the electrolysis of brine, write half equations, including state symbols, for the reactions:
   a at the anode
   b at the cathode.

3 We can also electrolyse *molten* sodium chloride.
   a Compare the products formed with those from the electrolysis of sodium chloride solution.
   b Explain any differences.

Key points

● When we electrolyse brine we get three products – chlorine gas, hydrogen gas and sodium hydroxide solution (an alkali).

● Chlorine is used to make bleach, which kills bacteria, and to make plastics.

● Hydrogen is used to make margarine.

● Sodium hydroxide is used to make bleach, paper and soap.

C14.5 Electroplating

Learning objectives

After this topic, you should know:

- why objects are electroplated
- how to electroplate a metal object.

Figure 1 Chromium-plated objects look very shiny and attractive. The chromium layer does not corrode away so it protects the steel beneath from rusting.

Figure 2 So-called 'tin' cans actually contain very little tin. The layer on the steel can be only a few thousandths of a millimetre thick! The tin keeps air and water away from the iron in steel and stops it rusting – at least until the tin gets scratched! Tin is quite a soft metal, unlike chromium.

Most of us will use an electroplated object at some time each day. You might use a chromium-plated kettle to boil water or ride a bicycle with chromium-plated handlebars. You could open a tin-plated steel can for a meal or put on some gold- or silver-plated jewellery.

An electroplated object is coated with a thin layer of metal by electrolysis.

Why do we electroplate objects?

There can be different reasons why we electroplate objects. These include:

- to protect the metal beneath from corroding
- to make the object look more attractive
- to increase the hardness of a surface and its resistance to scratching
- to save money by using a thin layer of a precious metal instead of the pure expensive metal. This also helps people who are allergic to nickel – a metal often used to make cheap jewellery.

Electroplating saves money by making cheaper jewellery. However, using electroplating to protect large metal surfaces against rusting and damage makes things more expensive. In the long term, though, this can still make economic sense for some objects because we don't have to replace them so often.

Electroplating a metal object

You can try to nickel plate some copper foil in the experiment below.

Practical

Nickel plating copper metal

Your teacher will melt some wax in a metal tray. Using tongs you can dip in a piece of copper foil.

Let the wax set. Then scratch a simple design in the wax. You want the design to be plated with nickel so get this area as free from wax as possible.

Set up the apparatus as shown in the diagram. Using a small current for a long time will give best results.

When you have finished, rinse the copper foil in water, dry, then scrape off the rest of the wax.

- What happens at the negative electrode?

Safety: Wear eye protection. Nickel sulfate solution is harmful.

Wax
Nickel anode
Copper to be plated
Nickel sulfate solution

Explaining the nickel-plating experiment

The metal object to be plated (the copper foil in this case) is used as the cathode (negative electrode). The anode (positive electrode) is made from the plating metal (in this case nickel). The electrolysis takes place in a solution containing ions of the plating metal. In the previous experiment we use nickel sulfate solution.

At the anode (+) made of the plating metal:

Nickel atoms in the electrode are oxidised. They lose 2 electrons each and form nickel ions (Ni^{2+}) which leave the anode and go into the solution. The half equation is:

$$Ni(s) \rightarrow Ni^{2+}(aq) + 2e^-$$

At the cathode (–) to be plated:

Nickel ions (Ni^{2+}) from the solution are reduced. They gain 2 electrons and form nickel atoms which are deposited on the copper cathode. The half equation is:

$$Ni^{2+}(aq) + 2e^- \rightarrow Ni(s)$$

Here are the half equations at each electrode if an object is electroplated by copper:

At the anode (positive electrode): $\quad Cu(s) \rightarrow Cu^{2+}(aq) + 2e^-$

At the cathode (negative electrode) to be plated: $\quad Cu^{2+}(aq) + 2e^- \rightarrow Cu(s)$

The electrolyte used contains copper(II) ions, such as a solution of copper(II) sulfate.

??? Did you know ...?

It is not only metal objects that can be electroplated. We can now electroplate plastic objects as well. The object to be plated is first coated in a 'paint' containing tiny particles of graphite. Once dry, the object has a layer of graphite that will conduct electricity. It can then be electroplated.

Summary questions

1 Name **four** metals that are used to electroplate objects.

2 List the reasons why objects get electroplated.

3 Look at the experiment described in the Practical box on the previous page.
   a Where are nickel atoms oxidised?
   b What is formed when nickel atoms are oxidised?

4 Draw a simple electrical circuit that could be used to copper plate a steel ball.

5 In making 'chrome' objects, chromium metal is used to electroplate a steel object. The steel is first electroplated with nickel because chromium does not stick well on steel.
   a Give the half equation at the cathode for the nickel-plating process. Include state symbols in your answer.
   b Give the half equation at the cathode for the chromium-plating process, including state symbols.
   (The formula of a chromium ion is Cr^{3+}.)

Key points

● We can electroplate objects to improve their appearance, to protect their surface and to use smaller amounts of precious metals.

● The object to be electroplated is made the cathode (negative electrode) in an electrolysis cell. The plating metal is made the anode (positive electrode). The electrolyte contains ions of the plating metal.

Summary questions

1 Select **A** or **B** to describe correctly the anode and cathode in electrolysis for statements **a–f**.

      A Anode (+)   **B** Cathode (–)

a Positive ions move towards this.

b Oxidation happens here.

c This is connected to the negative terminal of the power supply.

d This is connected to the positive terminal of the power supply.

e Reduction happens here.

f Negative ions move towards this.

2 a Which of the following ions would move towards the anode (+) and which towards the cathode (–) during electrolysis?

    potassium iodide calcium fluoride oxide magnesium aluminium bromide

b Write a half equation for the discharge of:
  i magnesium ions
  ii bromide ions

3 The diagram shows the electrolysis of sodium chloride solution in the laboratory.

    + Carbon rod as positive electrode (+)   Carbon rod as negative electrode (–) –

a Identify the products **A**, **B** and **C** on the diagram.

b Give two uses for substance **A**.

c What would be the pH of the solution around the cathode?

d How would you carry out a positive test on product **B**?

e Write the half equations, including state symbols, for the changes at the anode and cathode.

4 Water can be slightly acidified and broken down into hydrogen and oxygen using electrolysis. The word equation for this reaction is:

$$water \rightarrow hydrogen + oxygen$$

a Write a balanced symbol equation for this reaction, including state symbols.

b In water, a small percentage of molecules ionise (split up). Write a balanced symbol equation, including state symbols, for the ionisation of water molecules.

c Write half equations to show what happens at the positive and negative electrodes in the electrolysis of water.

d When some water is electrolysed it produces 2 moles of hydrogen. How much oxygen is produced?

e Where does the energy needed to split water into hydrogen and oxygen come from during electrolysis?

5 Copy and complete the following half equations:

a $Li^+ \rightarrow Li$

b $Sr^{2+} \rightarrow Sr$

c $F^- \rightarrow F_2$

d $O^{2-} \rightarrow O_2$

6 Electrolysis can be used to produce a thin layer of metal on the surface of a metal object.

Using words and diagrams, describe how you would cover a small piece of iron with tin using an electrolyte of tin(II) nitrate. Make sure that you write down the half equations that describe the changes at the anode and cathode, and include the words 'oxidation' and 'reduction'.

AQA Examination-style questions

1 The diagram shows apparatus for the electrolysis of lead bromide.

When the lead bromide is heated, it melts and observations can be recorded.

a A brown gas is seen at the anode. Name this gas and write a symbol equation for its formation. (3)

b Silvery globules are seen at the cathode. Name the substance in the globules and write a symbol equation for its formation. (3)

c The bulb does not light until the lead bromide is molten. What happens in the connecting wires when the bulb is lit? (1)

d Why does no electrolysis occur until the lead bromide has melted? (1)

e Why is the reaction at the cathode described as reduction? (1)

2 A student used the following apparatus to electrolyse dilute sulfuric acid.

a What is the formula of the only positive ion in dilute sulfuric acid? (1)

b Write the equation for the reaction of the OH^- ion that occurs at the anode. (2)

c Which ion in dilute sulfuric acid is attracted to an electrode but is not discharged? (1)

d Predict what happens to the concentration of the sulfuric acid as electrolysis occurs. (1)

e Why is the volume of hydrogen gas collected approximately double the volume of the oxygen gas? (1)

3 The electrolysis of sodium chloride solution is used to manufacture hydrogen and chlorine.

a Why is the H^+ ion discharged in preference to the Na^+ ion at the cathode? (1)

b Why is the Cl^- ion discharged in preference to the OH^- ion at the anode? (1)

c Name the solution formed in this process. (1)

d i State one use for the hydrogen formed. (1)
ii State one use for the chlorine formed. (1)

4 Objects can be electroplated. For example, a copper spoon can be plated with nickel.

a i What should be used as the anode and cathode in this process? (1)
ii Suggest the name of a solution that could be used as the electrolyte. (1)
iii Write the half equation for the reaction at the anode. (1)

b Suggest one physical property of an object that would change when it is electroplated. (1)

c Objects made of plastic can be electroplated. Why are they coated with graphite before they are electroplated? (1)

5 Aluminium is made by the electrolysis of aluminium oxide.

Aluminium oxide is an ionic compound containing aluminium ions (Al^{3+}) and oxide ions (O^{2-}).

The diagram below shows the apparatus used to electrolyse aluminium oxide.

Use information in the diagram and your knowledge and understanding of this extraction to explain, as fully as you can, how aluminium and carbon dioxide are formed in this process. (6)

Marks awarded for this answer will be determined by the quality of communication as well as the standard of the scientific response.

C15.1

Tests for positive ions

Learning objectives

After this topic, you should know:

- how to identify different positive ions by:
  - flame tests
  - precipitation reactions.

Scientists working in environmental monitoring, industry, medicine and forensic science need to analyse and identify substances. To identify unknown substances, there are a variety of different chemical tests.

Flame tests

Some metal ions produce flames with a characteristic colour. To carry out a flame test you:

- Put a small amount of the compound to be tested in a nichrome wire loop. (The wire loop should be dipped in concentrated hydrochloric acid and heated to clean it first. Then it should be dipped in the acid again before dipping in the metal compound.)
- Then hold the loop in the roaring blue flame of a Bunsen burner.
- Use the colour of the Bunsen flame to identify the metal ion in the compound.

Metal ion	Flame colour
Lithium (Li$^+$)	crimson
Sodium (Na$^+$)	yellow
Potassium (K$^+$)	lilac
Calcium (Ca^{2+})	brick red
Barium (Ba^{2+})	apple green

Figure 1 A flame test can identify most Group 1 or Group 2 metals in a compound

Reactions with sodium hydroxide

The reactions with sodium hydroxide solution can also help us identify some positive ions. Aluminium ions, calcium ions and magnesium ions all form *white precipitates* with sodium hydroxide solution. So, if a white precipitate forms we know an unknown compound contains either Al^{3+}, Ca^{2+} or Mg^{2+} ions.

For example, the ionic equation for the reaction with aluminium ions is:

$$Al^{3+}(aq) + 3OH^-(aq) \rightarrow Al(OH)_3(s)$$

If we add more and more sodium hydroxide then the precipitate formed with aluminium ions dissolves. However, the white precipitate formed with calcium or magnesium ions will not dissolve. Calcium and magnesium ions can be distinguished by a flame test. Calcium ions give a brick-red flame but magnesium ions produce no colour at all.

Some metal ions form *coloured precipitates* with sodium hydroxide.

If we add sodium hydroxide solution to a substance containing:

- copper(II) ions, a blue precipitate appears
- iron(II) ions, a green precipitate is produced
- iron(III) ions, a brown precipitate is formed.

For example, with iron(II) ions, the ionic equation is:

$$Fe^{2+}(aq) + 2OH^-(aq) \rightarrow Fe(OH)_2(s)$$

Figure 2 This distinctive precipitate that forms when we add sodium hydroxide solution tells us that Cu^{2+} ions are present

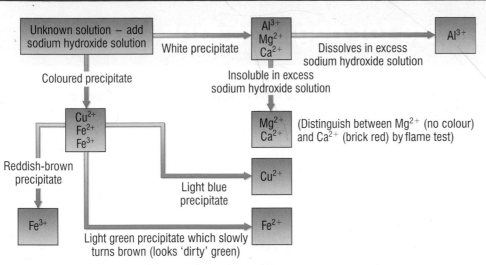

Figure 3 Sodium hydroxide solution provides a very useful test for many positive ions

Practical

Identifying positive ions

Try to identify the metal ions in some unknown compounds provided for you.

Safety: Wear chemical splash proof eye protection.

Summary questions

1 **a** What colour precipitate does dilute sodium hydroxide produce with aluminium, calcium and magnesium ions?
   b How can we distinguish between these three metal ions?
   c Write an ionic equation, including state symbols, for the precipitation of magnesium ions from solution by aqueous hydroxide ions.

2 **a** Draw a flow chart to describe how to carry out a flame test.
   b If the flame test was carried out on barium chloride, describe what you would see.

3 Complete the missing cells **a** to **j** in the table below:

Add sodium hydroxide solution	Flame test	Metal ion
nothing observed	lilac	**f**
white precipitate	brick red	**g**
a	**d**	Fe^{3+}
white precipitate which dissolves in excess sodium hydroxide solution	nothing observed	**h**
green precipitate which slowly turns reddish-brown	nothing observed	**i**
b	**e**	Na^+
c	crimson	**j**

Key points

- Most Group 1 and Group 2 metal ions can be identified in their compounds using flame tests.

- Sodium hydroxide solution can be used to identify different metal ions, depending on the precipitate that is formed.

Tests for negative ions

Learning objectives

After this topic, you should know:

- how to identify different negative ions, in particular:
  - carbonates
  - halides
  - sulfates.

We can also do chemical tests to identify some negative ions in ionic compounds.

Carbonates

If we add a dilute acid to a carbonate, it fizzes and produces carbon dioxide gas. This is a good test to see if an unknown substance is a carbonate.

Acid

Limewater

Carbonate

Figure 1 The test for a carbonate

∞ **links**

For more information on carbonates, look back to 6.4 'Metal carbonates'.

If the carbonate is sodium carbonate, the reaction we get is:

$$Na_2CO_3(s) + 2HCl(aq) \rightarrow 2NaCl(aq) + H_2O(l) + CO_2(g)$$

We can represent the reaction by just showing the ions that change in the reaction in an ionic equation:

$$2H^+(aq) + \underset{\text{carbonate ion}}{CO_3^{2-}(s)} \rightarrow CO_2(g) + H_2O(l)$$
$$\text{acid}$$

In limewater, the carbon dioxide reacts with calcium hydroxide. It forms a white precipitate of calcium carbonate which turns the limewater cloudy.

Halides (chlorides, bromides and iodides)

A very simple test shows whether chloride, bromide or iodide ions are present in a compound. First we add dilute nitric acid, and we then add silver nitrate solution. If a precipitate forms, there are halide ions present.

(We add the nitric acid to dissolve the compound and to remove any carbonate ions as they would also form a precipitate with the silver ions, and so interfere with the test.)

The colour of the precipitate tells us which halide ion is present:

- chloride ions (Cl^-) give a white precipitate.
- bromide ions (Br^-) give a cream precipitate.
- iodide ions (I^-) give a pale yellow precipitate.

If the unknown halide was sodium chloride, the precipitation reaction would be:

$$NaCl(aq) + AgNO_3(aq) \rightarrow NaNO_3(aq) + AgCl(s)$$

Here is the ionic equation, where X^- is the halide ion:

$$Ag^+(aq) + X^-(aq) \rightarrow AgX(s)$$

Examiner's tip

In the test for a halide ion: add dilute **nitric** acid before the silver **nitrate**. Do not add any other acid as they will produce precipitates with silver nitrate solution.

Figure 2 One simple test with silver nitrate solution can tell us if an unknown substance contains chloride, bromide or iodide ions

aiaylaiA

Sulfates

We can test for sulfate ions by adding dilute hydrochloric acid, followed by barium chloride solution. (We add the dilute hydrochloric acid first to remove carbonate ions that would form a precipitate with the barium ions.) A white precipitate tells us sulfate ions are present. The white precipitate is the insoluble salt barium sulfate, $BaSO_4$.

If the unknown compound was potassium sulfate, then the equation for the precipitation reaction would be:

$$K_2SO_4(aq) + BaCl_2(aq) \rightarrow 2KCl(aq) + BaSO_4(s)$$

Here is the ionic equation:

$$Ba^{2+}(aq) + SO_4^{2-}(aq) \rightarrow BaSO_4(s)$$

Figure 3 The white precipitate of barium sulfate forming

Practical

Identifying unknown ionic compounds

Now you know the tests for some positive and negative ions, you can try to identify some unknown compounds.

Safety: Wear chemical splash proof eye protection.

Summary questions

1 List the reagents you would need to assemble in a lab to test a sample of an unknown substance for carbonate, halide and sulfate ions.

2 An unknown compound is a white solid which dissolves in water to produce a colourless solution. When this solution is acidified with nitric acid and then silver nitrate is added, a pale yellow precipitate is produced. A flame test on the unknown compound produces a lilac flame. Deduce the name of the unknown compound and give your reasoning.

3 Write a word equation and a balanced symbol equation, including state symbols, for the following reactions:
   a magnesium chloride solution + silver nitrate solution
   b potassium carbonate powder + hydrochloric acid
   c aluminium sulfate solution + barium chloride solution

4 Write ionic equations, including state symbols, to summarise the reactions that help identify:
   a bromide ions
   b sulfate ions
   c carbonate ions

5 In the test for halide ions, explain why nitric acid (rather than other acids) is added to a sample before we add silver nitrate solution.

Examiner's tip

In the test for the sulfate ion: add **hydrochloric** acid before the barium **chloride**. Do not add sulfuric acid – it contains sulfate ions!

Key points

- We identify carbonates by adding dilute acid, which produces carbon dioxide gas. The gas turns limewater cloudy.

- We identify halides by adding nitric acid, then silver nitrate solution. This produces a precipitate of silver halide (chloride = white, bromide = cream, iodide = pale yellow).

- We identify sulfates by adding hydrochloric acid, then barium chloride solution. This produces a white precipitate of barium sulfate.

C15.3 Separating mixtures

Learning objectives

After this topic, you should know:

- what a mixture is

- how to separate the components in a range of mixtures by:
  - filtration
  - distillation
  - crystallisation.

When analytical chemists are given an unknown sample to identify, it is often a mixture of different substances.

A mixture is made up of two or more elements or compounds which are not chemically combined together.

Mixtures are different to chemical compounds. Look at the table below:

Compounds	Mixtures
Compounds have a fixed composition (the ratio of elements present is always the same in any particular compound).	Mixtures have no fixed composition (the proportions vary depending on the amount of each substance mixed together).
Need chemical reactions to separate the elements in a compound.	The different elements or compounds in a mixture can be separated again more easily (by physical means using the differences in properties of each substance in the mixture).
There are chemical bonds between atoms of the different elements in the compound.	There are no chemical bonds between atoms of the different substances in a mixture.

Before the substances in a mixture are identified, they are separated from each other. As it states in the table, we can use physical means to achieve the separation. The techniques available include:

- filtration
- distillation
- crystallisation
- chromatography (see 15.4).

These techniques all rely on differences in the physical properties of the substances in the mixture, such as solubilities or boiling points.

Filtration

This technique is used to separate substances that are insoluble in a particular solvent from those that are soluble. For example, you have probably tried to separate a mixture of sand and salt (sodium chloride) before in science lessons (see Figure 1).

The sand collected on the filter paper can be washed with distilled water (to remove any salt left in solution on it) and dried in a warm oven to obtain the pure sand.

Crystallisation

To obtain a sample of pure salt from the sand/salt mixture, following filtration, we would need to get the sodium chloride from the solution in water (called the filtrate). The water is evaporated from the sodium chloride solution by heating in an evaporating dish on a water bath. The water bath is a gentler way of heating than heating the evaporating dish directly on a tripod and gauze.

Figure 1 Filtering a mixture of sand, salt and water in the lab

Figure 2 Filtering in the home – some people like filter coffee made from ground-up coffee beans. The solid bits that are insoluble in water get left on filter paper as a residue.

Heating should be stopped when the solution is at the point of crystallisation, i.e. when small crystals first appear around the edge of the solution or when crystals appear in a drop of solution extracted from the dish with a glass rod. Look at Figure 3. The rest of the water is then left to evaporate off the saturated solution at room temperature to get a good sample of crystals. A flat-bottomed crystallisation dish or Petri dish can be used for this final step to give a large surface area for the water to evaporate from.

Figure 3 Crystallising sodium chloride from its solution in water

Distillation

Crystallisation separates a soluble solid from a solvent but sometimes we need to collect the solvent itself instead of just letting it evaporate off into the air. For example, some countries with a lack of freshwater sources purify seawater to obtain usable water. Distillation allows us to do this.

In distillation a solution is heated and boiled to evaporate the solvent. The vapour given off is then cooled and condensed back into a liquid for collection (see Figure 4). The dissolved solids remain in the heated flask.

Distillation can also be used to separate mixtures of miscible liquids, such as ethanol and water. Miscible refers to liquids that dissolve in each other; they do not form separate layers as in immiscible liquids. The liquids will have different boiling points, so we can use this to distil off and collect the liquid with the lowest boiling point first.

However, it is difficult to get pure liquids from mixtures of liquids by simple distillation, as vapour is given off from liquids before they actually reach their boiling point. This is especially the case where the liquids in the mixture have similar boiling points. So to aid separation we can add a fractionating column to the apparatus in Figure 4. This is usually a tall glass column filled with glass beads, fitted vertically on top of the flask being heated. The vapours must pass over and between the glass beads before they reach the condenser. The substance with the higher boiling point will condense more readily on the glass beads and drop back down into the flask beneath.

links

To remind yourself about crystallisation, look back to 6.2 'Making salts from metals or insoluble bases' and 6.3 'Neutralisation, precipitation and making salts'.

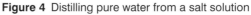

Figure 4 Distilling pure water from a salt solution

Summary questions

1 Define what a mixture is.

2 A mixture has 'no fixed composition'. What does this mean?

3 a Draw the apparatus you could use to separate ethanol and water.
  b Explain why you would be able to collect a more pure sample of ethanol using this apparatus than by using simple distillation.

4 Sulfur is soluble in the flammable liquid xylene but not in water. Sodium nitrate is soluble in water but not in xylene.
  Describe TWO ways to separate a mixture of sulfur powder and sodium nitrate to collect pure samples of each solid.

Key points

- A mixture is made up of two or more elements or compounds which are not chemically combined together.

- Mixtures can be separated by physical means, such as filtration, crystallisation and distillation.

C15.4 | Paper chromatography

Learning objectives

After this topic, you should know:

- how paper chromatography works

- how to calculate R_f values in paper chromatography

- Some of the advantages of instrumental methods of analysis.

Paper clip
Solvent front
Water (the solvent)
Orange   Blue

Figure 1 A chromatogram is the paper record of the separation. If the components of the mixture are not coloured we can sometimes spray the chromatogram with a detecting agent that colours the components to reveal their positions on the paper.

Scientists have many instruments that they can use to identify unknown compounds. Many of these are more sensitive, automated versions of techniques we use in school labs, such as paper chromatography.

Carrying out paper chromatography

One technique that is used to identify mixtures in solution is paper **chromatography**. It works because some compounds in a mixture will dissolve better than others in the solvent chosen (see Figure 1).

A capillary tube is used to dab a spot of the solution on a pencil line near the bottom of a sheet of absorbent chromatography paper. The paper is then placed in a solvent at the bottom of a beaker or tank. The solvent is allowed to soak up the paper, running past the spot of mixture. Their relative solubility determines how far the components in the mixture travel up the paper. The more soluble a substance is in the solvent, the further up the paper it is carried. Different solvents can be used to maximise separation.

Practical

Detecting dyes in food colourings

In this experiment you can make a chromatogram to analyse various food colourings.

Set up the experiment as shown in Figures 1 and 2:

- What can you deduce from your chromatography experiment?

Chromatography paper

Blue   Green   Red   Orange

Labels and line drawn in pencil

Figure 2 Setting up a chromatogram

Identification using a chromatogram

Once the compounds in a mixture have been separated using chromatography, they can be identified. We can compare the chromatogram with others obtained from known substances. For this we must have used the same solvent at the same temperature as used to generate the data held in a database or book of data.

The data is presented as an R_f **(retention factor)** value. This is a ratio, calculated by dividing the distance a spot travels up the paper by the distance the solvent front travels. Look at Figure 3 to see how to get the measurements to calculate an R_f value.

Solvent front
A
12 cm
8 cm   B
3 cm
Base line

Figure 3 The R_f value, in a particular solvent at a given temperature, of an unknown substance can be compared with values in a database to identify the substance

The R_f value of A $= \dfrac{8}{12} = 0.67$ The R_f value of B $= \dfrac{3}{12} = 0.25$

Instrumental methods

Many industries need rapid and accurate methods for analysing their products. They use modern instrumental analysis for this task, including gas chromatography (see 15.5).

Instrumental techniques are also important in fighting pollution. Careful monitoring of the environment using sensitive instruments is now common. This type of analysis is also used all the time in healthcare.

Modern instrumental methods have a number of benefits over older methods:
- they are highly accurate and sensitive
- they are quicker
- they enable very small samples to be analysed.

Against this, the main disadvantages of using instrumental methods are that the equipment:
- is usually very expensive
- takes special training to use
- gives results that can often be interpreted only by comparison with data from known substances.

Figure 4 Compared with the methods of 50 years ago, modern instrumental methods of analysis are quick, accurate and sensitive – three big advantages. They also need far fewer people to carry out the analysis than traditional laboratory analysis.

links

For more information on the instruments used by chemists to analyse substances, see 15.5 'Instrumental analysis'.

Examiner's tip

Although simpler to use than bench chemistry methods, instrumental methods still need trained technicians to operate them.

Summary questions

1 Describe how we can separate the dyes in a food colouring and identify them.

2 What is the R_f value of this substance X?

Solvent front

9.7 cm

7.5 cm

Base line

3 The R_f values of two substances, A and B, were taken from a chromatogram run in a 50% water, 50% ethanol solvent at 20 °C. The R_f value of A was 0.54 and B was 0.79. What can you deduce about A and B from these values and how could you use them to identify A and B?

4 What are the main advantages and disadvantages of using instrumental analysis compared with traditional practical methods?

Key points

- Scientists can analyse unknown substances in solution by using paper chromatography.

- R_f values can be measured and matched against databases to identify specific substances.

- Modern instrumental techniques provide fast, accurate and sensitive ways of analysing chemical substances.

C15.5 Instrumental analysis

Learning objectives

After this topic, you should know:

- how gas chromatography can be used to separate compounds in a sample mixture

- how a mass spectrometer can be used to identify the compounds in the sample.

Analysing mixtures

Samples to be analysed are often mixtures of different compounds. So the first step is to separate the compounds. Then they can be identified using one of the many instrumental techniques available. Chemists have developed a technique called gas chromatography–mass spectrometry (GC–MS) to do this task.

- Firstly, they use **gas chromatography** to separate compounds that are easily vaporised.

- Then the separated compounds pass into another instrument – the **mass spectrometer**, which can identify each of them. The mass spectrometer is useful for identifying both elements and compounds. The pattern of peaks it produces identifies the sample.

Gas chromatography

This separation technique is similar to paper chromatography. However, instead of a solvent moving over paper, it has a gas moving through a column packed with a solid.

Figure 1 This is the apparatus used in gas chromatography. The solid in the column can be coated in a liquid and is sometimes then known as gas–liquid chromatography.

- First of all, the sample mixture is vaporised.

- A 'carrier' gas moves the vapour through the coiled column.

- The compounds in the sample have different attractions to the material in the column. The compounds with stronger attractions will take longer to get through the column. We say that they have a longer **retention time**.

- The compounds with weak attractions to the material in the column travel through it more quickly and leave first. They have shorter retention times.

The separated compounds can be recorded as peaks at different times on a chart as they leave the column. Look at Figure 2 to see a gas chromatograph.

We can identify the unknown substances in the sample by comparing the retention times on the chromatograph with the results for known substances. The analysis must have taken place under exactly the same conditions to compare retention times.

Figure 2 This is a gas chromatograph of a mixture of three different substances. There was more of substance A than B or C in the sample mixture, as shown by the size of the peaks. Also, as substance A was first to leave the column, it had the weakest attraction for the solid packed in the column.

Mass spectrometry

To ensure that we identify the unknown substances, the gas chromatography apparatus can be attached directly to a mass spectrometer. This identifies substances very quickly and accurately and can detect very small quantities in the sample.

Measuring relative molecular masses

A mass spectrometer also provides an accurate way of measuring the relative molecular (formula) mass of a compound. The peak with the largest mass corresponds to the positive ion formed when the original molecule has just one electron removed. As you know, the mass of an electron is so small that it can be ignored when we look at the mass of atoms or molecules. This peak is called the **molecular ion peak**. It is found as the last peak on the right as you look at a mass spectrum. The molecular ion peak of the substance analysed in Figure 3 is at 45. So the substance has a relative molecular mass of 45.

Figure 3 The pattern of peaks (called the mass spectrum) is formed as the molecules are split apart in the mass spectrometer. This unique 'fragmentation' pattern acts like a 'fingerprint' for unknown compounds. The pattern is quickly matched against a database of known compounds stored on computer.
Note: You don't need to remember the details of how a mass spectrometer works.

Summary questions

1 Explain how the technique of gas chromatography can be used to separate a mixture of volatile compounds.

2 Why is the technique of gas chromatography less useful than some other instrumental analysis techniques for identifying very unstable substances?

3 Gas chromatography–mass spectroscopy (GC–MS) can be used to test athletes for illegal substances.
Why would a guilty athlete be worried before a test even though they had stopped using a banned substance a month before?

4 Explain how a mass spectrometer can be used to find the relative molecular mass of a compound.

Key points

- Compounds in a mixture can be separated using gas chromatography.

- Once separated, compounds can be identified using a mass spectrometer.

- The mass spectrometer can be used to find the relative molecular mass of a compound from its molecular ion peak.

Summary questions

1 What would be entered in **a** to **f** to complete the table.

Add dilute acid	Add sodium hydroxide solution	Add dilute nitric acid followed by silver nitrate solution	Flame test	Substance
Nothing observed	Nothing observed	Pale yellow precipitate	Yellow	e
Fizzing – gas turns limewater cloudy	Pale blue precipitate formed	Not needed	Nothing observed	f
a	b	c	d	Calcium chloride

2 An unknown compound gave the following positive tests when analysed:

• The Bunsen flame turned crimson in a flame test.
• When dissolved in dilute hydrochloric acid and barium chloride solution was added, a white precipitate was formed.

Name the unknown compound.

3 The label on a jar of white crystals has been damaged by water and cannot be read. A science technician thinks it is probably a jar of potassium bromide.

a Describe how the technician could positively identify the crystals as potassium bromide.

b Give the formula of potassium bromide.

c What type of bonding will be found in potassium bromide?

4 a What are the differences between a mixture and a compound?

b Name the technique you would use to separate and collect:
  i hydrated copper(II) sulfate, $CuSO_4.5H_2O$, from its aqueous solution
  ii a precipitate of lead iodide from the solution formed when aqueous solutions of lead nitrate and sodium iodide are mixed
  iii water from a solution of potassium chloride
  iv ethanol from a mixture of water and ethanol.

c Write a balanced symbol equation, including state symbols, for the reaction in **b** part **ii** above.

5 Look at the mass spectrum below of an alkane:

a What is the relative molecular mass of the alkane?

b Using the general formula for an alkane, i.e. $C_nH_{(2n+2)}$, work out the formula of the alkane analysed in the mass spectrometer?

6 Look at the gas chromatograph from a mixture of volatile compounds:

a How many substances were in the mixture analysed?

b Explain how the substances have been separated.

c We can use paper chromatography to identify solutes using R_f values from a database. Look at the chromatogram below and calculate the R_f value of the unknown substances X and Y.

AQA Examination-style questions

1 Potash alum is a compound with the formula $KAl(SO_4)_2$

A student dissolved some potash alum in water and did some tests on the solution.

a Some of the solution was sprayed into a bunsen flame.
  i State the colour of the flame. (1)
  ii Write the formula of the ion responsible for this colour. (1)

b The student added a small amount of some sodium hydroxide solution to some potash alum solution.
  i State the observation that could be made. (1)
  ii Write the name of the compound responsible for this observation. (1)

c Another student added some sodium hydroxide solution to some potash alum solution and recorded his observation as a colourless solution.

Explain why he did not make the same observation as the student in **b**. (2)

d Describe how the student should do a test to show that the potash alum contains sulfate ions. (3)

2 A solution contains dissolved sodium carbonate, iron(II) chloride and iron(III) chloride.

a After some dilute nitric acid is added, bubbles are seen.
  i Name the gas that forms. (1)
  ii Describe how you could test for this gas. (2)

b Next, some silver nitrate solution is added. A white precipitate forms.
  i Name the white precipitate. (1)
  ii Write the simplest ionic equation for the formation of the white precipitate. (2)

c A student adds some sodium hydroxide solution to test for positive ions.

Why will this test not clearly identify the three positive ions in the solution? (3)

3 Many methods of separation depend on a property that is different for each substance in a mixture.

For each of the mixtures in this question, suggest a suitable method of obtaining the first substance from the mixture and state the property that the method depends on.

a water from a mixture with sodium chloride (2)

b calcium carbonate from a mixture with sodium chloride solution (2)

c blue ink from a mixture with red ink (2)

4 An instrumental technique used to separate mixtures is gas chromatography.

a Why does the mixture separate as it passes through the column? (1)

b What piece of equipment can be linked to the column to identify the substances in the mixture? (1)

c In one analysis the equipment records three peaks. What does this tell you about the mixture? (1)

d State two advantages of this method of analysis over traditional methods. (2)

5 A scientist used chromatography to identify the artificial colours in a flavoured drink.

The result of the experiment is shown in the diagram.

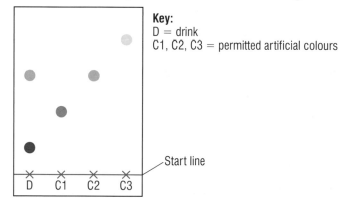

Key:
D = drink
C1, C2, C3 = permitted artificial colours

Start line

D C1 C2 C3

Describe how to do the experiment that gave this result. (6)

Marks awarded for this answer will be determined by the quality of communication as well as the standard of the scientific response.

Investigations

Learning objectives

After this topic, you should know:

- what 'continuous' and 'categoric variables' are

- what is meant by 'repeatable evidence', 'reproducible evidence' and 'valid evidence'

- what the link is between the independent and dependent variable

- what a 'hypothesis' and a 'prediction' are

- how to reduce risks in hazardous situations.

Science works for us all day, every day. Working as a scientist you will have knowledge of the world around you and particularly about the subject you are working with. You will observe the world around you. An enquiring mind will then lead you to start asking questions about what you have observed.

Science usually moves forward by slow steady steps. Each small step is important in its own way. It builds on the body of knowledge that we already have.

Thinking scientifically

Deciding on what to measure

Variables can be one of two different types:

- A **categoric variable** is one that is best described by a label (usually a word). The type of metal is a categoric variable, e.g. magnesium or zinc.

- A **continuous variable** is one that we measure, so its value could be any number. Temperature (as measured by a thermometer or temperature sensor) is a continuous variable, e.g. 37.6 °C, 45.2 °C. Continuous variables can have values (called a quantity) that can be given by any measurements made (e.g. mass, volume, etc.).

When designing your investigation you should always try to measure continuous **data** whenever you can. If this is not always possible, you should then try to use ordered data. If there is no other way to measure your variable then you have to use a label (categoric variable).

Making your investigation repeatable, reproducible and valid

When you are designing an investigation you must make sure that others can repeat any results you get – this makes it **reproducible**. You should also plan to make each result **repeatable**. You can do this by getting consistent sets of repeat measurements.

You must also make sure you are measuring the actual thing you want to measure. If you don't, your data can't be used to answer your original question. This seems very obvious but it is not always quite so easy. You need to make sure that you have controlled as many other variables as you can, so that no-one can say that your investigation is not **valid**.

How might an independent variable be linked to a dependent variable?

The **independent variable** is the one you choose to vary in your investigation.

The **dependent variable** is used to judge the effect of varying the independent variable.

These variables may be linked together. If there is a pattern to be seen (for example as one thing gets bigger the other also gets bigger), it may be that:

- changing one has caused the other to change

- the two are related, but one is not necessarily the cause of the other.

Starting an investigation

Observation

As scientists we use observations to ask questions. We can only ask useful questions if we know something about the observed event. We will not have all of the answers, but we know enough to start asking the correct questions.

When you are designing an investigation you have to observe carefully which variables are likely to have an effect.

What is a hypothesis?

A **hypothesis** is an idea based on observation that has some really good science to try to explain it.

When making hypotheses you can be very imaginative with your ideas. However, you should have some scientific reasoning behind those ideas so that they are not totally bizarre.

Remember, your explanation might not be correct, but you think it is. The only way you can check out your hypothesis is to make it into a prediction and then test it by carrying out an investigation.

observation + knowledge → hypothesis → prediction → investigation

Starting to design an investigation

An investigation starts with a question, followed by a **prediction**. You, as the scientist, predict that there is a **relationship** between two variables.

You should think about a preliminary investigation to find the most suitable range and interval for the independent variable.

Making your investigation safe

Remember that when you design your investigation, you must:
- look for any potential **hazards**
- decide how you will reduce any **risk**.

You will need to write these down in your plan:
- write down your plan
- make a risk assessment
- make a prediction
- draw a blank table ready for the results.

Key points

- Continuous data can give you more information than other types of data.
- You must design investigations that produce repeatable, reproducible and valid results if you are to be believed.
- Be aware that just because two variables are related, does not mean that there is a causal link.
- Hypotheses can lead to predictions and investigations.
- You must make a risk assessment, make a prediction and write a plan.

Setting up investigations

Fair testing

A **fair test** is one in which only the independent variable affects the dependent variable. All other variables are controlled.

This is easy to set up in the laboratory, but almost impossible in fieldwork. Investigations in the environment are not that simple and easy to control. There are complex variables that are changing constantly.

So how can we set up the fieldwork investigations? The best you can do is to make sure that all of the many variables change in much the same way, except for the one you are investigating. Then at least the plants you might be monitoring for the effects of pollution are getting the same weather, even if it is constantly changing.

If you are investigating two variables in a large population then you will need to do a survey. Again, it is impossible to control all of the variables. Imagine scientists were investigating the effect of a new drug on diabetes. They would have to choose people of the same age and same family history to test. The larger the sample size tested, the more valid the results will be.

Control groups are used in these investigations to try to make sure that you are measuring the variable that you intend to measure. When investigating the effects of a new drug, the control group will be given a placebo. The control group think they are taking a drug but the placebo does not contain the drug. This way you can control the variable of 'thinking that the drug is working' and separate out the effect of the actual drug.

Designing an investigation

Accuracy

Your investigation must provide **accurate** data. Accurate data is essential if your results are going to have any meaning.

How do you know if you have accurate data?

It is very difficult to be certain. Accurate results are very close to the true value. It is not always possible to know what that true value is.

- Sometimes you can calculate a theoretical value and check it against the experimental evidence. Close agreement between these two values could indicate accurate data.
- You can draw a graph of your results and see how close each result is to the line of best fit.
- Try repeating your measurements with a different instrument and see if you get the same readings.

How do you get accurate data?

- Using instruments that measure accurately will help.
- The more carefully you use the measuring instruments, the more accuracy you will get.

Precision

Your investigation must provide data with sufficient **precision**. If it doesn't then you will not be able to make a valid conclusion.

How do you get precise and repeatable data?

- You have to repeat your tests as often as necessary to improve repeatability.
- You have to repeat your tests in exactly the same way each time.
- Use measuring instruments that have the appropriate scale divisions needed for a particular investigation. Smaller scale divisions have better **resolution**.

Making measurements

Using instruments

You cannot expect perfect results. When you choose an instrument you need to know that it will give you the accuracy that you want, i.e. it will give you a true reading.

When you choose an instrument you need to decide how precise you need to be. Some instruments have smaller scale divisions than others. Instruments that measure the same thing can have different sensitivities. The resolution of an instrument refers to the smallest change in a value that can be detected. Choosing the wrong scale can cause you to miss important data or make silly conclusions.

You also need to be able to use an instrument properly.

Errors

Even when an instrument is used correctly, the results can still show differences. Results may differ because of a **random error**. This is most likely to be due to a poor measurement being made. It could be due to not carrying out the method consistently.

The **error** may be a **systematic error**. This means that the method was carried out consistently but an error was being repeated.

Anomalies

Anomalies are results that are clearly out of line. They are not those that are due to the natural variation that you get from any measurement. These should be looked at carefully. There might be a very interesting reason why they are so different. If they are simply due to a random error then they should be ignored.

If anomalies can be identified while you are doing an investigation, then it is best to repeat that part of the investigation. If you find anomalies after you have finished collecting the data for an investigation, then they must be discarded.

Using data

After this topic, you should know:

- what is meant by the 'range' and the 'mean' of a set of data
- how data should be displayed
- which charts and graphs are best to identify patterns in data
- how to identify relationships within data
- how scientists draw valid conclusions from relationships
- how to evaluate the reproducibility of an investigation.

Presenting data

Tables

Tables are really good for getting your results down quickly and clearly. You should design your table before you start your investigation.

The range of the data

Pick out the maximum and the minimum values and you have the **range**. You should always quote these two numbers when asked for a range. For example, the range is between … (the lowest value) and … (the highest value) and don't forget to include the units!

The mean of the data

Add up all of the measurements and divide by how many there are.

Bar charts

If you have a categoric independent variable and a continuous dependent variable then you should use a **bar chart**.

Line graphs

If you have a continuous independent and a continuous dependent variable then use a **line graph**.

Scatter graphs

These are used in much the same way as a line graph, but you might not expect to be able to draw such a clear line of best fit. For example, to find out if the melting point of an element is related to its density you might draw a scatter graph of your results.

Using data to draw conclusions

Identifying patterns and relationships

Now you have a bar chart or a graph of your results you can begin looking for patterns in your results. You must have an open mind at this point.

Firstly, there could still be some anomalous results. You might not have picked these out earlier. How do you spot an anomaly? It must be a significant distance away from the pattern, not just within normal variation.

A line of best fit will help to identify any anomalies at this stage. Ask yourself – do the anomalies represent something important or were they just a mistake?

Secondly, remember a line of best fit can be a straight line or it can be a curve – you have to decide from your results.

The line of best fit will also lead you into thinking what the relationship is between your two variables. You need to consider whether your graph shows a linear relationship. This simply means can you be confident about drawing a straight line of best fit on your graph? If the answer is yes, then is this line positive or negative?

A **directly proportional** relationship is shown by a positive straight line that goes through the origin (0, 0).

Your results might also show a curved line of best fit. These can be predictable, complex or very complex!

Drawing conclusions

Your graphs are designed to show the relationship between your two chosen variables. You need to consider what that relationship means for your conclusion. You must also take into account the repeatability and the validity of the data you are considering.

You will continue to have an open mind about your conclusion.

You will have made a prediction. This could be supported by your results, it might not be supported, or it could be partly supported. It might suggest some other hypothesis to you.

You must be willing to think carefully about your results. Remember it is quite rare for a set of results to completely support a prediction and be completely repeatable.

Look for possible links between variables. It may be that:
- changing one has caused the other to change.
- the two are related, but one is not necessarily the cause of the other.

You must decide which is the most likely. Remember a positive relationship does not always mean a causal link between the two variables.

Your conclusion must go no further than the **evidence** that you have. Any patterns you spot are only strictly valid in the range of values you tested. Further tests are needed to check whether the pattern continues beyond this range.

The purpose of the prediction was to test a hypothesis. The hypothesis can:
- be supported,
- be refuted, or
- lead to another hypothesis.

You have to decide which it is on the evidence available.

Evaluation

If you are still uncertain about a conclusion, it might be down to the repeatability, reproducibility and the validity of the results. You could check reproducibility by:
- looking for other similar work on the Internet or from others in your class,
- getting somebody else to redo your investigation,
- trying an alternative method to see if you get the same results.

Calcium carbonate reacts with dilute hydrochloric acid. The equation for the reaction is

$$CaCO_3(s) + 2\,HCl(aq) \rightarrow CaCl_2(aq) + H_2O(l) + CO_2(g)$$

A student investigated how changing the concentration of dilute hydrochloric acid altered how quickly carbon dioxide gas was made.

The gas was collected over water and its volume measured every 20 seconds.

1 (a) The diagram shows the apparatus during one experiment.

What volume of carbon dioxide gas has been collected?

23 cm³

(1)

> The volume is correct and units have been given. Level has been read to bottom of the meniscus.

The graph shows the results the student obtained.

> There are two marks available for the answer, so there will normally be two things that need to be said to gain full marks. This candidate has spotted that while the final volume of gas collected is the same (the graphs level off at the same height) the line for the more concentrated acid is steeper – this means that at any time before the reaction is complete, more gas has been collected when the more concentrated acid is used.

1 (b) Describe the effect of changing the concentration of the dilute hydrochloric acid on the volume of carbon dioxide collected during the experiment.

When the concentration of the acid is higher the gas is collected more quickly but the same final volume of gas is collected.

(2)

> Due to the fact that carbon dioxide is slightly soluble in water, a small amount of it will dissolve in the water in the water bath. This will reduce the volume of gas that can be collected in the measuring cylinder.

1 (c) Carbon dioxide gas is slightly soluble in water. What effect will this have on the volume of gas collected?

It will reduce the volume of gas collected.

(1)

1 (d) The student carried out her investigation so that it was a fair test. Select one variable that must be kept constant for the experiment to be a fair test and explain why it must be kept constant.

The surface area of the calcium carbonate must be kept constant. If the surface area was higher, then there would be more collisions of hydrogen ions with calcium carbonate per second. This would make the reaction faster.

(3)

Another student investigated the mass of calcium carbonate used on the final volume of carbon dioxide gas collected. The method she followed was:

1. Place 25.0 cm³ of dilute hydrochloric acid in a boiling tube.

2. Add a known mass of calcium carbonate to the dilute acid in the boiling tube.

3. Connect the boiling tube to a gas syringe as shown in the diagram

Hydrochloric acid

The graph shows the results she obtained.

Mass of calcium carbonate in grams

1 (e) Name an item of laboratory apparatus most suitable for measuring 25.0 cm³ of hydrochloric acid.

A volumetric pipette could be used.

(1)

1 (f) Draw a line of best fit through the points on the graph.

The line drawn is straight (it has been done with the aid of a rule) and it ignores the anomalous point.

(1)

1 (g) Describe the relationship between the mass of calcium carbonate used and the volume of carbon dioxide gas collected.

As the mass of calcium carbonate is doubled, the volume of gas collected also doubles.

(2)

An alternative way to say this is "they are directly proportional". A straight line through the origin shows a directly proportional relationship. If the line is straight but does not pass through the origin then we can say it is a linear relationship (but it is not directly proportional).

1 (h) There is an anomalous point on the graph. Circle the anomalous point and explain what could have happened to cause the anomalous point.

The point that is some distance from the line has been correctly identified.

The explanation gives a correct reason why the volume of gas collected could have been too small and explains why the reason given would result in too small a volume. Other possible explanations include the mass of calcium carbonate being too small so less carbon dioxide would be made.

The bung may not have been replaced correctly. This would have allowed some of the gas to escape, and so less was collected.

(3)

1 (i) What should the student have done to check the precision of her results and improve the accuracy of the data she has plotted?

The experiment should have been repeated at least three times and then a mean value calculated for the volume of gas collected for each mass of calcium carbonate.

(2)

Repeating the experiment does not necessarily make the results more accurate, but it does let us check to see if the results are precise. Calculating a mean using the repeated results will reduce any random errors and so the mean values should be more accurate.

1 (j) Use the graph to predict the volume of gas that would be collected if 0.55 g of calcium carbonate were used in the experiment. Show all of your working.

The volume of gas would be 110 cm³.

(2)

> This scores both marks because the candidate has extrapolated the graph line and then read off the correct value from the graph. The value has been read from the graph accurately.

The student then repeated the experiment using 0.55 g of calcium carbonate. She obtained a much smaller volume of gas than she expected. Her teacher suggested that this was because she had not used enough acid to react with all the calcium carbonate

1 (k) Explain how she could check whether her teacher's suggestion was correct.

She could repeat the experiment using a larger volume of acid.
If the teacher is correct then the volume of gas will increase.

(2)

> This scores both marks as the candidate has said what should be done and the result that should be obtained if the teacher is correct.

The student calculated the volume of gas, at 25 °C, she should have made in some of the runs. The table shows the volumes she collected and how much should have been made.

Mass calcium carbonate/g	Volume carbon dioxide collected/cm³	Theoretical volume of carbon dioxide/cm³
0.10	20	24
0.20	40	48
0.30	60	72

> All of the gas volumes are too small. This means there is a problem with the procedure being used.

1 (l) What type of error do her results show?

It is a systematic error.

(1)

1 (m) Explain how an error of this type could have occurred in each run.

As soon as the calcium carbonate has been added to the acid carbon dioxide gas is made. Some of this gas escapes before the bung is placed in the boiling tube connected to the gas syringe.

(2)

> This answer scores both marks as it gives a problem that would cause a systematic error and explains how that error makes the gas volume too small. Another correct answer would be if the gas was being collected at a temperature below 25°C as at a lower temperatures the gas will have a smaller volume

Glossary

A

Accurate A measurement is considered accurate if it is judged to be close to the true value.

Acid A sour substance which can attack metal, clothing or skin. When dissolved in water, its solution has a pH value less than 7. Acids are proton (H^+ ion) donors.

Activation energy The minimum energy needed for a reaction to take place.

Alkali metal Elements in Group 1 of the periodic table, e.g. lithium (Li), sodium (Na), potassium (K).

Alkali Its solution has a pH value more than 7.

Alkane Saturated hydrocarbon with the general formula C_nH_{2n+2}, e.g. methane, ethane and propane.

Alkene Unsaturated hydrocarbon which contains a carbon–carbon double bond. Its general formula is C_nH_{2n}, e.g. ethene C_2H_4.

Alloy A mixture of metals (and sometimes non-metals). For example, brass is a mixture of copper and zinc.

Aluminium A low density, corrosion-resistant metal used in many alloys, including those used in the aircraft industry.

Amphoteric An oxide that displays both acidic and basic properties.

Anhydrous Describes a substance that does not contain water.

Anode The positive electrode in electrolysis.

Anomalies Results that do not match the pattern seen in the other data collected or are well outside the range of other repeat readings. They should be retested and if necessary discarded.

Aqueous solution The mixture made by adding a soluble substance to water.

Atmosphere The relatively thin layer of gases that surround planet Earth.

Atom The smallest part of an element that can still be recognised as that element.

Atomic number The number of protons (which equals the number of electrons) in an atom. It is sometimes called the proton number.

B

Balanced (equation) A symbol equation in which there are equal numbers of each type of atom on either side of the equation.

Bar chart A chart with rectangular bars with lengths proportional to the values that they represent. The bars should be of equal width. Also called a bar graph.

Base The oxide, hydroxide or carbonate of a metal that will react with an acid, forming a salt as one of the products. (If a base dissolves in water it is called an alkali). Bases are proton (H^+ ion) acceptors.

Biodegradable Materials that can be broken down by microorganisms.

Biodiesel Fuel for cars made from plant oils.

Biofuel Fuel made from animal or plant products.

Bioleaching Process of extraction of metals from ores using microorganisms.

Blast furnace The huge reaction vessels used in industry to extract iron from its ore.

Bond dissociation energy The energy required to break a specific chemical bond.

Brine A solution of sodium chloride in water.

Burette A long glass tube with a tap at one end and markings to show volumes of liquid; used to add precisely known volumes of liquids to a solution in a conical flask below it.

C

Carbon monoxide A toxic gas whose formula is CO.

Carbon steel Alloy of iron containing controlled, small amounts of carbon.

Cast iron The impure iron taken directly from a blast furnace.

Catalyst A substance that speeds up a chemical reaction but remains chemically unchanged itself at the end of the reaction.

Catalytic converter Fitted to exhausts of vehicles to reduce pollutants released.

Cathode The negative electrode in electrolysis.

Cement A building material made by heating limestone and clay.

Chromatography The process whereby small amounts of dissolved substances are separated by running a solvent along a material such as absorbent paper.

Climate change The change in global weather patterns that could be caused by excess levels of greenhouse gases in the atmosphere.

Closed system A system in which no matter or energy enters or leaves.

Collision theory An explanation of chemical reactions in terms of reacting particles colliding with sufficient energy for a reaction to take place.

Compound A substance made when two or more elements are chemically bonded together. For example, water (H_2O) is a compound made from hydrogen and oxygen.

Control group If an experiment is to determine the effect of changing a single variable, a control is often set up in which the independent variable is not changed, thus enabling a comparison to be made. If the investigation is of the survey type a control group is usually established to serve the same purpose.

Copper-rich ore Rock that contains a high proportion of a copper compound.

Covalent bond The bond between two atoms that share one or more pairs of electrons.

Covalent bonding The attraction between two atoms that share one or more pairs of electrons.

Cracking The reaction used in the oil industry to break down large hydrocarbons into smaller, more useful ones. This occurs when the hydrocarbon vapour is either passed over a hot catalyst or mixed with steam and heated to a high temperature.

D

Data Information, either qualitative or quantitative, that has been collected.

Delocalised electron Bonding electron that is no longer associated with any one particular atom.

Desalination The removal of salts from water to make it suitable for drinking and other uses.

Diffusion The automatic mixing of liquids and gases as a result of the random motion of their particles.

Directly proportional A relationship that, when drawn on a line graph, shows a positive linear relationship that crosses through the origin.

Displacement reaction A reaction in which a more reactive element takes the place of a less reactive element in one of its compounds or in solution.

Distillation Separation of a liquid from a mixture by evaporation followed by condensation.

Dot and cross diagram A drawing to show only the arrangement of the outer shell electrons of the atoms or ions in a substance.

Double bond A covalent bond made by the sharing of two pairs of electrons.

E

Electrolysis The breakdown of a substance containing ions by electricity.

Electrolyte A liquid, containing free-moving ions, which is broken down by electricity in the process of electrolysis.

Electron A tiny particle with a negative charge. Electrons orbit the nucleus in atoms or ions.

Electronic structure A set of numbers to show the arrangement of electrons in their shells (or energy levels), e.g. the electronic structure of a potassium atom is 2, 8, 8, 1.

Electroplating The process of depositing a thin layer of metal on an object during electrolysis.

Element A substance made up of only one type of atom. An element cannot be broken down chemically into any simpler substance.

Empirical formula The simplest ratio of elements in a compound.

End point The point in a titration where the reaction is complete and titration should stop.

Endothermic A reaction that takes in energy from the surroundings.

Energy level see Shell.

Equilibrium The point in a reversible reaction in which the forward and backward rates of reaction are the same. Therefore, the amounts of substances present in the reacting mixture remain constant.

Error – random Causes readings to be spread about the true value, due to results varying in an unpredictable way from one measurement to the next. Random errors are present when any measurement is made, and cannot be corrected. The effect of random errors can be reduced by making more measurements and calculating a new mean.

Error – systematic Causes readings to be spread about some value other than the true value, due to results differing from the true value by a consistent amount each time a measurement is made. Sources of systematic error can include the environment, methods of observation or instruments used. Systematic errors cannot be dealt with by simple repeats. If a systematic error is suspected, the data collection should be repeated using a different technique or a different set of equipment, and the results compared.

Error Sometimes called an uncertainty.

Ethene An alkene with the formula C_2H_4.

Evidence Data which has been shown to be valid.

Exothermic A reaction that *gives out* energy to the surroundings.

F

Fair test A fair test is one in which only the independent variable has been allowed to affect the dependent variable.

Fermentation The reaction in which the enzymes in yeast turn glucose into ethanol and carbon dioxide.

Flammable Easily ignited and capable of burning rapidly.

Fraction Hydrocarbons with similar boiling points separated from crude oil.

Fractional distillation A way to separate liquids from a mixture of liquids by boiling off the substances at different temperatures, then condensing and collecting the liquids.

Fullerene Form of the element carbon that can exist as large cage-like structures, based on hexagonal rings of carbon atoms.

Functional group An atom or group of atoms that give organic compounds their characteristic reactions.

G

Galvanised Iron or steel objects that have been protected from rusting by a thin layer of zinc metal at their surface.

Gas chromatography The process of separating the components in a mixture by passing the vapours through a column and detecting them as they leave the column at different times.

Gas A state of matter.

Giant covalent structure A huge 3D network of covalently bonded atoms (e.g. the giant lattice of carbon atoms in diamond or graphite).

Giant lattice A huge 3D network of atoms or ions (e.g. the giant ionic lattice in sodium chloride).

Giant structure See Giant lattice.

Global dimming The reflection of sunlight by tiny solid particles in the air.

Group All the elements in the columns (labelled 1 to 7 and 0) down the periodic table.

H

Half equation An equation that describes reduction (gain of electrons) or oxidation (loss of electrons), such as the reactions that take place at the electrodes during electrolysis. For example: $Na^+ + e^- \rightarrow Na$.

Halogens The elements found in Group 7 of the periodic table.

Hazard A hazard is something (for example, an object, a property of a substance or an activity) that can cause harm.

High-alloy steel Expensive alloy of iron mixed with relatively large proportions of other metals e.g. stainless steel which contains nickel and chromium along with the iron.

Homologous series A group of related organic compounds that have the same functional group, e.g. the molecules of the homologous series of alcohols all contain the –OH group.

Hydrated Describes a substance that contains water in its crystals, e.g. hydrated copper sulfate.

Hydration A reaction in which water (H_2O) is chemically added to a compound.

Hydrocarbon A compound containing only hydrogen and carbon.

Hypothesis A proposal intended to explain certain facts or observations.

I

Incomplete combustion When a fuel burns in insufficient oxygen, producing carbon monoxide as a toxic product.

Inert Unreactive.

Intermolecular forces The attraction between the individual molecules in a covalently bonded substance.

Interval The quantity between readings, for example, a set of 11 readings equally spaced over a distance of 1 m would have an interval of 10 cm.

Ion A charged particle produced by the loss or gain of electrons.

Ion-exchange resin A water softener which works by replacing calcium and magnesium ions with sodium or hydrogen ions, removing the hardness.

Ionic bond The electrostatic force of attraction between positively and negatively charged ions.

Ionic bonding The electrostatic force of attraction between positively and negatively charged ions.

Ionic equation An equation that shows only those ions or atoms that change in a chemical reaction.

Isotope Atoms that have the same number of protons but different number of neutrons, i.e. they have the same atomic number but different mass numbers.

L

Limewater The common name for calcium hydroxide solution.

Line graph Used when both variables are continuous. The line should normally be a line of best fit, and may be straight or a smooth curve. (Exceptionally, in some (mainly biological) investigations, the line may be a 'point-to-point' line.)

Liquid A state of matter.

Low-alloy steel Alloy of iron containing small amounts (1 to 5 per cent) of other metals.

M

Macromolecule Giant covalent structure.

Mass number The number of protons plus neutrons in the nucleus of an atom.

Mass spectrometer A machine that can be used to analyse small amounts of a substance to identify it and to find its relative molecular mass.

Mean The arithmetical average of a series of numbers.

Metal ore A rock in which there is sufficient metal compound (or occasionally metal) to make it economically viable to extract the metal.

Mixture When some elements or compounds are mixed together and intermingle but do not react together (i.e. no new substance is made). A mixture is not a pure substance.

Mole The amount of substance in the relative atomic or formula mass of a substance in grams.

Molecular formula The chemical formula that shows the actual numbers of atoms in a particular molecule (e.g. C_2H_4).

Molecular ion peak The peak on the mass spectrum of a substance which tells us the relative molecular mass of the substance. The peak is produced by the heaviest positive ion shown on the mass spectrum.

Molecule A group of atoms bonded together e.g. PCl_5.

Monomers Small reactive molecules that react together in repeating sequences to form a very large molecule (a polymer).

N

Nanoscience The study of very tiny particles or structures between 1 and 100 nanometres in size – where 1 nanometre = 10^{-9} metres.

Neutral A solution with a pH value of 7 which is neither acidic nor alkaline. Alternatively, something that carries no overall electrical charge – neither positively nor negatively charged.

Neutralisation The chemical reaction of an acid with a base in which they cancel each other out, forming a salt and water. If the base is a carbonate or hydrogen carbonate, carbon dioxide is also produced in the reaction.

Neutron A dense particle found in the nucleus of an atom. It is electrically neutral, carrying no charge.

Nitrogen oxide Gaseous pollutant given off from motor vehicles; a cause of acid rain.

Noble gases The very unreactive gases found in Group 0 of the periodic table.

Non-renewable Something which cannot be replaced once it is used up.

Nucleus (of an atom) The very small and dense central part of an atom which contains protons and neutrons.

O

Ore Ore is rock which contains enough metal to make it economically worthwhile to extract the metal.

Oxidation The reaction when oxygen is added to a substance (or when electrons are lost).

Oxidised A reaction where oxygen is added to a substance (or when electrons are lost from a substance).

P

Particulate Small solid particle given off from motor vehicles as a result of incomplete combustion of its fuel.

Percentage yield The actual mass of product collected in a reaction divided by the maximum mass that could have been formed in theory, multiplied by 100.

Periodic table An arrangement of elements in the order of their atomic numbers, forming groups and periods.

pH scale A number which shows how strongly acidic or alkaline a solution is. Acids have a pH value of less than 7 (pH 0 is strongly acidic). Alkalis have a pH value above 7 (pH 14 is strongly alkaline). A neutral liquid has a pH value of 7.

Phytomining The process of extracting metals from ores using plants.

Pipette A glass tube used to measure accurate volumes of liquids.

Polymer A substance made from very large molecules made up of many repeating units e.g. poly(ethene).

Polymerisation The reaction of monomers to make a polymer.

Precipitate An insoluble solid formed by a reaction taking place in solution.

Precise A precise measurement is one in which there is very little spread about the mean value. Precision depends only on the extent of random errors – it gives no indication of how close results are to the true value.

Precision A precise set of repeat readings will be closely grouped together.

Prediction A forecast or statement about the way something will happen in the future. In science it is not just a simple guess, because it is based on some prior knowledge or on a hypothesis.

Product A substance made as a result of a chemical reaction.

Propene An alkene with the formula C_3H_6.

Proton A tiny positive particle found inside the nucleus of an atom.

R

Range The maximum and minimum values of the independent or dependent variables; important in ensuring that any pattern is detected.

Reactant A substance we start with before a chemical reaction takes place.

Reactivity series A list of elements in order of their reactivity. The most reactive element is put at the top of the list.

Recycle The process in which waste materials are processed to be used again.

Reduction A reaction in which oxygen is removed (or electrons are gained).

Relationship The link between the variables that were investigated. These relationships may be: causal, i.e. changing x is the reason why y changes; by association, i.e. both x and y change at the same time, but the changes may both be caused by a third variable changing; by chance occurrence.

Relative atomic mass, A_r The average mass of the atoms of an element compared with carbon-12 (which is given a mass of exactly 12). The average mass must take into account the proportions of the naturally occurring isotopes of the element.

Relative formula mass, M_r The total of the relative atomic masses, added up in the ratio shown in the chemical formula, of a substance.

Repeatable A measurement is repeatable if the original experimenter repeats the investigation using the same method and equipment and obtains the same results.

Reproducible A measurement is reproducible if the investigation is repeated by another person, or by using different equipment or techniques, and the same results are obtained.

Resolution This is the smallest change in the quantity being measured (input) of a measuring instrument that gives a perceptible change in the reading.

Respiration The process by which food molecules are broken down to release energy for the cells.

Retention time The time it takes a component in a mixture to pass through the column during gas chromatography.

Reversible reaction A reaction in which the products can re-form the reactants.

R_f (retention factor) A measurement from chromatography: it is the distance a spot of substance has been carried above the baseline divided by the distance of the solvent front.

Risk The likelihood that a hazard will actually cause harm. We can reduce risk by identifying the hazard and doing something to protect against that hazard.

Rusting The corrosion of iron.

S

Sacrificial protection An effective way to prevent rusting whereby a metal more reactive than iron (such as zinc or magnesium) is attached to or coated on an object.

Salt A salt is a compound formed when some or all of the hydrogen in an acid is replaced by a metal (or by an ammonium ion). For example, potassium nitrate, KNO_3 (from nitric acid).

Saturated hydrocarbon Describes a hydrocarbon with only single bonds between its carbon atoms. This means that it contains as many hydrogen atoms as possible in each molecule.

Shape memory alloy Mixture of metals which responds to changes in temperature.

Shell (or energy level) An area in an atom, around its nucleus, where electrons are found.

Smart polymer Polymers that change in response to changes in their environment.

Smelting Heating a metal ore in order to extract its metal.

Solid A state of matter.

Stainless steel A chromium-nickel alloy of steel which does not rust.

State symbol The abbreviations used in balanced symbol equations to show if reactants and products are solid (s), liquid (l), gas (g) or dissolved in water (aq).

States of matter Tells us whether a substance is a solid, a liquid or a gas.

Steel An alloy of iron with small amounts of carbon or other metals, such as nickel and chromium, added.

Sulfur dioxide A toxic gas whose formula is SO_2. It causes acid rain.

Symbol equation A balanced chemical equation showing the formula of each reactant and product in the reaction, e.g. $H_2 + Cl_2 \rightarrow 2HCl$

T

Thermal decomposition The breakdown of a compound by heating it.

Thermosetting polymer Polymer that can form extensive cross-linking between chains, resulting in rigid materials which are heat-resistant.

Thermosoftening polymer Polymer that forms plastics which can be softened by heating, then remoulded into different shapes as they cool down and set.

Titration A method for measuring the volumes of two solutions that react together.

Transition element Element from the central block of the periodic table. It has typical metallic properties and forms coloured compounds.

U

Universal indicator A mixture of indicators that can change through a range of colours depending on the pH of a solution. Its colour is matched to a pH number using a pH scale. It shows how strongly acidic or alkaline liquids and solutions are.

Unsaturated hydrocarbon A hydrocarbon whose molecules contains at least one carbon–carbon double bond.

V

Valid Suitability of the investigative procedure to answer the question being asked.

Variable – categoric Categoric variables have values that are labels. For example, names of plants or types of material.

Variable – continuous Can have values (called a quantity) that can be given by measurement (for example, light intensity, flow rate, temperature, etc.).

Variable – control A variable which may, in addition to the independent variable, affect the outcome of the investigation and therefore has to be kept constant or at least monitored.

Variable – dependent The variable for which the value is measured for each and every change in the independent variable.

Variable – independent The variable for which values are changed or selected by the investigator.

Variable Physical, chemical or biological quantity or characteristic.

Viscosity The resistance of a liquid to flowing or pouring; a liquid's 'thickness'.

W

Word equation A way of describing what happens in a chemical reaction by showing the names of all reactants and the products they form.

Y

Yield See Percentage yield.

Answers

1 Fundamental ideas (1)

1.1

1 E.g.

	General properties	Average distance between particles	Arrangement of particles	Movement of particles
Solid	Fixed shape; incompressible	Particles are touching	Regular pattern	Vibrate on the spot
Liquid	No fixed shape; can flow; very difficult to compress	Most particles are touching	Irregular, random	Slip and slide over and around each other
Gas	No fixed shape; spreads out to fill its container; easily compressed	Large distances	Irregular, random	Can move very quickly. In a random manner, between collisions

2 As the particles of gas are cooled down their average speed decreases until at its condensation point the particles become much closer together. They form a liquid in which the particles are moving randomly, slipping over and around each other. As the liquid is cooled, the average speed of the particles decreases until at its freezing point the particles stop moving around randomly and remain in fixed positions, vibrating on the spot. As the solid is cooled the average rate of the vibrations slows down.

3 a freeze/solidify   d boil/evaporate
   b condense   e sublime
   c melt

4 As the temperature is increased, the particles in a gas gain energy and their average speed is increased and they take up more space if the pressure remains constant. Therefore, the density decreases as the same mass of gas occupies a larger volume.
By compressing a gas the pressure is increased as particles collide with the walls of their container more frequently. So, the same mass of gas occupies a smaller volume and the density of the gas increases.

5 The strength of the attractive forces between particles varies in different substances so those with stronger forces of attraction will have higher melting points than those with weaker forces of attraction.

6 Plan a fair test varying one factor e.g. temperature of the water or surface area of the paper towel, keeping all other variables constant. Monitor the rate of evaporation by measuring the mass of the wet paper towel on the electric balance at regular time intervals.

1.2

1 a The food particles released from the hot food diffuse through the air outside the shop and passers-by detect these with their sense of smell.
   b The particles of water move around faster in hot water than in cold water so they collide into the sugar particles in the solid more frequently and with more energy. This breaks down the regular arrangement of sugar particles in the solid and spreads them out more quickly as the sugar solution is formed.
   c Hot water releases water particles into the air as its most energetic particles are moving fast enough to escape from their neighbouring water particles at the surface. The glass in the window is colder than the air so any water particles diffusing through the air to the window will cool down and slow down; then the vapour will condense back to liquid on the glass.
   d Petrol is a volatile liquid so particles can evaporate from its surface quite easily. It is also flammable. In a petrol station there are likely to be particles from petrol diffusing through the air which could be ignited by any naked flame or a lighted cigarette.

2 a The movement of one substance through another due to the random motion of the particles in liquids or gases.
   b The average speed of the particles in a gas is greater than that in a liquid so the mixing together of particles happens more quickly in gases.

3 The jittery movement of the pollen grains must be caused by collisions with the particles in liquid water which are too small to be seen under the microscope.

4 As hydrogen bromide is heavier than hydrogen chloride the white ring of smoke would form nearer the end of the tube releasing particles (molecules) of hydrogen bromide.
ammonia + hydrogen bromide → ammonium bromide
$NH_3(g)$ + $HBr(g)$ → $NH_4Br(s)$

1.3

1 a

Metals	Non-metals
Barium	Phosphorus
Vanadium	Krypton
Mercury	
Potassium	
Uranium	

   b Non-metal because it does not have the physical properties of a metal e.g. it does not conduct electricity.

2 A mixture of elements can be separated by physical means because atoms from the different elements are not chemically bonded to each other whereas they are if they have reacted together.

3 One diagram showing an element in which all the atoms present must of the same type and another showing a compound containing more than one type of atom chemically combined.

4 A tiny central nucleus surrounded by orbiting electrons.

5 a Na from Latin *natrium*   c Pb from Latin *plumbum*
   b Au from Latin *aurum*   d K from Latin *kalium*

1.4

1

Sub-atomic particle	Location	Relative charge
Proton	In the nucleus	+1
Neutron	In the nucleus	0
Electron	Orbiting the nucleus	−1

2 a It increases by 1.
   b It increases by 8.

3 Atoms contain an equal number of protons (carrying a relative charge of +1) and electrons (carrying a relative charge of −1) so the opposite charges cancel each other out.

4 Cobalt, Co, atomic number = 27, mass number = 59.

5 a 7 protons, 7 electrons and 7 neutrons.
   b 17 protons, 17 electrons and 18 neutrons.
   c 47 protons, 47 electrons and 61 neutrons.
   d 92 protons, 92 electrons and 143 neutrons.

1.5

1 a The first or innermost shell.
   b 2 in the first then 8 in the second.

2 a   b

   c   d

3 a 2, 8, 8, 1   b 1 electron

4 phosphorus, P

5 a Because they all have 1 electron (the same number of electrons) in the highest energy level (outermost shell) of their atoms.
   b lithium + oxygen → lithium oxide
      sodium + oxygen → sodium oxide
      potassium + oxygen → potassium oxide

1.6

1

Sub-atomic particle	Relative mass	Relative charge
Proton	1	+1
Neutron	1	0
Electron	Very small (1/2000)	−1

2 **a** 5 protons and 6 neutrons   **d** 17 protons and 20 neutrons
   b 7 protons and 7 neutrons   **e** 53 protons and 74 neutrons
   c 12 protons and 12 neutrons

3 Atoms of the same element with different numbers of neutrons/Atoms with the same number of protons but different numbers of neutrons/ Atoms with the same atomic number but different mass numbers

4 **a** Density
   b They have the same electronic structures so have the same number of electrons in their highest energy level/outermost shell.

5 **a** 0.00024 g/cm³   **c** Radioactive
   b Highly flammable

Answers to end of chapter summary questions

1 **a** The change from a solid directly to a gas.
   b

 613 °C

   c Boiling, melting and sublimation.

2 **a** Particles (molecules) of hydrogen sulfide and sulfur dioxide diffuse through the particles (molecules) of air in the long tube. Where they meet, they collide and react with each other to form the yellow powder.
   b Diffusion.
   c Because the particles (molecules) of sulfur dioxide travel down the tube/diffuse more slowly than the particles (molecules) of hydrogen sulfide (showing sulfur dioxide molecules have a greater mass than hydrogen sulfide molecules)
   d A long tube showing a jagged, random path.
   e The yellow powder would appear sooner because the molecules of gas move faster at higher temperatures.

3 **a** Bromine – liquid, Caesium – solid, Fluorine – gas, Strontium – solid, Xenon – gas
   b Caesium
   c The two gases have much lower densities because they have large spaces between their particles, unlike the solids and liquid whose particles are touching (so many more particles fit into the same volume compared with the gases).
   d Bromine – Br, Caesium – Cs, Fluorine – F, Strontium – Sr, Xenon – Xe
   e Bromine – non-metal, Caesium – metal, Fluorine – non-metal, Strontium – metal, Xenon – non-metal

4 **a** **i** Protons and neutrons
      ii 2 electrons in the first shell and 8 in the second.
   b **i** It is neutral because the number of protons (+) and electrons (−) is the same in an atom so the charges cancel out.
      ii Atomic number is the number of protons.
         Mass number is the number of protons plus neutrons.

5 **a** **i** Non-metal   **v** Noble gases, Group 0
      ii Metals   **vi** Helium, Argon, Krypton, Xenon, Radon
      iii 10 protons   **vii** 2,8
      iv 10 neutrons   **viii** They are very stable arrangements of electrons
   b **i** 88
      ii 2 electrons because it is in Group 2
      iii Metal
      iv 2, 8, 8, 2

Answers to end of chapter examination-style questions

1 Solid   *(1 mark)*
   Gas   *(1 mark)*
   Liquid   *(1 mark)*
2 **a** Element – all atoms are the same.   *(1 mark)*
      Compound – two different atoms/elements combined together.   *(1 mark)*
   b Ammonia is a compound because only one type of molecule, each containing two types of atom.   *(1 mark)*
      Air is a mixture because more than one type of molecule.   *(1 mark)*
   c **i** Condensation/liquefaction   *(1 mark)*
      ii Evaporation/boiling   *(1 mark)*
      iii Sublimation   *(1 mark)*

3 **a** Blue   *(1 mark)*
      Darker at bottom of beaker/lighter at top of beaker   *(1 mark)*
   b Becomes smaller/disappears   *(1 mark)*
   c Dissolving/solution   *(1 mark)*
      Diffusion   *(1 mark)*
4 **a** White solid/smoke   *(1 mark)*
      Closer to ammonia end   *(1 mark)*
   b g   g   s   *(1 mark)*
   c They travel further than hydrogen chloride molecules. *(1 mark)*
5 **a** Atoms of same element with same numbers of protons *(1 mark)*
      but different numbers of neutrons.   *(1 mark)*
   b Same number of electrons (in outer shell).   *(1 mark)*
   c **i** 10   *(1 mark)*
      ii 10   *(1 mark)*
      iii 10   *(1 mark)*
      iv 22   *(1 mark)*
   d $^{10}_{20}$Ne   *(1 mark)*
6 **a** 2   *(1 mark)*
   b 8   *(1 mark)*
   c 3   *(1 mark)*
   d 5   *(1 mark)*
   e 16   *(1 mark)*

2 Fundamental ideas (2)

2.1

1 **a** The average relative mass of an atom of an element, taking into account the proportions of different isotopes naturally occurring in that element, compared on a scale in which an atom of carbon 12 has a value of exactly 12.
   b Because of the averaging of the relative masses of different isotopes in a naturally occurring sample.

2 **a** 256   **c** 159.5
   b 62   **d** 180
3 **a** 8 times
   b **i** 4 moles   **ii** 0.005 moles
   c **i** 0.3 moles   **ii** 500 000 moles
4 **a** 13.5 g   **c** 0.1 g
   b 5000 g or 5 kg   **d** 74.4 g

2.2

1 5.9%   **4** PCl_3
2 21.2%   **5** Al_2O_3
3 SO_3

2.3

1 **a** Because no atoms are created or destroyed in a chemical reaction so equal numbers and types of atoms must appear on both sides of the equation.
   b $H_2 + Cl_2 \rightarrow 2HCl$
2 **a** 17.6 g   **b** $MgCO_3(s) \rightarrow MgO(s) + CO_2(g)$
3 **a** $2KNO_3 \rightarrow 2KNO_2 + O_2$ **c** $4Fe + 3O_2 \rightarrow 2Fe_2O_3$
   b $4Li + O_2 \rightarrow 2Li_2O$
4 $2Na(s) + 2H_2O(l) \rightarrow 2NaOH(aq) + H_2(g)$

2.4

1 2 molecules of HCl or 2 moles of HCl molecules
2 4.0 g
3 **a** $2H_2O_2(aq) \rightarrow 2H_2O(l) + O_2(g)$
   b 3.4 g
4 **a** $Ca(s) + 2H_2O(l) \rightarrow Ca(OH)_2(aq) + H_2(g)$
   b 2.0 g

2.5

1 A reaction in which reactants form products but the products also react to form the reactants.
2 The mixture of water and phenolphthalein would appear colourless to start with, then would turn pink-purple in the alkaline sodium hydroxide solution, and finally turn back to colourless in the excess acid.
3   HPhe   ⇌ $H^+(aq)$ + $Phe^-(aq)$
   colourless   pink-purple
4 E.g. toothbrushes, mugs, strip thermometers
5 White anhydrous copper sulfate powder turns blue in the presence of water:

$$CuSO_4 + 5H_2O \rightleftharpoons CuSO_4.5H_2O$$
           white   blue

Blue cobalt chloride paper turns pink in the presence of water
$$CoCl_2.2H_2O + 4H_2O \rightleftharpoons CoCl_2.6H_2O$$
           blue   pink

2.6

1 To conserve the Earth's resources and reduce waste and pollution.

2 The reaction may be reversible (as products form they react to re-form the reactants again); some reactants may react to give unexpected products; some of the product may be lost in handling or left behind in the apparatus; the reactants may not be pure; there may be losses in separating the product that we want from the reaction mixture.

3 80 g

4 21% (21.2%)

5 a $2NaHCO_3 \rightarrow Na_2CO_3 + H_2O + CO_2$

b 86.8%

Answers to end of chapter summary questions

1 a 34 g   **e** 106 g
  b 64 g   **f** 342 g
  c 28 g   **g** 118 g
  d 40 g

2 a 0.25 moles   **c** 0.05 moles
  b 0.001 moles

3 a 80%   **b** 0.76 g

4 $AlBr_3$

5 a $2Na + Cl_2 \rightarrow 2NaCl$
  b $4Al + 3O_2 \rightarrow 2Al_2O_3$
  c $2Al(OH)_3 \rightarrow Al_2O_3 + 3H_2O$
  d $2Ba(NO_3)_2 \rightarrow 2BaO + 4NO_2 + O_2$
  e $2C_4H_{10} + 13O_2 \rightarrow 8CO_2 + 10H_2O$

6 95.7%

7 a $C_2H_4(g) + H_2O(g) \rightleftharpoons C_2H_5OH(g)$
  b 75%

8 a 1 mole
  b 196 kg
  c 96%
  d Any two valid reasons, e.g. the 2nd stage is a reversible reaction/does not go to completion; reactants/products might be lost in the process at any stage; the sulfur might be impure.

Answers to end of chapter examination-style questions

1 a 32   *(1 mark)*
  b 74   *(1 mark)*
  c M_r of NaOH = 40   *(1 mark)*
    $n = \dfrac{20}{40} = 0.5$ *(1 mark)*
  d M_r of NH_4NO_3 = 80   *(1 mark)*
    mass = $2 \times 80 = 160$ g   *(1 mark)*

2 a $2HBr + H_2SO_4 \rightarrow 2H_2O + Br_2 + SO_2$ *(1 mark)*
  b M_r of CH_3Br = 95   *(1 mark)*
    $\% = \dfrac{80}{95} = 84\ \%$ *(1 mark)*
  c % of oxygen = 31.8   *(1 mark)*

	Br	Na	O
	$\dfrac{15.2}{23}$	$\dfrac{53.0}{80}$	$\dfrac{31.8}{16}$
ratio	0.66	0.66	1.99

                                             (1 mark)
    Empirical formula = $NaBrO_3$ *(1 mark)*

3 a Fire/explosion   *(1 mark)*
  b Water   *(1 mark)*
    Hydrogen reacting with oxygen in oxide.   *(1 mark)*
  c Weigh and heat in hydrogen again.   *(1 mark)*
    Until mass is constant.   *(1 mark)*
  d i 0.64 g   *(1 mark)*
    ii $\dfrac{0.64}{16} = 0.04$ *(1 mark)*
    iii $\dfrac{5.08}{63.5} = 0.08$ *(1 mark)*
    iv Cu:O ratio is 2:1   *(1 mark)*
    Empirical formula = Cu_2O *(1 mark)*

4 a i Ammonia   *(1 mark)*
    Hydrogen chloride   *(1 mark)*
    ii Ammonium chloride   *(1 mark)*
    iii $NH_3 + HCl \rightarrow NH_4Cl$ *(1 mark)*
  b Top of tube too hot for ammonium chloride to form/solid forms outside the tube.   *(1 mark)*

5 a Amount of carbon monoxide = $\dfrac{56}{28} = 2$ mol   *(1 mark)*
    mass of hydrogen = $4 \times 2 = 8$ g   *(1 mark)*
  b M_r of methanol = 32   *(1 mark)*
    mass of methanol = $2 \times 32 = 64$ g   *(1 mark)*
  c % yield = $\dfrac{16 \times 100}{64}$ *(1 mark)*
    = 25%   *(1 mark)*

---

3 Structure and bonding

3.1

1 a Covalent bond
  b Ionic bond

2 The atoms of Group 1 lose their single electron in the outermost shell (highest energy level) by transferring it to a Group 7 atom, which has 7 electrons in the outermost shell (highest energy level). The atoms become ions which have the stable electronic arrangements of a noble gas.

3 a 2, 8 for the Al^{3+} ion (3 electrons lost)
  b 2, 8 for the F^- ion (1 electron gained)
  c 2, 8, 8 for the K^+ ion (1 electron lost)
  d 2, 8 for O^{2-} (2 electrons gained)

3.2

1

Atomic number	Atom	Electronic structure of atom	Ion	Electronic structure of ion
9	F	2,7	F^-	2,8
3	Li	2,1	Li^+	2
16	S	2, 8, 6	S^{2-}	2, 8, 8
20	Ca	2,8,8,2	Ca^{2+}	2, 8, 8

2 Metal atoms lose electrons when they form ions (therefore their ions have more positively-charged protons than negatively-charged electrons) resulting in positively-charged ions. Non-metal atoms gain electrons when they form ions (therefore their ions have more negatively-charged electrons than positively-charged protons) resulting in negatively-charged ions.

3 a Groups 1, 2 and 3; the charge on their ions = (group number)+
  b Groups 5, 6 and 7; the charge on their ions = (8 − group number)−

4 a In KBr the 1− charge on the Br^- ion is cancelled out by the 1+ charge on K^+ ion whereas 2 K^+ ions are needed to cancel out the 2− charge on an O^{2-} ion.
  b In MgO the 2− charge on the O^{2-} ion is cancelled out by the 2+ charge on Mg^{2+} ion whereas 2 Cl^- ions are needed to cancel out the 2+ charge on an Mg^{2+} ion.

5 a

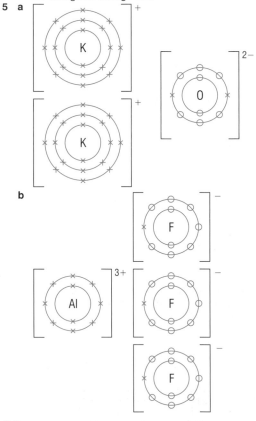

  b

3.3

1 There are strong electrostatic forces of attraction between the oppositely charged ions in the giant lattice, acting in all directions, which result in a lot of energy being required to separate the ions in the process of melting.

2 The ions in the solid are fixed in position and are only free to move (and carry their charge to electrodes) when they are molten or dissolved in water.

3 There is a higher concentration of ions from the dissolved salts in seawater than there are in freshwater.

4 Positive electrode – chloride ions, bromide ions, oxide ions, iodide ions
Negative electrode – lithium ions, calcium ions, sodium ions, zinc ions, barium ions

5 Aluminium oxide because it contains 3+ ions as opposed to the 1+ ions in sodium oxide so we can expect stronger electrostatic forces of attraction between the metal ions and the oxide ions (the smaller size of the aluminium ions also contributes towards this).

3.4

1 Hydrogen iodide, sulfur dioxide and nitrogen(III) chloride because these contain only non-metallic elements.

2 a

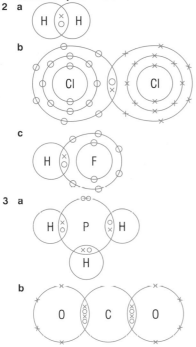

b

c

3 a

b

4 Hydrogen attains the electronic structure of helium.
Chlorine attains the electronic structure of argon.

5 The electrostatic attraction between the bonding pair of negatively charged electrons for each of the positively charged nuclei on either side of the pair hold the atoms together.

3.5

1 Forces of attraction between molecules.

2 a Oxygen.
  b Chlorine.
  c Hydrogen sulfide; hydrogen; sulfur.

3 a It has a giant covalent structure with strong covalent bonds holding the atoms strongly into the regular giant lattices.
  b Nitrogen gas has a very strong triple covalent bond between its nitrogen atoms within each N_2 molecule but only very weak forces of attraction between the N_2 molecules/weak intermolecular forces between N_2 molecules. Therefore molecules easily separated from each other.

4 Good electrical insulator/does not conduct electricity as there is no overall charge on its molecules.

5 There are only weak intermolecular forces between HCl molecules but very strong ionic bonds, which form strong electrostatic forces of attraction in all directions, in the giant ionic lattice of sodium chloride.

3.6

1 a Diamond, graphite, fullerenes
  b Allotropes

2 Very high melting point and boiling point, hard, insoluble in water, electrical insulator.

3 a Delivering drugs to parts of the body where they are needed.
  b The shape of the C_{60} molecule was similar to a building in Montreal designed by the architect Buckminster Fuller in 1967.

4 The layers of graphite atoms have weak forces between them so can slip and slide over each other to act as a lubricant.

5 The carbon atoms in graphite's layers are arranged in hexagons, with each carbon atom forming three strong covalent bonds to its nearest neighbours. As carbon atoms have four electrons in their outer shell available for bonding, this leaves one spare outer electron on each carbon atom. This electron is free to move along the layers of carbon

atoms. So these free-moving delocalised electrons can drift along the layers enabling graphite to conduct electricity. In diamond all the outer shell electrons are involved in covalent bonding so there are no free electrons.

3.7

1 The study of particles between 1 and 100 nm in size.

2 As an antibactericide in fridges and in sprays in operating theatres.

3 a They have a large surface area to volume ratio.
  b Explosions caused by sparks/particles escaping into the air or dangers of being breathed in.

4 a In sun-screens to block ultraviolet light and in face creams to deliver active ingredients deeper beneath the surface of the skin.
  b Delivering drugs to the tumour itself inside the body or being absorbed by tumours and then absorbing energy from lasers to damage the tumour by affecting its proteins.

5 Student's views expressed in a balanced argument.

Answers to end of chapter summary questions

1 a 1   **d** 6
  b 2   **e** 4
  c 7

2 a

Giant covalent	Giant ionic	Simple molecules
silicon dioxide	magnesium oxide	ammonia
graphite	lithium chloride	hydrogen bromide

  b Ammonia, and hydrogen bromide.
  c Graphite because although it has a giant covalent structure it does conduct electricity.
  d

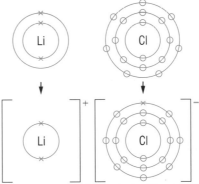

3 a hydrogen iodide, chlorine(VII) oxide, phosphorus(V) fluoride
  b They contain only non-metallic elements.
  c Ionic bonding.
  d i HI   **ii** CaBr$_2$

4

	chloride, Cl^-	oxide, O^{2-}	sulfate, SO_4^{2-}	phosphate(V), PO_4^{3-}
potassium, K^+	KCl	K_2O	K_2SO_4	K_3PO_4
magnesium, Mg^{2+}	$MgCl_2$	MgO	$MgSO_4$	$Mg_3(PO_4)_2$
iron(III), Fe^{3+}	$FeCl_3$	Fe_2O_3	$Fe_2(SO_4)_3$	$FePO_4$

5 a   **b**

Answers to end of chapter examination-style questions

1 a Electrons transfer   *(1 mark)*
  From lithium to oxygen   *(1 mark)*
  Each lithium atoms loses 1 electron, each oxygen atom gains 2 electrons.   *(1 mark)*
  b Li^+ *(1 mark)*
  O^{2-} *(1 mark)*
  c Ions attract each other strongly.   *(1 mark)*
  Many bonds need to be broken.   *(1 mark)*
  d Ions cannot move when solid.   *(1 mark)*
  Ions move to the electrodes when molten.   *(1 mark)*

2 a Diagram showing 2 electrons between H and F.   *(1 mark)*
  6 more electrons in outer shell of F.   *(1 mark)*
  b Covalent   *(1 mark)*
  c Attractions between molecules are weak.   *(1 mark)*
  Easily overcome/need little energy to break.   *(1 mark)*
  d H–Br   *(1 mark)*

3 a Covalent bonds *(1 mark)*
Many/strong bonds *(1 mark)*
Hard to overcome/need a lot of energy to break. *(1 mark)*
b No ions *(1 mark)*
No electrons free to move. *(1 mark)*
4 a Carbon *(1 mark)*
In hexagonal rings. *(1 mark)*
b In drug delivery *(1 mark)*
c 1–200 nanometres *(1 mark)*
d High surface area to volume ratio. *(1 mark)*

4 Air and water

4.1

1

Nitrogen	Oxygen	Argon	Carbon dioxide	Other gases
78%	21%	0.9%	0.04%	0.06%

2 a Fractional distillation.
b They are solidified out of the mixture as it is cooled down.
c i Nitrogen   **ii** Oxygen
3 a Molecules made up of two atoms (N_2 and O_2).
b Argon exists as single atoms because its atoms have very stable electronic structures so its atoms do not need to lose or gain electrons by bonding to each other.
4 Percentages of gas can vary for a variety of reasons e.g. water vapour content can be high over oceans compared with over large land masses; carbon dioxide levels and oxygen levels may vary in tropical forests because of photosynthesis; pollutant gases can be high in cities with heavy traffic/industry.

4.2

1 a carbon + oxygen → carbon dioxide
$C(s)$ + $O_2(g)$ → $CO_2(g)$
b hydrogen + oxygen → water
$2H_2(g)$ + $O_2(g)$ →$2H_2O(l)$ (accept $H_2O(g)$)
c calcium + oxygen → calcium oxide
$2Ca(s)$ + $O_2(g)$ → $2CaO(s)$
d iron + oxygen → iron(III) oxide
$4Fe(s)$ + $3O_2(g)$ → $2Fe_2O_3(s)$
2 a A and C, because the solutions are alkaline and are likely to come from oxides of Group 1 or 2 metals.
b D
c B and E, because they form acidic solutions in water.
3 a $Li_2O(s) + H_2O(l) → 2LiOH(aq)$
b pH = 10 – 14
4 Magnesium is oxidised as it has oxygen added to it to form magnesium oxide. Copper(II) oxide is reduced as it has oxygen removed from it to form copper.

4.3

1 Sterilise with chlorine.
2 a Distillation.
b See if its boiling point is 100°C.
c They only test for the presence of water and don't tell you anything about water's purity.
3 They contain dissolved minerals (salts).
4 Letters outlining the points made in the table on page 51.
5 Make groups of people receiving the fluoride as similar as possible to those not receiving fluoride; make the sample as large as possible; monitor the dosages of fluoride accurately; repeat test measurements; repeat with different groups of matched people; monitor over different periods of time. Carry out a survey to collect information to set up matching groups.

4.4

1 Set up test tubes in which an iron object e.g. a nail is in contact with:
– just water (by boiling a sample of water to drive off any dissolved air and then covering the surface in oil so no more air can re-dissolve into the water, and stoppering the test tube)
– just air (by setting up a test tube with calcium chloride to absorb any water vapour from the air in a stoppered test tube, making sure that the nail is not in contact with the calcium chloride)
– both air and water (by having the nail partly in water and partly in air – or covering the nail in unboiled water and leaving the test tube unstoppered)
2 a Hydrated iron(III) oxide
b The composition can vary depending on conditions and there is no one formula that we can say is the same in all samples of rust.
3 a Coat in paint, oil or grease, plastic, a less reactive metal, or a more reactive metal.

b i Oil/grease as the chain is constantly rubbing against the cogs when a bicycle is moving so coatings such as paint would wear off quickly; the oil/grease also lubricates the moving parts.
ii Paint because this is a cheap method/coating in grease would be too messy for people brushing against the railings.
iii Sacrificial protection e.g. by attaching blocks of zinc/magnesium/ aluminium to the pipe – this is expensive to set up but is easier to maintain in inaccessible locations and more effective than other methods in the harsh conditions caused by constant contact with seawater.
4 a Set up test tubes with a nail and:
– sodium chloride solution
– water
Use the same volumes and all conditions controlled to make it a fair test. Judge the amount of rust formed after a week in each test tube.
b Set up a series of test tubes with a nail in each plus increasingly concentrated solutions of sodium chloride e.g. with no sodium chloride in the first test tube and then measuring ever increasing masses of sodium chloride into the same volume of water in each successive tube, and shaking to dissolve, until the salt solution becomes saturated in the final tube. Leave the tubes in a test tube rack for a week and then judge the degree of rusting in each test tube.

Answers to end of chapter summary questions

1 a Because air only contains 21% oxygen so the oxygen is diluted down in air by the unreactive nitrogen gas.
b i $2Ba + O_2 → 2BaO$ **iii** $S + O_2 → SO_2$
ii $N_2 + O_2 → 2NO$ **iv** $4Li + O_2 → 2Li_2O$
c The pH will be 11–14, as lithium oxide is the oxide of a metallic oxide, which if soluble in water will form an alkaline solution according to the equation:
$$Li_2O(s) + H_2O(l) → 2LiOH(aq)$$
2 a By fractional distillation of liquid air which has been cooled to –200°C. The fractionating column is cooler at the top than the bottom and nitrogen leaves the column from the top as a gas as it boils off first, and oxygen leaves as a liquid at the bottom.
b i Water vapour is H_2O, carbon dioxide is CO_2, oxygen is O_2, argon is Ar and nitrogen is N_2.
ii Oxygen, argon and nitrogen are elements.
Water and carbon dioxide are compounds.
3 a To reduce the boiling point of the seawater and so keep down energy needed in the process.
b Sodium chloride/salt solution speeds up the process of rusting as does the high process temperatures.
c You do not have to use energy to boil the seawater thus saving money and conserving energy resources if fossil fuels are used to supply the heat energy (and reducing the pollution produced by burning fossil fuels).
4 a i Tube A   **iii** Tube B
ii Tube C
b To remove the dissolved air/oxygen in it.
c To keep it away from any moisture on the calcium chloride.
d Both air/oxygen and water are needed for iron to rust.
e Sodium chloride.
f Set up two test tubes one with a nail in contact with air and water and the other in contact with air and sodium chloride solution (use the same volume of water and sodium chloride solution). Leave them in the same conditions for a set time then see which nail has formed more rust.
g i Oil/grease as the cogs are constantly rubbing against each other when the machine is working so coatings such as paint would wear off quickly; the oil/grease also lubricates the cogs.
ii A thin coating of tin as the unreactive tin will not dissolve into any food by reacting with e.g. acidic juices.
iii Sacrificial protection using a more reactive metal/attach bars of a more reactive metal as these do not need a complete covering over the iron (cutting costs on difficult repairs that would be needed if a barrier was pierced underground) and last a long time before they need replacing.

Answers to end of chapter examination-style questions

1 a Nitrogen, oxygen, argon *(1 mark)*
b Carbon dioxide *(1 mark)*
Water (vapour) *(1 mark)*
c Boiling point *(1 mark)*
d Air is liquefied *(1 mark)*
Then heated to boil the gases *(1 mark)*
Each element leaves the column separately. *(1 mark)*
2 i Bright/white flame *(1 mark)*
White smoke/solid *(1 mark)*
ii $2Mg + O_2 → 2MgO$ *(1 mark)*

b **i** $MgO + H_2O \rightarrow Mg(OH)_2$ *(1 mark)*
$S + O_2 \rightarrow SO_2$ *(1 mark)*
ii Magnesium oxide – blue *(1 mark)*
Sulfur dioxide – red *(1 mark)*
iii Magnesium oxide is basic *(1 mark)*
Sulfur dioxide is acidic *(1 mark)*
c **i** Amphoteric *(1 mark)*
ii Acids *(1 mark)*
Alkalis *(1 mark)*
3 a **i** Anhydrous copper(II) sulfate *(1 mark)*
Turns blue *(1 mark)*
ii Heat it/cool it *(1 mark)*
Boils at 100°C/freezes at 0°C *(1 mark)*
b Ion exchange resin/silver/carbon *(1 mark)*
Calcium compounds/bacteria/chlorine *(1 mark)*
c **i** Improves dental health *(1 mark)*
ii Fluorosis/bone damage/variable intake/mass
medication *(1 mark)*
4 a **i** Iron oxide *(1 mark)*
ii Oxygen *(1 mark)*
Water *(1 mark)*
b **i** Galvanising *(1 mark)*
ii Zinc more reactive than iron *(1 mark)*
Zinc reacts instead of iron *(1 mark)*

5 The periodic table

5.1
1 a Repeated at regular intervals.
b **i** A vertical column of elements.
ii A horizontal row of elements.
2 There are many more metals.
3 They have the same number of electrons in the highest energy level (outermost shell)
4 a 2 **b** 3 **c** 1 **d** 2
e 8 **f** 2 **g** 8 **h** 7
5 Because of their very stable electron arrangements.

5.2
1 To keep them out of contact with air/oxygen and water vapour.
2 The melting point decreases with increasing atomic number/going down the group.
3 They all have 1 electron in their outermost shell (highest energy level) which they lose when forming ions.
4 The metal would explode on contact with water as hydrogen gas is liberated very quickly. The alkali metals get more reactive going down the group so caesium, being near the bottom of Group 1, is extremely reactive. (Alkaline caesium hydroxide would also be formed in the reaction).
caesium + water → caesium hydroxide + hydrogen
$2Cs(s) + 2H_2O(l) \rightarrow 2CsOH(aq) + H_2(g)$
5 a $2Cs(s) + I_2(g) \rightarrow 2CsI(s)$ **b** $2Cs(s) + Br_2(g) \rightarrow 2CsBr(s)$

5.3
1 a They are good conductors of electricity and heat, are hard and strong, have high densities and have high melting points.
b Mercury has a lower than expected melting point.
2 a Iron(II) chloride.
b Chromium(III) oxide.
3 Copper(I) oxide, Cu_2O and copper(II) oxide, CuO.
4 Vanadium(V) oxide, V_2O_5.

5.4
1 a Their melting points increase.
b Their reactivity decreases.
2 a Fluorine – gas; Chlorine – gas; Bromine – liquid; Iodine – solid.
b The halogens.
3 a

b
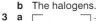
4 a Lithium + bromine → lithium bromide
b Bromine water + potassium iodide → potassium bromide + iodine solution

5 a $2Na(s) + I_2(g) \rightarrow 2NaI(s)$
b $Cl_2(aq) + 2NaI(aq) \rightarrow 2NaCl(aq) + I_2(aq)$

5.5
1 Helium – despite the fact that it has the smallest positive charge on its nucleus, its outer electrons are nearest to the nucleus and have no inner shells of electrons shielding them from the nuclear charge.
2 The electron in the outermost shell in potassium is attracted less strongly to the positive nucleus than in lithium. The attraction is weaker in potassium because the distance between the outer electron and the nucleus is greater. As well as that, the outer electron in potassium experiences a greater shielding effect from more inner shells of electrons, making it easier for potassium to lose its outer electron than it is for lithium.
3 Going down the group, the outermost shell gets further away from the attractive force of the nucleus so it is harder for a bromine atom to gain an electron. The outer shell in bromine will also be shielded by more inner electrons, again reducing the attraction of the nucleus for an electron so bromine is less reactive than fluorine.
4 a Ca is more reactive than Mg – the Group 2 elements get more reactive going down the group, as their atoms react by losing their two outer shell electrons, which get easier to lose because of the increasing distance between the nucleus and the outer electrons and the greater shielding effect in Ca compared with Mg.
b Group 6 non-metals get less reactive going down the group, as their atoms can react by gaining two electrons, and this is more difficult for sulfur atoms than for oxygen atoms, as sulfur's outer shell is further from the attractive force of its nucleus and is shielded by more inner electrons.

Answers to end of chapter summary questions
1 a **i** Group 7 **iii** Group 1
ii Group 0 **iv** Between Groups 2 and 3
b **i** Transition elements **iii** Group 0/noble gases
ii Group 1/alkali metals **iv** Group 7/halogens
2 a 7 electrons as it is in Group 7.
b Solid
c **i** Ionic
ii White
iii NaAt
iv $2Na + At_2 \rightarrow 2NaAt$
v Yes, because chlorine is more reactive than astatine so would displace it from solution as the element.
3 a **i** Soft **iii** Low melting point.
ii Good electrical conductivity.
b **i** 1+
ii

Rubidium compound	Chemical formula
rubidium iodide	RbI
rubidium fluoride	RbF
rubidium hydroxide	RbOH

iii White; they will all dissolve in water.
b **i** $2Rb(s) + 2H_2O(l) \rightarrow 2RbOH(aq) + H_2(g)$
ii $2Rb(s) + Cl_2(g) \rightarrow 2RbCl(s)$
c Rubidium will react more vigorously than potassium because it can lose its outer electron more easily as it is further from the nucleus than potassium's outer electron and it is shielded from the nuclear charge by an extra inner shell of electrons than potassium's.
4 a **i** **ii**

b

5 a **i** Copper(II) sulfate is blue and sodium sulfate is white.
ii Copper can form more than one type of ion (2+ or 1+ ion) whereas sodium can only form a 1+ ion.
b Copper will have a much higher melting point, greater hardness and higher density than sodium.
c Sodium is much more reactive than copper. For example, sodium reacts vigorously with water, giving off hydrogen gas and forming an alkaline solution of sodium hydroxide whereas copper does not react with water.

Answers to end of chapter examination-style questions

1 a Melting point/boiling point/density (any two of)   *(2 marks)*
   b i Fizzing/bubbles/effervescence
       Metal floats or moves on the surface
       Metal gets smaller or disappears
       (any two)   *(2 marks)*
     ii Potassium melts   *(1 mark)*
       Flame   *(1 mark)*
     iii Blue   *(1 mark)*
       Alkali present/OH$^-$ ions formed   *(1 mark)*
     iv $2K + 2H_2O \rightarrow 2KOH + H_2$
       Four correct formulae   *(1 mark)*
       Balancing   *(1 mark)*
   c Potassium loses an electron further away from nucleus.   *(1 mark)*
     Lost electron less strongly attracted to nucleus.   *(1 mark)*
     Lost electron repelled/shielded by more inner electrons.   *(1 mark)*
2 a Fe^{2+} *(1 mark)*
     Fe^{3+} *(1 mark)*
   b $Fe(OH)_2$ is green   *(1 mark)*
     $Fe(OH)_3$ is brown   *(1 mark)*
   c i Valency/charge on the ion   *(1 mark)*
     ii Catalysts   *(1 mark)*
3 a $Ca + Cl_2 \rightarrow CaCl_2$
     Three correct formulae   *(1 mark)*
     Balancing   *(1 mark)*
   b i No reaction   *(1 mark)*
     ii Sodium chloride + bromine   *(1 mark)*
     iii Potassium bromide + iodine   *(1 mark)*
   c Electron gained by fluorine gets closer to nucleus.   *(1 mark)*
     Gained electron more strongly attracted to nucleus.   *(1 mark)*
     Gained electron repelled/shielded by fewer inner electrons.   *(1 mark)*

6 Acids, bases and salts

6.1

1 a An alkali is a base that dissolves in water.
   b They dissolve in water to produce hydroxide ions.
   c
$$KOH(s) \xrightarrow{\text{water}} K^+(aq) + OH^-(aq)$$
2 a $H^+(aq)$ ions
   b
$$HI(g) \xrightarrow{\text{water}} H^+(aq) + I^-(aq)$$
3 Distilled water pH 7; sodium hydroxide solution pH above 7 e.g. 14; ethanoic acid pH below 7 e.g. 4.
4 A pH sensor and datalogger would be more accurate as the matching of colours against a pH chart by eye is subjective and difficult to judge. A pH sensor is more likely to produce more repeatable measurements over a narrower range than using universal indicator paper.

6.2

1 a acid + a base → a salt + water
   b acid + a metal → a salt + hydrogen
2 Copper sulfate solution is heated in an evaporating dish on a water bath. Some of the water is evaporated off from the copper sulfate solution until the point of crystallisation when crystals appear at the edge of the solution. The copper sulfate solution is then left at room temperature for the remaining water to evaporate off slowly, leaving crystals in the dish.
3 a Copper metal does not react with dilute acid.
   b Potassium metal is so reactive it will explode in dilute acid.
4 a $Mg(s) + 2HCl(aq) \rightarrow MgCl_2(aq) + H_2(g)$
   b $Li_2O(s) + H_2SO_4(aq) \rightarrow Li_2SO_4(aq) + H_2O(l)$

6.3

1 a acid + alkali → a salt + water   b $H^+(aq) + OH^-(aq) \rightarrow H_2O(l)$
2 a Ammonium nitrate
   b It is used as a fertiliser to provide plants with nitrogen.
   c 35%
   d $NH_4OH + HNO_3 \rightarrow NH_4NO_3 + H_2O$ or $NH_3 + HNO_3 \rightarrow NH_4NO_3$
3 $LiOH(aq) + HCl(aq) \rightarrow LiCl(aq) + H_2O(l)$
   Add a known volume of dilute hydrochloric acid (e.g. from a burette) to a measured volume of lithium hydroxide solution which has a few drops of an indicator added (e.g. methyl orange) until the indicator just changes colour. Note how much acid is needed to neutralise a known volume of lithium hydroxide solution. Repeat until consistent volumes of acid are used. Then repeat without the indicator and evaporate off water from the lithium chloride solution by heating until the point of crystallisation is reached. Then leave at room temperature for the rest of the water to evaporate off.
4 a Add solutions of lead nitrate and e.g. sodium chloride, filter, wash the precipitate of lead chloride collected on the filter paper with distilled water and leave in a warm oven or leave to dry at room temperature.

   b E.g. $Pb(NO_3)_2(aq) + 2NaCl(aq) \rightarrow PbCl_2(s) + 2NaNO_3(aq)$
   c Ionic bonding.
5 Add an alkali (e.g. sodium hydroxide or lime) and filter off the precipitate of chromium(III) hydroxide formed.

6.4

1 a metal carbonate + acid → a salt + water + carbon dioxide
   b
$$\text{metal carbonate} \xrightarrow{\text{heat}} \text{metal oxide} + \text{carbon dioxide}$$
2 sodium carbonate + hydrochloric acid → sodium chloride + water + carbon dioxide
   $Na_2CO_3(s) + 2HCl(aq) \rightarrow 2NaCl(aq) + H_2O(l) + CO_2(g)$
3 $CuCO_3(s) \rightarrow CuO(s) + CO_2(g)$
4 $CuCO_3(s) + 2HNO_3(aq) \rightarrow Cu(NO_3)_2(aq) + H_2O(l) + CO_2(g)$
5 Limewater is a solution of alkaline calcium hydroxide. Carbon dioxide is a weakly acidic gas so it reacts with the alkaline limewater, forming a suspension of solid particles of insoluble calcium carbonate which precipitates out of solution making it cloudy.
   The reaction is:
    calcium hydroxide + carbon dioxide → calcium carbonate + water
     (limewater)   (an insoluble white precipitate)
    $Ca(OH)_2(aq) + CO_2(g) \rightarrow CaCO_3(s) + H_2O(l)$

6.5

1 Precise
2 a Meniscus
   b i (Volumetric) Pipette and burette.
     ii Read to the bottom of the meniscus, with the eye level with that point.
3 a Measure a known volume of sodium hydroxide solution into a conical flask using a pipette, and add a few drops of an acid/base indicator. Then pour the dilute nitric acid into a burette, recording the reading on the burette. Then slowly add small amounts of acid into the flask, swirling it to make sure that the two solutions are mixed. Continue until the indicator in the flask changes colour. Repeat the titration until you get two identical results.
   b $NaOH(aq) + HNO_3(aq) \rightarrow NaNO_3(aq) + H_2O(l)$
4 a e.g. methyl orange, phenolphthalein.
   b Two distinctly different colours in acidic and alkaline conditions in order to make the end point clear to the experimenter.

6.6

1 $KOH(aq) + HNO_3(aq) \rightarrow KNO_3(aq) + H_2O(l)$
2 0.004 (4×10^{-3}) moles
3 0.004 (4×10^{-3}) moles
4 $0.32 \, mol/dm^3$

Answers to end of chapter summary questions

1 a i Nickel(II) oxide
     ii $NiO(s) + H_2SO_4(aq) \rightarrow NiSO_4(aq) + H_2O(l)$
     iii Neutralisation
   b Add excess nickel(II) oxide to warm sulfuric acid and filter off the excess solid. Then heat the nickel(II) sulfate solution in an evaporating dish on a water bath until the point of crystallisation is reached. Stop heating and allow the remaining water to evaporate from the solution at room temperature to leave the crystals of nickel(II) sulfate.
2 a $2LiOH(aq) + H_2SO_4(aq) \rightarrow Li_2SO_4(aq) + 2H_2O(l)$
   b $Fe_2O_3(s) + 6HNO_3(aq) \rightarrow 2Fe(NO_3)_3(aq) + 3H_2O(l)$
   c $Zn(s) + 2HCl(aq) \rightarrow ZnCl_2(aq) + H_2(g)$
   d $Ba(NO_3)_2(aq) + K_2SO_4(aq) \rightarrow BaSO_4(s) + 2KNO_3(aq)$
3 a $CaCO_3$
   b i $CaCO_3(s) + 2HCl(aq) \rightarrow CaCl_2(aq) + H_2O(l) + CO_2(g)$
     ii

Dilute hydrochloric acid   Calcium carbonate   Limewater

     iii calcium hydroxide + carbon dioxide → calcium carbonate + water
       $Ca(OH)_2(aq) + CO_2(g) \rightarrow CaCO_3(s) + H_2O(l)$
   c i calcium carbonate → calcium oxide + carbon dioxide
       $CaCO_3(s) \rightarrow CaO(s) + CO_2(g)$
     ii Thermal decomposition.
     iii 5.5 tonnes.
     iv Making cement; glass; extracting iron from its ore; building material; raising pH of acidic soil or lakes.
4 a $KOH(aq) + HCl(aq) \rightarrow KCl(aq) + H_2O(l)$
   b i 0.01 moles   ii 0.01 moles
   c i $0.8 \, mol/dm^3$ ii $44.8 \, g/dm^3$

Answers to end of chapter examination-style questions

1 a solution 1   pH = 2
   solution 2   pH = 7
   solution 3   pH = 12 *(1 mark)*
   b Universal indicator *(1 mark)*
     It has more colours/it indicates pH values *(1 mark)*
   c solution 4 *(1 mark)*
2 a i   Magnesium chloride *(1 mark)*
         Hydrogen *(1 mark)*
     ii Zinc nitrate *(1 mark)*
         Water *(1 mark)*
     iii Copper(II) sulfate *(1 mark)*
         Water + carbon dioxide *(1 mark)*
   b Bubbles *(1 mark)*
   c To make sure all the acid reacts. *(1 mark)*
   d i   Magnesium chloride *(1 mark)*
     ii Zinc oxide *(1 mark)*
     iii Blue *(1 mark)*
   e Evaporate some of the water (on a water bath) *(1 mark)*
     Cool the liquid/heat to the point of crystallisation *(1 mark)*
     Filter off the crystals/then leave at room temperature *(1 mark)*
     Dry them on filter paper/until all water has evaporated. *(1 mark)*
3 a $MgCl_2(aq) + 2NaF(aq) \rightarrow MgF_2(s) + 2NaCl(aq)$
     All four formulae *(1 mark)*
     Balancing *(1 mark)*
     All four state symbols *(1 mark)*
   b i   Lead nitrate *(1 mark)*
         Sodium sulfate/other soluble sulfate or sulfuric acid *(1 mark)*
     ii To remove soluble reactant. *(1 mark)*
4 a $H^+ + OH^- \rightarrow H_2O$ *(1 mark)*
   b i   Potassium hydroxide *(1 mark)*
         Smaller volume used *(1 mark)*
     ii Nitric acid – burette *(1 mark)*
         Potassium hydroxide – (volumetric) pipette *(1 mark)*
   c i   26.10 and 26.20 *(1 mark)*
     ii $(26.10 + 26.20) \div 2$ *(1 mark)*
         $26.15\,cm^3$ *(1 mark)*
   d $\dfrac{0.120 \times 25.00}{28.50}$ *(1 mark)*
     $0.105\,mol/dm^3$ *(1 mark)*

7 Metals

7.1

1 a lithium + water → lithium hydroxide + hydrogen
     $2Li(s) + 2H_2O(l) \rightarrow 2LiOH(aq) + H_2(g)$
   b zinc + steam → zinc oxide + hydrogen
     $Zn(s) + H_2O(g) \rightarrow ZnO(s) + H_2(g)$
2 a Gas given off/fizzing; magnesium gets smaller and smaller then disappears; heat energy released/gets hot.
   b metal + an acid → a salt + hydrogen
   c magnesium + sulfuric acid → magnesium sulfate + hydrogen
     $Mg(s) + H_2SO_4(aq) \rightarrow MgSO_4(aq) + H_2(g)$
3 a Because they are so unreactive they don't react with water at all.
   b Because they are so reactive they will react with water vapour (and oxygen) in the air.
   c Zinc will react with acidic foods whereas tin will not at room temperature.
4 Aluminium is protected by a tough/impervious layer of aluminium oxide.

7.2

1 a No reaction.
   b $Zn(s) + CuSO_4(aq) \rightarrow ZnSO_4(aq) + Cu(s)$
   c $Mg(s) + FeCl_2(aq) \rightarrow MgCl_2(aq) + Fe(s)$
2 Carbon is more reactive than zinc but not as reactive as magnesium so can displace zinc from its compounds but not magnesium from its compounds.
3 a Tungsten is below hydrogen in the reactivity series.
   b $WO_3 + 3H_2 \rightarrow W + 3H_2O$
4 a $Zn(s) + Fe^{2+}(aq) \rightarrow Zn^{2+}(aq) + Fe(s)$
   b Zinc atoms lose 2 electrons to form zinc(II) ions. Zinc atoms have been oxidised as oxidation is the loss of electrons. Iron(II) ions are reduced as they form iron atoms when they gain 2 electrons from zinc (and reduction is the gain of electrons).

7.3

1 A metal ore is a rock which contains enough of a metal or metal compound to make it worth extracting the metal.
2 It is a very unreactive metal.
3 Very low reactivity; used for jewellery

4 a zinc oxide + carbon → zinc + carbon monoxide
   b $ZnO(s) + C(s) \rightarrow Zn(l) + CO(g)$
5 a lead sulfide + oxygen → lead oxide + sulfur dioxide
   b $2PbS(s) + 3O_2(g) \rightarrow 2PbO(s) + 2SO_2(g)$
   c $2PbO + C \rightarrow 2Pb + CO_2$

7.4

1 It is used in electrical wiring to deliver the electricity we need to run our appliances.
2 a Smelting of copper ores; electrolysis of solutions containing copper ions.
   b Copper can be extracted from lower-grade ores than would be economical by traditional methods of extraction.
   c It is very unreactive/low in the reactivity series.
   d Negative electrode/cathode because copper ions are positively charged (like all metal ions).
3 a $2CuS(s) + 3O_2(g) \rightarrow 2CuO(s) + 2SO_2(g)$
   b $Fe(s) + CuSO_4(aq) \rightarrow FeSO_4(aq) + Cu(s)$
4 a At the negative copper electrode: $Cu^{2+}(aq) + 2e^- \rightarrow Cu(s)$
     At the positive copper electrode: $Cu(s) \rightarrow Cu^{2+}(aq) + 2e^-$
   b Reduction takes place at the negative electrode because copper ions *gain electrons* to become copper atoms.
     Oxidation takes place at the positive electrode because copper atoms *lose electrons* to become copper ions.
5 In phytomining, plants can absorb copper ions from low-grade copper ore as they grow. Then the plants are burned and the metals can be extracted from the ash by leaching copper ions in solution from the ash by adding sulfuric acid. Then we can use displacement by scrap iron and electrolysis to extract pure copper metal. This method will become more important as our copper-rich deposits become more scarce.

7.5

1 E.g. fill with water to create a recreational resource for fishing, sailing, wildlife reserve, etc./replace topsoil and replant vegetation.
2 56 hours.
3 The aluminium oxide from the ore must be molten and then electrolysed, using large amounts of energy compared with the energy required in the recycling process.
4 Copper is found in a variety of alloys with varying amounts of different metals, making the recycling of pure copper more difficult. Making new alloys is one solution or improving the percentage of copper in the recycled mixture by adding pure copper and then electrolysing to complete the purification process.
5 E.g. less scarring of the landscape from open cast mining; less pollution of water running through waste heaps; less fossil fuels burnt during extraction so reducing atmospheric pollution.

7.6

1 The particles are arranged in regular patterns.
2 a Because the metal atoms donate their outer shell electrons into a 'sea' of electrons so have more protons (+) than electrons (−).
   b Electrons that are free-moving within a structure and are no longer associated with any particular atom.
3 Magnesium atoms have 2 electrons in their outer shell (highest energy level). These are donated into the 'sea' of delocalised electrons which are free to move around. The electrostatic attraction of the negatively charged delocalised electrons for the positively charged Mg^{2+} ions bonds the ions in the giant metallic lattice.
4 The 'glue' model can help us imagine the positively charged metal ions being stuck in position in the giant lattice but a glue itself becomes solid when it sets so is not helpful in visualising the fluid movement of the delocalised electrons throughout the structure.

7.7

1 a Because the layers of atoms (positively charged ions) can slide over each other relatively easily.
   b i   Malleable
     ii Ductile
2 a The differently sized atoms inserted into the regular arrangement of metal atoms (positively charged ions) is disrupted, making it more difficult for the layers to slip past each other.
   b A mixture of metals that once deformed will revert to its original shape at a certain temperature.
3 Nitinol can apply a force to the teeth once it warmed up in the mouth as it changes to its original shape whereas a traditional metal must be adjusted manually to change the force applied to the teeth.
4 They conduct electricity because the 'sea' of delocalised electrons can drift through the metal's giant structure because they are free-moving. They conduct heat because the free-moving delocalised electrons gain energy when heated and can move around more quickly within the metal spreading the energy through the metal quickly.

7.8

1 a Good conductors of heat and electricity; high melting points, strong; high density.
   b The central block between Groups 2 and 3.
   c Aluminium.
2 a It is very unreactive and is malleable.
   b To make gold more hard-wearing.
3 The silver and gold would be too expensive to use (except in small amounts in specialist uses).
4 They are 'light-weight' alloys due to the low density of aluminium, so more passengers and/or cargo can be carried on the aircraft; and the alloying makes them strong enough to withstand the high stresses put on an aeroplane in flight.
5 The copper alloys are harder-wearing so won't be worn away as quickly as softer coins made from pure copper. In alloying copper, differently-sized atoms of other metals are introduced into the regular layers of copper atoms, distorting the layers and making it more difficult for them to slide over each other.

7.9

1 a It contains too much carbon.
   b Cast iron contains about 4% carbon whereas pure iron contains only iron. This makes cast iron very hard and brittle as opposed to pure iron which is relatively soft and malleable.
   c E.g. man-hole covers
2 a Haematite (iron ore/iron(III) oxide); coke (carbon); limestone (calcium carbonate); air
   b Carbon monoxide.
      $CO_2(g) + C(s) \rightarrow 2CO(g)$
   c Iron(III) oxide + carbon → iron + carbon dioxide
      $2Fe_2O_3(s) + 3C(s) \rightarrow 4Fe(l) + 3CO_2(g)$
   d As a gas, carbon monoxide can diffuse throughout the blast furnace and come into contact with lots of iron(III) oxide, as opposed to solid carbon which can only react with iron(III) oxide it is directly in contact with.

3

Type of steel	Main useful properties
Low carbon steel	Relatively soft and malleable
High carbon steel	Hard/strong
Chromium–nickel steel	Corrosion resistant

4 a They will not rust so are easier to sterilise and stay sharp.
   b i Low carbon steel as it can be stamped into shapes.
      ii High carbon steel as it is very strong and hard.

Answers to end of chapter summary questions

1 a Vigorous reaction, metal changes to metal oxide.
      X + steam → X oxide + hydrogen
      $X(s) + H_2O(g) \rightarrow XO(s) + H_2(g)$
   b Fizzes readily, X gets smaller and eventually dissolves away completely into the acid.
      X + sulfuric acid → X sulfate + hydrogen
      $X(s) + H_2SO_4(aq) \rightarrow XSO_4(aq) + H_2(g)$
   c Because we do not know how much less reactive than calcium and more reactive than magnesium X is, so bubbles of hydrogen may be given off too slowly to be seen immediately or they might be liberated slowly on contact with water.
   d i You would expect the more reactive metal X to displace the less reactive copper from solution – so the solution will lose its blue colour, X will dissolve into solution and copper metal will be deposited as a brown solid.
         $X(s) + Cu(NO_3)_2(aq) \rightarrow X(NO_3)_2(aq) + Cu(s)$
      ii $X(s) + Cu^{2+}(aq) \rightarrow X^{2+}(aq) + Cu(s)$
      iii $X(s) \rightarrow X^{2+}(aq) + 2e^-$ X atoms lose 2 electrons so they are oxidised
         $Cu^{2+}(aq) + 2e^- \rightarrow Cu(s)$ Cu^{2+} ions gain 2 electrons so they are reduced.
   e i Just above copper.
      ii No change/no reaction as Y is less reactive than magnesium so cannot displace it from a solution of one of its compounds.
2 a Carbon + copper oxide will react.
      $C(s) + 2CuO(s) \rightarrow 2Cu(s) + CO_2(g)$
   b Iron + zinc nitrate will not react.
   c Iron + magnesium oxide will not react.
   d Magnesium + copper(II) sulfate will react.
      $Mg(s) + CuSO_4(aq) \rightarrow MgSO_4(aq) + Cu(s)$
3 a i aluminium + iron(III) oxide → aluminium oxide + iron
         $2Al + Fe_2O_3 \rightarrow Al_2O_3 + 2Fe$
      ii Displacement/redox reaction.
   b Aluminium and copper(II) oxide would react more vigorously than aluminium and iron(III) oxide.

c No change/no reaction.
d You would expect it to react in air, water and acid more readily than it does so you would not expect it to be used outdoors or for drinks cans.
4 a i Bioleaching   iii Smelting
      ii Phytomining   iv Electrolysis
   b Bioleaching and phytomining.
5 a Gold   d Copper
   b Nitinol   e Magnesium
   c Aluminium   f Chromium
6 a $CaCO_3 \rightarrow CaO + CO_2$ b $CaO + SiO_2 \rightarrow CaSiO_3$

Answers to end of chapter examination-style questions

1 a i Concentration/temperature/volume (any two of) (2 marks)
      ii Surface area   (1 mark)
   b i Magnesium   (1 mark)
      ii X has the same observation   (1 mark)
   c Timer   (1 mark)
      Gas syringe/measuring cylinder/boiling tube   (1 mark)
2 a $Zn + CuSO_4 \rightarrow ZnSO_4 + Cu$
      Reactants   (1 mark)
      Products   (1 mark)
   b $Fe + Cu^{2+} \rightarrow Fe^{2+} + Cu$ (1 mark)
   c i Reduction and oxidation occur   (1 mark)
      ii Iron is oxidised   (1 mark)
          Because it loses electrons   (1 mark)
   d i Carbon dioxide/carbon monoxide   (1 mark)
      ii Carbon, zinc, hydrogen   (1 mark)
          Carbon is above zinc because carbon displaces zinc from zinc oxide (1 mark)
          Zinc is above hydrogen because zinc displaces hydrogen from acids   (1 mark)
3 a Plants grow   (1 mark)
      and absorb copper compounds from the ore   (1 mark)
      Plants burned to give ash containing copper compounds (1 mark)
      can use low-grade ores/high-grade ores in short supply (1 mark)
   b i Atoms/ions in layers   (1 mark)
          Layers slide   (1 mark)
      ii Delocalised/free electrons   (1 mark)
          Move   (1 mark)
   c i Alloy   (1 mark)
      ii Atoms of other metals are different in size   (1 mark)
          Make it harder for layers of copper atoms to slide (1 mark)

8 Rates of reaction

8.1

1 a

   calcium carbonate + hydrochloric acid → calcium chloride + water + carbon dioxide
   $CaCO_3(s) + 2HCl(aq) \rightarrow CaCl_2(aq) + H_2O(l) + CO_2(g)$
   b All the acid had been used up in the reaction.
   c The line will be horizontal.
2 a i

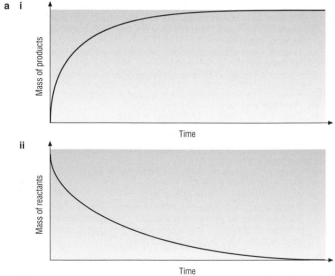

      ii

   b The slope of the line tells us the rate of the reaction at that particular time.

8.2

1 Temperature, concentration, surface area, pressure (if gases involved), catalyst (some reactions affected by light).

2 a Only iron atoms on the surface can react

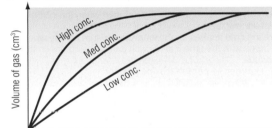

If you cut the nail up, more iron atoms are exposed and ready to react

b To control all the other variables/keep the other variables constant in order to make it a fair test.

3 The 'activation energy' is the minimum energy needed for reactant particles to react so any collisions with insufficient energy will not react so having no effect on the rate of reaction; only those colliding particles with the activation energy will react.

4 Well-chewed food will be in smaller pieces so will have a greater surface area. Therefore it will have more food molecules exposed to attack by the acid particles in your stomach than unchewed food.

8.3

1 a Because the frequency of collisions increases and more particles collide with energy greater than the activation energy.

b by a factor of 2/doubles/twice the rate.

2 a Because a precipitate of sulfur forms in the solution (so light is blocked from passing through the solution).

b It gets shorter.

c The reactant thiosulfate and acid particles move around more quickly so they collide more often and there is a higher proportion of collisions with energy greater than the activation energy needed for a reaction to take place/for effective collisions to occur.

3 The chemical reactions that take place in the cooking process will occur more quickly as the water under pressure can be heated to a higher temperature than 100 °C.

8.4

1 a The green line/highest concentration because its slope is steepest.

b To stop any acid spray escaping whilst allowing the carbon dioxide gas to escape/a rubber bung would trap the carbon dioxide gas given off until the bung blew off under the increasing pressure as the reaction proceeded.

c The electric balance responds to small changes in mass.

2

```
Volume of gas (cm³)

  High conc.
       Med conc.
              Low conc.

                    Time (mins)
```

3 The higher the concentration of a gas, the more particles there are in a given volume and each particle of gas will contribute to the overall pressure exerted by the gas. If we double the concentration of a gas, we double the number of particles in a given volume. The particles are moving randomly at high speeds so the force per unit area caused by their collisions with the walls of the container will also double.

4 There are many more collisions between the particles of acid in the undiluted cleaner and the limescale (calcium carbonate) in a given time resulting in a faster reaction than with diluted cleaner. This is because the number of acid particles in a given volume is far higher in the undiluted cleaner than in a diluted cleaning solution.

8.5

1 It remains chemically unchanged.

2 To make them as effective as possible by increasing their surface area as much as possible.

3 The reactants are used up as they turn into products but catalysts remain chemically unchanged at the end of a reaction. So catalysts can go on to catalyse further conversion of reactants to products (eventually they do become 'poisoned' by impurities and need to be replaced, but not often).

4 E.g. Manufacture of ammonia/Haber process;
nitrogen + hydrogen ⇌ ammonia – uses an iron catalyst.
Manufacture of sulfuric acid/Contact process;
sulfur dioxide + oxygen ⇌ sulfur trioxide – uses a vanadium(v) oxide catalyst.
Manufacture of nitric acid;
ammonia + oxygen ⇌ nitrogen(ii) oxide (nitrogen monoxide) + water – uses platinum/rhodium as a catalyst.

Manufacture of margarine;
unsaturated oil + hydrogen → hydrogenated fat – uses nickel as a catalyst.

5 They speed up the production process, making it more economical; save energy; reduce pollution from, and save limited resources of, fossil fuels.

Answers to end of chapter summary questions

1 a E.g. measuring the mass of the reaction mixture over time/measuring the volume of gas given off in a gas syringe (or measuring cylinder over water) over time.

b Use more concentrated acid; increase the temperature of the acid; use a larger surface area of magnesium (e.g. cut the magnesium ribbon up into smaller pieces).

c i The student could repeat the reaction at different temperatures, keeping the other variables constant i.e. concentration and volume of acid, mass and surface area of magnesium ribbon.

ii The higher the temperature of acid, the greater the rate of reaction/faster the reaction.

iii As the temperature of the acid is increased the particles of acid (hydrogen ions) in solution gain more energy and move around more quickly (on average). Therefore they will collide with particles (atoms) of the magnesium ribbon more frequently. Not only that, a higher proportion of the collisions will have energy greater than the activation energy so more collisions in any given time will be successful/result in a reaction.

2 a Carbon dioxide; limewater turns cloudy.

b i calcium carbonate + nitric acid → calcium nitrate + water + carbon dioxide

ii $CaCO_3(s) + 2HNO_3(aq) \rightarrow Ca(NO_3)_2(aq) + H_2O(l) + CO_2(g)$

c They used two solutions of nitric acid with different concentrations, keeping all other variables constant, in a conical flask. This was placed on an electric balance, marble chips added, with a cotton wool plug in the mouth of the flask and the loss in mass (which is equivalent to the mass of gas produced) was monitored for 2.5 minutes, taking readings every 30 seconds.

d Student graphs (both lines drawn as smooth curves and labelled)

e The rate of reaction in Investigation B is half that in Investigation A.

f The final mass of gas produced in Investigation B is half of that produced in Investigation A.

g The initial concentration of the acid in Investigations A is twice/double the concentration of acid in Investigation B.

h In Investigation A there are twice as many acid particles ($H^+(aq)$ ions) as in Investigation B in the same volume of acid. So, there will be twice the number of collisions in a given time between the acid particles in solution and particles at the surface of the marble chips. Therefore the rate of reaction in Investigation A is twice the rate in Investigation B.

3 a They kept the temperature, concentration of acid, volume of acid, mass of zinc constant and only varied the surface area of the zinc in each different test.

b Hydrogen; a lighted spill pops.

c $Zn(s) + H_2SO_4(aq) \rightarrow ZnSO_4(aq) + H_2(g)$

d Line 1.

e The largest pieces of zinc.

f The line would be the steepest, rising to the same level as the other three lines, levelling off before them.

g The smaller the pieces of zinc, the larger its surface area and the more zinc particles (atoms) are exposed to react with the acid particles ($H^+(aq)$ ions) moving around randomly in the solution. Therefore the frequency of collision between reactant particles increases, causing an increase in the rate of reaction.

4 a A substance that increases the rate of a reaction but remains chemically unchanged at the end of the reaction.

b $2H_2O_2(aq) \rightarrow 2H_2O(l) + O_2(g)$

c E.g. Measure the time to collect a fixed volume of oxygen gas using the same mass of potential catalyst (with the same surface area) in the same concentration of hydrogen peroxide solution at the same temperature in each test.

d Filter off the insoluble metal oxides after the reaction, wash with distilled water and dry in a warm oven/leave to dry/dab with filter paper to dry.

Answers to end of chapter examination-style questions

1 a Acid concentration   (1 mark)
Temperature   (1 mark)

b Curve is steeper   (1 mark)
Curve becomes horizontal before the others   (1 mark)

c Greater surface area   (1 mark)

d i Student 1   (1 mark)
Bigger (%) error in recording short times   (1 mark)

ii $1 \div 11$ *(1 mark)*
     $= 0.09$ *(1 mark)*
iii Rate increases as concentration increases *(1 mark)*
     In direct proportion *(1 mark)*
iv Concentration doubled/twice as many (acid) particles *(1 mark)*
     More collisions between (acid) particles *(1 mark)*
     In a given time/more frequent *(1 mark)*

2 a i S/sulfur *(1 mark)*
     Does not dissolve/appears as a precipitate *(1 mark)*
ii SO_2/sulfur dioxide *(1 mark)*
     Acid rain *(1 mark)*
b i They move more quickly *(1 mark)*
ii Collisions are more energetic *(1 mark)*

3 a A substance that speeds up a chemical reaction *(1 mark)*
     But is not used up during the reaction *(1 mark)*
b They reduce costs/they last a long time/they help to make a lot of products in a shorter time *(1 mark)*
c Greater surface area *(1 mark)*

9 Crude oil and fuels

9.1

1 a A mixture of hydrocarbons.
b We rely on fractions from crude oil for most of our fuels, as well as many other products made from them.
c Because it is a mixture of different substances with different boiling points.

2 As the mixture, crude oil contains a wide range of hydrocarbons. Its components all have differing properties, such as boiling points, so it is better to separate the crude oil into fractions which can have different specific uses.

3 a $C_nH_{(2n+2)}$
b hexane, C_6H_{14}; heptane, C_7H_{16}; octane, C_8H_{18}; nonane, C_9H_{20}; decane, $C_{10}H_{22}$

4 a

b 46
c 15
d Because they are compounds of hydrogen and carbon atoms only which have the maximum number of hydrogen atoms possible in their molecules/contain only single covalent C–C bonds.

9.2

1 a i the larger the hydrocarbon, the higher the boiling point.
ii the larger the hydrocarbon, the lower the volatility.
iii the larger the hydrocarbon, the higher the viscosity.
b Short-chain hydrocarbon molecules – it will burn with a clean flame/not smoky.

2 Student table that effectively shows the patterns in the boiling points (gets higher), volatility (gets lower), viscosity (gets more viscous) and flammability (gets less flammable) as the size of the hydrocarbon molecules increase.

3 Hot crude oil is heated and enters a fractionating column near the bottom as a vapour. The temperature decreases going up the column. The gases condense when they reach the temperature of their boiling points so different fractions are collected as liquids at different levels in a continuous process. The hydrocarbons with the smallest molecules have the lowest boiling points and are collected at the top of the column where the temperature is lower. Nearer the bottom of the fractionating column, the fractions with the higher boiling points are collected.

9.3

1 a Carbon dioxide and water.   **b** Sulfur.
2 a Acid rain.   **b** Oxides of nitrogen.
3 a From oxidation of sulfur impurities when fuels burn.
b When nitrogen in the air is oxidised in the very high temperatures inside a vehicle engine.
c When fuel, such as diesel, undergoes incomplete combustion.
4 a $CH_4(g) + 2O_2(g) \rightarrow CO_2(g) + 2H_2O(l)$
b $2CH_4(g) + 3O_2(g) \rightarrow 2CO(g) + 4H_2O(l)$
c Carbon monoxide is a highly toxic gas. As it is colourless and odourless, people cannot detect it and so become poisoned.

9.4

1 Because ethanol can be made from plants which actually absorb carbon dioxide as they photosynthesise which offsets the carbon dioxide released when it is burned, whereas burning petrol is releasing carbon dioxide from hydrocarbons trapped beneath the surface for millions of years.

2 The energy comes from the Sun, which is used by the plants, such as oilseed rape, in the process of photosynthesis as the biofuel crop is growing.
3 a When hydrogen burns, the only product is water vapour:
$$2H_2 + O_2 \rightarrow 2H_2O$$
b Storage of the gas;
safety as it is highly flammable;
production of large volumes of hydrogen using renewable energy sources.

Answers to end of chapter summary questions

1 a i $C_nH_{(2n+2)}$ **ii** $C_{18}H_{38}$ **iii** C_8H_{18}
b Student graph.
c The higher the number of carbon atoms (the larger the alkane molecule), the higher its boiling point.
d Actual boiling point of pentane is $36\,^\circ C$ – see student graph for accuracy.

2 a i A compound made up of hydrogen and carbon atoms only.
ii They have the maximum number of hydrogen atoms possible in their molecules/contain only single covalent bonds between carbon atoms.
b i Propane, C_3H_8.
ii Atoms of carbon and hydrogen.
iii Single covalent bonds.

3 a B, because a fractionating column gets cooler nearer the top and the vapour of B will condense at a lower temperature than A.
b B as it is made up of smaller alkane molecules than A because it has a lower boiling point – and smaller hydrocarbons are more flammable.
c i A is more viscous than B.
ii B is more volatile than A.

4 a Climate change.
b i Sulfur dioxide.
ii Remove sulfur impurities before burning the fossil fuel or preventing the sulfur dioxide gas formed from entering the atmosphere.
iii Oxides of nitrogen – formed when nitrogen in the air inside a combustion engine is oxidised at very high temperatures.

5 a To condense the steam formed in the combustion of ethanol and collect it as a liquid.
b Blue cobalt chloride paper turns pink/white anhydrous copper(II) sulfate turns blue.
c It turns cloudy as carbon dioxide is produced when the carbon atoms in ethanol are oxidised.
d Compare the time it takes for the limewater to turn cloudy when ethanol burns with the time it takes with just air being drawn through the apparatus.
e ethanol + oxygen $\rightarrow$ carbon dioxide + water
$C_2H_5OH + 3O_2 \rightarrow 2CO_2 + 3H_2O$
f Swap the spirit burner with ethanol in for a wax candle.
g propane + oxygen $\rightarrow$ carbon dioxide + water
$C_3H_8 + 5O_2 \rightarrow 3CO_2 + 4H_2O$
h Carbon monoxide.

6 a Ethanol, because it can be made from plants e.g. sugar cane and sugar beet.
b The carbon dioxide released when it burns was taken in from the atmosphere as it grew.
c Water is the only product of combustion so no more carbon dioxide is added to the atmosphere when it burns.
d How to store the gas (large volume or very high pressures in cylinders);
explosive with oxygen in an accident;
how to generate the hydrogen.
e hydrogen + oxygen $\rightarrow$ water
$2H_2 + O_2 \rightarrow 2H_2O$
f A fuel cell.

Answers to end of chapter examination-style questions

1 a i (compound containing) hydrogen and carbon *(1 mark)*
     only/but no other elements *(1 mark)*
ii only single bonds/no double bonds *(1 mark)*
b i C_nH_{2n+2} *(1 mark)*
ii C_3H_8 *(1 mark)*
iii
H–C–C–C–C–H (or methylpropane) *(1 mark)*
c i (liquid to vapour) evaporation/boiling *(1 mark)*
     (vapour to liquid) condensation *(1 mark)*
ii Viscous *(1 mark)*
     High boiling point *(1 mark)*

2 **a** Carbon dioxide *(1 mark)*
Water *(1 mark)*
b $CH_4 + 2O_2 \rightarrow CO_2 + 2H_2O$
four formulae correct *(1 mark)*
balancing *(1 mark)*
c (solid) Carbon *(1 mark)*
(gaseous) Carbon monoxide *(1 mark)*
d **i** High temperature *(1 mark)*
ii Acid rain *(1 mark)*
e **i** Remove it before fuel is burned *(1 mark)*
ii Remove it before it enters the atmosphere *(1 mark)*
3 **a** It comes from plants *(1 mark)*
b Sugar (cane) *(1 mark)*
Fermentation *(1 mark)*
c **i** Crude oil/fossil fuels becoming depleted *(1 mark)*
ii Less food can be grown *(1 mark)*
d **i** No carbon dioxide formed *(1 mark)*
ii Storage is difficult/expensive/heavy *(1 mark)*
Risk of explosion *(1 mark)*

10 Other products from crude oil

10.1
1 **a** To meet our demands for fuels (petrol and diesel) from crude oil.
b The hydrocarbon vapours are passed over a hot catalyst or mixed with steam at very high temperatures.
2 **a** **i** B
ii A hydrocarbon that contains at least one C=C double bond.
iii Alkene
b **i** A **ii** Alkane
c Thermal decomposition
3 24 hydrogen atoms in $C_{12}H_{24}$
4 $C_{12}H_{26} \rightarrow C_8H_{18} + 2C_2H_4$

10.2
1 **a** A monomer is a small reactive molecule that joins together with other monomers to form a polymer.
A polymer is a very large molecule made up of many repeating units.
b Polymerisation
c

Ethene   Poly(ethene)

d E.g. carrier bags, dustbins, clingfilm, bottles, washing-up bowls.
2 Two carbon atoms are needed for a hydrocarbon to have a C=C double bond whereas in alkanes only one carbon atom is needed to form a saturated hydrocarbon as in CH_4.
3 **a**

b

c E.g. carpet, milk crate, ropes.
d The C=C double bond 'opens up' in neighbouring propene molecules and forms single bonds, joining the monomers together in a long chain.

10.3
1 **a** In a tangled mess.
b **i** Thermosoftening polymers have their individual chains held in place by relatively weak intermolecular forces whereas thermosetting polymers have strong covalent bonds (cross-links) between the chains.
ii Thermosoftening plastics soften when heated and tend to be soft but thermosetting polymers are heat-resistant (eventually charring at high enough temperatures) and rigid.
2 The handles would soften if thermosoftening polymers were used as heat is conducted through the metal pan to its handle.
3 Polymer A has stronger intermolecular forces than polymer B so it takes more energy to soften it. Polymer C has strong covalent bonds holding its chains in position so it will not soften on heating.

4 **a** The reaction conditions are different (temperature, pressure, catalyst).
b Both HDPE and LDPE are thermosoftening polymers.
c HDPE has straighter chains which can pack more closely together, hence its higher density, whereas LDPE has randomly branched chains so the chains cannot pack regularly together so there is more space in its structure, hence its lower density.

10.4
1 **a** **i** A polymer that is developed with a specific use in mind.
ii A polymer which changes in response to changes in its surroundings.
b **i** It is light, tough and transparent.
ii E.g. Clothing, duvet filling.
iii Thermosoftening polymer because it can be melted and re-worked.
2 **a** A loose network of cross-linked polymers with water trapped in its structure.
b Dressings for burns, contact lenses.
3 Once the top layer is peeled off, the light-sensitive polymer beneath loses its stickiness when in contact with light so can easily be removed from the skin.
4 The stitches are inserted loosely and tighten when warmed to body temperature.

10.5
1 Waste plastic mostly ends up in landfill sites where it takes many years to break down.
2 Polymers that can be broken down by microbes in the soil.
3 **a** Because they are biodegradable.
b Lactic acid.
4 **a** Little or not enough oxygen to aid decomposition process.
b Decomposition might start before the plastics useful life has expired.
c It can be incorporated into the structure of non-biodegradable plastics so that microbes feed on it once disposed of and speed up decomposition.
Polymers derived from cornstarch are themselves biodegradable.

Answers to end of chapter summary questions

1 **a** C_3H_6
b

c Unsaturated molecule as it contains a C=C double bond.
d Add bromine water, stopper and shake – the propene will decolourise the bromine water whereas the propane has no effect/bromine water remains orange in colour.
e **i** Polymerisation
ii Poly(propene)
iii Monomers
iv The poly(propene) is a solid at room temperature whereas propene is a gas.
2 $n\,C_2H_4 \rightarrow -(CH_2 - CH_2)_n-$
3 **a** ethene + steam $\rightleftharpoons$ ethanol
$C_2H_4(g) + H_2O(g) \rightleftharpoons C_2H_5OH$
b 75%
c Advantage – it is a continuous process and a quicker process.
Disadvantage – it uses a non-renewable resource as its raw material (crude oil) and uses more energy in the process.
4 **a** Water molecules can pass out of the tiny pores in the material (as when we breathe out water vapour) so the wearer does not get clammy.
b No, because it does not change in response to changes in its environment.
5 **a** The crops have been genetically modified.
b Not in theory as it absorbs the same amount of carbon dioxide when the crop grows as it releases when it decomposes. However, processing and transporting the crop to extract the polymer will use fossil fuels which will result in some excess carbon dioxide being released.
c Probably as the recycling bypasses the processing/fermentation stages but it would itself require some costs in terms of extracting the polymer.

Answers to end of chapter examination-style questions

1 **a** (type 1)
heat *(1 mark)*
with a catalyst *(1 mark)*
(type 2)
mix with steam *(1 mark)*
very high temperature *(1 mark)*

b i (carbon-carbon) double (covalent) bond *(1 mark)*

ii

iii C_4H_8 *(1 mark)*

c C_4H_8 or $2C_2H_4$ *(1 mark)*

d Bromine (water) *(1 mark)*
Alkanes show no change in colour *(1 mark)*
Alkenes decolourise it *(1 mark)*

e Ethene *(1 mark)*
Steam *(1 mark)*
Heat/catalyst *(1 mark)*

2 a No double bonds/saturated *(1 mark)*
Much bigger/long chains *(1 mark)*

b i LD = low density and HD = high density *(1 mark)*

ii Melt when heated *(1 mark)*

c i Does not melt/decompose *(1 mark)*

ii Cross links/chains joined together *(1 mark)*

d Broken down by microbes *(1 mark)*
Reduce space taken up in landfill *(1 mark)*

3 **0 marks** No relevant content
Level 1 (1–2 marks) One type of polymer is correctly identified and there is a brief account of the properties, structure and bonding of polymers.
Level 2 (3–4 marks) Both types of polymer are correctly identified and there are some references to the properties, structure and bonding of polymers.
Level 3 (5–6 marks) Both types of polymer are correctly identified and there is a clear, balanced and detailed account of the properties, structure and bonding of polymers.
Examples of chemistry points made in the response:
- Polymer 2 should be made using low-density thermosoftening polymer
- Polymer 1 should be made using thermosetting polymer
- Low-density (thermosoftening) polymer chains have many branches
- High-density (thermosoftening) polymer chains have no/few branches
- Thermosetting polymer chains have cross links / covalent bonds between the chains
- HD polymer chains can pack closely together
- LD polymer chains do not pack closely together
- Thermosetting polymers cannot change shape because the cross links do not break when heated

11 Alcohols, carboxylic acids and esters

11.1

1 a Esters
b Alcohols
c Carboxylic acids

2 a Propanol
b Ethyl ethanoate
c Methanoic acid

3 a

c

b

11.2

1 Ethanol, CH_3CH_2OH or C_2H_5OH.
2 Fuels, solvents and ethanol in alcoholic drinks.
3 a sodium + methanol → sodium methoxide + hydrogen
$2Na + 2CH_3OH \rightarrow 2CH_3ONa + H_2$
b methanoic acid, HCOOH
c methanol + oxygen → carbon dioxide + water
$2CH_3OH + 3O_2 \rightarrow 2CO_2 + 4H_2O$
4 Place methanol, ethanol and propanol in separate spirit burners and weigh then accurately. Heat a known volume of water for a set time and record the rise in temperature of the water. Re-weigh the spirit burners with their remaining alcohols. Calculate the rise in temperature that would have been produced if one gram of each alcohol had burned. The alcohol with the largest temperature rise per gram is the one that releases most energy when it burns.

11.3

1 a Carbon dioxide
b Potassium propanoate
c $2C_2H_5COOH + K_2CO_3 \rightarrow 2C_2H_5COOK + H_2O + CO_2$
2 a
methanoic acid + ethanol $\xrightarrow{\text{sulfuric acid catalyst}}$ ethyl methanoate + water
b i Ethyl ethanoate **ii** Propyl methanoate
c They evaporate/give off vapour easily.
d Flavourings and perfumes (polyester fabrics).
3 Propanoic acid is a weak acid because it does not ionise completely when added to water. The majority of its molecules remain intact and only a fraction form $H^+(aq)$ ions and propanoate (negative) ions. Therefore propanoic acid does not produce as high a concentration of $H^+(aq)$ ions in its solution as a solution of a strong acid of equal concentration.

Answers to end of chapter summary questions

1 a A
b C
c Esters
d B
e A is $CH_3CH_2CH_2CH_2CH_2COOH$
C is $CH_3CH_2CH_2CH_2CH_2CH_2CH_2OH$

2 a i Sodium fizzes/effervesces/gives off bubbles of gas, and gets smaller and smaller as a solution is formed.
ii Hydrogen
iii Sodium ethoxide
iv Na^+
v $2Na + 2C_2H_5OH \rightarrow 2C_2H_5ONa + H_2$
b The reaction with lithium would be slower/gas given off more slowly/ longer for lithium to dissolve into the solution.

3 a

b i

ii methanoic acid + potassium carbonate → potassium methanoate + water + carbon dioxide
$2HCOOH + K_2CO_3 \rightarrow 2HCOOK + H_2O + CO_2$
c i E ethanol.
ii C methanoic acid, because ethanol is neutral so has the highest pH of 7 – the rest are acids so have a pH below 7, but methanoic acid is the only weak acid; the other three being strong acids will have lower pH values.

4 a Ethyl ethanoate.
b Ethanol and ethanoic acid.
c
ethanoic acid + ethanol $\xrightarrow{\text{sulfuric acid catalyst}}$ ethyl ethanoate + water
$CH_3COOH + C_2H_5OH \rightleftharpoons CH_3COOC_2H_5 + H_2O$
d It evaporates easily.
e Methanol and propanoic acid.

5 E.g. Add sodium carbonate to a solution of each liquid – only propanoic acid would fizz (giving off carbon dioxide gas); then add sodium to the other two remaining liquids, only propanol would fizz (giving off hydrogen); the remaining liquid is ethyl ethanoate (smell to check).

6 a There are 0.5 moles of solute in 1 dm^3 of solution.
b Methanoic acid will have a higher pH value than nitric acid.
c Nitric acid is a strong acid. The HNO_3 molecules all ionise in water:
$HNO_3(aq) \rightarrow H^+(aq) + NO_3^-(aq)$
However, methanoic acid is a weak acid so most of its molecules stay un-ionised. Only a few molecules will ionise and split up in their solutions in a reversible reaction.
$HCOOH(aq) \rightleftharpoons HCOO^-(aq) + H^+(aq)$
So there are fewer $H^+(aq)$ ions in a given volume of methanoic acid solution compared with the same volume of nitric acid solution.

Answers to end of chapter examination-style questions

1 a (any two of)
same general formula
same functional group
same/similar chemical reactions *(2 marks)*
b i CH_3OH/CH_4O *(1 mark)*
ii

(1 mark)

c (any two of)
bubbles
sodium disappears/gets smaller
solid moves around *(2 marks)*
d Carbon dioxide *(1 mark)*
Water *(1 mark)*
e $CH_3CH_2OH + 3O_2 \rightarrow 2CO_2 + 3H_2O$
all formulae correct *(1 mark)*
balancing *(1 mark)*
f **i** Ethanoic acid *(1 mark)*
ii Vinegar *(1 mark)*
2 a (ethanol) – no change *(1 mark)*
(ethanoic acid) – bubbles *(1 mark)*
b **i** 5 *(1 mark)*
ii 1 *(1 mark)*
c Ethanoic acid is weaker because the ionisation is not
complete/fewer H^+ ions formed *(1 mark)*
Nitric acid is stronger because ionisation is complete/more
H^+ ions formed *(1 mark)*
3 a **i** Methanoic acid *(1 mark)*
Propanol *(1 mark)*
ii
    O H H H
    ‖ | | |
H–C–O–C–C–C–H
       | | |
       H H H *(1 mark)*
b Ethyl ethanoate *(1 mark)*
c (food) flavourings *(1 mark)*
Perfumes *(1 mark)*

12 Energy changes in chemical reactions

12.1
1 a Exothermic
b Endothermic
c E.g. oxidation, combustion, neutralisation, respiration.
d E.g. any thermal decomposition, photosynthesis.
2 The beaker would feel cold as the process of dissolving absorbed energy from its surroundings which included the beaker and your hand holding it.
3 The enthalpy of the reactants was greater/higher than the products, with the difference released as energy which raised the temperature of the surroundings. ΔH would have a negative value.
4 a $MgCO_3(s) \rightarrow MgO(s) + CO_2(g)$
b $+117\,kJ/mol$

12.2
1 a It uses the energy released in the oxidation of iron, forming hydrated iron(III) oxide in an exothermic reaction. Sodium chloride (common salt) is used as a catalyst.
b A supersaturated solution is made to crystallise by pressing a small metal disc. The crystals spread throughout the solution, releasing energy. The crystals are re-dissolved in hot water, ready to use again.
c The disposable hand warmer lasts longer when activated than the reusable one. However it can only be used once. Opposite applies to reusable hand warmers.
d Self-heating cans.
2 a To treat injuries with cold packs; to chill drinks in cans.
b Dissolving ammonium nitrate in water.
c **i** NH_4NO_3 **ii** E.g. fertiliser.
3 a Calcium oxide
b $CaO(s) + H_2O(l) \rightarrow Ca(OH)_2(aq)$
c It would form a harmful alkaline solution.

12.3
1 a Their size/numerical value/magnitude is the same but they have opposite signs.
b Water
c It reacts with water vapour in the air.
d Energy is released
2 a $W + X \rightleftharpoons Y + Z$
b It will absorb 50 kJ ($+50\,kJ/mol$).
3 a 4 moles.
b $CoCl_2.2H_2O + 4H_2O \rightleftharpoons CoCl_2.6H_2O$.
c Warm them up.

12.4
1 a A = 6720 J (6.72 kJ); B = 3360 J (3.36 kJ); C = 5670 J (5.67 kJ)
b A = 28 000 J (28 kJ); B = 18 667 J (18.67 kJ); C = 21 000 J (21 kJ)
c A > C > B
d A = 1344 kJ/mol; B = 784 kJ/mol; C = 1218 kJ/mol

e A > C > B
f They are likely to be much too low in magnitude because of large energy losses to the surroundings in the simple calorimeter.

12.5
1 Because it is a good thermal insulator it will reduce the rate of energy transferred to or from the surroundings.
2 a $NaOH(aq) + HCl(aq) \rightarrow NaCl(aq) + H_2O(l)$
b Neutralisation
c $2.0\,mol/dm^3$
d 1155 J
e $-23.1\,kJ/mol$

12.6
1 Draw energy level diagrams for the following reactions:
a

b

2 **a** and **b**

c It reduces the activation energy/energy needed for colliding particles to react so increasing the proportion of collisions in a sample with sufficient energy to cause a reaction and hence increases the rate of reaction.
3 a Energy must be supplied from the surroundings and absorbed by the molecule whose bonds are being broken to overcome the attraction between atoms; so the separated atoms formed will have a higher energy content than the original molecule.
b

c Bonds broken: 4 C–H; 2 O=O
Bonds made: 2 C=O; 4 O–H

12.7
1 Endothermic
2 The energy required to break a specific bond.

3 **a** $H_2 + Cl_2 \rightarrow 2HCl$ $\Delta H = -185\,kJ/mol$
  b $2H_2 + O_2 \rightarrow 2H_2O$ $\Delta H = -486\,kJ/mol$

Answers to end of chapter summary questions

1 **a and b**

c 504 J
2 **a**

b

c

3 **a** $C_{12}H_{22}O_{11} + 12O_2 \rightarrow 12CO_2 + 11H_2O$
  b To break the bonds in reactants/to supply the activation energy.
  c The process of making new bonds in carbon dioxide and water releases energy.
  d 85 kJ
4 **a** $-210\,kJ/mol.$
  b The energy absorbed in breaking the bonds in hydrogen peroxide is less than the energy released when the new bonds in water and oxygen are made.
5 **a** 27.3 kJ
  b 2730 kJ/mol

Answers to end of chapter examination-style questions

1 **a** **i** Exothermic reactions give out heat/produce temperature rise
    Endothermic reactions take in heat/produce temperature fall   *(2 marks)*
  ii Enthalpy change   *(1 mark)*

iii Negative sign means exothermic/positive sign means endothermic   *(1 mark)*
  b **i** Energy of reactants higher than energy of products   *(1 mark)*
  ii Activation energy   *(1 mark)*
  iii Catalyst used (in B)   *(1 mark)*
  iv C   *(1 mark)*
  c −31 kJ/mole   *(1 mark)*
2 **a** **i** 12.5 °C   *(1 mark)*
  ii 2   *(1 mark)*
  b **i** $100 \times 4.18 \times 14.5 = 6061\,J$
    Temperature change   *(1 mark)*
    Substitution   *(1 mark)*
    Correct answer   *(1 mark)*
  ii $6200 \div 0.40 = 15500\,J/gram = 15.5\,kJ/gram$
    Substitution   *(1 mark)*
    Conversion from J to kJ   *(1 mark)*
    Correct answer   *(1 mark)*
  c Heat lost (to atmosphere)   *(1 mark)*
3 **a** $(4 \times 412) + (2 \times 496)$ *(1 mark)*
    = 2640   *(1 mark)*
  b $(2 \times 743) + (4 \times 463)$ *(1 mark)*
    = 3338   *(1 mark)*
  c −698 kJ/mole   *(1 mark)*

13 The production of ammonia

13.1
1 The rate of the reverse reaction is equal to the rate of the forward reaction.
2 They remain constant.
3 Because although the concentrations of reactants and products are unchanged overall in the reaction mixture, the forward and reverse reactions are still taking place but at the same rate.
4 Pump more chlorine gas into the mixture as this will increase the rate of the forward reaction and more iodine trichloride will be produced.

13.2
1 Decreases products.
2 Increases the amount of hydrogen gas formed.
3 **a** As pressure increases the colour of a mixture lightens as the forward reaction producing more N_2O_4 results in fewer gas molecules.
  b The colour of a mixture darkens as the reverse reaction producing more NO_2 is endothermic.
4 No effect, as the number of gas molecules is the same on either side of the balanced equation.

13.3
1 Nitrogen gas – from air.
  Hydrogen gas – from natural gas.
2 **a** $N_2(g) + 3H_2(g) \rightleftharpoons 2NH_3(g)$
  b 450 °C, 200 atmospheres, iron catalyst.
3 **a** Cooled, condensed and collected as a liquid.
  b They are recycled to the reaction mixture.
4

13.4
1 **i** Increases the yield of ammonia as there are fewer molecules of gas on the right hand side of the balanced equation so increasing the pressure will favour the forward reaction.
  ii Increases the rate of production of ammonia as at higher pressures there are more gas molecules in the same volume so collisions will occur more frequently, increasing the rate of reaction.
2 To increase the rate of production of ammonia (even though both forward and reverse rates are increased).
3 **a** 31%
  b 10%
  c 94%
  d 82%
  e These conditions are a compromise so that the yield of ammonia is lower than would be ideal but the rate of reaction is reasonable at this temperature and pressure (with the aid of the iron catalyst).

Answers to end of chapter summary questions

1 a There is solid, liquid and gas present.
  b More ICl_3 is made as the position of equilibrium shifts to favour the forward reaction which produces no molecules of gas, thereby reducing the pressure.
  c The position of equilibrium would shift to the left in order to replace lost chlorine gas.
2 a $A(g) + B(g) \rightleftharpoons 2C(g)$
  b i No effect.   ii Increase the rate.
  c i Increase the amount of C formed.
    ii Increase the rate.
3 a Increase in temperature will favour the reverse reaction, making more sulfur dioxide and oxygen, as this reaction is endothermic, absorbing energy and thereby decreasing the temperature. Therefore, yield will be lower. The rate of reactions will be increased as the gas molecules will move around faster so there will be more frequent collisions, with more being successful in producing a reaction as more have energy greater than the activation energy.
  b Increase in pressure will favour the forward reaction as this produces fewer molecules of gas (2 molecules of sulfur trioxide on the right hand side of the equation as opposed to 3 molecules of sulfur dioxide and oxygen on the left), thereby increasing the yield. The rate of reactions will be increased as there will be more gas molecules in a given volume, producing more frequent collisions.
  c use of a catalyst has no effect on the position of equilibrium but will increase the rate of both forward and reverse reactions by the same amount as it lowers the activation energy so a higher proportion of the gas molecules have sufficient energy to collide successfully and react.
4 The pressure could be decreased as the left hand side of the equation has fewer (9) molecules of gas than the right hand side (10), so would tend to decrease the pressure.
  The temperature could be decreased as the forward reaction is exothermic so releases energy thereby increasing the temperature.
  The platinum catalyst will not affect the yield as it increases the rate of both forward and reverse reactions equally.
5 a i Increases the yield of ammonia.
    ii Decreases the yield of ammonia.
    iii Looking at pressure, choose one temperature and follow the pattern down a column as the pressure increases.
      Looking at temperature, choose one pressure and follow the pattern across a row as the temperature increases.
  b The pressure is not raised any higher for economic reasons – making a plant to withstand higher pressures costs more, generating higher pressures takes more energy and increases safety risks.
    The temperature can't be decreased, although this would improve the yield of ammonia, as the rate of reaction would be too slow.
  c No effect on the yield of ammonia.
6

Answers to end of chapter examination-style questions

1 a The rates of the forward and reverse reactions are the same *(1 mark)*
    The concentrations of the reactants and products do not change *(1 mark)*
  b i It becomes brown/darker *(1 mark)*
    ii The reaction is endothermic *(1 mark)*
      The equilibrium shifts to the right (as the temperature increases) *(1 mark)*
  c The colour becomes pale yellow/paler *(1 mark)*
    There are more gas molecules on the right *(1 mark)*
    The equilibrium shifts to the left (as the pressure increases) *(1 mark)*
2 a i Air *(1 mark)*
    ii Natural gas/water *(1 mark)*

b Iron catalyst *(1 mark)*
    450°C *(1 mark)*
    200 atmospheres *(1 mark)*
  c Nitrogen and hydrogen *(1 mark)*
  d cool/lower temperatures *(1 mark)*
  e $N_2 + 3H_2 \rightarrow 2NH_3$
    All symbols correct *(1 mark)*
    Balancing *(1 mark)*
3 a The temperature decrease raises the yield *(1 mark)*
    Because the reaction is exothermic *(1 mark)*
    So the equilibrium shifts to the right *(1 mark)*
    The pressure increases raises the yield *(1 mark)*
    Because there are fewer molecules of gas on the right *(1 mark)*
    So the equilibrium shifts to the right *(1 mark)*
  b It increases it *(1 mark)*
  c It increases the rates of the forward and reverse reactions *(1 mark)*
    By the same amount *(1 mark)*

14 Electrolysis

14.1
1 a The breakdown of a compound by electricity.
  b Electrolyte
  c Ionic
2   **Cathode (–)**   **Anode (+)**
  a zinc   iodine
  b lithium   bromine
  c iron   fluorine
  d sodium   oxygen
  e potassium   chlorine.
3 $2NaCl(l) \rightarrow 2Na(l) + Cl_2(g)$
4 a $CuCl_2(aq)$ and $AgNO_3(aq)$
  b Copper and silver are below hydrogen in the reactivity series.
5 In the solid, the ions are in fixed positions in the giant ionic lattice; but when molten or in aqueous solution the ions are free to move around within the liquid and can carry their charge to the oppositely charged electrode.

14.2
1 a i They lose electrons.   ii Oxidation
  b i They gain electrons.   ii Reduction
2   **Cathode**   **Anode**
  a lithium   oxygen
  b copper   chlorine
  c hydrogen   oxygen
3 a $2Cl^- \rightarrow Cl_2 + 2e^-$ e $K^+ + e^- \rightarrow K$
  b $2Br^- \rightarrow Br_2 + 2e^-$ f $2H^+ + 2e^- \rightarrow H_2$
  c $Mg^{2+} + 2e^- \rightarrow Mg$ g $2O^{2-} \rightarrow O_2 + 4e^-$
  d $Al^{3+} + 3e^- \rightarrow Al$ h $4OH^- \rightarrow O_2 + 2H_2O + 4e^-$

14.3
1 a Because in solid aluminium oxide the ions are fixed in position in the giant lattice so can only move to electrodes if molten when they are free to move around within the liquid.
  b To lower the melting point of aluminium oxide and save energy.
2 Oxygen is produced at the hot carbon anodes and reacts with the carbon to produce carbon dioxide gas, in effect gradually burning away the anodes.
3 a Cathode: $Al^{3+}(l) + 3e^- \rightarrow Al(l)$
    Anode: $2O^{2-}(l) \rightarrow O_2(g) + 4e^-$
  b Oxide ions are oxidised as they lose electrons and aluminium ions are reduced as they gain electrons.
4 a Lots of energy is needed to purify the aluminium oxide which involves heating to decompose aluminium hydroxide formed in the process; melting the aluminium oxide/cryolite mixture; electrical energy in the electrolytic cells.
  b Aluminium in nature is combined/bonded to other elements in compounds that are difficult to break down. It was not until scientists could use electrical cells to pass electricity through substances that aluminium could be extracted from one of its molten compounds by electrolysis.

14.4
1 a Chlorine, hydrogen and sodium hydroxide solution.
  b Chlorine is used to make bleach and plastics;
    hydrogen is used to make margarine;
    sodium hydroxide is used to make bleach, paper and soap.
2 a At anode: $2Cl^-(aq) \rightarrow Cl_2(g) + 2e^-$
  b At cathode: $2H^+(aq) + 2e^- \rightarrow H_2(g)$

3 a Molten sodium chloride will produce sodium metal and chlorine, whereas sodium chloride solution produces chlorine, hydrogen and sodium hydroxide solution.

b The difference at the cathode in aqueous solution is caused by the presence of $H^+(aq)$ ions from the ionisation of water , so hydrogen is produced and not sodium as with molten sodium chloride. Sodium hydroxide solution is formed from the excess aqueous sodium ions and hydroxide ions left in solution when aqueous hydrogen and chloride ions are discharged.

14.5

1 Nickel, chromium, silver, gold, tin, copper (any four).

2 To protect from corrosion; to improve appearance; to increase durability; to save money by using a thin layer of a precious metal.

3 a At the anode/positive electrode.

b Aqueous nickel(II) ions, $Ni^{2+}(aq)$.

4

Copper anode

Steel ball cathode

Copper sulfate solution

5 a $Ni^{2+}(aq) + 2e^- \rightarrow Ni(s)$ **b** $Cr^{3+}(aq) + 3e^- \rightarrow Cr(s)$

Answers to end of chapter summary questions

1 a B   **d** A
b A   **e** B
c B   **f** A

2 a Anode: iodide, fluoride, oxide, bromide
Cathode: potassium, calcium, magnesium, aluminium

b i $Mg^{2+} + 2e^- \rightarrow Mg$ **ii** $2Br^- \rightarrow Br_2 + 2e^-$ or $2Br^- - 2e^- \rightarrow Br_2$

3 a **A** = chlorine, **B** = hydrogen and **C** = sodium hydroxide solution

b E.g. making bleach and plastics, sterilising water.

c 11–14

d Lighted spill burns with a 'pop'.

e Anode: $2Cl^-(aq) \rightarrow Cl_2(g) + 2e^-$ or $2Cl^-(aq) - 2e^- \rightarrow Cl_2(g)$
Cathode: $2H^+(aq) + 2e^- \rightarrow H_2(g)$

4 a $2H_2O(l) \rightarrow 2H_2(g) + O_2(g)$

b $H_2O(l) \rightleftharpoons H^+(aq) + OH^-(aq)$

c Anode: $4OH^-(aq) \rightarrow 2H_2O(l) + O_2(g) + 4e^-$
Cathode: $2H^+(aq) + 2e^- \rightarrow H_2(g)$.

d 1 mole

e Electrical supply/battery/cell/power pack

5 a $Li^+ + e^- \rightarrow Li$

b $Sr^{2+} + 2e^- \rightarrow Sr$

c $2F^- \rightarrow F_2 + 2e^-$ or $2F^- - 2e^- \rightarrow F_2$

d $2O^{2-} \rightarrow O_2 + 4e^-$ or $2O^{2-} - 4e^- \rightarrow O_2$

6 Description to include:
Diagram of circuit with tin anode, iron cathode and tin(II) nitrate solution.
At anode; oxidation i.e. loss of electrons; $Sn \rightarrow Sn^{2+} + 2e^-$ or $Sn - 2e^- \rightarrow Sn^{2+}$
At cathode; reduction i.e. gain of electrons; $Sn^{2+} + 2e^- \rightarrow Sn$

Answers to end of chapter examination-style questions

1 a Bromine   *(1 mark)*
$2Br^- \rightarrow Br_2 + 2e^-$
both formulae correct   *(1 mark)*
balancing   *(1 mark)*

b Lead   *(1 mark)*
$Pb^{2+} + 2e^- \rightarrow Pb$
both formulae correct   *(1 mark)*
balancing   *(1 mark)*

c Electrons move   *(1 mark)*

d Ions cannot move when solid/ions move when molten   *(1 mark)*

e Ions gain electrons   *(1 mark)*

2 a H^+ *(1 mark)*

b $4OH^- \rightarrow 2H_2O + O_2 + 4e^-$
All formulae correct   *(1 mark)*
Balancing   *(1 mark)*

c Sulfate/SO_4^{2-} *(1 mark)*

d It increases   *(1 mark)*

e It takes twice as many electrons to discharge the same volume of oxygen compared with hydrogen/same number of electrons discharges twice the volume of H^+ ions as OH^- ions e.g. 2 moles of electrons give 1 mole of H_2 but only 0.5 mole of O_2 *(1 mark)*

3 a Hydrogen less reactive/sodium more reactive   *(1 mark)*

b Greater concentration of Cl^- ions   *(1 mark)*

c Sodium hydroxide   *(1 mark)*

d i Fuel/making margarine   *(1 mark)*

ii Bleach/making plastics

4 a i Nickel for the anode and copper spoon for the cathode *(1 mark)*

ii Nickel chloride/nitrate/sulfate   *(1 mark)*

iii $Ni \rightarrow Ni^{2+} + 2e^-$ *(1 mark)*

b Appearance/durability   *(1 mark)*

c Graphite conducts electricity/plastic does not conduct electricity   *(1 mark)*

5 **0 marks** No relevant content.

Level 1 (1–2 marks) There is a brief description of the electrolysis of aluminium oxide.

Level 2 (3–4 marks) There is some description of the electrolysis of aluminium oxide.

Level 3 (5–6 marks) There is a clear, balanced and detailed description of the electrolysis of aluminium oxide.

Examples of chemistry points made in the response:
- aluminium oxide is melted / made liquid
- cryolite is used as a solvent / to decrease the amount of energy or electricity used
- carbon / graphite used as the positive electrode
- aluminium ions are attracted to the negative electrode
- at the negative electrode aluminium is formed or aluminium ions gain electrons
- oxide ions are attracted to the positive electrode
- oxygen is formed at the positive electrode or oxide ions lose electrons
- the oxygen reacts with carbon to make carbon dioxide or carbon dioxide formed at positive electrode
- $Al^{3+} + 3e^- \rightarrow Al$
- $2O^{2-} \rightarrow O_2 + 4e^-$

15 Analysis

15.1

1 a White

b Add sodium hydroxide solution – all will form a white precipitate but the aluminium hydroxide precipitate formed would dissolve in excess sodium hydroxide solution (Al^{3+} identified). Take the original magnesium and calcium compounds and carry out a flame test – the calcium ions will produce a brick red flame (Ca^{2+} identified) and the magnesium ions will not colour the flame (so Mg^{2+} identified).

c $Mg^{2+}(aq) + 2OH^-(aq) \rightarrow Mg(OH)_2(s)$

2 a Dip a wire loop in concentrated hydrochloric acid and heat to clean it → dip the loop into conc. acid again before dipping in the metal compound to be tested → hold the loop in the edge of a roaring Bunsen flame → match the colour of the flame to the known flame test colours of metal ions.

b (apple) green flame.

3 a brown precipitate.   **f** K^+
b nothing observed (no change). **g** Ca^{2+}
c nothing observed (no change). **h** Al^{3+}
d nothing observed (no change). **i** Fe^{2+}
e yellow   **j** Li^+

15.2

1 Dilute hydrochloric acid, limewater, dilute nitric acid, silver nitrate solution, barium chloride solution.

2 Potassium iodide (potassium ions have a lilac flame test; and silver iodide, a pale yellow precipitate, is formed with silver nitrate solution).

3 a magnesium chloride + silver nitrate → magnesium nitrate + silver chloride
$MgCl_2(aq) + 2AgNO_3(aq) \rightarrow Mg(NO_3)_2(aq) + 2AgCl(s)$

b potassium carbonate + hydrochloric acid → potassium chloride + water + carbon dioxide
$K_2CO_3(s) + 2HCl(aq) \rightarrow 2KCl(aq) + H_2O(l) + CO_2(g)$

c aluminium sulfate + barium chloride → aluminium chloride + barium sulfate
$Al_2(SO_4)_3(aq) + 3BaCl_2(aq) \rightarrow 2AlCl_3(aq) + 3BaSO_4(s)$

4 a $Ag^+(aq) + Br^-(aq) \rightarrow AgBr(s)$

b $Ba^{2+}(aq) + SO_4^{2-}(aq) \rightarrow BaSO_4(s)$

c $2H^+(aq) + CO_3^{2-}(s) \rightarrow CO_2(g) + H_2O(l)$

5 To dissolve the compound and to remove any carbonate ions as they would also form a precipitate with the silver ions, interfering with the test. Also, any other acids added would produce precipitates with silver nitrate solution e.g sulfuric acid would make a precipitate of silver sulfate.

15.3

1 A mixture is made up of two or more elements or compounds which are not chemically combined together.

2 The relative proportions of each substance/component of the mixture can be in any ratio (it is not fixed as in a compound).

3 a

b At 78°C/the boiling point of ethanol, much of the water vapour rising up the fractionating column would condense and return to the heated flask instead of entering the condenser to be collected with the ethanol.

4 Method A – Add water to the mixture, stir and filter. Sulfur residue will be left on the filter paper. Wash with distilled water and leave sulfur to dry. Evaporate water from the filtrate of sodium nitrate solution on a water bath until the point of crystallization. Then leave the saturated solution to crystallise.
Method B – Add xylene to the mixture, stir and filter. Sodium nitrate residue will be left on the filter paper. Wash with xylene and leave sodium nitrate to dry. Evaporate xylene from the filtrate of sulfur solution using water bath (electrically heated/no naked flame) in a fume cupboard to crystallise.

15.4

1 Use a capillary tube to dab a spot of the food colouring on a pencil line near the bottom of a sheet of chromatography paper, then place in a solvent at the bottom of a beaker or tank. Allow the solvent to run up the paper, past the spot of mixture to separate the dyes. Allow the paper to dry and measure the distance from the pencil line to the solvent front and to each dye left on the paper. Divide the distance each dye moved by the distance of the solvent front to get the R_f values, then match the values against tables of data to identify the dyes.

2 0.77

3 The solubility of B in the solvent is greater than the solubility of A in the same solvent. To identify A and B their R_f values are matched against values of known substances in the 50–50 water ethanol solvent at 20°C in a database or data book.

4 Modern instrumental methods are highly accurate and sensitive, quicker and can identify minute traces of samples. However, the instruments are usually very expensive and take special training to use, producing results that can often be interpreted only by comparison with data from substances already in a database.

15.5

1 The mixture is vaporised and a carrier gas moves the vapour through a coiled column packed with particles of a solid (that might be coated in a liquid). The compounds in the sample have different attractions to the material in the column. The compounds with stronger attractions will take longer to get through the column so they have a longer retention time. The separated compounds can be recorded as peaks on a chart as they leave the column. The unknown substances in the sample can be identified by comparing the chromatograph with the results for known substances in a database or tables of data. The gas chromatography must have been conducted in exactly the same conditions to compare retention times with reference data.

2 They might be broken down when they are heated to vaporise them before entering the column.

3 Because the technique is so sensitive it can detect any tiny quantities of the illegal substance that might still be present in the athlete's body.

4 Analyse the compound in a mass spectrometer and look for the molecular ion peak on the mass spectrum, i.e. the peak caused by the positive ion with the heaviest mass, whose mass will correspond to the relative molecular mass of the compound.

Answers to end of chapter summary questions

1 a Nothing observed/dissolves
b white precipitate forms
c white precipitate forms
d (brick) red flame
e sodium iodide
f copper(II) carbonate

2 Lithium sulfate

3 a Lilac flame test to identify potassium ions.

Add nitric acid, then silver nitrate solution – a cream precipitate will identify bromide ions.

b KBr
c Ionic

4 a Compounds have a fixed composition whereas mixtures do not (their proportions vary). Compounds cannot be easily separated into their elements/needing chemical reactions but mixtures can be separated by physical means, as there are no chemical bonds between different substances in a mixture.

b i crystallisation   **iii** (simple) distillation
ii filtration   **iv** (fractional) distillation
c $Pb(NO_3)_2(aq) + 2NaI(aq) \rightarrow PbI_2(s) + 2NaNO_3(aq)$

5 a 72   **b** C_5H_{12}

6 a 5
b The mixture is vaporised and a carrier gas moves the vapour through a coiled column packed with particles of a solid (that might be coated in a liquid). The compounds in the sample have different attractions to the material in the column. The compounds with stronger attractions will take longer to get through the column so they have a longer retention time. The separated compounds can be recorded as peaks on a chart as they leave the column, with the one with the longest retention time furthest to the right as you look at the chromatograph.
c R_f of X = 0.6
R_f of Y = 0.2

Answers to end of chapter examination-style questions

1 a i Lilac *(1 mark)*
ii K^+ *(1 mark)*
b i White precipitate *(1 mark)*
ii Aluminium hydroxide *(1 mark)*
c Too much added *(1 mark)*
So white precipitate dissolved *(1 mark)*
d Add dilute hydrochloric acid *(1 mark)*
And barium chloride solution *(1 mark)*
White precipitate forms *(1 mark)*

2 a i Carbon dioxide *(1 mark)*
ii Limewater *(1 mark)*
turns cloudy *(1 mark)*
b i Silver chloride *(1 mark)*
ii $Ag^+ + Cl^- \rightarrow AgCl$
reactants *(1 mark)*
products *(1 mark)*
c Sodium ions do not form a precipitate *(1 mark)*
The two iron ions form a precipitate *(1 mark)*
The colour is not green or brown/colour is a mixture of green and brown *(1 mark)*

3 a Distillation *(1 mark)*
Difference in boiling point *(1 mark)*
b Filtration *(1 mark)*
Difference in solubility *(1 mark)*
c (paper) chromatography *(1 mark)*
difference in solubility in solvent/R_f values *(1 mark)*

4 a They pass through at different speeds/retention times *(1 mark)*
b Mass spectrometer *(1 mark)*
c There are 3 substances in the mixture *(1 mark)*
d It is fast *(1 mark)*
only small quantities are needed *(1 mark)*

5 0 marks No relevant content.
Level 1 (1–2 marks) There is a brief description of how to do the chromatography experiment.
Level 2 (3–4 marks) There is some description of how to do the chromatography experiment.
Level 3 (5–6 marks) There is a clear, balanced and detailed description of how to do the chromatography experiment.
Examples of chemistry points made in the response:
- use chromatography paper
- draw pencil line near the bottom
- place drops of the drink and colours on the line
- pour some water into a large beaker or tank
- place the paper in the tank
- with the spots of colour above the water level
- fit the tank with a lid
- leave until the water reaches almost to the top
- leave to dry

Index

Photo acknowledgements

C1.2.2 sciencephotos/Alamy; C1.3.1 iStockphoto; C1.5.3 Martyn F. Chillmaid/Science Photo Library; C2.5.1 Andrew Lambert Photography/Science Photo Library; C2.5.2 sciencephotos/Alamy; C3.4.1 Leonard Lee Rue/Science Photo Library; C3.4.5 Dirk Wiersma/Science Photo Library; C3.6.2 Olga D. van de Veer/Fotolia.com; C3.7.1 AFP/Getty Images; C3.7.2 amaxim/Fotolia.com; C3.7.3T Laguna Design/Science Photo Library; C3.7.3B Pasieka/Science Photo Library; C4.1.2 H. Raguet/Eurelios/Science Photo Library; C4.2.1 Martyn F. Chillmaid; C4.3.1 snezhok/iStockphoto; C4.3.2 CARDOSO CARDOSO/BSIP Medical/Photolibary; C4.4.1 Oleg Shpak/Alamy; C4.4.4 Martyn F. Chillmaid; C4.SQ3 DenGuy/iStockphoto; C5.2.2 Martyn F. Chillmaid/Science Photo Library; C5.2.3 Martyn F. Chillmaid; C5.3.3 Dirk Wiersma/Science Photo Library; C6.1.1T Andrew Lambert Photography/Science Photo Library; C6.1.1B Martyn F. Chillmaid/Science Photo Library; C6.3.1 Adrian Sherratt/Alamy; C6.3.2 iStockphoto; C6.4.1 Peter Arnold Images/Photolibrary/Getty Images; C6.4.DYK iStockphoto; C6.4.2 Andrew Lambert Photography/Science Photo Library; C7.3.1 Britain on View/Photolibrary/Getty Images; C7.3.3 iStockphoto; C7.4.1 Lee Prince/fotolia.com; C7.5.2 UIG via Getty Images; C7.5.3 Copper Development Association; C7.5.4 iStockphoto; C7.6.3 Martyn F. Chillmaid; C7.7.1 Bloomberg via Getty Images; C7.7.4T Joe Gough/Fotolia.com; C7.7.4B iStockphoto; C7.7.5 Pascal Goetgheluck/Science Photo Library; C7.8.2 Jeff Greenberg/Photolibrary/Getty Images; C7.8.3 iStockphoto; C7.8.4 iStockphoto; C7.8.5 michellepix/fotolia.com; C7.9.1 Luis Veiga/Getty Images; C7.9.2 Ton Kinsbergen/Science Photo Library; C7.9.3 iStockphoto; C7.9.4 iStockphoto; C8.2.1 Michelle Lester/Fotolia.com; C8.2.2 iStockphoto; C8.3.1 Photolibrary/Getty Images; C8.3.2 iStockphoto; C8.4.1 Cordelia Molloy/Science Photo Library; C8.5.1 Dr Keith Wheeler/Science Photo Library; C8.5.2 Sheila Terry/Science Photo Library; C9.1.1 Tim Graham/Getty Images; C9.2.3 iStockphoto; C9.3.2 John Millar/Getty Images; C9.3.3 Photolibrary/Getty Images; C9.4.1 USDA; C9.4.3 Bloomberg/Getty Images; C10.1.1 Paul Rapson/Science Photo Library; C10.2.1 Cordelia Molloy/Science Photo Library; C10.2.3 Charles D. Winters/Science Photo Library; C10.3.1 fotomatrix/Fotolia.com; C10.3.4 innershadows/Fotolia.com; C10.4.1 Image Source/Alamy; C10.5.1 iStockphoto; C10.5.2 AP Photo/Josh Reynolds; C11.1.4 Martyn F. Chillmaid/Science Photo Library; C11.2.1 Anyka/iStockphoto; C11.2.2 Andrew Lambert Photography/Science Photo Library; C11.3.2 Craig Lovell/Agstockusa/Science Photo Library; C12.1.1 Nina Ryan; C12.1.2 iStockphoto; C12.1.3 Photolibrary/Getty Images; C12.2.1 Martyn F. Chillmaid; C12.2.3 Fuse/Getty Images; C12.3.2 Martyn F. Chillmaid/Science Photo Library; C12.3.4 Andrew Lambert Photography/Science Photo Library; C13.3.1 ICI; C13.4.1 Maximilian Stock Ltd/Science Photo Library; C14.1.1 iStockphoto; C14.3.1 iStockphoto; C14.4.2 iStockphoto; C14.5.1 iStockphoto; C14.5.2 aberenyi/fotolia.com; C15.1.1 David Taylor/Science Photo Library; C15.1.2 Andrew Lambert Photography/Science Photo Library; C15.2.2 Andrew Lambert Photography/Science Photo Library; C15.2.3 Charles D. Winters/Science Photo Library; C15.3.2 Martyn F. Chillmaid; C15.4.4L Mary Evans Picture Library; C15.4.4R Photolibrary/Getty Images